Professional MEL Solutions for Production

Kevin Mannens
with Ed Caspersen

Wordware Publishing, Inc.

Library of Congress Cataloging-in-Publication Data

Mannens, Kevin.
    Professional MEL solutions for production / by Kevin Mannens, with Ed Caspersen.
        p. cm.
    Includes index.
    ISBN-13: 978-1-59822-066-7 (pbk.)
    ISBN-10: 1-59822-066-7
    1. Computer animation.   2.   Maya (Computer file)   3. Computer graphics.
    4. Scripting languages (Computer science)   I. Caspersen, Ed.   II. Title.
    TR897.7.M353 2009
    006.6'96—dc22   2009000851

© 2009, Wordware Publishing, Inc.

All Rights Reserved

1100 Summit Ave., Suite 102
Plano, Texas 75074

No part of this book may be reproduced in any form or by
any means without permission in writing from
Wordware Publishing, Inc.

Printed in the United States of America

ISBN-13: 978-1-59822-066-7
ISBN-10: 1-59822-066-7
10 9 8 7 6 5 4 3 2 1
0902

All inquiries for volume purchases of this book should be addressed to Wordware
Publishing, Inc., at the above address. Telephone inquiries may be made by
calling:

(972) 423-0090

To my mother and father, for instilling in me a vigorous passion for life.

Contents

Contents

Acknowledgments

Writing a book can be a lonely and arduous task, yet I could not have done it alone. Scores of people went out of their way to help me, throughout my career as well as for this book. I would like to take this opportunity to thank them.

First of all, I would like to bow down to my mentor, Chris Kniffen. It was due to his doting yet persistent tutelage that I originally developed a keen interest in MEL, and without fail he has nourished it ever since. I doubt that I will ever be able to convey my appreciation fully, but I owe him my eternal gratitude.

This book would have been impossible without the constant counseling and reviewing of Craig Davies, who also wrote the code for Chapter 9. I am in awe of his technical knowledge and greatly indebted for his expertise, understanding, and patience.

My co-author, Ed Caspersen, deserves a well-meant pat on the back for contributing Chapter 6 and for being a constant source of stimulating conversation. In retrospect, one can do nothing but cherish those 3 a.m. chat sessions about radian conversions and ternary operations, while at the same time having a quiet chuckle about one's own geekiness.

A very special thanks goes out to the FX and R&D crew at The Moving Picture Company: Nigel Ankers, Rob Hopper, Jonathan Wills, Harry Mukhopadhyay, Jimmi Gravesen, Oliver Winwood, Mark Newport, Ciaran Divine, and Niall Flinn, for providing a stimulating and jovial working environment and creating a fertile breeding ground for technical challenges.

From that same crew, I would like to do a special shout-out to Chris "Sexy" Armsden, for being a constant source of amusement, even when you were lying face down on the pavement covered in your own fluids.

I would also like to pay tribute to über-Mayans Michael K. O'Brien and Julian Mann for their support throughout the years.

Last but not least, a warm, fuzzy thanks for my Lilliputian muse, for supporting me through nights of reviewing and for listening to me when I was ranting about the idiosyncrasies in Maya.

About the Authors

A Belgian native, Kevin Mannens originally pursued an academic career at the University of Leuven, where he received a degree in philosophy. Due to a mind-boggling sequence of fortunate events, he regained consciousness and worked at the Alias|Wavefront (AW) European Support Center as an application engineer for three years. Traveling around Europe, Kevin con-sulted and trained AW clients such as The Moving Picture Company, Double Negative, CFC, Cinesite, and many more. In desperate need of a warmer climate and new professional challenges, Kevin moved to the Philippines for a job as Technical Director at ImagineAsia. He hasn't looked back since and swears by his lifestyle as a lyrical vagabond, alternating between TD and scuba instructor, most recently in China, Malaysia, the Philippines, New Zealand, Taiwan, and Thailand. His feature film credits include *10,000 BC*, *The Chronicles of Narnia: Prince Caspian*, and *G-Force*. Recently, Kevin founded TD-College (http://www.td-college.com/), the premier on-line school for technical directors, where he spearheads the FX program. Kevin is currently working toward his DSAT Trimix instructor certification in the Gulf of Thailand.

Ed Caspersen is a freelance programmer with a degree from the ITT Technical Institute at the Grand Rapids campus in Michigan. He is a member of the National Technical Honor Society and volunteers his time at the campus as a mentor. Ed was born into a military family in Texas in 1976. After moving around the country for several years, Ed and his family settled down in the  small town of Scottville, Michigan, and remained there until he finished high school. At the age of 19, Ed joined the U.S. Marine Corps as an infantryman. From 1996 to 2000 he was a member of the Chemical Biological Incident Response Force. After two and a half years, he was promoted into a position in the operations element of the unit and worked in the planning and execution of large-scale operations. Ed currently works as a MEL and Python mentor at TD-College. He lives in Ludington, Michigan, with his three dogs and a rabbit.

Introduction

As the title ever so slightly suggests, this book is an attempt to show the reader how MEL is used in production. At least how I have been using it for the last seven years. Unlike other books, this book will spend relatively little time explaining dry, theoretical programming concepts. The focus of the book is to illustrate how MEL is being *used* in feature film production. As such, I opted for a no-nonsense, down-in-the-trenches, curse-when-it-breaks approach.

This book assumes no previous programming experience, but intermediate to advanced knowledge of Maya. This assumption will allow me to skip the pleasantries and delve right into the juicy bits. That being said, Chapters 1 through 3 do explain the basics of MEL (syntax, variables, data types, procedures) in great detail and use practical examples of what I like to call "applied MEL." The remaining chapters cover real-world production scripts, with ascending degrees of complexity. This content approach allows me to write for a broad audience: from the MEL novice who wants to learn MEL to the advanced scripter who is interested in scripting strategies for production problems.

Let's take a closer look at what each chapter covers.

As previously mentioned, Chapters 1 and 2 cover the obligatory basics of MEL: its grammar and structure, commands, data types, variables, and procedures. These are basically all you need to know of a language to start talking. Chapter 1 also elaborates on which editors are available to write your code in, how to use the MEL command reference, and how to turn lead into gold. In Chapter 2, you learn about conditionals, loops, and procedures. At the end of this chapter, you will stutter your first words. This is where you want to bring your mum into the room so she can start beaming with pride.

In Chapter 3, we write two very simple scripts to put the accumulated knowledge from the previous two chapters into practice. If this were basketball training, these two scripts would be your first attempt at a layup. The idea is to drive home the theoretical concepts we learned in the previous chapters and get firm fundamentals we can build on.

Chapter 4 is the deep end of a pool filled with hungry piranhas. We will jump in head first, dressed like a giant meatball. This chapter is a line-by-line dissection of a script I wrote a while back called bookmarkManager that sets up characters and fights with light sabers. In the course of this chapter, I cover concepts like building UIs with formLayouts, operations on strings, and scriptJobs.

By now you are well underway to becoming irresistible to the opposite sex, so in Chapter 5 I treat you to a little tool that generates debris (pebbles, rocks, and needles) used for ground-foot interaction of smaller characters, created while I was working on a recent Hollywood production.

Chapter 6 is a gracious and elaborate contribution from my coauthor, Ed Caspersen. In it, Ed covers step-by-step how and why he wrote a very useful script called Extended Layer Manager. At the very least, ELM provides users with an efficient interface that allows for extended control over the layers within Maya.

From Chapter 7 onward, we are talking face-down-in-the-muck, hard-core material. You will have to flex your cerebral muscles and dig deep in those repressed childhood memories, but I guarantee you that it will all be worth it. Chapter 7 introduces recursion and uses that technique to build a procedural curve tree. Achieving this in MEL requires a fair bit of trigonometry, but the cool kind of trigonometry — the kind you can use in pick-up lines.

Chapter 8 demonstrates how you can combine MEL and expressions to set up scalable FX rigs. It is important to understand that there are differences between MEL and expressions, so I start that chapter by explaining precisely what expressions are and how they differ from MEL. To exemplify a practical application of expressions, in this chapter we set up a moderately complex rig that can be scaled for big shots in production.

The script covered in Chapter 9 is MEL, but from a software engineering point of view. It was written by a very talented programmer named Craig Davies and creates annotation markers under the Maya timeline to aid animators with lip-synching. It is a tremendous insight to realize how programming principles (like logical indices, complex attributes, and memory considerations) can be translated to MEL in such a way that the efficiency and stability of the script improves exponentially. This chapter is the triple whammy with whipped cream on top.

Remember that programming is not a spectator sport; you will only learn it when you are right in the middle. In all honesty, working through this book will require some effort and a fair bit of study. Learning (and using) MEL is one of those experiences that can be extremely frustrating, yet — in the end — exceptionally rewarding. It is my profound hope that this book will help you bypass at least some of those frustrations and get you closer to the gratifying experience MEL can be.

If you have any questions or comments about the content of the book, we have set up a site with a message board at http://mel4prod.mayawiki.com/. Please feel free to drop by anytime!

Chapter 1

Under the Hood

1.1 Lifting Maya's Skirt

1.1.1 Introduction

This book is not an exhaustive reference book that covers all aspects of Maya programming. Instead, it provides detailed explanations of a number of scripts I have written and used in production. The idea is to provide the novice scripter a structured and synoptic view into production scripting and to give the experienced scripter a quick reference of tested scripting techniques.

With the knowledge you will gain from this book, you will be able to expand upon Maya's already impressive list of tools by creating new UIs, automating tasks, and generally making life easier for yourself or whoever you are writing code for.

Learning MEL is much like learning a new language. Initially, it will take some effort to learn the new vocabulary and syntax, but with practice it will soon come naturally. As with any language, you need a firm foundation to build upon, and that is what this first chapter is all about. I use real-life production scripts to illustrate the basic concepts and thoroughly explain the theory behind them. In later chapters, we will tackle more advanced tasks, while attempting to maintain theoretical and conceptual clarity.

This first chapter is all about lifting Maya's skirt and taking a good look under it.

We will start by taking a closer look at what really happens when you perform actions while using Maya. This will lead us to an analysis of some common MEL commands and the workflow for querying and creating attributes through MEL. With that knowledge we should be ready to write our very first MEL script. After that we take a closer look at important programming concepts like procedures, data types, iterations, and conditional statements.

This chapter and the next one will take the most effort because unfortunately we will have to cover some dry and rather theoretical material. There is no way around this really, but if you are having a hard time, think about how it would feel to go to an exotic country for the first time and be able to speak the local language perfectly. No fumbling with worthless dictionaries or clumsy sign language; you can get what you want, when you want it. With MEL, you will get this control. With MEL, you are the authority.

1.1.2 **Resources**

Apart from this book, where can you get information on MEL?

- The first and most important resource is the Maya Developer Resources in the Maya help. Due to the fact that there are over 1,300 commands, each with at least 10 flags, you will spend more time reading the Maya command reference than you do coding. Especially in the beginning. I strongly suggest you make a handy bookmark in your browser for this page because you will be using it all the time. Throughout this book I show you how to use the help regarding MEL.

- As demonstrated in this book, the best way to learn is to get your hands dirty and dissect and brutalize the scripts that come with Maya and those you can find on the net. On Windows (for Maya 2008), you can find them in: C:\Program Files\Autodesk\ Maya2008\scripts.

> **Note:** Please note that most of these scripts are quite advanced and that you should never adjust these scripts unless you know exactly what you are doing (and you have backed them up).

- By far, the best resource for MEL and Maya on the web is http://www.highend3d.com/. From here you can download thousands of MEL scripts of all levels of complexity, but be aware that the quality of coding varies from script to script. Highend3D also has a mailing list, specifically aimed at Maya developers, to which you should subscribe. There is also a mailing list archive with a search function at http://www.highend3d.com/maya/list_servers/. If you have a question, chances are the question has been asked before, so searching that mailing list before asking is a good idea.

- There is also a vibrant MEL forum at http://www.cgtalk.com/.

- A real MEL wiki at http://mayamel.tiddlyspot.com/.

- Matt Estella's Maya wiki: http://www.tokeru.com/t/bin/view.

1.1.3 Using an Appropriate Editor

To write MEL, you should never actually use the Script Editor, as its functionality is far too limited. For even simple scripting, you will need a text editor for programmers. Here are some of the most popular editors used by MEL programmers:

- **Crimson Editor** (http://www.crimsoneditor.com/) is a professional source code editor for Windows. It offers many powerful features for programming such as highlighting, undo/redo, user tools, macros, spell checker, and more.

- **jEdit** is another neat free editor (http://www.jedit.org/). jEdit is much more than just a text editor, though. Through various plug-ins and macros, jEdit can be integrated into Maya and function as a full-featured programming environment. jEdit will also function on every operating system that Maya does, so it's easy to use wherever you are using Maya. Detailed docs can be found at http://www.highend3d.com/maya/tutorials/using_tools_scripts/Configuring-jEdit-with-Maya-319.html.

- In this book I will be using an integrated editor called **MEL Studio Pro**, which is actually a plug-in for Maya and replaces the Script Editor completely. You can find more information about MEL Studio Pro at http://www.digimation.com/. The downside of MEL Studio Pro is that it is for 32-bit Windows only.

■ A recent addition to the MEL editors list is **MaxYa**, which offers a free learning edition at http://www.tarzworkshop.com/. Besides the fact that it does MEL and Python, the immensely cool thing about MaxYa is that it works independently from Maya, which means that Maya does not have to be open to use it. MaxYa is not a plug-in, yet it is perfectly integrated in Maya. It executes and sends results back without any command port communication. Highly recommended!

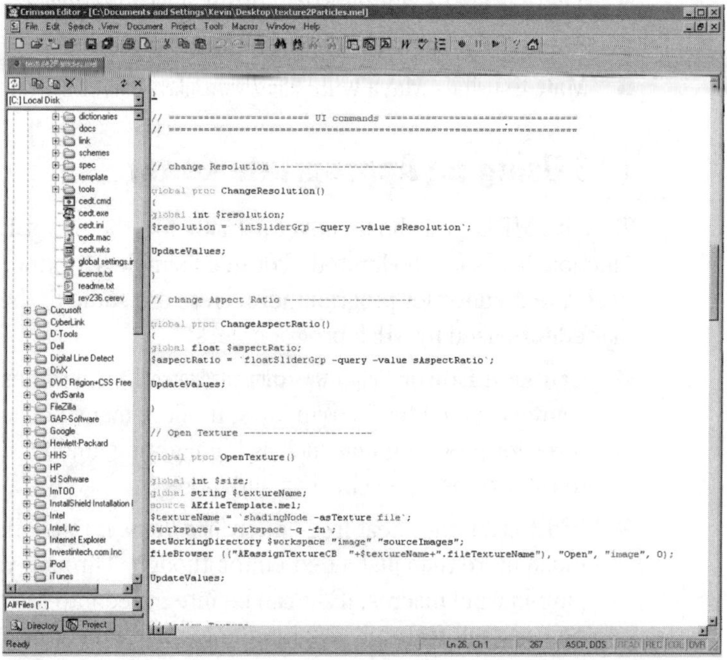

Figure 1-1: Crimson Editor

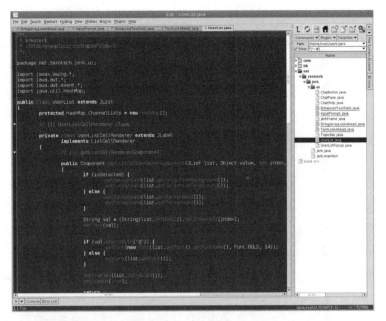

Figure 1-2: jEdit

Figure 1-3: MEL Studio Pro

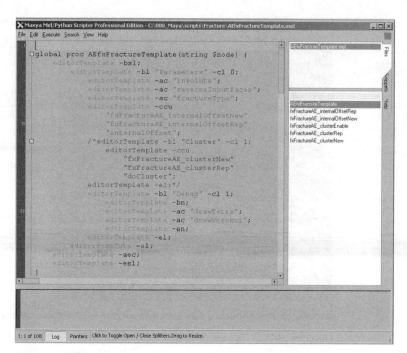

Figure 1-4: MaxYa

All of these editors offer at least the following functionality:

- Syntax highlighting. Comments, procedures, and commands are highlighted in user-definable colors.
- Automatic command completion.
- A panel that shows an overview of the procedures, scripts, and expressions. Double-clicking jumps to that part in the script.
- Find and replace functions.

The Script Editor offers, well, almost none of these features other than a crappy search and replace. They only added line numbers in Maya 8 or so. Bottom line is: Don't use the Script Editor for coding unless you want to end up in the loony bin. I strongly advise you to download and install one of the editors mentioned above before reading further.

1.2 **What Can MEL Do for You?**

MEL is Maya's scripting language. This means that you can type a MEL command in the Script Editor and execute that command as soon as you hit Enter. This differs from a compiled language like C++, because a compiled language would require you to convert your code into machine code, a language a computer understands. Because MEL is a scripting language, it is easier to use and to learn. This does not mean, however, that learning to use it is not time-consuming. Like with all programming, the bulk of your time will be spent debugging and refining your code, and smashing your head against the monitor because of code absurdities. For most programmers, however, these riddles and anomalies are a large part of the fun — especially when they occur at 3 a.m. the night before a big review.

In other words, Maya's embedded language is its programming interface that enables the user to:

- Automate repetitive tasks
- Expand Maya's capabilities
- Perform very complex tasks
- Create a custom Maya interface

Actually, all of Maya's functionality can be accessed through MEL. Moreover, some commands/nodes can *only* be accessed through MEL.

1.2.1 **Some Examples of MEL Scripts**

Let's take a look at some MEL scripts (going from simple to more complex) to get a better idea of the endless possibilities. It is not my intention to exhaustively explain the functions of each of these scripts in depth, but just illustrate what is possible.

At the same time I show you how you can use scripts that you download from the net.

The basic workflow is this:

1. *Source the script.* You can do so by choosing File > Source, or by opening the script, selecting all, and hitting Enter. Mind you, that is Enter on the numerical keypad, *not* Return. If you hit Return, you will lose everything.

2. If there is an interface, *execute the main interface procedure.* (I will explain in Chapter 2 what a procedure is.) Otherwise, use the command line/Script Editor to execute the main procedure and its arguments.

km_CVamountInSceneHUD

The km_CVamountInSceneHUD script creates a heads-up display that shows the CVs in your scene. A distinction is made between surface CVs and curve CVs. The HUD can be turned on/off from the Display menu.

km_bookmarkManager

This script does just that: It manages your bookmarks. Cameras are listed on the left side, and the bookmarks of the selected cam on the right. All of the menus are under the right mouse button. Left-clicking on a bookmark displays it in the active view panel. In Chapter 4 of this book we will completely dissect this script and look at it line by line.

AdvancedSkeleton

AdvancedSkeleton (by AnimationStudios www.animationstudios.com.au/) is a collection of Maya tools for doing character setup. The main features of AdvancedSkeleton are:

- You are not limited to a pre-made FitSkeleton; you can create any FitSkeleton you like.

- The local rotation axis and rotation orders are set by the FitSkeleton, so you can control these.

- You can go back and forth from AdvancedSkeleton to the FitSkeleton and make changes and then rebuild the AdvancedSkeleton.

- Unlimited body configurations; from three heads and five legs to 100 fingers or anything you can think of.

- Comes with a drag-and-drop SelectorDesigner that lets you easily create custom Selector user interfaces.

- And a PoserDesigner that creates UIs for storing and retrieving poses.

OverBurn

OverBurn (by Peter Shipkov http://petershipkov.com/) is a combination of particles, fluids, and particleSamplerInfo nodes. It substitutes the default particleCloud shader with a fluids shader. As a result, the final look of the particles is much more believable. Using this technique we can create a wide range of interesting volumetric effects like explosions, fireballs, dust, smoke, lava, ice, etc.

1.3 Not Your Everyday Maya

In this section we'll take a closer look at the Script Editor and external editors and why you should use them. We'll also give you an example of a special marking menu. Finally, we'll take a closer look at the dependency graph.

1.3.1 A Closer Look at the Script Editor

Let's take a closer look at what actually happens if you do something simple in Maya like creating a sphere.

1. Open up the Script Editor.

2. Choose **Edit > Clear All** to make all changes apparent.

3. Create a NURBs sphere with the menu commands in the UI and look at the output in the Script Editor. What you get is a line like this:

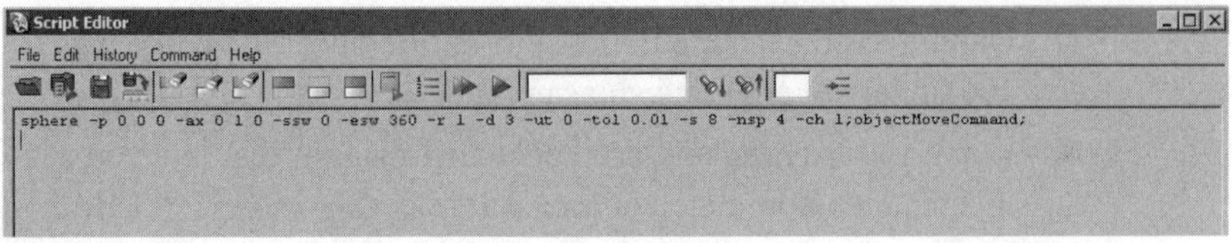

Figure 1-5

The line above is the `sphere` command with some of its flags. We will talk more about commands in section 1.4 of this chapter, "MEL Commands."

4. Open the Developer Resources help and look for the `sphere` command. The help page shows you the command syntax, return value, flags, and other information about the command.

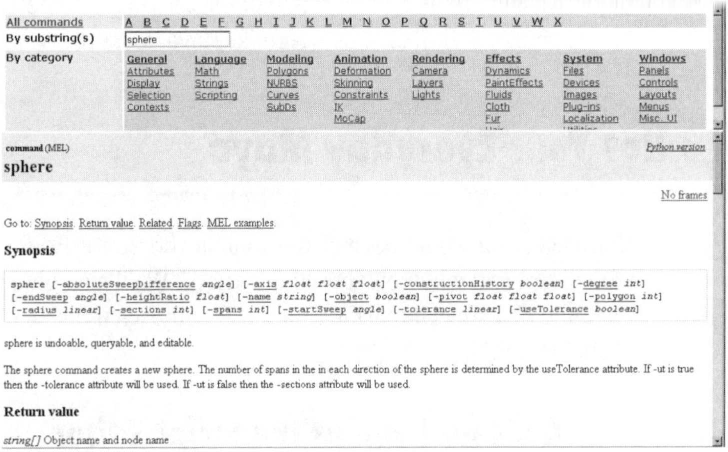

Figure 1-6

5. Delete the sphere you just created.

6. Type **sphere** in the Script Editor, then highlight it and press **Enter.**

Everything you do in Maya is reflected in the Script Editor because the UI is nothing more than MEL commands and procedures in fancy buttons, sliders, and windows. You can learn a whole lot by looking at what happens in the Script Editor.

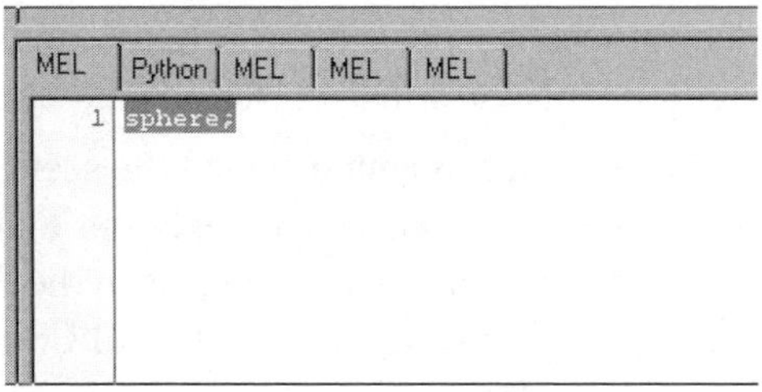

Figure 1-7

1.3.2 When Marking Menus Don't Listen

Let's use this knowledge to do something more practical.

I love marking menus. I dream in marking menus. I take them out to dinner and pay for their entertainment. We all know how we make marking menus:

Get your command in the shelf (by holding down Ctrl+Shift+Alt) and drag it into the Marking Menu window.

Figure 1-8 shows a custom marking menu.

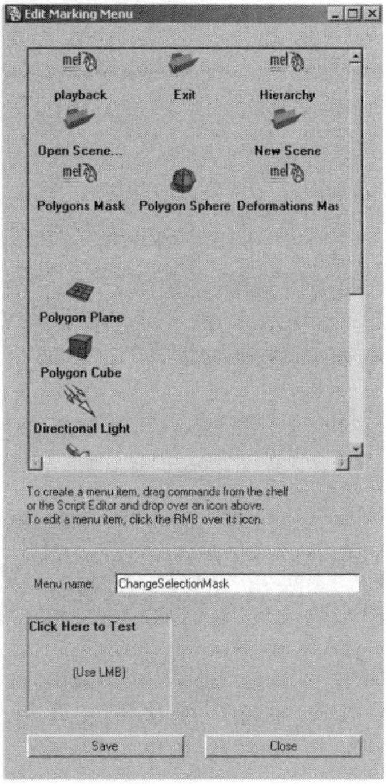

Something that I used to use all the time (when I was still rendering with the Maya renderer) is the Create Render Node window. To speed up my workflow, I'd like to have fast access to that functionality with a marking menu. The problem is that when I try the procedure outlined above, the Script Editor spews this at me:

Figure 1-8

```
// Error: This action has no effect. //
```

Cheeky!

1. Let's take a look at what happens in the Script Editor when we call the Create Render Node window: Nothing!

2. Because there is so much happening behind the scenes, Maya hides most of the internal commands in the Script Editor. You can, however, tell Maya to show *all* commands in the Script Editor window by choosing **History > Echo All Commands.**

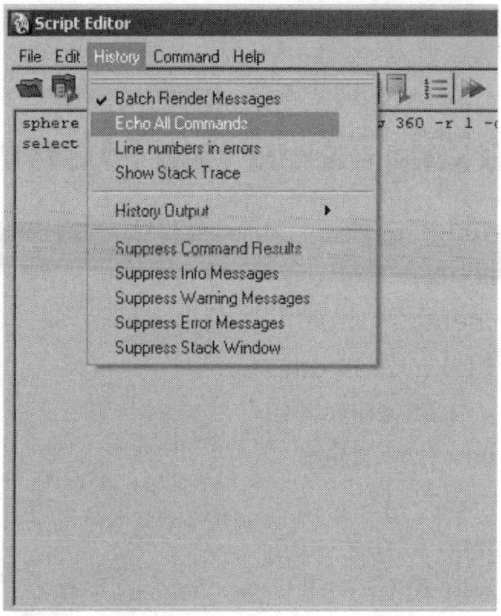

Figure 1-9

3. Now do **Create > Create Render Node** again and look in the Script Editor.

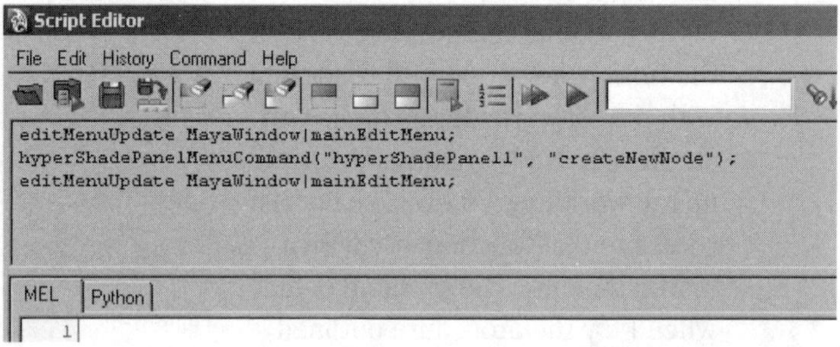

Figure 1-10

4. The code that is of interest to us is this:

```
hyperShadePanelMenuCommand("hyperShadePanel1", "createNewNode");
editMenuUpdate MayaWindow|mainEditMenu;
```

5. With your middle mouse button (MMB), drag this in the Script Editor's input area and execute it. The Create Render Node window should appear.

6. Using the MMB, drag these two lines to the shelf.

7. Now you can open the Marking Menu window and create a marking menu like you normally would.

1.3.3 Maya as a System of Nodes

To make the transition from GUI to scripting a bit easier, the single most important thing you have to understand is that:

> Maya is a system of nodes with attributes that can be connected and animated. This system is called the "dependency graph."

My good friend Tom Kluyskens always compares Maya with a set of LEGO blocks. One block (node) can be independent and have some characteristics (attributes) such as its color, shape, weight, etc., but things start getting interesting when you put those separate blocks (nodes) together to build something.

Knowing that a scene is nothing more than a collection of nodes and connections is paramount when scripting. Often the UI hides most of what happens in the dependency graph, but when scripting you will have to delve right into it. Hence a firm understanding is essential.

Every part of a Maya scene (be it a texture, camera, expression, or geometry) is internally represented as a node. Each node has attributes, which store the characteristics of that specific node. As mentioned before, the system of these nodes, their attributes, and the connections in between is called the dependency graph. Often, to write a MEL script to automate a task, you will look at what happens in the dependency graph and then reproduce it in MEL for your specific purpose.

We all know you can manipulate the keyable attributes of a node in the channel box, and most of the other attributes in the Attribute Editor. I say most attributes, because certain attributes can only be accessed through MEL.

Using the Graph Editor, let's take a closer look at the dependency graph of a simple scene like an animated ball.

1. With the Hypergraph and Attribute Editor open, create a NURBs sphere.

2. In the Hypergraph you can see that several nodes were created. (Like the flow of a river, nodes whose attributes' values connect to the current node are "upstream" nodes, and nodes that connect to the current node are "downstream" nodes.)

    ■ nurbsSphere1: This is the transform node. The attributes of a transform node store all the information of where an object is in space (world and local) and how it is scaled and rotated.

    ■ nurbsSphereShape1: This is the shape node. The shape node contains a node's actual geometric shape and the properties about its construction and rendering.

    ■ initialShadingGroup: This is a shading group node that contains all objects that will be shaded with that particular shader.

3. If you hold your cursor over the connections, you can see which attributes of which nodes are connected.

Figure 1-11

4. Set some keyframes on the sphere.

Setting a keyframe on a node (now represented as a trapezoid in the Hypergraph) connects an animation curve to each channel that is getting animated. When you play back the scene, Maya's time1 node (the scene's clock), tells the animation curve which frame's numbers value to look up. Then the animation curve sets (in this particular case) the translate value to the right value.

5. Click on the sphere in the Hypergraph (HG) and choose **Show up and downstream connections**.

6. Hold your mouse over the connections to get a clear idea of what is going on.

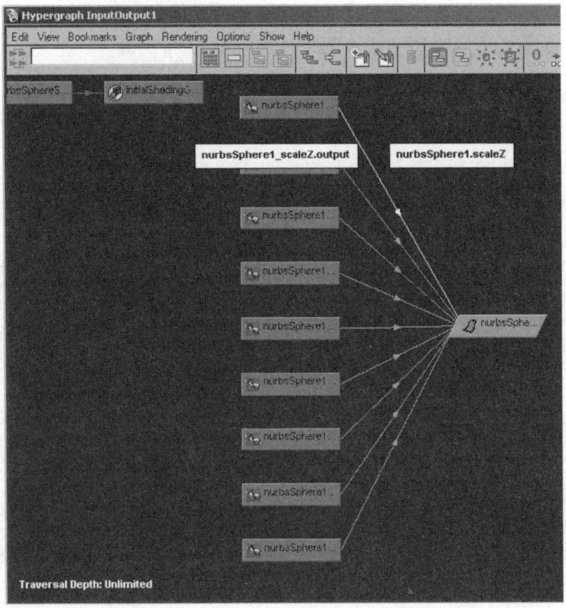

Figure 1-12

Now let's examine a more "elaborate" example: a joint hierarchy bound to a cylinder.

By the way, to get detailed information about nodes and their attributes, go to Help > Developer Resources > Nodes and Attributes.

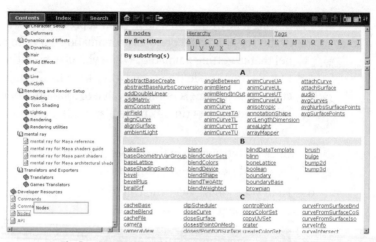

Figure 1-13: The Developer Resources Nodes help page

1. With the HG open, create a cylinder, put three joints inside, and Smooth Bind.

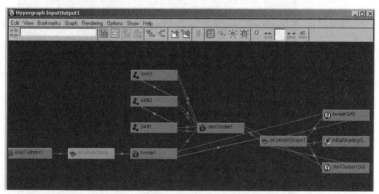

Figure 1-14

2. From left to right (upstream to downstream) let's take a look at what is going on:

   ■ On the far left we have the polyCylinder history node connected to the original cylinder's shape node, which has been renamed and hidden. (Hidden nodes are grayed out.)

   ■ tweak1 is a tweak node, which is automatically created when you perform any kind of deformation. A tweak node is placed in the history of all deformed shapes so that the user can control the ordering of the CV translation and the deformers.

■ The tweak node and the joint hierarchy are connected to the skinCluster node. A skin cluster node allows you to associate a percentage per joint transform for each CV in the geometry.

■ The new pCylinderShape1 node contains the newly deformed geometry.

■ The two remaining nodes are hidden set nodes that define the sets of points that each joint influences. A set is basically a collection of objects.

3. With a joint selected, click on the scene hierarchy in the HG. This displays the transform hierarchy of the nodes in your scene. You should be familiar with its parent/child relationships.

1.4 MEL Commands

Note: The code shown throughout this book is available on the companion disc.

1.4.1 What Is a MEL Command?

When you execute a MEL command, you are actually executing one of Maya's C++ functions. For example, when you create a sphere from the UI, you are indirectly calling Maya's `sphere` command.

1.4.2 The Structure of a MEL Command

The basic structure of a MEL command is this:

```
melCommand -flag value;
```

For example:

```
sphere -radius 2;
```

Make sure you always terminate a command with a semicolon to signify the end of the command. Maya reads a line of code until it hits a semicolon.

Let's look at the `sphere` command in the help files and take a closer look at some of its flags. In the help pages, each command also has some examples beneath the list of flags. This is the best resource for learning how to use commands and their flags.

Again, please make sure you create a quick bookmark to the Maya Developer Resources page.

All flags have a long name and a short name, both of which are valid. As you get more used to writing MEL, you will learn to use the shorthand. For example:

```
sphere -radius 2;
```

is the same as:

```
sphere -r 2;
```

Now, in MEL, create a half sphere called halfSphere by setting the `-startSweep` and `-endSweep` flags.

```
sphere -name "halfSphere"
    -startSweep 0
    -endSweep 180;
```

In the help page for the `sphere` command's flags is a column that shows the argument types. These argument types describe the data type of each argument the command can include. For more information about data types, see section 1.5.2 in this chapter.

Chapter 1

All commands	A B C D E F G H I J K L M N O P Q R S T U V W X
By substring(s)	sphere

By category	General	Language	Modeling	Animation	Rendering	Effects	System	Windows
	Attributes	Math	Polygons	Deformation	Camera	Dynamics	Files	Panels
	Display	Strings	NURBS	Skinning	Layers	PaintEffects	Devices	Controls
	Selection	Scripting	Curves	Constraints	Lights	Fluids	Images	Layouts
	Contexts		SubDs	IK		Cloth	Plug-ins	Menus
				MoCap		Fur	Localization	Misc. UI

cone, cylinder, nurbsCube, nurbsPlane, torus

Flags

absoluteSweepDifference, axis, constructionHistory, degree, endSweep, heightRatio, name, object, pivot, polygon, radius, sections, spans, startSweep, tolerance, useTolerance

Long name (short name)	argument types	Properties
-pivot (-p)	float float float	Q E
The primitive's pivot point		
-axis (-ax)	float float float	Q E
The primitive's axis		
-radius (-r)	linear	Q E
The radius of the object *Default:* 1.0		
-startSweep (-ssw)	angle	Q E
The angle at which to start the surface of revolution *Default:* 0		

Figure 1-15

You can very easily create your own window with a sphere button to do exactly the same thing. To create a window, we use the, well, `window` command. We will spend quite a bit of time creating UIs, so you better get comfy.

```
window sphereWindow;
columnLayout;
button -label "create sphere" -command sphere;
showWindow sphereWindow;
```

1.4.3 Create, Edit, and Query Mode

Let's take another look at the `sphere` command in the MEL command reference. The last column, Properties, contains the letters Q, E, and C.

- Q stands for Query. A command in Query mode allows you to query the properties of an existing object.

- E stands for Edit. In Edit mode, a command can change the given property of an existing object in a scene.

- C stands for Create. Unless you explicitly specify the Query or Edit mode, a command operates in Create mode. In other words, Create mode is the default.

You cannot mix modes within a single command. Not all commands support the various modes. That is why the available modes are specified in the Properties column of the command reference.

All commands	A B C D E F G H I J K L M N O P Q R S I U V W X
By substring(s)	sphere

By category	General	Language	Modeling	Animation	Rendering	Effects	System	Windows
	Attributes	Math	Polygons	Deformation	Camera	Dynamics	Files	Panels
	Display	Strings	NURBS	Skinning	Layers	PaintEffects	Devices	Controls
	Selection	Scripting	Curves	Constraints	Lights	Fluids	Images	Layouts
	Contexts		SubDs	IK		Cloth	Plug-ins	Menus
				MoCap		Fur	Localization	Misc. UI

cone, cylinder, nurbsCube, nurbsPlane, torus

Flags

absoluteSweepDifference, axis, constructionHistory, degree, endSweep, heightRatio, name, object, pivot, polygon, radius, sections, spans, startSweep, tolerance, useTolerance

Long name (short name)	argument types	Properties
-pivot (-p)	float float float	Q E
The primitive's pivot point		
-axis (-ax)	float float float	Q E
The primitive's axis		
-radius (-r)	linear	Q E
The radius of the object		
Default: 1.0		
-startSweep (-ssw)	angle	Q E
The angle at which to start the surface of revolution		
Default: 0		

Figure 1-16

Because they are so common, the query and edit flags are almost always used in their short version: -e and -q.

Examples for Query

Going back to our previous command, create a half sphere in MEL:

```
sphere -name "halfSphere" -startSweep 0 -endSweep 180;
```

To query any of its attributes, try this:

```
sphere -q -startSweep;
// Result: 0 //

sphere -q -radius;
// Result: 1 //
```

Here's another example. While writing scripts for animation, something you will do all the time is query the current time in the timeslider:

```
currentTime -q;
// Result: 136 //
```

Chapter 1

Examples for Edit

Going back to our favorite halfSphere:

```
sphere -e -startSweep 25;
// Result: Values edited. //
```

To change the name, switch to Edit mode:

```
sphere -e -name "quarterSphere";
// Result: Values edited. //
```

A typical example of using Edit mode is changing the name of a button after it has been pressed.

When writing MEL you use these modes in almost every command, so don't worry about it if it isn't clear yet. It will become clear after the gazillionth time.

1.4.4 MEL Syntax

How you write commands, flags, arguments, and procedures is called "syntax." With any language, you have to take certain rules into account to make the language understandable. In English, for example, we read from left to right and from top to bottom. In Japanese, you read from top to bottom and from right to left. In English, this is correct: "A pretty girl crossed the street." But "A girl pretty the street crossed" sounds a bit dodgy. MEL is the same in the sense that you have to adhere to certain rules to make the language understandable for Maya.

Just like in a book, in addition to correct language syntax, you format the language with paragraphs and headings to make it easier for the reader and yourself to understand.

We will cover MEL syntax and formatting to a much greater extent in later chapters, but here is a tantalizing taste:

Semicolons

All MEL commands must end with a semicolon.

Flag Names

Especially in the beginning, avoid using the short form for command flags. When you or someone else later edits or modifies the script, you won't have to remember or look up all the short names.

```
select -allDependencyNodes;  // as opposed to select -adn
revolve -useLocalPivot;      // as opposed to revolve -ulp
```

White Space

Use lots of white space to break up commands and programming structures. Create white space with spaces, tab characters, and blank lines. White space has no effect on the execution of the script, but it can greatly improve readability, as shown in Figure 1-17.

```
// -----> Used in annoNudge.mel

global proc int[] annoDisplayGetNeighbors(string $node, int $logIdx) {

    // time range of the marker we're interested in
    float $min = `getAttr ($node+".block["+$logIdx+"].in")`;
    float $max = `getAttr ($node+".block["+$logIdx+"].out")`;

    int $all[];
    annoDataGetExistingElements($node, $all);

    // find our left/right neighbor markers
    float $big = 1000000;
    float $neighborTime[2] = {-$big,$big};
    int $neighborIdx[2] = {-1,-1};
    int $idx;
    for ($idx in $all) {
        if ($idx == $logIdx) {
            continue;
        }
        string $elemPlug = $node+".block["+$idx+"]";
        float $in  = `getAttr ($elemPlug+".in")`;
        float $out = `getAttr ($elemPlug+".out")`;

        // find the highest marker that is still lower than
        // the one we're interested in
        if ($in < $min && $out < $max) {
            if ($in > $neighborTime[0]) {
                $neighborTime[0] = $in;
                $neighborIdx[0] = $idx;
            }
```

Figure 1-17: Use white space to improve the readability of the code.

Comments

Comments in your script are invaluable to explain what is happening. When you go back to a script after some time, they will prove the ultimate way to pick up the train of thought. When you pass your scripts on to others, they will also be able to understand them. I also use comments to add to-do's to my scripts, such as feature enhancements or bug fixes.

I will continually remind you to include comments because they are absolutely vital when programming. An illustration of this is an anecdote told by someone who placed second in a national programming competition. He said that there were people who had met all the criteria for error checking and UI features, but didn't even place due to lack of comments in their code.

I can guarantee that you will go completely mental if you have to read even a small amount of code without comments. If you code in a team and others have to read and/or debug your uncommented code, you will be stripped, spanked, and tossed in a barrel filled with tar and feathers.

Bottom line: Comment your code!

There are two ways to add comments. For single-line comments, use two forward slashes (//). For comments that consist of more than one line, use the forward slash and asterisk combination (/* comments here */).

```
//----------------------------------------------------------------
//listCams lists all cameras in the scene and places them in
//tslCameras, with all their RMB functionality
//----------------------------------------------------------------
global proc listCams ()
{   //list all cameras
    string $camera[] = `listCameras`;
    //loop though all cameras and put each in
    //tslCameras
    for ($eachCamera in $camera)
        {
        textScrollList -e
            -append $eachCamera
            //when the camera is selected
            //call the populateBookmarkList proc that populates the bookmark TSL
            //-selectCommand ("populateBookmarkList; string $sel[]=`textScrollList -q -si ts
            -selectCommand ("populateBookmarkList")
            //string $sel[]=`textScrollList -q -si tslCameras`;")
            tslCameras;
        //add RMB functionailty to each of the cameras in the TSL
        //Mind the -parent flag that parents the popupMenu tot the
        //cameta TSL (tslCameras)
        popupMenu -p tslCameras camPop;
            menuItem -l "Look through" -command lookThoughCamera;
            menuItem -l "Toggle ResGate" -command toggleResGate;
            menuItem -l "Open AE" -command openAECam;
            menuItem -l "rename" -command renameCamera;

        }

    //since the active camera will be the selected item in the camera TSL
    //its bookmarks wll be loaded in the bookmark TSL
    populateBookmarkList;
}
```

Figure 1-18: Include comments!

Multiple-Line Commands

Regardless of how many lines you use for a command, the end of a command is determined by the semicolon. If you have a command with a larger number of flags, using tabs and aligning the flags under each other makes the code a whole lot more readable.

I will also hammer on cleanliness and readability in coding throughout this book. This stems from dreadful personal experiences of having to look for bugs in code (even my own). Sifting through 3,000 lines of code without comments or proper formatting is a nightmare, as you can well imagine.

1.4.5 Your First Script!

> **IMPORTANT NOTE:** Due to the limited width of the pages in this book, most of the scripts will exhibit some kind of text wrapping. You can find the scripts on the disc that comes with this book. I strongly suggest you open the scripts in your text editor and read the code on your screen.

Let's put the above acquired knowledge into practice. We will create a window with:

- A create sphere button
- A button that prints "Whoozaaaa!!"

Hey, you have to start somewhere.

```
//create window with a title
//optional: turn off minimize and maximize button
window -title "doTheSphere" firstWin;

//create a layout to put controls in
columnLayout -adjustableColumn mainCol;

//create button
button -command "polySphere" sphereButton;

//create button
// Note the funky backslashes before the quotes
// More about that in 1.5.3 (below)
button -command "print \"Whoozaaaa!!\"" printButton;
```

```
//show window
showWindow firstWin;
```

Go on! Get your mum and show it to her. I know you want to.

1.4.6 **Common MEL Commands**

There are a couple of commands that you will need in every script
you write. Let's take a brief look at these commands and their
usage.

> **Note:** You can look up the commands in the command reference for a full list of
> their flags.

setAttr sets an attribute to a specified value.

```
//create a spotlight
defaultSpotLight(1, 1,1,1, 0, 40, 0, 0, 0, 0,0,0, 1, 0);

//set the intensity to 4
setAttr "spotLightShape1.intensity" 4;

//set the color to blue
//the -type flag specifies an array of three doubles
setAttr "spotLightShape1.color" -type double3 0.0 0.0 1.0;

//make the tz attribute unkeyable
setAttr -keyable off "spotLight1.translateZ";

//lock the scale values
setAttr -lock on "spotLight1.scaleX";
setAttr -lock on "spotLight1.scaleY";
setAttr -lock on "spotLight1.scaleZ";
getAttr helps you find out the current value of an attribute.
//continuing from the above script
getAttr "spotLightShape1.intensity";
//to cast the value in a variable, do this:
float $intensity = `getAttr "spotLightShape1.intensity"`;
```

connectAttr, as you can probably guess, connects two attributes to each other. An important flag is the `-force` flag, which will break the existing connection (if there is one) to perform the new one.

```
//create locator
spaceLocator -position 0 0 0;

//create sphere
polySphere;

//connect translate of sphere to scale of locator
connectAttr -force pSphere1.translate locator1.scale;
//move sphere around to get wacky stuff
```

ls returns the list of objects in the scene. Some common flags for the `ls` command are:

```
//-selection (-sl): Lists objects that are currently selected.
//this flag is used so much that the short version is used
//exclusively
ls -selection

//-cameras (-ca): Lists camera shapes
ls -cameras;

//-lights (-lt): Lists all lights
ls -lights;

//-materials (-mat): Lists all materials
ls -materials;
```

xform is a very powerful command with dozens of flags. It allows you to query or change transformations that are more complicated than the normal move, rotate, and scale. It can also be used to query some values that cannot be set directly, such as the transformation matrix or the bounding box.

```
//create a sphere
polySphere;

//select a vertex
//-replace indicates that the specified items should replace
```

```
//the existing items on the active list.
select -replace pSphere1.vtx[228];

//query the world space position of that vertex
xform -query -worldSpace  -translation  pSphere1.vtx[228];

//query the bounding box
//The values returned are in the following order:
//xmin ymin zmin xmax ymax zmax.
xform -query -boundingBox  pSphere1;
```

1.5 **Variables and Data Types**

1.5.1 **Definition and Syntax**

Variables are the cornerstone of each MEL script. In layman's terms, a variable is like a drawer that allows you to store stuff for later usage. More technically, variables are dynamic storage places for values. Variables are an important aspect of all programming languages.

In MEL syntax, you must use a dollar sign ($) in front of your variable name. Additionally, a variable cannot start with a number or special character, and they are case sensitive. For example, $myVariable is considered to be different from $MyVariable. $_thisHere is valid but $12Joint is not.

What I mean above by "dynamic" is that variables allow your script to work in multiple scenarios. For example:

```
//create some objects

polySphere;
polyPlane;
defaultSpotLight(1, 1,1,1, 0, 40, 0, 0, 0, 0,0,0, 1, 0);
defaultDirectionalLight(1, 1,1,1, "0", 0,0,0);
spaceLocator -position 0 0 0;

//select some objects in your scene
//store selected objects in variable
```

```
string $selectedObjects[] = `ls -sl`;
// Result: spotLight1 spotLight2 spotLight3 spotLight4 //

//select some OTHER objects in your scene
//store selected objects in variable
string $selectedObjects[] = `ls -sl`;
// Result: front side pSphere1 pPlane1 directionalLight1 //
```

When you create variables (also called *declaring* variables in programmer lingo) you must tell Maya what kind of object you are planning on storing (also called *assigning* or *casting*) in the variable. These kinds of values or objects are called *data types*. You cannot mix data types within the same variable.

1.5.2 Data Types

Integers (int) are numbers without a fractional part.
    For example:

```
5
-20
0
20004
```

In a variable:

```
int $frameNumber = 10;
```

Floating-point numbers (float) are numbers that have a fractional part.
    For example:

```
3.145544
2.0
-6548.22545
0.0
```

In a variable:

```
float $scaleX = 7.545;
```

A **vector** (vector) is a triple of floating-point numbers. Vectors usually indicate an X, Y, Z location or an RGB color value.

For example:

```
<<2.5, 45, 45.22>>
```

Mind the syntax. Vectors are separated by commas and enclosed with double angle brackets (<< and >>):

```
vector $position = <<1.23,4.5,7.88>>;
```

> **IMPORTANT NOTE:** To get the individual elements (x or y or z) "out of" a vector, you have to do this:
>
> ```
> vector $position = <<1.23, 4.5, 7.88>>;
> //mind the syntax
> print ($position.x);
> //1.23
> print ($position.y);
> //4.5
> print ($position.z);
> //7.88
> ```

A **string** (string) is a sequence of characters surrounded by quotes.
For example:

```
"Whooozaaaaaaaa!"
"123548qwertyuiop"
```

You can add strings together (*concatenate* in programmer jargon) with the plus sign (+):

```
string $add = "I love ";
string $this = "MEL";
string $result = $add + $this;
// Result: I love MEL //
```

1.5.3 Special Characters

If a string contains a "special" character such as a quote mark, tab character, or backslash, you use the backslash as an escape sequence.

For a quote mark, use \" like this:

```
print "Print a quotation mark\"";
```

For a new line, use \n like this:

```
print "go to a new\nline";
```

For a tab character, use \t like this:

```
print "This is a \t tab";
```

For a carriage return, use \r like this:

```
print "Return this \rbaby";
```

For a backslash, use \\ like this:

```
print "Gimme a backslash \\";
```

Here is an example:

```
print "I want to play \\ \" \r\r \\\non a new line";
```

I strongly suggest you try out these special characters and look at the results in the Script Editor to get a feel for how they work and what they do.

1.5.4 Arrays

An *array* is a variable like a normal variable, except it can hold more than one value. A string array can, for example, store a list of selected objects, but it can still only store strings. You cannot mix data types in variables, not even in arrays.

You declare an array by using square brackets after the variable. For example:

```
string $sel[];
float $floatArray[];
```

To access values from an array, you need to specify the element in the array.

> **IMPORTANT NOTE:** Arrays are zero-based, meaning that the first element is [0], and not [1].

```
//create some objects and select them (all in MEL, no UI)
polySphere;
duplicate -returnRootsOnly;
//-rr is returnRootsOnly: return only
//the root nodes of the new hierarchy.
duplicate -returnRootsOnly;
duplicate -returnRootsOnly;

//select all spheres
select -replace pSphere1 pSphere2 pSphere3 pSphere4;

//cast the selected objects in a string array called
// $selectedObjects
string $selectedObjects[] =`ls -sl`;

//get the size of the array
size $selectedObjects;
// Result: 4 //

//take a look at the elements or the array using the print command
print $selectedObjects[0];
//pSphere1
print $selectedObjects[1];
print $selectedObjects[2];
print $selectedObjects[3];
```

1.5.5 Giving Your Variables Descriptive Names

It is a good idea to give your variables descriptive names that will make sense when you (or others) have to wrestle through your scripts. For example, `string $x` doesn't say as much as `string $availableLights`.

The common way to separate words in MEL is with underscores or capitalization. For example:

```
$selected_joints
$selectedJoints
```

For clarity, you should use only one way of denoting variables throughout your script.

1.5.6 **Capturing the Result of a Command in a Variable**

To capture the result of a command, the most common method is to enclose the command with back quotes (top left of your keyboard, under the tilde). Using back quotes tells Maya to execute the command within the back quotes and assign the value to a variable.

```
//create a cube
polyCube;

//rotate it a tad
setAttr "pCube1.rotateY" 50;

//cast the value in a variable (mind the back quotes)
float $rotateY = `getAttr pCube1.rotateY`;
// Result: 50 //
```

This character (the back quote) is one of the biggest "gotchas" in MEL for new users, probably because it appears insignificant.

If you forget the back quotes, you will get an error like this:

```
// Error: float $rotateY = getAttr pCube1.rotateY; //
// Error: Invalid use of Maya object "getAttr". //
```

Chapter 2
Conditional Statements, Iterations, and Procedures

2.1 Conditional Statements

2.1.1 Definition

A conditional statement, also known as an "if statement," lets your script make its own decisions based on a comparison between two values. In more technical terms, with a conditional, a certain action will be performed only when a condition is met.

In plain English, a conditional statement would sound like this:

> IF it rains outside, THEN take an umbrella. ELSE don't take one.

The correct syntax in MEL is as follows:

```
//declare variable
int $x = 4;
//perform if statement
if ($x > 5)
    {
        print "X is greater than 5";
    }
else
    {
```

```
    print "X is not greater than 5";
}
```

The following example shows a conditional that will change the color of a sphere based on its scale in Z:

```
//create sphere
//put scale Z in variable
float $scaleZ = `getAttr pSphere1.sz`;

//change color to red when scaleZ is larger than 2
if ($scaleZ > 2)
    setAttr lambert1.color 1 0 0;

else
    setAttr lambert1.color 0 0 0;
```

As you can see, the comparison is always mathematical in nature. The left side is compared to the right side and a decision is made as to whether the values are equal, larger, or smaller. If they meet the condition, the statement is considered true and the given command will be executed.

MEL uses a large number of operators, including comparison, logic, binary, and others. The assignment operator is the equal sign (=). The >=, <=, <, and > operators are called comparison operators. The == and != operators are equality and inequality, respectively. The logical operators include || (or), && (and), and ! (not).

> **Note:** Be careful not to confuse the = and == operators. The = operator assigns a value to a variable. For example, $a = 10 assigns the value 10 to the variable $a. The == operator tests the equality of two values. For example, ($a == 10) tests whether $a is equal to 10.

Let's use all this knowledge in two more interesting and practical examples.

2.1.2 **Killing a Particle Based on the Position of a Locator**

Although there are some very big differences between MEL scripting and expressions (which will be exhaustively discussed in Chapter 8, "MEL and Expressions"), we can use what we have learned about conditionals to tackle a common problem with particles.

Motivation

Say you have a glass of soda and you are creating the rising bubbles with particles. At the soda surface you would want the particles to fizzle out or die.

Solution

We achieve this by creating a locator and a conditional that says:

"IF the particle's Y position is greater than the locator's Y position, THEN kill it."

English Transliteration of Script

To translate this into something Maya understands, we need to know:

1. The particle's position
2. The locator's position
3. How to kill all particles

> **IMPORTANT NOTE:** This is an expression, so write it in the particle shape Expression Editor, NOT in the Script Editor.

```
// IN THE CREATION EXPRESSION
//give particles enough lifespanPP so they can DIE
//cruel, innit?
particleShape1.lifespanPP = 100000;

// IN THE RUNTIME EXPRESSION
```

```
//get locator translation values and put in variable
vector $locatorPosition = <<locator1.translateX,
    locator1.translateY, locator1.translateZ>>;
//get particle position
vector $particlePosition = particleShape1.position;

//access Y values and perform conditional
if ($particlePosition.y>$locatorPosition.y)
    particleShape1.lifespanPP=0;
```

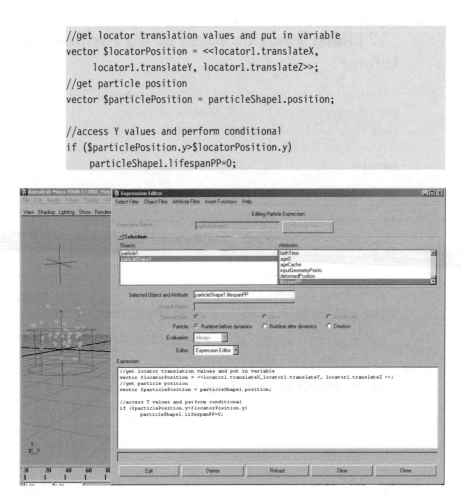

Figure 2-1

You can find the scene file called killParticleAtLocator.ma on the companion disc.

2.1.3 **Toggling the Resolution Gate**

Motivation

In the rendering phase of a project I find myself displaying and hiding the res gate dozens of times. Since the res gate control is hidden three clicks away in the View menu, I made a hotkey for it. The problem with this is that it doesn't work on a newly created camera; it only works with the camera you made the hotkey for.

Solution

I need to know what camera is active and display/hide the res gate for that specific camera.

Elements Needed

■ The active model panel. More specifically, the model panel the curser is over.

■ The camera that is active in that model panel.

■ How to show/hide the res gate for that camera.

English Transliteration of Script

1. Get the active camera.

2. IF the camera has its res gate displayed, hide it.

3. IF the res gate is hidden, display it.

Code and Comments

```
// get the active panel
// -withFocus: return the name of the panel that currently has focus
string $whichPanel = `getPanel -withFocus`;

//get camera of active modelPanel
string $nameCamera = `modelPanel -q -camera ($whichPanel)`;

//query the state of the resolution gate
//if there is one (==1)
if (`camera -q -displayResolution $nameCamera`==1)
//then turn it off
    camera -e -displayResolution off $nameCamera;
```

```
else
//else turn it on
    camera -e -displayResolution on $nameCamera;
```

Finer Points

■ Instead of –withFocus, you could use –underPointer, which returns the name of the panel that the pointer is currently over.

■ Mind the back quotes around commands that are executed.

■ Since value==1 is so common, there is a shorthand version for it:

```
if (`camera -q -displayResolution $nameCamera`)
```

The shorthand for value!=1 is:

```
if (!`camera -q -displayResolution $nameCamera`)
```

■ Mind the –edit flag to change/edit an existing value.

2.2 Looping Statements

Loops (also called *iterations*) allow you to repeatedly execute statements while a certain test condition is true. MEL supports for loops, for-in loops, and while loops.

■ **For-in loops** are designed to repeat a chunk of code, incrementing or decrementing a variable each time, until a condition (that you specify) is satisfied.

■ **For loops** allow you to repeat a chunk of code for each member in an array.

■ **While loops** allow you to repeat a chunk of code until some condition is satisfied

2.2.1 While Loops

A while loop works just like an if statement, except that it repeatedly executes the code inside the loop until the condition is satisfied.

```
int $x = 0;
while ($x < 20)
{
    $x = $x+1;
    print ($x + "\n");
}
```

When using while loops, always be careful to ensure that the condition actually *can* be satisfied; otherwise, it will run forever and Maya will lock up.

2.2.2 **For Loops**

For loops are handy when you want something done a certain number of times.

The for loop has the following syntax:

```
for (start value; conditional used to break out of loop;
increment value)
```

So every time the loop is executed, the initial value of the variable $i is incremented until the maximum number is reached. The conditional is checked to see if it passes. If it passes, then the bit in between the curly brackets is executed; if the conditional is not satisfied, then it skips to the next bit of code (outside of the loop).

In MEL you use a variable (which does not need to be explicitly declared) to keep track of how many times the statement has repeated. This can be anything to your liking, but most programmers use $i or $x:

```
//create a loop that prints a statement 20 times
for ($x=0; $x <20; $x = $x+1)
{
//mind the syntax of concatenating
print ("I am now at number" + $x +"\n");
}
```

MEL provides shorthand for the following:

```
$x = $x +1;  // is the same as $x++
$x = $x -1;  // is the same as $x--
$x = $x +5;  // is the same as $x+=5
```

```
$x = $x -5;  // is the same as $x-=5
```

For example:

```
//----------------------------------------------------------------
//create a loop that puts 20 spheres on top of each other
for ($x=0; $x <20; $x++)
    {
    sphere -name ("sphereNumber_" + $x) -pivot 0 $x 0;
    //since $x is increasing by 1 in each loop, so will the
    //position of the pivot and the suffix of the name
    }
//----------------------------------------------------------------
//create a loop that creates 50 cubes in a spherical area
for ($x=0; $x <50; $x++)
    {
    //sphrand will return a random vector (3 values)
    //within a sphere of specified radius (10 here)
    vector $rand = sphrand(10);
    nurbsCube -pivot ($rand.x)($rand.y)($rand.z);
    }
//----------------------------------------------------------------
//create a helix using the sine and cosine functions
for ($x=0; $x <20; $x++)
    {
    float $sin = sin($x);
    float $cos = cos($x);
    sphere -pivot $sin $x $cos;
    }
//----------------------------------------------------------------
//Something USEFUL now please!
//aaaah... a spiral

//create a circle
// use command, NOT UI
circle;
//move it away from the center
move 4 0 0;
//put the rotate center in the world's center
move 0 0 0 nurbsCircle1.rotatePivot;

for ($x=0; $x <50; $x++)
```

```
    {
    duplicate;
    rotate -relative 0 30 0;
    move -relative 0 .3 0;
    }
select -all;
loft;
```

2.2.3 For-in Loops

For-in loops allow you to perform a function on each member of an array.

The syntax is as follows:

```
for (element in array)
statement;
```

Or in MEL:

```
for ($eachMember in $array)
    {
    //statement;
    }
```

It is not necessary to explicitly declare the element variable (`$eachMember`), and it can have any name you choose.

For example:

```
//create some objects and select them
//list selected objects and put them in an array
string $sel[]=`ls -sl`;

//loop through the array and
//print out the name of the objects
for ($each in $sel)
    {
    print ("The current item is " + $each + ".\n");
    }

//----------------------------------------------------------
//do same with a for-in loop
string $sel[]=`ls -sl`;
for ($i=0; $i<size($sel); $i++)
```

```
{
    print ("The current item is " + $sel[$i] + ".\n");
}
```

2.2.4 Something More Useful: Putting an Array in a textScrollList

```
//----------------------------------------------------------
//create a UI that puts all meshes in a TSL
//----------------------------------------------------------

//find out how to list all polys, using the nodeType command
//To do this: select shape node, NOI transform
nodeType `ls -sl`;
// Result: mesh //

//list all meshes in scene
string $allMeshes[] = `ls -type "mesh"`;
// Result: pCylinderShape1 pCylinderShape2 pSphereShape1 //

//create UI
//if window exists, delete it.
if (`window -exists meshUI`)
    deleteUI meshUI;

//create window
window -title "Lists all meshes" meshUI;

//create a layout for the controls
columnLayout -adjustableColumn 1 mainCol;

//inside the layout, put a textScrollList
textScrollList -height 150 meshTSL;

//loop though each mesh (stored in $allMeshes)
//and place in TSL
for ($eachMesh in $allMeshes)
    textScrollList -edit -append $eachMesh meshTSL;

//show window
showWindow meshUI;
```

2.2.5 **An Example of Nesting Loops**

```
//------------------------------------------------------------
// NESTING LOOPS
// In this example we will use TWO for loops
// One to go through a list of selected objects
// Second to list all the keyable attributes on each of those objects
// Based on that information we will create a UI.
//------------------------------------------------------------

//the usual window stuff
if (`window -exists sliderUI`)
    deleteUI sliderUI;
window sliderUI;

//create a layout
columnLayout mainCol;

//create some descriptive text
text -label "Keyable Attributes:";

//get all selected objects
string $selectedObjects[]=`ls -sl`;

//loop though each of the selected objects
//and find its keyable attributes
for ($eachObject in $selectedObjects)
{
string $keyableAttributes[] =`listAttr -keyable $eachObject`;

//for each selected object, create a separator and a title
separator -width 400 -style "out";
text -label $eachObject;

//loop though each keyable attribute
// and create an attrFieldSliderGrp
    for ($eachKeyableAttribute in $keyableAttributes)
    {
    attrFieldSliderGrp -min -100 -max 100 -at
        ($eachObject+"."+$eachKeyableAttribute);
        //button -l "Keyframe" -w 100 -c ("setKeyframe " +
```

```
//    $eachObject+"."+$eachKeyableAttribute);
    }
}
showWindow sliderUI;
```

2.2.6 Variable Scope

An important programming pitfall to watch for is variable scope.
Variable scope is the area within a script that knows of a variable. If a
variable is created within a for loop, it only exists within that loop.
Once the for loop ends, the variable no longer exists. The same
goes for if statements and procedures.

```
//variable scope with string
for ($x=0; $x<10; $x++)
    {
    print ($x +"|");
    string $fubar[] = {"Whoazzzooo"};
    }

print $fubar;

// Error: print $fubar; //
// Error: "$fubar" is an undeclared variable. //


//-------------------------------------------------------
// to avoid this, declare the variable OUTSIDE
// the for statement

string $foo[];
for ($x=0; $x<10; $x++)
    {
    print ($x +"|");
    $foo = {"Whakkaaaa"};
    }
print $foo;
```

2.2.7 **The Internal Names of Controls**

Why do I always begin UI creation with a conditional on the existence of a window? For example:

```
if (`window -exists windowName`)
```

When you create a control in Maya (be it a button, a column layout, or a window), Maya always give this control an internal name for reference purposes. This internal name is *not* the name specified in the -title or -label flag. The -title name is purely there for visual purposes. The command structure is as follows:

```
window -title "windowTitle" internalName;
columnLayout -adj 0 internalColumnName;
```

Chapter 2

> **Important:**   *Always* give your controls internal names because you will need to refer to them frequently.

```
//create a window without internal name
window -t "kmWindow";
showWindow;

//list all the windows currently open
lsUI -windows;
// Result: CommandWindow MayaWindow window1 //

//window1 is the window we just created

//-----------------------------------------------------------------
//now give your window an internal name
window -title "kmWindow" myInternalName;
showWindow myInternalName;

//list all the windows currently open
lsUI -windows;
// Result: CommandWindow MayaWindow myInternalName //

//With the window open
//Try to execute myInternalName again:
```

```
window -t "kmWindow" myInternalName;
showWindow myInternalName;
// Error: Object's name is not unique:  myInternalName //

//This is exactly why we always build in the conditional:

//See if the window exists
window -exists myInternalName;
// Result: 1 //

//if it exists, delete it
if (`window -exists myInternalName` ==1); //long version
deleteUI myInternalName;

//OR - in shorthand
if (`window -exists myInternalName`); //short version
deleteUI myInternalName;
```

Note that you can, but are not required to, place the internal name inside quotes. Both of the following are valid:

```
window -t "kmWindow" myInternalName; //works
window -t "kmWindow" "myInternalName"; //works too
```

2.3 Procedures

2.3.1 Definition

A *procedure* is a group of MEL commands that can be executed by typing one command. It's similar to a macro that gets stored in Maya memory and can be called upon with a simple command. Procedures are very useful because:

- They help break your script up into easy-to-manage chunks of code that are easier to debug when something goes wrong.

- They allow you to reuse chunks of code in more than one part of your script.

The command structure of a procedure is as follows:

```
global proc procedureName (arguments)
{
commands;
}
```

For example:

```
global proc getShape (string $object)
{
//check if it is a shape
string $getShapes[] = `listRelatives -s $object`;

//if it isn't, print you are silly
if (`size $getShapes`==0)
    error ("Ola pendejo! This is already a shape");
else
    print ("The shape of " +$object + " is " + $getShapes[0]);
}
```

You can find a wealth of additional and more generic information on procedures at http://en.wikipedia.org/wiki/Function_ (computer_science).

2.3.2 **Arguments**

Arguments are additional user input that a procedure can require. Essentially, they are variables (values) that are supplied to the procedure when it is executed. You can use more than one argument in a procedure, but if you don't use any arguments you just add open and close parentheses () after your procedure name. When you declare a procedure with arguments, you need to provide the arguments; otherwise you get the following error:

```
// Error: renameAll; //
// Error: Wrong number of arguments on call to renameAll. //
```

For example:

```
//--------------------------------------------------------------------
// Examples of procs with arguments
//--------------------------------------------------------------------
global proc bigDenseSphere (float $radius, float $divX, float $divY)
```

```
{
    polySphere -r $radius -sx $divX -sy $divY;
}
//for example:
bigDenseSphere 10 50 50;


//------------------------------------------------------------------
global proc scarFace (string $who)
{
    print ("Say hello to " + $who + " !!");
}
// for example:
scarFace "My Little Friend";


//------------------------------------------------------------------
// Something more useful:
// A rename procedure

proc renameAll (string $newName)
{
//get all selected objects
string $sel[] =`ls -sl`;

//loop through selected objects
//and rename
for ($each in $sel)
    {
    rename $each ($newName +"_#");
    }
}
//for example:
renameAll foo
//------------------------------------------------------------------
```

2.3.3 Return Procedures

A procedure can also return a value, which can then (for example) be passed to a variable of another procedure. If you specify a return type for a procedure, then you *must* use a return operator some-where in the procedure's code block to return a value. Also, the data type of the returned value needs to be specified in the syntax of the procedure declaration. (See the data type in bold in the following example.)

For example:

```
//Note the explicit declaration of the data type of the return
global proc string getShape (string $object)
{
//check if it is a shape
string $getShapes[] = `listRelatives -s $object`;

//if it isn't, print you are silly
if (`size $getShapes`==0)
    error ("Ola pendejo! This is already a shape");
else
    return $getShapes[0];
}
```

Executing the above procedure results in:

```
getShape ("pCylinder1");
// Result: pCylinderShape1 //
```

2.3.4 Local and Global Procedures

Once you define a global procedure, you can call it anywhere: from any script file, within any function, or from the command line.

If you leave the `global` keyword off the beginning of a procedure declaration, the procedure is local to the file in which it is defined. This is very useful for making "helper" procedures that do work for other procedures. You can expose just one or two global procedures, hiding the helper code from other people using your scripts. Having fewer global procedures also uses less memory.

```
// This is a local procedure
// that is only visible to the code in this file.
proc red5()
    {
    print ("red5 standing by...\n");
    }
```

2.4 Bringing It All Together: A Renaming Tool

Let's gather all we have learned so far and create a rename procedure in a cute little UI.

```
//NOTE: TITLING AND PARAPHRASING OF CODE
//------------------------------------------------------------------
// km_rename contains the UI
//------------------------------------------------------------------
global proc km_rename ()
{
    if (`window -exists km_renameUI`)
        deleteUI km_renameUI;
    window -mxb off km_renameUI;

    columnLayout -adj 1 mainCol;
        textScrollList -h 150 renameTSL;
        button -l "GetObjects" -c populateTSL getbutton;
        text -l "New name:(dont add #)";
        textField newNameTextfield;
        button -l "Rename" -c renameThis renameButton;
    showWindow km_renameUI;
}


//------------------------------------------------------------------
// populateTSL puts the selected items in the textScrollList (TSL)
//------------------------------------------------------------------
global proc populateTSL ()
{
    //get selected objects
    string $sel[] =`ls -sl`;

    //put each selected object in TSL
    for ($each in $sel)
        textScrollList -e -a $each renameTSL;
}


//------------------------------------------------------------------
// renameThis renames all the items in the TSL
// based on the input in the textField
```

```
//-------------------------------------------------------------------
proc renameThis ()
{
    //get all objects in TSL
    string $itemsInTSL[] =`textScrollList -q -ai renameTSL `;

    //get the new name from the textField
    string $newName = `textField -q -text newNameTextfield`;

    //loop through objects in TSL
    //and rename
    for ($eachItems in $itemsInTSL)
    {
        rename $eachItems ($newName +"_#");
    }
    //remove all objects from TSL when renaming is done
    textScrollList -e -ra renameTSL;
}
```

2.5 Strategies for Designing MEL Scripts

2.5.1 Top-Down Design

When programming, one of the most common approaches to lay out a strategy and structure is called *top-down design*. With this technique, you break the problem down into successively smaller parts until each problem is easy to tackle.

In other words, a top-down approach is essentially breaking down a system to gain insight into its compositional subsystems. In a top-down approach, an overview of the system is first formulated, specifying but not detailing any first-level subsystems. Each subsystem is then refined in yet greater detail, sometimes in many additional subsystem levels, until the entire specification is reduced to base elements. It is inherent that no coding can begin until a sufficient level of detail has been reached in the design of at least some part of the system.

Complex problems can thus be solved using top-down design, also known as stepwise refinement, where we:

1. Break the problem into parts.

2. Then break the parts into parts.

3. Solve each of the parts, which will be easy to do.

2.5.2 Advantages of Top-Down Design

Breaking the problem into parts helps us to clarify what needs to be done, and at each step of refinement, the new parts become less complicated and therefore easier to figure out. Thus parts of the solution may turn out to be reusable. Breaking the problem into parts also allows more than one person to work on the solution. By separating the low-level work from the higher level objects, the design becomes modular, which means development can be self-contained. A top-down modular approach means you create a "skeleton" code that illustrates clearly how low-level modules integrate. This approach also reduces coding errors, because each module has to be processed separately.

2.5.3 Non-MEL Example of Top-Down Design

Problem

- We own a home improvement company.

- We do painting, roofing, and basement waterproofing.

- A section of town has recently flooded (zip code 21222).

- We want to send out pamphlets to our customers in that area.

Top-Down Solution

1. Get the customer list from a file.

2. Sort the list according to zip code.

3. Make a new file of only the customers with the zip code 21222 from the sorted customer list.

4. Print an envelope for each of these customers.

Further Breakdown

- Should any of these steps be broken down further? Possibly.

- How do I know? Ask yourself whether or not you could easily write the algorithm for the step. If not, break it down again.

- When you are comfortable with the breakdown, write the pseudocode for each of the steps (modules) in the hierarchy.

- Typically, each module will be coded as a separate function.

Another example of top-down design:

Problem

Write a program that draws a picture of a house.

Solution

1. Draw the outline of the house.
2. Draw the chimney.
3. Draw the door.
4. Draw the windows.

Pseudocode

- Call Draw Outline
- Call Draw Chimney
- Call Draw Door
- Call Draw Windows

Some Observations

The door has both a frame and knob. We could break this into two steps. But don't the windows look the same? They just have different locations. We can reuse the code that draws a window. Simply copy the code three times and edit it to place the window in the correct location, or use the code three times, "sending it" the correct location each time. This is an example of code reuse.

2.5.4 **Top-Down Design Applied to MEL Scripting**

In general, my scripting workflow goes through the following steps:

1. Create the top-down design on paper (plus preliminary drawing/outline of UI).
2. Type out/restructure top-down design (in Word or in an editor).
3. Construct pseudocode based on top-down design.
4. Write code.

2.5.5 **Step-by-Step Creation of the km_allCameras Script**

Outline

By default, Maya creates the front/side/top orthographic cameras. Often, however, users need the back/left/bottom cameras. Although these are relatively simple to create, km_allCameras makes the creation of these cameras a single click away with a simple UI. Some extra options are also provided.

 Figure 2-2

Top-Down Design

Main UI:

1. Create procedure for back cam.
2. Create procedure for left cam.
3. Create procedure for bottom cam.
4. Create procedure that combines all three procedures.

Finer Points

1. Create check box that hides/shows camera icons.
2. Build in check so same camera cannot be created two times. First, check if camera exists. If it does, display a confirmDialog; else, create the camera.

Code and Comments

```
//------------------------------------------------------------------
// km_allCameras is the main UI
//------------------------------------------------------------------
global proc km_allCameras ()


//create window with 4 buttons and one check box
{
//conditional on existence of window
if (`window -exists km_allCamerasUI`)
    deleteUI km_allCamerasUI;

//create window
window -wh 170 170 -mxb off -mnb off km_allCamerasUI;

//hide all camera items to get check box to work consistently
hideShow -cameras -hide;

//create layout for controls
columnLayout -adj on mainCol;

    //create check box for hide/show camera icons
    checkBox
        -l "Show/Hide Cams"
        -onc "hideShow -cameras -show"
        -ofc "hideShow -cameras -hide";

    //create button that creates all cameras
    button
        -l "Create ALL"
        -c "createBottom;\createBack;\createLeft;";

    //text -l "";
    //insert some text as title for individual camera buttons
```

```
        text -l "Create separately";

        //create back/left/bottom buttons
        button -l "Back Cam" -c  createBack;
        button -l "Left Cam" -c  createLeft;
        button -l "Bottom Cam" -c  createBottom;

    showWindow km_allCamerasUI;
    }

//-------------------------------------------------------------------
// createBottom is the proc that creates the bottom camera
//-------------------------------------------------------------------
// CODE REUSE: to be copied and changed accordingly for the other
// cameras

global proc createBottom()
{
//check if the bottom camera already exists
    // if it does, display the confirmDialog
    // (with the winExists procedure - see below)
if (objExists ("bottom"))
    winExists;
else
    {
    //put camera creation in a variable, so...
    string $bottom[] = `camera -n bottom`;
    //...we can easily use it in the viewSet command
    // This command positions the camera to one of the pre-defined
    // positions.
    viewSet -bottom $bottom[0];
    //since the camera created with viewSet is called "bottom1",
    //we rename it
    rename "bottom1" "bottom";

    //to be consistent with the show/hide check box,
    //hide the just created camera
    hide bottom;
    }
}
```

```
//-------------------------------------------------------------------
// createLeft is the proc that creates the left camera
//-------------------------------------------------------------------
global proc createLeft()
{
if (objExists ("left"))
    winExists;
else
    {
    string $left[] = `camera -n left`;
    viewSet -ls $left[0];
    rename "left1" "left";
    hide left;
    }
}


//-------------------------------------------------------------------
// createBack is the proc that creates the back camera
//-------------------------------------------------------------------
global proc createBack()

{
if (objExists ("back"))
    winExists;
else
    {
    string $back[] = `camera -n back`;
    viewSet -b $back[0];
    rename "back1" "back";
    hide back;
    }
}


//-------------------------------------------------------------------
// winExists is the proc that creates the confirmDialog
// when the user tries to create a camera that already exists
//-------------------------------------------------------------------
global proc winExists ()
{
confirmDialog
    -title "Careful aye"
```

```
    -message "This camera already exists"
    -button "I won't do it again";
}
```

Chapter 3

First Blood

In this chapter we will write two very simple scripts to put the accumulated knowledge from the previous two chapters in practice. If this were basketball training, these two scripts would be your first attempt at a layup. The idea is to drive home the theoretical concepts we learned in the previous chapters and get firm fundamentals we can build on.

3.1 km_toggleFluidRes

3.1.1 Origin and Purpose

When setting up and tweaking fluids, I often start off with a low resolution container to get the fluid movement and texturing right. The main advantage of this is obviously simulation speed and less frustration. A fluid container has a resolution and a size in XYZ; resolution defines the resolution of the fluid container in voxels, and size defines the size of the fluid container in world space units. In order for fluids to look and simulate predictably, voxels need to be square (i.e., proportional). km_toggleFluidRes came into existence when I got tired of continuously changing the size and resolution of a container while tweaking fluids. The script simply doubles or halves the given resolution (and size) of the selected container. Sweet and simple.

3.1.2 **Brainstorm**

First we need to get the resolution and size of the selected fluidShape. We need to build in a check to make sure the user has selected a fluidShape and not another node. Based on UI input (a button), the user can either double or halve the current resolution. The user should also have the option to double or halve the size of the container. A warning should be displayed when the user is using non-proportional voxels.

3.1.3 **The Main Procedure: fluidResToggle**

Outline

fluidResToggle has one argument ($operation), which decides if the resolution and size of the container will be doubled or halved. The flow of this procedure is as follows:

- Get the selected fluidShape.
- Make sure it is actually a fluidShape. If it isn't, display an error message.
- Check if the user wants to double or halve the size of the container (based on input from UI).
- Get the resolution and the size of the selected container.
- Based on the size and the resolution, get the size of the voxels.
- Check if the voxels are proportional.
- If the voxels are not proportional, display a box stating such.
- Based on the argument of the procedure (double/half) and the result of the size check, double or halve the size/resolution.

New Commands

ls -sl -type: Using the ls command in combination with the -selected and -type flags allows you to filter out only certain node types in the list of selected objects. To find out the type of a selected node (e.g., mesh, nurbsCurve, fluidShape), simply select the node and execute:

```
nodeType `ls -sl`;
```

It is *very* important to note that when the user selects a node in the viewport, the nodeType of that node will almost always be "transform." Create a sphere, select it and execute:

```
nodeType `ls -sl`;
```

You will get:

```
// transform //
```

Now select the shape node of the sphere (in the Outliner or the Hypergraph) and execute the same command again. Now you will get the desired result:

```
nodeType `ls -sl`;
// mesh //
```

So, to find out the useful nodeType, we need to explicitly select the shape node. Let's take this example a step further by filtering out the meshes from a list of all DAG (directed acyclic graph) objects in a scene:

```
// The snippet below lists all objects in the scene
// and selects only the polys (meshes)

// Create some objects.
// Note that only the first are polygons (meshes)
polySphere;
polyCube;
emitter -pos 0 0 0 -type volume;
sphere;

// clear the selection list
select -clear;

// select all the DAG objects in the scene
string $allObjs[] = `ls -dagObjects`;
//loop over all the selected objects
for ($each in $allObjs)

    {
    // get the shape of each DAG
    string $getShapes[] = `listRelatives -s $each `;
    // if the DAG has a shape
```

```
if ($getShapes[0] != "")
    {
    // get the nodeType of the shape
    string $nodeType = `nodeType $getShapes[0]`;
    // if it is a mesh,
    if ($nodeType == "mesh")
        // add it to the selection
        select -add $each;
    }
}
```

We will use the `-sl -type` combination of flags to make sure the user has selected the actual fluidShape, which has the attributes we are interested in. (Note that there are other ways of doing this as well, but we will come to those later.)

I am also using this method to work around a little quirk in Maya fluid selection. To illustrate this quirk, try this:

- Create a 3D fluid container (Fluid Effects > Create 3D Container).

- Select the container.

- Open the Attribute Editor to see the attributes of the fluidShape.

- In the Script Editor, type `ls -sl`.

You will notice that Maya returns the transform node, although the shape is clearly selected/displayed in the Attribute Editor.

```
// fluid1 //
```

This is annoying, which is exactly why we make the user aware of this nuisance by starting the fluidResToggle procedure with:

```
// get selected fluid
string $selFluids[] = `ls -sl -type "fluidShape"`;
// check if fluid shape is selected
if ($selFluids[0] == "")
error "Make sure you EXPLICITLY select a fluidSHAPE in the
    attribute editor";
```

You will note that I use the `error` command to not only display an error, but also to halt the execution of the procedure.

confirmDialog: This command creates a little window with a message to the user and a specified button to dismiss the dialog.

For example:

```
confirmDialog
-title "Export complete"
-message "You can sit back now"
-button "OK"
-defaultButton "OK";
```

Figure 3-1

Clean Concatenation

In the `confirmDialog` chunk of code, the string argument of the `-message` flag was getting a bit long for the source file, so I spread it over two lines. Have a look at the code below to see how the concatenation was done. Concatenating long strings will help you to keep them more manageable.

```
confirmDialog
-title "Container not proportional"
-message ("Your container dimensions are not proportional.\n"
+ "This WILL cause problems!")
-button "I am a muppet";
```

New Operators

Before we dive into the code, let's have a closer look at some of the operators that will be used.

We already covered == in the previous chapter, but *repetitio mater studiorum est*. The = operator (single equal sign) assigns values to variables. For example, $a = 10 assigns the value 10 to the variable $a. The == operator (double equal sign) tests if two values are equal. For example, $a == 10 tests whether the value of $a is equal to 10.

For example:

```
// declare variable (we use the = sign)
int $number = 5;

// test if that variable is
// equal to a given number

if ($number == 5)
    print ("This variable is equal to 5")
```

To test if two values are not equal, we use !=.
For example:

```
// declare a string
string $test = ("testValue");
// test if the string has content
if ($test != "")
    print ("This variable is not empty");
```

To test if a condition is true (1) or false (0), you can use the following shorthand.
For example:

```
// declare variable
int $number = 6;

if (!$number) // same as: if ($number == 0)
    print ("The house wins");

if ($number) // same as: if ($number !=0)
    print ("Jackpot!");
```

This means we use integer 0 as Boolean false; every other integer (positive or negative) counts as true. ! is Boolean-negation/logical-not. So:

- if ($number) means if the number is true (i.e., not zero).
- if (!$number) means if the number is not true (i.e., false or zero).

For example:

```
//6 is true, so !6 (Boolean negation of true) is false, and prints 0
print(!6+"\n");
```

```
//0 is false, so !0 is true, and prints 1
print(!0+"\n");

//not not true -> not false -> true, prints 1
print(!!6+"\n");

//not not false -> not true -> false, prints 0
print(!!0+"\n");
```

&& is the operator for "and," which tests if *both conditions* mentioned have been satisfied. **||** is the operator for "or," which tests if *one of the conditions* mentioned has been satisfied.

For example:

```
// create a sphere and select it
polySphere;
// get the selected object
string $sphere[] = `ls -sl`;
// get the node type of the first element in the array
string $type = `nodeType $sphere[0]`;
// get the scale Z of the first element in the array
float $scaleZ = `getAttr ($sphere[0] + ".scaleZ")`;

// if that element is a transform AND
// scaleZ is bigger than 5
if ($type == "transform" && $scaleZ > 5)
// print the obvious
    print "That is one big ball!";
```

To test if the voxels of the container are square, we simply divide the size by the resolution and then check if each side is the same size:

```
// get resolution
vector $res = `getAttr ($selFluids[0] + ".resolution")`;

// get size
float $sizeX = `getAttr ($selFluids[0] + ".dimensionsW")`;
float $sizeY = `getAttr ($selFluids[0] + ".dimensionsH")`;
float $sizeZ = `getAttr ($selFluids[0] + ".dimensionsD")`;

// get the size of the voxels in XYZ
```

Chapter 3

```
float $cellSizeX = $sizeX/$res.x;
float $cellSizeY = $sizeY/$res.y;
float $cellSizeZ = $sizeZ/$res.z;

//check if the voxels are proportional
if (!($cellSizeX == $cellSizeY && $cellSizeY == $cellSizeZ))
    {
    confirmDialog
    -title "Container not proportional"
    -message ("Your container dimensions are not proportional.\n"
    + "This WILL cause problems!")
    -button "I am a muppet"
    ;
    }
```

Code and Comments

The full procedure is printed below. Please note that due to the width of the page, some text wrapping may have occurred. Please refer to the actual script on the companion disc for correct formatting.

```
//===============================================================
// fluidResToggle takes "half" or "double" as an argument and
// applies this operation to the container
// It also checks if the container is proportional
//===============================================================

global proc fluidResToggle (string $operation)
{
// get selected fluid
string $selFluids[] = `ls -sl -type "fluidShape"`;
// check if fluid shape is selected
if ($selFluids[0] == "")
error "Make sure you EXPLICITLY select a fluidSHAPE in the
    attribute editor";

// get value from check box
int $sizeCHBX = `checkBox -q -v sizeCHBX`;

// get resolution
vector $res = `getAttr ($selFluids[0] + ".resolution")`;
```

```
// get size
float $sizeX = `getAttr ($selFluids[0] + ".dimensionsW")`;
float $sizeY = `getAttr ($selFluids[0] + ".dimensionsH")`;
float $sizeZ = `getAttr ($selFluids[0] + ".dimensionsD")`;

// get the size of the voxels in XYZ
float $cellSizeX = $sizeX/$res.x;
float $cellSizeY = $sizeY/$res.y;
float $cellSizeZ = $sizeZ/$res.z;

//check if the voxels are proportional
if (!($cellSizeX == $cellSizeY && $cellSizeY == $cellSizeZ))
    {
    confirmDialog -title "Container not proportional"
    -message ("Your container dimensions are not proportional.\n"
    + "This WILL cause problems!")
    -button "I am a muppet"
    ;
    }

//double the resolution and the size of the container
if ($operation == "double" && $sizeCHBX == 0)
    {
    setAttr ($selFluids[0] + ".resolution") ($res.x * 2) ($res.y * 2)
        ($res.z * 2) ;
    setAttr ($selFluids[0] + ".dimensionsW") ($sizeX *2);
    setAttr ($selFluids[0] + ".dimensionsH") ($sizeY *2);
    setAttr ($selFluids[0] + ".dimensionsD") ($sizeZ *2);
    }
//double the resolution alone
if ($operation == "double" && $sizeCHBX == 1)
    {
    setAttr ($selFluids[0] + ".resolution") ($res.x * 2) ($res.y * 2)
        ($res.z * 2) ;
    }

if ($operation == "half" && $sizeCHBX == 0)
    {
    setAttr ($selFluids[0] + ".resolution") ($res.x / 2) ($res.y / 2)
        ($res.z / 2) ;
    setAttr ($selFluids[0] + ".dimensionsW") ($sizeX /2);
```

```
    setAttr ($selFluids[0] + ".dimensionsH") ($sizeY /2);
    setAttr ($selFluids[0] + ".dimensionsD") ($sizeZ /2);
    }

if ($operation == "half" && $sizeCHBX == 1)
    {
    setAttr ($selFluids[0] + ".resolution") ($res.x / 2) ($res.y / 2)
        ($res.z / 2);
    }
}
```

Again, please note that due to the width of the pages in this book, the formatting of the code above is not correct. To view the correct formatting, please open the actual code (which you can find on the companion disc) in your editor.

3.1.4 **The UI Procedure: km_toggleFluidRes**

Outline

This procedure creates a very simple UI that enables the user to halve or double the resolution (and optionally the size) of a fluid container. It consists of a check box and two buttons in a frameLayout. I deliberately introduce frameLayouts here because their very essence gives meaning to my life. They are also neat and useful UI controls with some unfortunate limitations, which I will cover below. The UI will look like Figure 3-2.

Figure 3-2

New Commands

checkbox: A check box is a simple control containing a text label and a check/tick box that indicates either on or off.

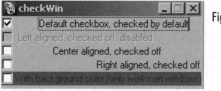

Figure 3-3

For example:

```
if (`window -exists checkWin`)
    deleteUI checkWin;

window -mxb 0 checkWin;
columnLayout -adjustableColumn true checkCol;
    checkBox
        -value 1
        -label "Default checkbox, checked by default";
    checkBox
        -enable 0
        -label "Left aligned, checked off, disabled"
        -align "left";
    checkBox
        -label "Center aligned, checked off "
        -align "center";
    checkBox
        -label "Right aligned, checked off"
        -align "right";
    checkBox
        -label "With background color (only works on windows)"
        -backgroundColor 1 0 0;

showWindow checkWin;
```

scrollLayout: This layout will display a horizontal and/or vertical scroll bar when necessary to bring into view the hidden controls. Since the scroll layout provides no real positioning of children, you should use another control layout as the immediate child. This means that scrollLayout is a bit of a limp layout, because on its own it's pretty useless. You need to use another layout to actually position UI controls in it. Same goes for the frameLayout (explained next). I will use scrollLayout, frameLayout, and setParent in the same UI code, outlined below.

frameLayout: The Attribute Editor and the Render Globals window are two examples of frameLayouts. A frameLayout displays a title and draws a border around its child controls. FrameLayouts can also be collapsible, which means that this layout will make the child of the frameLayout invisible and shrink the frameLayout size. The frameLayout can then be expanded to make its child visible. *Note that just like the scrollLayout, the frameLayout can have only one child control.* (How terribly annoying.) If you wish to have more than one child inside a frameLayout, you must use some other control layout as the immediate child of the frameLayout. We will use columnLayouts most of the time.

setParent: This command changes the default parent to be the specified parent. Two special parents are "/", which indicates the top of the hierarchy, and "..", which indicates one level up in the hierarchy. Trying to move above the top level has no effect. A control must be parented to a control layout. A control layout may be parented to another control layout or a window.

For example:

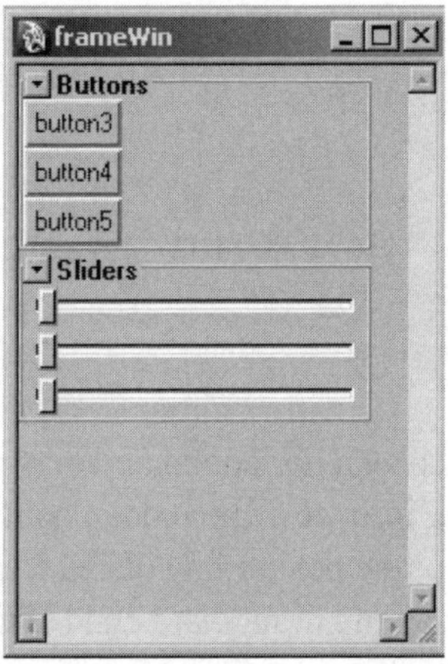

Figure 3-4

```
//check if the window exists, if it does...
if (`window -exists frameWin`)
    //..delete it
    deleteUI frameWin;

// create the window
window frameWin;

// the main layout is a scrollLayout:
scrollLayout mainScroll;
```

```
    //to position the children of the scrollLayout,
    // we use a columnLayout (mainCol)
    columnLayout -adjustableColumn 1 mainCol;
        //...which has 2 frameLayouts
        //first framelayout
        frameLayout
            -label "Buttons"
            -labelAlign "top"
        -borderStyle "etchedIn"
            -collapsable 1
            -collapse 1
            frameOne;
        //... which holds one columnLayout
        columnLayout buttonCol;
            //buttonCol holds 3 buttons
            button;
            button;
            button;
//revert UI-hierarchy back to mainCol
setParent mainCol;
        //first framelayout
        frameLayout
            -label "Sliders"
            -labelAlign "top"
        -borderStyle "etchedIn"
            -collapsable 1
            -collapse 0
            frameTwo;
        //... which holds one columnLayout
        columnLayout sliderCol;
            //sliderCol holds 3 intSliders
            intSlider;
            intSlider;
            intSlider;
//revert UI-hierarchy back to mainCol
setParent mainCol;

showWindow frameWin;
```

Code and Comments

The full procedure is printed below. Please note that due to the width of the pages in this book, some text wrapping may have occurred. Please refer to the actual script on the companion disc for correct formatting.

```
//================================================================
// toggleFluidRes creates a little UI with half/double buttons
//================================================================
global proc km_toggleFluidRes()
{
    // if the window control exists, delete it
    if (`window -ex km_toggleFluidResUI`)
        deleteUI km_toggleFluidResUI;

    // create window
    window -mxb 0 -wh 180 120 km_toggleFluidResUI;
    // frameLayout can only have 1 child,
    // so use a columnLayout to position children
    frameLayout -labelVisible 0 mainFrame;
        columnLayout -adj 1 mainCol;
            checkBox -l "Do not touch container size" -v 1 sizeCHBX;
            separator -style "out";
            // note the escape characters in front of the quotation
            // marks to correctly interpret the arguments
            button -l "double resolution" -c "fluidResToggle
                (\"double\")" doubleBTT;
            button -l "half resolution" -c "fluidResToggle
                (\"half\")" halfBTT;

    showWindow km_toggleFluidResUI;
}
```

3.2 **RandRBattr**

3.2.1 **Origin and Purpose**

This tool originated from the desire to have some rigid body (RB) randomization tools in one place. The code is very simple, yet centralizes often-used functions when using RBs:

1. Apply a random spin to all selected RBs.
2. Apply a random velocity to all selected RBs.
3. Put all selected RBs in a different collision layer to avoid interpenetration.

3.2.2 **Top-Down Design**

This script is so simple that it doesn't really warrant a top-down design. The parent UI is a scrollLayout with three collapsible frameLayouts inside.

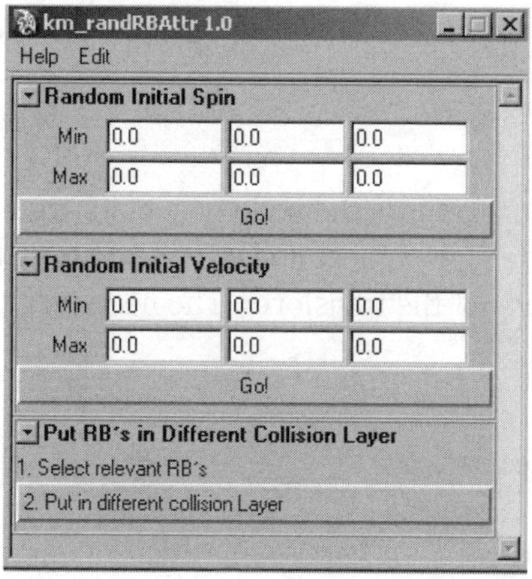

Figure 3-5

3.2.3 **The Procedures**

- The km_randSpin procedure uses input values to generate a random value and then applies that value to each selected RB.

- The km_randVelocity procedure uses input values to generate a random value and then applies that value to each selected RB.

- The km_differentCollisionLayer procedure loops through all selected RBs and assigns a different value to each collision layer.

- resetUI resets all the float fields in the UI.

New Commands

ls -sl -dag -exactType rigidbody: The -exactType flag lists all objects of the specified type, but not objects that are descendants of that type.

For example:

```
ls -exactType camera;
// frontShape perspShape sideShape topShape //
```

As explained before, if you want to know the type of a selected node, simply execute:

```
nodeType `ls -sl`;
```

nodeType: This command returns the node type of its argument. Note that to find the nodeType of most nodes, you will have to feed it the shape of a node and not the transform. The node type of a transform is "transform."

For example:

```
//get node type of selected object
nodeType `ls -sl`;


//=======================
//create a node
sphere;
//select node
string $ball[] = `ls -sl`;
//get shape of node
```

```
string $getShape[] = `listRelatives -s $ball[0]`;
//get node type of shape
string $type = `nodeType $getShape[0]`;
// nurbsSurface //
```

floatFieldGrp: If you look this command up in the docs, the description is something unintelligible. The first sentence, for example, reads: "All of the group commands position their individual controls in columns starting at column 1." Rest assured, this will by no means be the last time that you will find the docs useless. The best way to understand the command is to just execute the example and find out for yourself what is going on. That said, sometimes the examples are a bit of crap as well. Welcome to the wonderful world of MEL.

What you need to know is a floatFieldGrp is a combination (hence "group") of any number of floatFields. A floatField creates a field control that accepts only float values and is bound by a minimum and maximum value. It is like a textField, but for floats instead of strings.

For example:

```
string $window = `window`;
columnLayout floatCol;
    floatFieldGrp
        -numberOfFields 3
        -label "Scale"
        -extraLabel "cm"
        -value1 0.3
        -value2 0.5
        -value3 0.1
    floatFldEx;

showWindow $window;
```

Code and Comments

```
//==============================================================
// km_randRBAttr is the proc that holds the UI
//==============================================================
global proc km_randRBAttr ()
{
```

```
if (`window -exists km_randRBAttrUI`)
deleteUI km_randRBAttrUI;

string $about = "print \"km_rigidBodyTools || version
    1.0 || kevin_mannens@yahoo.com\"";

window -wh 200 200
    -t "km_randRBAttr 1.0"
    -mxb off
    km_randRBAttrUI;

menuBarLayout;
    menu -label "Help";
        menuItem -l "Help..." ;
        menuItem -divider 1;
        menuItem -l "About" -c $about ;
    menu -label "Edit";
        menuItem -l "Reset" -c "km_resetUI()" ;

        scrollLayout -horizontalScrollBarThickness 0
                -verticalScrollBarThickness 10
                -childResizable true
                mainScroll;
            columnLayout -adj 1 mainCol;

            frameLayout -l "Random Initial Spin"
                    -bs "etchedIn"
                    -collapsable 1
                    -marginHeight 5
                    randomSpinFrame;
            columnLayout -adj 1 spinCol;
                floatFieldGrp
                    -numberOfFields 3
                    -label " Min"
                    -cw 1 50
                    -cw 2 70
                    -cw 3 70
                    -cw 4 70
                    -columnAlign4 "right" "left" "left" "left"
                    -value1 0
                    -value2 0
```

```
                        -value3 0
                        minSpinFloat;
                    floatFieldGrp
                        -numberOfFields 3
                        -label " Max"
                        -cw 1 50
                        -cw 2 70
                        -cw 3 70
                        -cw 4 70
                        -columnAlign4 "right" "left" "left" "left"
                        -value1 0
                        -value2 0
                        -value3 0
                        maxSpinFloat;
                    button -l "Go!" -c "km_randSpin()" spinButton;

setParent mainCol;

        frameLayout -l "Random Initial Velocity"
            -bs "etchedIn"
            -collapsable 1
            -marginHeight 5
            randomVelocityFrame;

        columnLayout -adj 1 velocityCol;
            floatFieldGrp
                -numberOfFields 3
                -label " Min"
                -cw 1 50
                -cw 2 70
                -cw 3 70
                -cw 4 70
                -columnAlign4 "right" "left" "left" "left"
                -value1 0
                -value2 0
                -value3 0
                minVelFloat;
            floatFieldGrp
                -numberOfFields 3
                -label " Max"
                -cw 1 50
```

```
                        -cw 2 70
                        -cw 3 70
                        -cw 4 70
                        -columnAlign4 "right" "left" "left" "left"
                        -value1 0
                        -value2 0
                        -value3 0
                        maxVelFloat;
        button -l "Go!" -c "km_randVelocity()" velButton;

setParent mainCol;

            frameLayout
                -l "Put RBs in Different Collision Layer"
                -bs "etchedIn"
                -collapsable 1
                -marginHeight 5
                collisionFrame;

                columnLayout -adj 1 collisionCol;
                text -l "1. Select relevant RBs"
                    -al "left";
                button -l "2. Put in different collision layer"
                    -al "left"
                    -c "km_differentCollisionLayer()"
                    collisionButton;
setParent mainCol;
showWindow km_randRBAttrUI;
}

//================================================================
// km_randSpin generates a random value based on user input
// and applies it to the initialSpin attribute of
// each selected SB
//================================================================
global proc km_randSpin()
{
//declare vars
string $rigidBodys[];
float $xSpin, $ySpin, $zSpin;
```

```
//get UI info
float $minX = `floatFieldGrp -q -value1 minSpinFloat`;
float $minY = `floatFieldGrp -q -value2 minSpinFloat`;
float $minZ = `floatFieldGrp -q -value3 minSpinFloat`;
float $maxX = `floatFieldGrp -q -value1 maxSpinFloat`;
float $maxY = `floatFieldGrp -q -value2 maxSpinFloat`;
float $maxZ = `floatFieldGrp -q -value3 maxSpinFloat`;

//get all selected RBs
//-exactType: List all objects of the specified type,
//but not objects that are descendants of that type
$rigidBodys = `ls -sl -dag -exactType rigidBody`;
//loop through RBs and apply random value
for ($eachRigidBody in $rigidBodys)
    { //random value generation
    $xSpin = rand($minX, $maxX);
    $ySpin = rand($minY, $maxY);
    $zSpin = rand($minZ, $maxZ);

    //apply random value to relevant attribute
    $attr = $eachRigidBody + ".initialSpinX";
    setAttr $attr $xSpin;
    $attr = $eachRigidBody + ".initialSpinY";
    setAttr $attr $ySpin;
    $attr = $eachRigidBody + ".initialSpinZ";
    setAttr $attr $zSpin;
    }
}
//===============================================================
// km_randVelocity generates a random value based on user input
// and applies it to the initialVelocity attribute of
// each selected SB
//===============================================================
global proc km_randVelocity()
{
string $rigidBodys[];
float $xSpin, $ySpin, $zSpin;

float $minX = `floatFieldGrp -q -value1 minVelFloat`;
float $minY = `floatFieldGrp -q -value2 minVelFloat`;
float $minZ = `floatFieldGrp -q -value3 minVelFloat`;
```

Chapter 3

```
float $maxX = `floatFieldGrp -q -value1 maxVelFloat`;
float $maxY = `floatFieldGrp -q -value2 maxVelFloat`;
float $maxZ = `floatFieldGrp -q -value3 maxVelFloat`;

$rigidBodys = `ls -sl -dag -et rigidBody`;
for ($eachRigidBody in $rigidBodys)
    {
    $xVel = rand($minX, $maxX);
    $yVel = rand($minY, $maxY);
    $zVel = rand($minZ, $maxZ);

    $attr = $eachRigidBody + ".initialVelocityX";
    setAttr $attr $xVel;
    $attr = $eachRigidBody + ".initialVelocityY";
    setAttr $attr $yVel;
    $attr = $eachRigidBody + ".initialVelocityZ";
    setAttr $attr $zVel;
    }
}
//=============================================================
// km_differentCollisionLayer loops through all selected RBs
// and applies a $i as collision layer
//=============================================================
global proc km_differentCollisionLayer()
{
string $allRigidBodies[] = `ls -sl -dag -et rigidBody`;
int $amount = `size $allRigidBodies`;
for ($i=0; $i<$amount; $i++)
    {
    string $attr = $allRigidBodies[$i] + ".collisionLayer";
    setAttr $attr $i;
    print ($allRigidBodies[$i] +" done!\n");
    }
}


//=============================================================
// km_resetUI - resets the UI
//=============================================================
global proc km_resetUI()
{
floatFieldGrp
```

```
        -e
        -value1 0
        -value2 0
        -value3 0
        minSpinFloat;
floatFieldGrp
        -e
        -value1 0
        -value2 0
        -value3 0
        maxSpinFloat;
floatFieldGrp
        -e
        -value1 0
        -value2 0
        -value3 0
        minVelFloat;
floatFieldGrp
        -e
        -value1 0
        -value2 0
        -value3 0
        maxVelFloat;
}
//=================================================================
```

Hands-On MEL Coding: km_bookmarkManager

4.1 Orientation and Top-Down Design

4.1.1 Origin and UI Layout

Default Maya functionality allows you to set bookmarks on a camera. A camera bookmark is a way to mark a view for future use, allowing you to have a variety of camera views for a scene.

Maya's default bookmark functionality is, however, very limited. When designing a layout for a shot or doing serious previsualization of a product, you need a more detailed and efficient way to control camera bookmarks.

The final UI of the script looks like this:

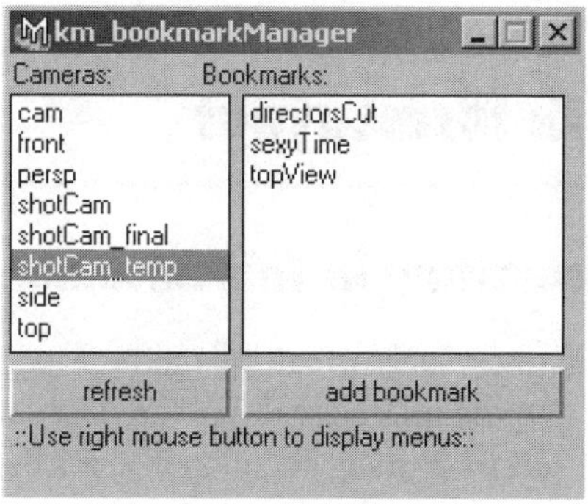

Figure 4-1

4.1.2 Top-Down Design of km_bookmarkManager

List all cameras in the textScrollList (TSL) on the left. The RMB (right mouse button) pop-up should contain:

- Rename camera (and update TSL with new name)
- Toggle resolution gate of selected camera
- Open Attribute Editor of selected camera
- Look though selected camera

List all bookmarks in the textScrollList (TSL) on the right. The RMB pop-up should contain:

- Rename selected bookmark (and update TSL with new name)
- Delete selected bookmark (and update TSL)
- Copy bookmark to other camera

In addition to the above, there should be:

- A force refresh button, although new camera and bookmark creation should happen instantly.
- A create new bookmark button that stores the current camera view as a bookmark (with a user-specified name). The bookmark TSL should update accordingly.
- Concise help should be displayed in a separate window.

4.2 Creating a UI with formLayout

4.2.1 A Note on Formatting in This Document

Although I try to maintain my actual formatting on these pages, this is not always possible due to the limited width of the pages in this book. Please refer to the script on the companion disc for the actual formatting.

When coding UIs, I also like to represent the "tree-branch" hierarchy of the layouts in the code formatting. I have tried to do this as much as possible in these documents as well.

Whenever possible, large chunks of code will be clearly marked with appropriate separators. I strongly suggest you adopt these formatting guidelines when writing your own code.

4.2.2 Introduction to formLayout

The formLayout is probably the most advanced and versatile form of layout MEL has to offer. It takes a little bit more effort to set it up, but formLayout harnesses enormous power and gives you the ultimate control over your UI. The setup is also a bit different from other controls. With formLayout, you first determine which controls will be "children" of the formLayout, and then you put the formLayout in Edit mode to actually position those controls. In other words, first we define the container that will hold the UI controls (like buttons and sliders) and then we edit that container to actually position the UI controls. This is different from a columnLayout, where you simply physically place the children of the layout under the actual layout.

formLayout works as follows:

```
window;
formLayout myForm;
button;
text;
textScrollList;

formLayout -e [position controls myForm];
showWindow;
```

You'll need a bit of background information to get formLayout working.

Controls (e.g., buttons, check boxes, text fields) have four edges: top, left, bottom, and right. There are only two directions in which children can be positioned: right to left or up and down. The attach flags take the direction of an attachment from the second argument, which names the edge to attach (e.g., left). Any or all edges of a child may be attached.

There are six ways to attach controls:

- Attach to Form (-af): Attaches an edge to the relevant side of the form layout. Thus -attachForm button3 "left" attaches the left edge of the button to the left edge of the form.

- Attach to Position (-ap): This attaches the control's given side to a position within the layout. I like to think of it more as "attachPercentage" because it uses a value from 0 to 100 (e.g., -ap button left 0 50). The first number, 0 in the example, is used as an offset value of the second value, which is a percentage.

- Attach to Another Control (-ac): This attaches the control's given side to a specified control (e.g., -ac button left 5 button2). In this example, we attach the left side of the button to the right side of button2 with an offset of 5.

- Attach to Opposite Side of Another Control (-aoc): This attaches the control's given side to the *same* side of a given control (e.g., -aoc button1 top 5 button2). This example places the top side of button1 at the top side of button2 with an offset of 5.

- Attach to Opposite Side of Form (-aof): Attaches an edge relative to the farthest side of the formLayout.

- Attach to Nothing (-an): Attaches an edge to nothing. The size of the child control will determine this edge's position.

Each edge attachment may have an offset that acts to separate controls visually.

There is no real default positioning relationship, so to have children appear in the form, they must have at least one edge attached in each direction.

I do realize this sounds as straightforward as reading Kant's *Metaphysische Anfangsgründe der Naturwissenschaft* on acid, but a bit of practice and a whole lot of cursing makes it easier after a while.

For example:

```
//do the usual window stuff
if (`window -exists formWindow`)
```

```
    deleteUI formWindow;

window formWindow;
    //create a formLayout
    formLayout myForm;

//START formLayout content----------------------------
    //comment controls out and create layout
    //by working through them one by one

    text -l "Selected Joints:" jointText;
    textScrollList -h 100 jointTSL;
    textField jointTF;
    button -l "left" leftButton;
    button -l "right" rightButton;
//END formLayout content----------------------------

//START formLayout positioning----------------------
formLayout -e
    //attach the top side of jointText to the relative
    //(i.e., top-)side of the formLayout
    -af jointText top 0

    //attach the left side of jointText to the relative
    //(i.e., left-)side of the formLayout
    -af jointText left 0

    //attach the right side of jointText to the relative
    //(i.e., right-)side of the formLayout
    -af jointText right 20

    //attach the left side of jointTSL to the relative
    //(i.e., left-)side of the formLayout
    -af jointTSL left 0

    //attach the top edge of jointTSL to the closest edge
    //(i.e., the bottom one) of the control called jointText
    -ac jointTSL top 5 jointText

    //attach the right side of jointTSL to the relative
    //(i.e., right-)side of the formLayout
```

Chapter 4

```
   -af jointTSL right 2

   //attach the top edge of jointTF to the closest edge
   //(i.e., the bottom one) of the control called jointTSL
   -ac jointTF top 2 jointTSL

   //attach the right side of jointTF to the relative
   //(i.e., right-)side of the formLayout
   -af jointTF right 2

   //attach the left side of jointTF to the relative
   //(i.e., left-)side of the formLayout
   -af jointTF left 0
   -af leftButton left 2
   -ac leftButton top 2 jointTF

   //"attach the right edge of the control named leftButton
   //to a position of 50% between the left and right margins
   //(from the left margin) of the formLayout with 0 pixel offset".
   -ap leftButton right 0 50
   -af rightButton right 2
   -ac rightButton top 2 jointTF

   //"Attach the bottom edge of rightButton to the
   //FURTHEST RELATIVE SIDE of leftButton with 0 offset".
   -aoc rightButton bottom 0 leftButton
   -ac rightButton left 2 leftButton
   myForm;

//END formLayout positioning----------------------
showWindow formWindow;
```

My mentor Chris Kniffen once told me something along these lines:
The best thing to do is to dumb it down to the most basic example to
see how things are working, and then convert that to your more
complex UI. You can also break the UI into sections if it is too complicated and complex. One could make the analogy of building a
puzzle, but to place the pieces (controls) you can only use commands. Each piece you put down must eventually connect to a piece
that is already on the table (the table being the formLayout command). You can build sections of the puzzle (different "child"

layouts), but before you can finish it, all the sections must be connected to each other on the table.

Chris recently updated his web page with an explanation of formLayouts. You can check it out here:

http://kniffen.ca/mayatutorials/mel/layouts/formlayout/
http://kniffen.ca/mayatutorials/mel/layouts/formlayout/formlayoutflags/

4.2.3 The km_bookmarkManager UI

Once you get a grip on formLayouts, the rest of the UI is a piece of cake.

> **Note:** Some text wrapping has occurred due to the width of the pages in this book; please check the script on the companion disc for the correct formatting.

```
if (`window -exists bookmarkManager`)
    deleteUI bookmarkManager;


window
    -t "km_bookmarkManager"
    -wh 198 180
    -mxb 0
    -resizeToFitChildren 1
    -sizeable 0
    bookmarkManager;


formLayout mainForm;


//START - MAINFORM CONTENT-------------------------------------------

    text -l "Cameras" camtext;
    text -l "Bookmarks" BMtext;
    textScrollList -h 110 tslCameras;
    textScrollList -h 110 tslBookmarks;
    button -l "refresh"
    //-command km_bookmarkManager
        refreshButton;
    button -l "add bookmark"
    //-command addNewBookmark
        addBookmarkButton;
```

```
    text -l "::Use right mouse button to display menus::" helpText;
    popupMenu -p helpText;
    menuItem -l "Help" -command displayHelpWindow;

//END - MAINFORM CONTENT-------------------------------------------

formLayout -e
    -af camtext top 0
    -af camtext left 0
    -ap camtext right 0 47
    -af BMtext top 0
    -ac BMtext left 0 camtext

    //change to 25 to get word in middle over TSL
    //-ac BMtext bottom 5 tslBookmarks
    -af BMtext right 0
    -af tslCameras left 3
    -ac tslCameras top 0 camtext

    //Attach to Position - Attaches an edge to a
    //position on the form layout.
    //Arguments are: control, edge, offset, position
    -ap tslCameras right 0 47
    -ac tslBookmarks left 5 tslCameras
    -ac tslBookmarks top 0 BMtext
    -af tslBookmarks right 3

    //Attach to Opposite Side of Another Control -
    //Attaches an edge relative to the furthest
    //side of another control.
    // Arguments are: control, edge, offset, control
    -aoc tslBookmarks bottom 0 tslCameras

    //attach the bottom edge of TSLBookmarks to the opposite
    //side of tslCameras with 0 offset
    -af refreshButton left 0
    -ac refreshButton top 5 tslCameras
    -ap refreshButton right 0 47
    -ac addBookmarkButton left 5 refreshButton
    -ac addBookmarkButton top 5 tslBookmarks
    -af addBookmarkButton right 0
```

```
//Attach to Opposite Side of Another Control -
//Attaches an edge relative to the furthest
//side of another control.
// Arguments are: control, edge, offset, control
-aoc addBookmarkButton bottom 0 refreshButton
-af helpText left 2
-ac helpText top 0 addBookmarkButton


    mainForm;
showWindow bookmarkManager;
```

4.3 The listCams and populateBookmarkList Procedures

4.3.1 The listCams Procedure

Outline

In essence, the listCams procedure consists of two parts:

■ A for loop that loops through all cameras in the scene and appends them to the tslCameras. Each camera also gets its RMB functionality with the popupMenu and menuItem commands. Clicking on an item in the tslCamera will populate the TSLbookmarks with the bookmarks of the selected camera.

■ A group of commands that makes the current active camera the selected item in the camera textScrollList (tslCameras). It also contains a for loop that makes the active camera the selected item in the TSL.

New Commands

popupMenu: This command creates a pop-up menu and attaches it to the current control if no parent is specified. The pop-up menu is displayed with the right mouse button by default.

menuItem: This command creates/edits/queries menu items for the popupMenu.

break: Sometimes you want to exit a loop immediately as soon as some condition is met. The `break` instruction exits a loop from any point in its block, bypassing the loop's condition. Execution resumes at the next statement after the loop. You can use a `break` instruction with while, do, and for loops.

Code and Comments

```
//----------------------------------------------------------------
//listCams lists all cameras in the scene and places them in
//tslCameras, with all their RMB functionality
//----------------------------------------------------------------
global proc listCams ()
{
    //clear the TSL of potentially existing elements
    textScrollList -e -ra tslCameras;
    //list all cameras
    string $camera[] = `listCameras`;
    //loop though all cameras and put each in tslCameras
    for ($eachCamera in $camera)
        {
        textScrollList -e -append $eachCamera
        //when the camera is selected call the populateBookmarkList
        //proc that populates the bookmark TSL
            -selectCommand ("populateBookmarkList";
            string $sel[] = `textScrollList -q -si tslCarmeras`;")
            tslCameras;
        //add RMB functionality to each of the cameras in the TSL
        //Mind the -parent flag that parents the popupMenu to the
        //camera TSL (tslCameras)
            popupMenu -p tslCameras camPop;
            menuItem -l "Look through" -command lookThoughCamera;
            menuItem -l "Toggle ResGate" -command toggleResGate;
            menuItem -l "Open AE" -command openAECam;
            menuItem -l "rename" -command renameCamera;
        }

    //get the current camera selected in the list
    string $currentPanel = `getPanel -wf`;
    string $currentCamera = `modelPanel -q -cam $currentPanel`;
    for ($c in $camera)
```

```
        {
        //if the current camera (i.e., the camera of the active
        //modelPanel)
        if ($currentCamera == $c)
        {
        textScrollList -e -si $currentCamera tslCameras;
        break;
        }
    else
        textScrollList -e -showIndexedItem 1 tslCameras;
    }
    //since the active camera will be the selected item in the camera
    //TSL its bookmarks will be loaded in the bookmark TSL
    populateBookmarkList;
}
```

4.3.2 The populateBookmarkList Procedure

This procedure queries the selected camera and displays its bookmarks.

Outline

1. Get the selected camera from the camera TSL.

2. Get all bookmarks of that camera with the `listConnections` command.

3. Alphabetize those bookmarks, loop through them, and place them in the right TSL (the bookmark TSL). Show each camera's RMB functionality in the form of a pop-up menu.

New Commands

sort: Returns an array containing the elements of the input array sorted in ascending order.

For example:

```
string $sortThisString[] ={"z","a","r","b","y"};
// Result: z a r b y //
sort $sortThisString;
// Result: a b r y z //
int $sortThisInteger[] = {10,50,100,1};
```

```
// Result: 10 50 100 1 //
sort $sortThisInteger;
// Result: 1 10 50 100 //

//to rearrange and reassign at the same time, do this:
$sortThisInteger = `sort $sortThisInteger`;
```

listConnections: This command returns a list of all attributes/objects of a specified type that are connected to the given object(s).

For example:

```
//create an emitter as example:
emitter;

//list all incoming connections and print each on a new line
string $incoming[] =`listConnections -source 1 -plugs 1 emitter1`;
for ($each in $incoming)
    print ($each +"\n");
```

Code and Comments

```
global proc populateBookmarkList ()
{
    //remove any potential elements from the bookmark TSL
    textScrollList -e -removeAll tslBookmarks;

    //get selected camera from camera TSL
    string $selCamera[] = `textScrollList -q -selectItem tslCameras`;

    //get all bookmarks of selected camera and sort them alphabetically
    string $bookmarks[] = sort(`listConnections ($selCamera[0]+
        ".bookmarks")`);

    //TIP: Open Hypergraph to see connections
    //for example: listConnections persp.bookmarks
    //loop through all bookmarks and put them in the bookmark TSL
    //with all their RMB functionality

    for ($eachBookmark in $bookmarks)
        {
        textScrollList -e
```

```
    -append $eachBookmark
    -selectCommand lookThroughBookmark
    tslBookmarks;

    string $selectedBookmark[] = `textScrollList -q -selectItem
        tslBookmarks`;

    popupMenu -p tslBookmarks bmPop;
    menuItem -l "rename" -command "renameBookmark()";
    menuItem -l "delete" -command "deleteBookmark" ;
    menuItem -l "Copy bookmark to:" -command "openTargetCameraTSL";
    }
}
```

4.4 Renaming Elements in the TSL: The renameCamera and renameBookmark Procedures

4.4.1 The renameCamera Procedure

Outline

This procedure will be the command under the Rename menu item of the pop-up menu from the camera TSL. The renameCamera procedure checks which camera is selected in the camera TSL and opens a promptDialog window asking the user for a new name. Based on that input, the camera will be renamed and the camera TSL will be updated accordingly (i.e., remove old name and replace with new name). A conditional prevents the startup cameras (persp, side, front, top) from being renamed.

New Commands

promptDialog: The promptDialog command creates a modal dialog with a message to the user, a text field in which the user may enter a response, and a variable number of buttons to dismiss the dialog.

For example:

```
promptDialog
    -title "Rename Camera"
    -message "Enter New Name:"
    -button "OK" -button "Cancel"
    -defaultButton "OK" -cancelButton "Cancel"
    -dismissString "Cancel";

    //To catch which button is pressed, throw it a variable
    //and query the textField

string $result = `promptDialog
    -title "Rename Camera"
    -message "Enter New Name:"
    -button "OK" -button "Cancel"
    -defaultButton "OK"
    -cancelButton "Cancel"
    -dismissString "Cancel"`;
    // Result: OK //
if ($result =="OK")
    {
        $text = `promptDialog -query -text`;
        print $text;
    }
```

stringArrayRemove: Removes the string items in the first string array from the second string array. A new string array with the items removed is returned.

For example:

```
//FIRST EXAMPLE---------------------------------------------------
string $list[] = { "a", "b", "c", "d", "e", "f", "g" };
string $items[] = { "a", "c", "e", "g" };
stringArrayRemove($items, $list);
// Result : { b, d, f } //

//SECOND EXAMPLE--------------------------------------------------
//list all cams in new scene
string $camerasInScene[] =`listCameras`;
// Result: front persp side top //
//stringArrayRemove needs arrays so we make an array of one
```

```
// mind the squiggly brackets
string $removeThis[1]={"persp"};
// Result: persp //
string $result[] =stringArrayRemove ($removeThis, $camerasInScene);
// Result: front side top //
```

Code and Comments

```
//-----------------------------------------------------------------
// proc that has the camera rename function
//-----------------------------------------------------------------
global proc renameCamera ()
{
    //get the selected cam in the camera TSL
    string $selCamera[] = `textScrollList -q -selectItem tslCameras`;

    //get all the cameras in the camera TSL
    string $allCams[]=`textScrollList -q -ai tslCameras`;

    //if the camera is a startup camera (persp, side, front, top)
    //display an error message and abort renaming
    if (`camera -q -startupCamera $selCamera[0]`)
        error ("Cannot rename read-only camera.");

    //declare variables to avoid problems with scope
    string $text;
    string $renamed;

//display promptDialog
string $result = `promptDialog
    -title "Rename Camera"
    -message "Enter New Name:"
    -button "OK" -button "Cancel"
    -defaultButton "OK" -cancelButton "Cancel"
    -dismissString "Cancel"`;

//if the OK button is pressed...
if ($result == "OK")
    {
    //...query the text input from the promptDialog
    $text = `promptDialog -query -text`;
    //rename the selected camera based on the input
```

Chapter 4

```
    //from the promptDialog
    $renamed=`rename $selCamera[0] $text`;

    //-------------------------------------------
    //Below is the stuff to clean up, repopulate
    //and arrange the camera TSL
    //-------------------------------------------
    //Because the stringArrayRemove requires 2 arrays,
    //we declare an array of 1 and assign the selected camera to it
    string $removed[1]={$selCamera[0]};

    //then we remove the old (not renamed) bookmark from the list
    $allCams=stringArrayRemove ($removed, $allCams);

    //place the renamed bookmark at the end of the list
    $allCams[size($allCams)]=$renamed;

    //sort camera TSL
    $allCams=sort($allCams);
    //-------------------------------------------
    }

//time to do the actual repopulating of the camera TSL
//First, we remove all items from the camera TSL
textScrollList -e -ra tslCameras;

//Then we loop though all cameras and add them to the TSL
for ($ac in $allCams)
textScrollList -e -a $ac tslCameras;

//Finally, we select the just renamed camera in the TSL
textScrollList -e -si $renamed tslCameras;
}
```

4.4.2 **The renameBookmark Procedure**

The renameBookmark procedure is exactly the same as the
renameCamera procedure, except for the check on default cameras.

```
//------------------------------------------------------------
// proc that has the bookmark rename function
//------------------------------------------------------------

global proc renameBookmark ()
    {   //get selected camera TSL
    string $selCam[]=`textScrollList -q -si tslCameras`;
    //get selected BM from TSL
    string $selectedBookmark[] = `textScrollList -q -selectItem
        tslBookmarks`;
    //get ALL BM's from TSL
    string $allBookmarks[]=`textScrollList -q -ai tslBookmarks`;

    // explicitly declare text var
    string $text;
    string $renamed;
    //call promptDialog and cast result in var
    string $result =
    `promptDialog
    -title "Rename bookmark"
    -message "Enter New Name:"
    -button "OK" -button "Cancel"
    -defaultButton "OK" -cancelButton "Cancel"
    -dismissString "Cancel"`;

    //if the OK button is pressed...
    if ($result == "OK")
        {//...query the text input
        $text = `promptDialog -query -text`;
        //rename BM with result of text input
        //and put new name in var
        $renamed=`rename $selectedBookmark[0] $text`;
            //stringArrayRemove requires 2 arrays, so we make
            //$removed an array of 1: $removed[1]
        string $removed[1]={$selectedBookmark[0]};
            //then remove the old (not renamed) bookmark from the list
```

```
        $allBookmarks=stringArrayRemove ($removed, $allBookmarks);
            //place the renamed bookmark at the end of the list
        $allBookmarks[size($allBookmarks)]=$renamed;
        $allBookmarks=sort($allBookmarks);
        }


    //----repopulating of "new" BM TSL
    //remove all objects from BM TSL
    textScrollList -e -ra tslBookmarks;
    //loop through all BM's...
    for ($bm in $allBookmarks)
        //...and append to BM TSL
    textScrollList -e -a $bm tslBookmarks;
    //select original selected cam in cam TSL
    textScrollList -e -si $selCam[0] tslCameras;
    //select fresh BM in BM TSL
    textScrollList -e -si $renamed tslBookmarks;
}
```

4.5 The Remaining RMB Functionality of the Camera TSL: the toggleResGate, openAECam, and lookThroughCamera Procedures

4.5.1 The toggleResGate Procedure

Outline

This procedure determines which camera is active and displays/hides its resolution gate (based on the settings in the Render Globals window).

New Commands

getPanel: The -withFocus flag of the getPanel command returns the name of the panel that currently has focus. If no panel has focus, then the last panel that had focus is returned.

modelPanel: This command creates (or displays information about) a panel consisting of a model editor. The `-cam` flag tells us which camera is being used in the modelPanel we will get from the `getPanel` command.

Code and Comments

```
global proc toggleResGate ()
{
    // get the active panel
    // -withFocus: return name of panel that currently has focus
    string $whichPanel = `getPanel -withFocus`;

    //get camera of active modelPanel
    string $nameCamera = `modelPanel -q -camera ($whichPanel)`;

    //query the state of the resolution gate
    //if the resolution gate is on (==1)
    if (`camera -q -displayResolution $nameCamera`)
    // ...then turn it off
    camera -e -displayResolution off $nameCamera;
    else
    // ...else turn it on.
    camera -e -displayResolution on $nameCamera;
}
```

4.5.2 The openAECam Procedure

Outline

This procedure selects the camera that is active in the camera TSL and opens its Attribute Editor.

New Commands

openAEWindow: This is an undocumented command that I found by using `echo all commands`. It does just what its name implies: It opens the Attribute Editor of the selected node.

Code and Comments

```
global proc openAECam ()
{
    //First, cast selected item in camera TSL in an array
    string $selCamera[] = `textScrollList -q -selectItem tslCameras`;

    //Then, select it
    select $selCamera[0];

    //and open its AE
    openAEWindow;
}
```

4.5.3 The lookThroughCam Procedure

Outline

This procedure takes the selected camera in the TSL and looks
through it in the model panel with focus. Figure 4-2 shows the
default model panels. Note that in the figure, the perspective camera is the model panel with focus.

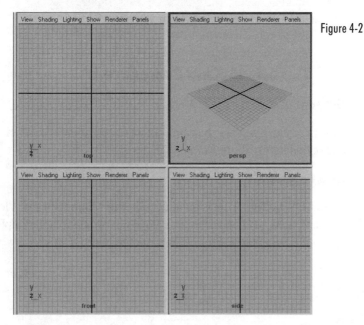

Figure 4-2

New Commands

lookThru: This command sets a particular camera to look through in a view. If used with a model panel, the syntax is as follows:

```
lookThru [modelEditor] [camera]
```

Code and Comments

```
global proc lookThroughCamera ()
{
    //get selected camera
    string $selCamera[] = `textScrollList -q -selectItem tslCameras`;

    //get the modelPanel with focus in the UI
    string $focusPanel =`getPanel -withFocus`;

    //look though the selected camera in that modelPanel
    string $lookThroughCam = `lookThru $selCamera[0] $focusPanel`;
}
```

4.6 The lookThroughBookmark and deleteBookmark Procedures

4.6.1 The lookThroughBookmark Procedure

Outline

lookThroughBookmark looks through the currently selected bookmark in the active model panel in a similar way that the lookThroughCamera procedure does.

New Commands

cameraView: This command creates a preset view for a camera that is then independent of the camera. The view stores a camera's eye point, center of interest point, up vector, tumble pivot, horizontal aperture, vertical aperture, focal length, orthographic width, and whether the camera is orthographic or perspective. These settings

Chapter 4

can be applied to any other camera through the -setCamera flag. In other words, this commands stores, queries, and edits bookmarks.

The syntax in our case is like this:

```
cameraView [camera to be edited] [to what the camera needs to be set]
//so, in our case that would be:
cameraView [selected camera in TSL] [selected bookmark in TSL]
```

Code and Comments

```
global proc lookThroughBookmark ()
{
    //get selected camera from camera TSL
    string $selCamera[] = `textScrollList -q -selectItem tslCameras`;

    //get selected bookmark from bookmark TSL
    string $selectedBookmark[] = `textScrollList -q -selectItem
        tslBookmarks`;

    //getPanel: returns the name of the panel that currently has focus.
    string $focusPanel =`getPanel -withFocus`;

    //First, look through the selected camera in the panel with focus
    string $lookThroughCam = `lookThroughModelPanel $selCamera[0]
        $focusPanel`;

    //Then, edit the cameraView of the selected camera, so it looks
    //through the selected bookmark
    //syntax: cameraView [camera to be edited]
    //    [to what the camera needs to be set]
    string $lookThroughBookmark = `cameraView -e -camera $selCamera[0]
        -setCamera $selectedBookmark[0]`;
}
```

4.6.2 **The deleteBookmark Procedure**

Outline

The deleteBookmark procedure deletes the active bookmark from the TSL and repopulates the list accordingly.

New Commands

None.

Code and Comments

```
global proc deleteBookmark ()
{
    string $selCamera[] = `textScrollList -q -si tslCameras`;
    string $selectedBookmark[] = `textScrollList -q -selectItem
        tslBookmarks`;
    string $allSelectedBookmarks[]=`textScrollList -q -ai
        tslBookmarks`;
    select $selectedBookmark[0];
    delete $selectedBookmark[0];

    //rebuild bookmark TSL without the just deleted bookmark
    //remove all BM's from TSL
    textScrollList -e -ra tslBookmarks;

    //loop though all BM's
    for ($i=0; $i<size($allSelectedBookmarks); $i++)
        {
        //if the current BM is not the just deleted BM...
        if ($allSelectedBookmarks[$i] != $selectedBookmark[0])
        //...add it to the TSL
            textScrollList -e -a $allSelectedBookmarks[$i]
                tslBookmarks;
        }

    //reselect the original camera
    textScrollList -e -si $selCamera[0] tslCameras;
}
```

Chapter 4

4.7 Copying Bookmarks from One Camera to Another: The copyBookmark and openTargetCameraTSL Procedures

Outline

The copyBookmark and openTargetCameraTSL procedures are closely linked, as the copyBookmark proc needs input from the openTargetCameraTSL proc to function. More specifically, openTargetCameraTSL gets called when the user holds down his RMB over a bookmark and displays a list of the available cameras. Based on the selected camera in that list and the selected bookmark, the bookmark gets copied over (with a suffix) when the Confirm button is pressed.

New Commands

None.

Code and Comments

```
//----------------------------------------------------------------
// openTargetCameraTSL opens target camera TSL
//----------------------------------------------------------------
global proc openTargetCameraTSL ()
{
    //Nothing special here. Just an iteration putting all
    //cameras in a TSL.
    //The copyBookmark is attached to the
    //command of the "Confirm" button
    if (`window -exists copyBookmarkWin`)
        deleteUI copyBookmarkWin;

    window -t "copyBookmarkWin" -wh 100 150 -mxb 0 -resizeToFitChildren
        1 copyBookmarkWin;
        columnLayout copyBookmarkCol;
        textScrollList -h 150 -w 100 tslTargetCameras;
            button -w 100 -l "Confirm" -c copyBookmark confirmButton;
```

```
        string $camera[] = `listCameras`;
        for ($eachCamera in $camera)
            {
            textScrollList -e -append $eachCamera tslTargetCameras;
            }
        showWindow copyBookmarkWin;
    }


//----------------------------------------------------------------
// copyBookmark checks which bookmark is selected and
// copies it to the camera in the targetCameraTSL.
//----------------------------------------------------------------
global proc copyBookmark ()
{
    //get selected bookmark
    string $selectedBookmark[] = `textScrollList -q -selectItem
        tslBookmarks`;
    //get targetCamera from tslTargetCameras
    string $targetCamera[] = `textScrollList -q -selectItem
        tslTargetCameras`;
    //set the target camera with the settings of the selected bookmark
    cameraView -e -camera $targetCamera[0] -setCamera
        $selectedBookmark[0];
    //add that setting to the targetCamera
    cameraView -camera $targetCamera[0] -name ($selectedBookmark[0] +
        "_copy")
    addBookmark;
    //delete the openTargetCameraTSL
    deleteUI copyBookmarkWin;
}
```

Chapter 4

4.8 The Add Bookmark Button and Its Functionality

Outline

This procedure makes the current cameraView a bookmark for the active camera, based on the name given by the user in the promptDialog.

New Commands

cameraView -camera -addName: When used with this syntax, the cameraView command sets the name of the view (i.e., the bookmark).

Code and Comments

```
global proc addNewBookmark ()
{
    //get selected camera
    string $selCamera[] = `textScrollList -q -selectItem tslCameras`;

    //explicitly declare variables to avoid problems with scope
    string $newBookmarkName;
    string $newBookmark;

    //display promptDialog
    string $result = `promptDialog
        -title "Create New Bookmark"
        -message "Enter New Name:"
        -button "OK" -button "Cancel"
        -defaultButton "OK" -cancelButton "Cancel"
        -dismissString "Cancel"`;

    //cast all bookmarks in TSL in variable
    //so the TSL can be repopulated
    string $allBmks[]=`textScrollList -q -ai tslBookmarks`;

    //based on new name...
```

```
if ($result == "OK")
{
$newBookmarkName= `promptDialog -query -text`;

//...add current view to selected camera
$newBookmark = `cameraView -camera $selCamera[0] -name
    $newBookmarkName - addBookmark`;

//add the new bookmark to the bottom of the list
$allBmks[size($allBmks)]=$newBookmark;

//sort the bookmarks
$allBmks=sort($allBmks);

//remove all bookmarks from list...
textScrollList -e -ra tslBookmarks;

//...and repopulate with new bookmark added
for ($bm in $allBmks)
    textScrollList -e -append $bm tslBookmarks;
}

//select the freshly created bookmark
textScrollList -e -si $newBookmark tslBookmarks;
}
```

Chapter 4

4.9 Automatically Adding Newly Created Camera to the Camera TSL with scriptJob

Outline

When the user creates a new camera with the UI, I want the bookmarkManager to update as well. This means that the newly created camera should be automatically added to the camera TSL (without the user having to press the Refresh button). In MEL, you do something like that with a command called scriptJob, which monitors the user's actions and runs a script when a certain action is performed. In programming language, this is often called a trigger; when the action is triggered, the script is run.

It essentially works like this:

If a DAG object is created (`scriptJob`), check if it is a camera (`checkForCam`).

If it is a camera, add it to the camera TSL (`rebuildNewCamList`).

A DAG (directed acyclic graph) object is another name for a transform node.

New Commands

scriptJob: This command creates a "script job," which is a MEL command or script. This job is attached to the named condition, event, or attribute. Each time the condition switches to the desired state (or the trigger is triggered), the script is run.

> **IMPORTANT:** You have to be careful when creating scriptJobs, because the triggering can happen so frequently that your scene can become unworkably slow. One way to remedy that is to parent the scriptJob to the UI you are using it in. That way, when the UI gets killed, the scriptJob gets killed.

Besides the `-parent` flag, we will also use the `-event` flag. This will run the script when the named event occurs. This string must be the name of a predefined Maya event. To get a list of the events that exist, use the `-listEvents` flag or check the command reference. The event in our case will be DagObjectCreated, which means that the script will be run whenever a new transform node is created.

The script that will run is a procedure of our own making: checkForCam. This procedure checks the history of our scene (with the `listHistory` command) and does a nodeType check. If the most recently created node is a camera, then the rebuildNewCamList procedure is called.

rebuildNewCamList is the procedure that adds the freshly created camera to our camera TSL in the bookmarkManager UI.

listHistory: If used without any flags, the `listHistory` command returns the most recently created transform node.

listRelatives: This command lists parents and children of DAG objects.

For example:

```
//create a camera
camera;
// Result: camera1 cameraShape1 //
listHistory;
// Result: cameraShape1 //

//We need the transform, not the shape node, so...
listRelatives -parent cameraShape1;
// Result: camera1 //
```

Code and Comments

```
//-------------------------------------------------------------------
// We parent scriptJob to the bookmarkWindow, so the scriptJob gets
// killed when the window gets closed
scriptJob -parent "bookmarkManager" -event "DagObjectCreated"
    "checkForCam";
//-------------------------------------------------------------------

global proc checkForCam()
{
    //initialize check at 0 because usually
    //the dag object won't be a camera
    int $isCamera=0;

    //check history
    string $history[]=`listHistory`;

    //if history object is a camera, change
    //camera check to 1.

    if (`nodeType $history[0]` == "camera")
    $isCamera=1;

    //if check is 1, rebuild camera list
```

```
    //(let's make this a separate proc...)

    if ($isCamera)
        rebuildNewCamList($history[0]);
}


//--------------------------------------------------------------
// rebuildNewCamList is for rebuilding the camera list with a new
// camera. It takes as its argument the newly created camera.
//--------------------------------------------------------------
global proc rebuildNewCamList(string $newCameraShape)
{
    //get camera's transform for name
    string $cameraName[]=`listRelatives -parent $newCameraShape`;

    //get list of cameras
    string $allCams[]=`textScrollList -q -ai tslCameras`;

    //add new camera to end of list and sort list
    $allCams[size($allCams)]=$cameraName[0];

    //e.g., if there are 6 cams: $allCams[5] = persp2Shape;
    $allCams=sort($allCams);

    //remove list from textScrollList
    textScrollList -e -ra tslCameras;

    //add new list to textScrollList
    for ($cam in $allCams) textScrollList -e -a $cam tslCameras;

    //select new camera
    textScrollList -e -si $cameraName[0] tslCameras;

    //there won't be any bookmarks yet, so skip initializing them
}
```

4.10 **The Help Window**

Outline

The displayHelpWindow procedure calls a simple scroll window with some lines of explanation about the script in it. It also mentions the version number of the script and gives an e-mail address for suggestions and bug reports.

This proc goes under the RMB of the text:

```
menuItem -l "Help" -command displayHelpWindow;
```

New Commands

scrollField: This command creates a scrolling field that handles multiple lines of text.

For example:

```
if (`window -exists scrollFieldExample`)
    deleteUI scrollFieldExample;

    window -wh 200 300 scrollFieldExample;
    paneLayout -configuration "horizontal4";
    scrollField -wordWrap true -text "Non-editable with word wrap"
        -editable false;
    scrollField -wordWrap false -text "Non-editable with no word wrap"
        -editable false;
    scrollField -wordWrap true -text "Editable with word wrap";
    scrollField -wordWrap false -text "Editable with no word wrap";

showWindow scrollFieldExample;
```

Code and Comments

```
global proc displayHelpWindow ()
{
    if (`window -exists helpWindow`)
        deleteUI helpWindow;

    window -wh 300 160
        -mxb off
```

```
        -mnb off
        helpWindow;

    columnLayout -adj 1 mainCol;
    //mind the concatenation with the + sign to avoid the long string
    scrollField -wordWrap true
        -h 160
        -editable false
        -text (":::::::::bookmarkManager 1.0:::::::::\n \nAll the good
            stuff is "
        +"under the almighty RIGHT mouse button. So, hold down RIGHT
            mouse button "
        +"over selected cam or bookmark to display menus.\nAll of
            it is "
        +"self-explanatory.\n \nTake it easy,
            \nkevin_mannens@yahoo.com");

    showWindow helpWindow;
}
```

Note: Some text wrapping has occurred due to the width of the pages in this book; please check the script on the companion disc for the correct formatting.

The last thing you have to do is attach all the procedures to their buttons and RMBs in the main UI.

Hands-On MEL Coding: km_debrisCreator

5.1 Orientation and Top-Down Design

5.1.1 Origin and UI Layout

During a recent production, it became apparent we needed a little tool to help us with debris creation for ground-foot interaction for the smaller characters. In particular, there were a lot of shots with rodents walking on a forest floor covered with pine needles and little rocks. We needed a tool that would create rocks and needles on the fly based on a couple of inputs. Those rocks and needles could then be fed into our proprietary rigid body software for the actual dynamic interaction. Hence, km_debrisCreator came into existence.

This script introduces some interesting techniques like the use of plug-ins in MEL scripts and concepts like model-view-controller. It also allows me to elaborate a bit more on good coding practices.

This is what the UI turned out like:

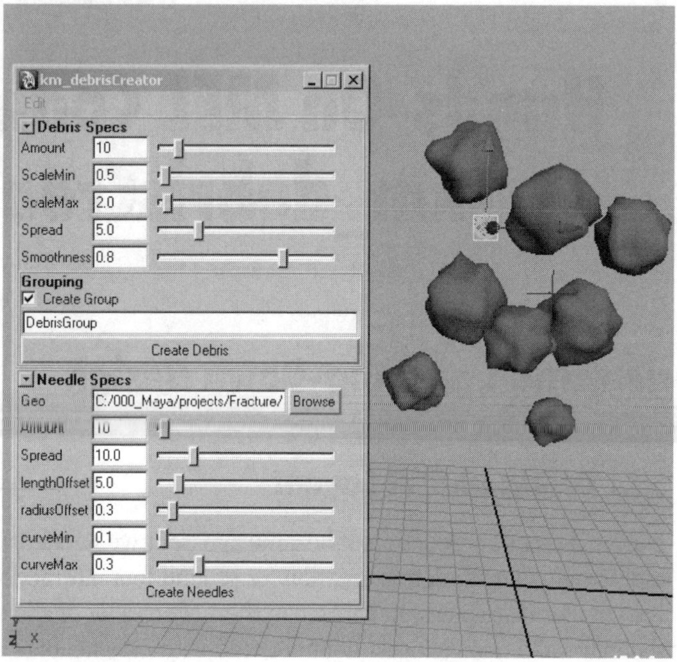

Figure 5-1

5.1.2 **Top-Down Design of km_debrisCreator**

We need a tool for creating needles and rocks. Top-down design is again a bit of an overstatement here because this tool is actually quite linear, both in UI and concept. In any case, the outline would look something like the following:

Functionality

Rocks

■ We should be able to create rocks at a specific location (locator) or at center

■ The number of rocks should be user-definable

■ Min and max scale of rocks should be user-definable

- Spreading of rocks around point in space should be user-definable
- User should have option to group rocks and name group
- Group name should include details of group, such as number of rocks in that group

Needles

- User should pick existing geometry that will be used as base geometry
- We should be able to create needles at a specific location (locator) or at center
- Spreading of needles around a point in space should be user-definable
- Number of needles should be user-definable
- User should be able to define a length-offset based on the length of the original geometry
- User should be able to define a radius-offset based on the radius of the original geometry
- User should be able to define the min and max curvature of the needle (use bend deformer for that)

User Interface

The UI should be as simple and synoptic as possible, so we will use two frameLayouts (one for rocks and one for needles), each containing a number of sliders and text fields.

5.2 Good Coding Practices

Before we dig into the code, I would like to spend a bit more time on good coding practices. Now that we have written some scripts, this information should make a lot more sense. As always: *Repetitio mater studiorum est.*

> **Note:** The text below is an adjusted version of two articles I found on the Internet, mixed with a personal brain dump. I tweaked the text a bit so it would fit our MEL context better. You can find the original articles here: http://www.nyu.edu/classes/nagler/quant2/coding_style.html by Jonathan Nagler and http://www.gamedev.net/reference/articles/article819.asp by Brent P. Newhall.
> I would like to thank both authors for granting me permission to use their articles in this book.

5.2.1 Design Your Code before You Start Coding

I can't repeat this enough: Never write code on the fly. You should always sketch out some pseudocode explaining what the code will do (at a higher level) before you start coding. The only exception to this rule is code that you've already written innumerable times (e.g., finding one element in an array).

Sketching out code before writing it will solidify in your mind exactly what you want to do, and will save you a lot of time sitting in front of a computer screen, trying different approaches to an algorithm. This approach of "pseudocode before code" works because when you're typing code, you're in "programmer mode," trying to get each individual line right. When you're writing out pseudocode on a legal pad, you're in "design mode," and you can look at things from a better perspective.

5.2.2 Comment Your Code as You Write It

Comments. Comments. Comments. I can't count the number of times I've berated a piece of code for not having enough comments, but I can't remember ever being annoyed at code that had too many comments. The point is simple: Write as many comments as possible.

Don't overdo it though and comment something that's obvious:

```
$i = 0; //Assign the value 0 to the integer variable
```

But try to explain yourself as you code:

```
// sometimes (on Linux anyway) a command that takes too long to execute
// from a popup menu item will completely lock up Maya and screw the X
```

```
// server, so we wrap the command in an evalDeferred as a workaround...

menuItem -l "Edit"
    -c ("evalDeferred \""+encodeString($editCmd)+"\"")
    -p $menu;
```

I recommend writing comments as you're writing the code itself, mainly because you're much less likely to go back in and add useful, meaningful comments later. Do it as you're coding, and the comments have a much better chance of being both meaningful and complete.

5.2.3 Each Procedure Should Have a Meaningful Explanatory Header Comment

Describe exactly what the procedure is supposed to do, what it assumes about incoming data, and any gotchas in the results. This way, rather than having to read a 50-line procedure to figure out what it does, all you have to do is read a one- or two-sentence description.

The pseudocode you sketched out when designing this procedure can also come in handy in writing the explanation. Some programmers include the pseudocode with the description.

5.2.4 Use Indents and Margins Appropriately

This quickly becomes a habit, but a surprising number of programmers don't indent properly. Each new loop, if statement, procedure, or block of UI code should be indented one level further (just hit the Spacebar or Tab key a few times). Make sure that you return to the previous level of indentation when you're done with each block, too.

Blank lines are also surprisingly useful in increasing the readability of your code. A couple of blank lines between each procedure will visibly separate them, and you'll be able to quickly see where one ends and another begins.

Chapter 5

5.2.5 **Keep Procedures Direct and to the Point**

I've lost count of the number of times I've seen procedures that have all sorts of processing (e.g., sorting an array) dumped into them. Separate out distinct procedures into their own procedures. Redesign a big procedure into several smaller procedures that are easier for others to read and understand.

5.2.6 **Always Use Descriptive Variable Names**

Code becomes orders of magnitude more difficult to debug when important variables are named $i, $t, $temp, $var, $var1, and so forth. If you have a variable to store the player's health, don't name it $h; name it $playerHealth.

Remember that most of the time you spend on programming is spent modifying existing code; very little time (comparatively) is actually spent adding new stuff. This means that you'll be spending a lot of time reading through your code, so it makes sense to invest the time and effort in teaching yourself how to write code that's readable. Readable code is easy to write, easy to debug, and easy to maintain. Everybody wins!

5.3 **Good Practices when Writing Procedures**

5.3.1 **The Difference between Procedures and Functions**

Many times you will find the words "procedure" and "function" used interchangeably. Although in the case of MEL it doesn't really matter much, these two concepts are in fact not the same. Many programming languages such as Pascal, FORTRAN, and Ada distinguish between functions or function subprograms, which return values (via a return statement), and subroutines or procedures, which do not. Other languages such as C and MEL do not make this distinction, and treat those terms as synonymous.

5.3.2 **Procedures Should Be Small, Simple, and Layered**

Ideally, procedures should be small, simple, layered, and built on other procedures. It is advisable (although sometimes not practical) to make a procedure do just *one clearly identifiable thing*. By layered, I just mean that once you've written some procedures that do something useful, you build on that and write other higher-level procedures in terms of those. But you can work the opposite way around too, writing a procedure that calls others you haven't written yet but know you'll need, before dropping down a level. You can even mix the layering methods if that's how you like working.

Also, you don't want to make a procedure so massive that you can't easily figure out what it does, but not so short that it hardly does anything and you've got too many. It's hard to say where the balance is; you just get a feel for when to break something into a new procedure and when not to.

5.3.3 **Modularity**

Modularity refers to the concept that tasks should be split up. If two tasks can be performed sequentially rather than simultaneously, then perform them sequentially. The logic for this is simple: Lots of things can go wrong. You want to be able to isolate what went wrong. You also want to be able to isolate what went right. After what specific change did things improve? This makes for much more readable code.

This means it is (almost) always good practice to break a procedure up into separate procedures whenever possible so that they can be reused and you can avoid duplicating the code. For example, say you have a node that you use to store and retrieve data. You would then create a procedure that you can call to get data from the node where everything's saved. That procedure would then be called from other places in the file rather than having what it does/its code duplicated. If you change your mind about how it should work, you only have to change it in one place as well.

Note that the paragraphs above are guidelines that in some cases will be very hard to achieve.

5.3.4 **K.I.S.S.**

Keep it simple and don't get too clever. In most cases, the simplest way is the best way. You may think of a very clever way to code something this week. Unfortunately, you may not be as clever next week and you might not be able to figure out what you did. Also, the next person to read your code might not be so clever. Finally, you might not be as clever as you think. For example, a complicated method of doing three steps at once might only work for five out of six cases. Or it might create nonsense values out of what should be missing data. Why take the chance? Computers are very fast. Any gains you make in efficiency will be dwarfed by the confusion caused later on in trying to figure out what exactly your code is doing so efficiently.

The bottom line? Do not try to be as clever as possible when coding. Try to write code that is as simple as possible. A procedure should not be constructed to express how eccentric an individual thinks he or she is. It should be constructed so other programmers can understand what is going on.

5.3.5 **Comments, Again**

There is probably nothing more important than having adequate comments in your code. Basically, one should have comments in front of any distinct task that the code is about to perform. Beyond this, one can have a comment to describe what a single line does. The basic rule of thumb is this: The line of code should be absolutely, positively self-explanatory to someone other than yourself without the comment. If there is any ambiguity, go ahead and put the comment in.

5.3.6 **Model-view-controller (MVC) Architecture**

MVC is a fancy term for keeping your UI procedures and work procedures separated.

Wikipedia describes MVC as follows:

Model-view-controller (MVC) is an architectural pattern used in software engineering. Successful use of the pattern isolates business logic from user interface considerations, resulting in an application where it is easier to modify either the visual appearance of the application or the underlying business rules without affecting the other. In MVC, the Model represents the information (the data) of the application and the business rules used to manipulate the data, the View corresponds to elements of the user interface such as text, checkbox items, and so forth, and the Controller manages details involving the communication to the model of user actions such as keystrokes and mouse movements.

My mentor Chris Kniffen describes it as follows:

Separate your UI procedures and work procedures as much as possible. Procedures should be stand-alone (i.e., executable as such from the command line) and not rely on the UI.

So, applying the MVC architecture to MEL you would have:

1. A UI proc that creates the UI.

2. An intermediate proc that gets executed when a button in the UI is pressed and that sucks the info from the UI and builds the stand-alone command, which gets fed into the work proc. This can also be described as a "switchboard procedure," one whose sole task is to parse some data and make a call to another procedure or a set of procedures based on the input.

3. A stand-alone procedure that does the work, and that can be run from the command line without the UI.

Using MVC is clean, practical, and fast because if you need to change the stand-alone procedure, it's not as much work to change the intermediate proc to compensate, and the UI probably wouldn't need to get changed unless things are added or removed.

Chapter 5

We will apply MVC in km_debrisCreator, so don't worry if the process isn't completely clear yet.

5.4 The debrisCreator Procedure: MVC in Action

5.4.1 Outline

Finally! Some coding.

The debrisCreator procedure is a stand alone procedure that creates a user-definable number of rocks, either at the origin or around a selected transform if the user has selected one. The debrisCreator procedure has the following arguments:

- $num: The number of rocks
- $scaleMin: The radius of the smallest rock
- $scaleMax: The radius of the largest rock; all other rocks have a radius between min and max
- $spreadValue: The size of the sphrand around the transform in case of transform-based placement
- $coarseValue: A value of the noise deformer that defines the coarseness/smoothness of the rocks
- $groupCheck: A Boolean that defines if a group should be created for the rocks
- $groupName: The group name for the aforementioned group

The inner workings of the procedure are as follows for each iteration (i.e., the number of rocks):

1. Create a cube.
2. Rotate it randomly.
3. Smooth it.
4. Apply a noise deformer (a plug-in called NoiseD).
5. Smooth the deformed cube.

6. If a transform was selected, pick a sphrand location and position the cube there.

7. Else, place at origin (on top of previous cube).

The noise deformer we will use is called NoiseD and can be downloaded here: http://www.hajimenakamura.com/hajime/cg/mll/noiseD/noiseD_e.shtml

5.4.2 **New Commands**

pluginInfo: No mysteries here; this command provides information about registered plug-ins. We will use this command to check if the NoiseD plug-in is loaded. If it is not, the script will spit out an error (because without the plug-in it can't create wee rocks).

For example:

```
// List the plugins that are currently loaded
pluginInfo -query -listPlugins;

// Turn on autoloading for a plug-in
pluginInfo -edit -autoload true myPlugin.so;

// check if a plug-in called NoiseD.mll is loaded
pluginInfo -query -loaded NoiseD.mll
```

nodeType: Again, pretty self-explanatory; this command returns the type of node of its argument. Note that to know the `nodeType` of most nodes, you will have to feed it the shape of a node and not the transform. The node type of a transform is "transform."

We use this command to verify that the selected node to position the rocks around is, indeed, a transform.

For example:

```
//get node type of selected object
nodeType `ls -sl`;

//======================
//create a node
sphere;
//select node
string $ball[] = `ls -sl`;
//get shape of node
```

Chapter 5

```
string $getShape[] = `listRelatives -shapes $ball[0]`;
//get node type of shape
string $type = `nodeType $getShape[0]`;
// nurbsSurface //
```

group: Yet another fairly obvious command. group, as you might have guessed, creates a group. We use the -name flag to name the group and the -empty flag to make sure the group gets created empty; i.e., without children. This will enable us to add each rock to a group that has been created outside the iteration that creates the rocks.

Let's make an example that combines group and nodeType, where only the locators of a bunch of selected nodes get added to the group.

For example:

```
// get selected objects
string $sel[] = `ls -sl`;

// create empty group
string $group = `group -n "locatorgroup" -em`;

//loop through selected objects
for ($each in $sel)
    {
    // get shape
    string $shape[] = `listRelatives -s $each`;
    // get type of shape
    string $type = `nodeType $shape[0]`;
    //if it is a locator
    if ($type == "locator")
    {   //parent to group
        parent $each $group;
        print ("Placed " + $shape[0] + " in " + $group + ".\n");
    }
    }
```

xform: Can be used to query/set any element in a transformation node. It can also be used to query some values that cannot be set directly, such as the transformation matrix, bounding box, or pivots. You will notice that in the docs some of the arguments are called "double." For simplicity's sake we will consider these to be equal to floats.

For example:

```
// create object to manipulate
sphere -n sphere1;
// set rotation of sphere
xform -r -rotate 0 90 0;
// change the rotate order but preserve the overall transformation
xform -p true -rotateOrder yzx;
```

rand: Returns random numbers evenly distributed over the range between a start number and an end number. If no start number is provided, the command will assume it to be 0. When applied to a vector, the command generates an independent random number for each of the three components. Although the syntax doesn't need it, I always put brackets around the arguments of the rand command. This is especially important in expressions.

For example:

```
rand (50);
// 35.888315 //
rand (-5654, 42);
// -5405.041488 //
rand <<1, 1, 1>>;
// <<0.677275, 0.733665, 0.935424>> //
rand <<1, 1, 1>> <<100, 200, 300>>;
// <84.82616, 87.194758, 31.286249>> //
```

sphrand: Generates random vectors evenly distributed inside a sphere of the specified radius. To understand how it works, imagine a sphere of a certain radius. Each time you run the sphrand command, it provides you with a vector (i.e., a point in space) within that sphere.

Let's put some of these commands together and create a group of locators (xform), around a random point in space (rand) and within a certain radius (sphrand).

```
//to create 10 locators, iterate 10 times
for($n=0; $n<=10; $n++)
    {
    // get a random point in space
```

```
    vector $randPos = `rand <<100, 100, 100>>`;
    // get a position around that point within a certain radius
    vector $randRad = `sphrand (.1)`;
    // to get the radius around the randPos, we add the values together
    // - offset to get them closer
    vector $pos = ($randPos + $randRad)/10;
    //create a loc
    string $locator[] = `spaceLocator`;
    //position it to the $pos
    xform -t ($pos.x) ($pos.y) ($pos.z) $locator[0];
    }
```

abs: Returns the absolute value of its argument (i.e., makes negative values positive). With a couple of brackets you can combine it with another number-generating command. We use this command because we don't want a negative value for the scale attribute we will set.

For example:

```
rand (-10, -100);
abs (rand (-10, -100));
```

deformer: This command creates a deformer of the specified type. In our case it will need the -type flag because we will use the NoiseD plug-in. The -type flag specifies the type of deformer to create. This flag is required in Create mode. Typically the type should specify a loaded plug-in deformer. This command should normally not be used to create one of the standard deformers such as sculpt, lattice, blendShape, wire, or cluster, since they have their own customized commands with useful specialized functionality.

I found this out the good, old-fashioned way: by looking in the Script Editor when I added the deformer.

For example:

```
// create a sphere
sphere;
// make sure it is selected
select -r nurbsSphere1;
// add the noise deformer
deformer -type noiseD;
// noiseD1 noiseHandle //
```

```
// set some noise attrs
setAttr "noiseD1.frequency" 2.1;
setAttr "noiseD1.amplitude" 1.6;
setAttr "noiseD1.FrequencyRatio" 4.6;
```

polySmooth: Smoothes a polygonal object. This command works on polygonal objects or faces. We will use it to smooth the cube so that it looks more like a rock or pebble before we deform it with NoiseD. The $-dv$ (divisions) flag specifies the number of recursive smoothing steps. There are many other flags to suit your needs.

For example:

```
// create some cubes, move them around and delete faces
// on some
polyCube -n plg1; move -3 0 2;
polyCube -n plg2; move -3 0 -2;
polyCube -n plg3; move 0 0 2; delete plg3.f[1];
polyCube -n plg4; move 0 0 -2; delete plg4.f[1];
polyCube -n plg5; move 3 0 2;
polyCube -n plg6; move 3 0 -2;

// change some global display polygonal attributes.
polyOptions -activeObjects -displayBorder 1;

// #### execute the lines below, one by one ####
// so you can see the effects on the cubes

// only one division:
polySmooth -dv 1 plg1.f[0:5];

// 2 divisions produces a round-ish object
polySmooth -dv 2 plg2.f[0:5];

// keep border edges
select plg3.f[0:4];
polySmooth -kb 1;

// don't keep border edges
select plg4.f[0:4];
polySmooth -kb 0;
```

```
// 1 division, continuity 0.2
select plg5;
polySmooth -c 0.2;

// 1 division, continuity 0.8
polySmooth -c 0.8 plg6.f[0:5];
```

makeIdentity: This is the command behind "freeze transformations," and is probably the first cryptic command in this chapter. The docs say it like this: "The `makeIdentity` command is a quick way to reset the selected transform and all of its children down to the shape level by the identity transformation." `makeIdentity` has an important flag called `-apply`. `makeIdentity` is the MEL command for freezing transformations, so that means if you pass `-apply` as true, any flags that come after are frozen. For example:

```
makeIdentity -apply 1 -t 1; //means translations are frozen.
```

In other words, `makeIdentity` freezes transforms from the selected DAG node downward, baking the transformations into the geometry's points, and resetting the translate/rotate/scale to 0 0 0, 0 0 0, 1 1 1, but leaving the pivots where they are.

You guessed it: I found this out by looking in the Script Editor when I called the command from the UI.

For example:

```
makeIdentity -apply 1 -t 1 -r 1 -s 1 -n 0;
```

5.4.3 Code and Comments

```
global proc debrisCreator(int $num,
            float $scaleMin,
            float $scaleMax,
            float $spreadValue,
            float $coarseValue,
            int $groupCheck,
            string $groupName)


{
//check if plug-in is loaded
// don't forget the ! operator
```

```
if (!`pluginInfo -q -loaded NoiseD.mll`)
    error (" NoiseD plug-in NOT loaded. Please load the plug-in" +
        "\n");
    else
        print ("NoiseD plug-in loaded. Ready to go...");

//get selected objects for locator positioning
    string $sel[] = `ls -sl`;

    //check the nodeType of the selection to make sure transforms can
    //be extracted
    string $selType="";
    if (`size $sel` >= 1)
        {
        $selType = `nodeType $sel[0]`;
        }

//create groups to store geo in
    string $newGroup = "";
    if ($groupCheck)
        $newGroup = `group -n ($groupName+ "#") -em`;

//main debris creation loop
    for($n=0;$n<$num;$n++)
        {
        //create original cube
        string $cube[] = `polyCube -n ("pebble" + "#")`;
        //rotate cube randomly around world space coordinates
        xform -ws -ro (rand(180)) (rand(180))(rand(180)) $cube[0];
        //smooth the cube to make it look like a sphere
        polySmooth -dv 2 -c 0.75 $cube[0];
        select -r $cube[0];

        //create, apply and set attrs of the noiseDeformer
        string $noiseD[] = `deformer -type noiseD `;
        float $noiseFreq = rand (2, 5);
        setAttr ($noiseD[0] + ".pointSpace") 0;
        setAttr ($noiseD[0] + ".noiseType") 1;
        setAttr ($noiseD[0] + ".noiseDirection") 1;
        setAttr ($noiseD[0] + ".amplitude") 2;
        setAttr ($noiseD[0] + ".gain") 1;
```

Chapter 5

```
      setAttr ($noiseD[0] + ".frequency") $noiseFreq;

      //smooth the deformed result
      polySmooth -dv 1 -c $coarseValue $cube[0];

      //delete the history of the cube/debris
      delete -ch $cube[0];
      //delete the deformer
      delete $noiseD[1] ;
      select -r $cube[0];

      //cast scaleMin and scaleMax in a var and apply to debris
      float $scale= abs(rand ($scaleMin, $scaleMax));
      xform -ws -s $scale $scale $scale $cube[0];
      //zero out the t  r, s
      makeIdentity -apply true -t 1 -r 1 -s 1 -n 0 $cube[0];

  if (`size $sel` >= 1 && $selType == "transform")
      {
      //get the locator's position and
      // add it to the sphrand for random positioning
      vector $locPos = `xform -q -ws -t $sel[0]`;
      vector $sphrand = sphrand ($spreadValue);
      vector $randPos = ($locPos + $sphrand);
      xform -t ($randPos.x) ($randPos.y) ($randPos.z) $cube[0];
      }

      // else just stack 'em.
      else
          {
          print ("No transform selected. Stacking debris" + "\n");
          xform -ws -t 0 ($n*($scaleMax + 1)) 0 $cube[0];
          }

      if ($groupCheck)
          parent $cube[0] $newGroup;
      }

//center pivot on group
xform -cp $newGroup;
//rename group here, because concatenation during original creation
```

```
//was messy
rename $newGroup ($newGroup + "_" + "amnt" + $num);
//clear selection
select -cl;
}
```

5.5 The needleCreator Procedure

5.5.1 Outline

In broad strokes, this procedure is the same as the debrisCreator procedure except that it uses a user-specified piece of geometry (a needle) to duplicate around a transform. It is interesting to note that this procedure was written some time after debrisCreator. It was only in a later stage that both procedures were brought together in one script. This is apparent in the slightly different workflow and coding style. This procedure only works with a selected object, for example for needle positioning.

It is important to note that needleCreator calls two other procedures, getNeedle and getNeedleAttr, which will be explained in later sections of this chapter.

The needleCreator procedure has the following arguments:

- `$amount`: The number of needles that will be created around the transform.

- `$spread`: The size of the sphrand around the transform in case of transform-based placement.

- `$lengthOffset`: The value that will be subtracted/added to the length of the base needle to generate the random length according to this formula:

  randMin = original length − lengthOffset
  randMax = original length + lengthOffset

- `$radiusOffset`: Same as `lengthOffset`, but for radius.

- `$curvatureMin`, `$curvatureMax`: The random curvature that will be generated between these min and max values.

The inner workings of the procedure are as follows for each iteration (i.e., the number of needles):

1. Generate the sphrand, radius offset, height offset, and curvature data.
2. Duplicate the imported needle geo.
3. Adjust its radius, height, and curvature.
4. Position it based on the sphrand and the positioning transform.
5. Parent it to the needle group.

5.5.2 New Commands

|| and &&: These are not really commands, but symbols that are used in conditionals and that respectively mean an "or" and "and".

For example: If it rains AND the street is flooded, then don't go out. Or, more in our context: If the size of the selected objects is smaller than 1 OR it is not a transform, then spit out an error.

Note that you can add as many as you want after each other: if...and...and...or...and...or, then.

For example:

```
// create 5 locators and select 4
string $objs[] = `ls -sl `;

if (`nodeType $objs[0]` == "transform" && `size $objs` >= 3)
    print "You have selected at least 3 transforms";
    else
    print "Thandie Newton's smooth silky hair";
```

clamp: Returns a number within a range. You can use the `clamp` function to confine an increasing, decreasing, or randomly changing number to a range of values. We will use it to make sure that our min radius does not go below 0 by clamping it at 0, and use some insanely big value for max.

For example:

```
float clamp(float minnumber, float maxnumber, float parameter)
```

The minnumber and maxnumber arguments specify the range of the returned value. Parameter is an attribute or variable whose value you want to clamp within the range.

If parameter is within the numerical range of minnumber and maxnumber, the function returns the value of parameter. If parameter is greater than the range, the function returns the maxnumber. If parameter is less than the range, the function returns the minnumber.

For example:

```
float $radiusMinOrig = -10;
clamp (0, 100000, $radiusMinOrig);
// 0 //
float $radiusMinOrig = 10;
clamp (0, 100000, $radiusMinOrig);
// 10 //
```

nonLinear: This command creates a functional deformer of the specified type that will deform the selected objects. It is handy to know that the deformer consists of three nodes:

- One node that is the deformer driver that gets connected to the history of the selected objects.

- A node that is the deformer handle transform that controls position and orientation of the axis of the deformation.

- A node for the deformer handle that maintains the deformation parameters.

Again, I found this out by looking in the Script Editor when I called the command from the UI. Are you beginning to see a trend here?
For example:

```
// create a poly cylinder and scale it up
// add bend deformer
nonLinear -type bend
    -lowBound -1
    -highBound 1
```

Chapter 5

```
    -curvature 5
    pCylinder1;
```

5.5.3 Code and Comments

```
global proc km_needleCreator (int $amount,
                             float $spread,
                             float $lengthOffset,
                             float $radiusOffset,
                             float $curvatureMin,
                             float $curvatureMax  )
{
//get sel object for positioning of needles
string $sel[] = `ls -sl`;

//do some checks on transform that will be used for positioning
//of duplicates
// || is the symbol for "or"
// && is the symbol for "and"
string $selType = `nodeType  $sel[0]`;
if (`size $sel` > 1 || $selType != "transform" || `size $sel` != 1)
    error "Please select only/at least one transform node";

string $loc = $sel[0];
print ("Objects will be duplicated around " + $loc + ".\n");

//import the selected geo and cast selected needle in var.
// See getNeedle proc for more detailed info
string $getNeedleVar = getNeedle();

print ($getNeedleVar + " is the object that will be duplicated. \n");
//clear selection
select -cl;

// main loop that creates duplicates
string $newGroup =`group -n ("needlesGroup "+"#") -em`;

for ($x =0; $x <=$amount; $x++)
    {
    // -------> SPREAD RELATED CODE
    vector $sphrand = sphrand ($spread);
```

```
    vector $locPos = `xform -q -t -ws $loc`;
    vector $randPos = ($locPos + $sphrand);


    vector $randRot = {rand (180,360),rand (100,360),rand (200,360)};

// -------> HEIGHT RELATED CODE


    //get height of original needle
    // See getNeedleAttr for more info on attr extraction
    float $needleHeight = getNeedleAttr ("height", $getNeedleVar);
    //subtract offset from original height to get min value
    float $heightMinOrig = ($needleHeight - $lengthOffset);
    // clamp any negative values to 0
    float $heightMin = clamp (0, 100000, $heightMinOrig);
    //add offset from original height to get max value
    float $heightMax = ($needleHeight + $lengthOffset);
    //get rand value based on min and max
    float $randHeight = rand ($heightMin, $heightMax);

// -------> RADIUS RELATED CODE


    float $needleRadius = getNeedleAttr ("radius", $getNeedleVar);
    //subtract offset from original radius to get min value
    float $radiusMinOrig = ($needleRadius - $radiusOffset);
    // clamp any negative values to 0
    float $radiusMin = clamp (0, 100000, $radiusMinOrig);
    //add offset from original radius to get max value
    float $radiusMax = ($needleRadius + $radiusOffset);
    //get rand value based on min and max
    float $randRadius = rand ($radiusMin, $radiusMax)/5;
    //$randRadius needs to be clamped, because the min value for
    //radius is .01
    float $randRadiusClamp = clamp (0.1,100000, $randRadius);
    //float $randRadius = rand (.05,.1);

// -------> CURVATURE RELATED CODE
    //float $randRadius = (rand (.009,.01) *($randHeight/1.5));
    //float $randCurve = rand (.1,.4);
    float $randCurve = rand ($curvatureMin, $curvatureMax);


// duplicate and adjust
```

```
    string $dup[] = `duplicate -un $getNeedleVar`;
    setAttr ($dup[3] + ".radius") $randRadiusClamp;
    setAttr ($dup[3] + ".height") $randHeight;
    setAttr ($dup[3] + ".subdivisionsHeight") 8;

// bend deformer stuff
    string $bendDef[] = `nonLinear -type bend -lowBound -1 -highBound 1
        -curvature $randCurve $dup[0]`;
    delete -ch $dup[0];
    xform -t ($randPos.x) ($randPos.y) ($randPos.z) $dup[0];
    xform -ro ($randRot.x) ($randRot.y) ($randRot.z) $dup[0];

// parent under group and center pivot
    parent $dup[0] $newGroup;
    xform -op $newGroup;
    }
    //delete original imported needle
    delete $getNeedleVar;

}
```

5.6 The getNeedle Procedure

5.6.1 Outline

getNeedle is an interesting procedure. This gets called in the main createNeedle procedure and provides the actual piece of geometry (the needle) that gets duplicated.

The problem I was faced with when writing this script was: How do I find the piece of geometry that was just imported?

When you import an object, even if it is just one object, you always import a scene (either an .ma or an .mb). Maya does not tell you what objects are in that scene. The solution is to:

1. Store all transforms in the scene in an array before the import.

2. Store all transforms in the scene in an array after the import.

3. Compare those two arrays. The resulting object is the imported one.

The command we use to compare two arrays is called stringArrayIntersector. This command is a royal pain. Using it is about as easy as building a space shuttle.

5.6.2 New Commands

stringArrayIntersector: This command creates and edits an object that is able to efficiently intersect large string arrays. The way that it works is as follows:

1. Create the intersector by casting it in a variable.

2. Get/declare the first array.

3. Set the stringArrayIntersector to Intersect mode (-edit -intersect) to store the first array in the stringArrayIntersector.

4. Set the stringArrayIntersector to Intersect mode (-edit -intersect) to store the second array in the stringArrayIntersector.

5. Query the content of the stringArrayIntersector to get the intersecting elements.

6. If you want to do another intersection, you have to reset it (-edit -reset) and repeat the craziness above.

7. If you are completely done with the stringArrayIntersector, you need to delete it with deleteUI.

Whoever designed this command needs to be shot.

For example:

```
// EXAMPLE 1
// Create an intersector
string $myIntersector = `stringArrayIntersector`;

// Intersect 2 string arrays using the intersector
string $initialArray[] = {"Peter", "Family", "guy"};
stringArrayIntersector -edit -intersect $initialArray $myIntersector;
stringArrayIntersector -edit -intersect {"Peter", "guy"} $myIntersector;

// Query the intersector to see what the intersection is so far
stringArrayIntersector -query $myIntersector;
```

```
// Result: Peter guy //

// Reset the intersector so that you can use it again with new string
// arrays
stringArrayIntersector -edit -reset $myIntersector;

// Delete the intersector as we are now done with it
deleteUI $myIntersector;

//================================================================
// EXAMPLE 2

string $myIntersector = `stringArrayIntersector`;
stringArrayIntersector -edit -reset $myIntersector;

string $initialArray[] = {"A", "B", "C", "D", "E", "F", "G", "H", "I"};
string $itemListArray[] = {"B", "E", "H", "I"};
string $commonItems[];

stringArrayIntersector -edit -intersect $initialArray $myIntersector;
stringArrayIntersector -edit -intersect $itemListArray $myIntersector;
$commonItems = `stringArrayIntersector -query $myIntersector`;

print $commonItems;
// Result: commonItems = B E H I //
//================================================================
```

stringArrayRemove: This command takes two arguments (two string arrays) and removes the items in the first string array from the second string array. A new string array with the items removed is returned. We use it to remove the pre-save array from the post-save array; the result will be the imported object.

For example:

```
string $list[] = { "a", "b", "c", "d", "e", "f", "g" };
string $items[] = { "a", "c", "e", "g" };
string $diff[] = stringArrayRemove($items, $list);
// Result : { b, d, f } //
```

Procedures That Return Values

Something we haven't covered yet, although common, is return procedures. It is possible to have a procedure return a value (or a list of values; i.e., an array) so you can pass this to a variable, another procedure, or even the same procedure.

The syntax is slightly different from normal procedures because you have to explicitly declare the data type that will be returned and finish the procedure with a return statement:

```
global proc float myReturnProc (arguments)
{
    //statements
    return $myFloatValue;
}
```

For example:

```
global proc int addThis (int $numberX, int $numberY)
{
    int $sum = $numberX + $numberY;
    return $sum;
}

//addThis (1,2);
// 3 //
//===============================================================
global proc string[] arrayRem (string $arrayOne[], string $arrayTwo[])

{
    string $returnThis[] = stringArrayRemove ($arrayOne,$arrayTwo);
    return $returnThis;
}
```

5.6.3 **Code and Comments**

> **Note:** In some of the code, the formatting is a bit strange due to the limitations of the book's page width.

```
global proc string getNeedle()

{
    // We need to explicitly declare the variable we will return
    // outside the conditional loop; otherwise, variable scope
    // will prevent us from returning the value, which gets
    // assigned in the conditional
    string $return;
    //get geo from text field
    string $needlePath = `textFieldButtonGrp -q -text browselFG`;

    //test if the selected file is an .ma
    string $isAscii[] = `file -q -type $needlePath`;
    if ($isAscii[0] == "mayaAscii")
    {   //<--only need to check filetype once, then block the rest
        //within that check scope

        //create intersector
        string $intersector = `stringArrayIntersector`;
        //get list of scene transforms
        string $prior[] = `ls -dag -type "transform"`;
        //add to intersector
        stringArrayIntersector -edit -intersect $prior $intersector;
        //do import stuff
        string $doImport = `file -import -type $isAscii[0]
            $needlePath`;
        //get new list of scene transforms
            string $post[] = `ls -dag -type "transform"`;
        //add to intersector
        stringArrayIntersector -edit -intersect $post $intersector;
        //remove all objects but new
        string $importedObj[] = stringArrayRemove
            (`stringArrayIntersector -query $intersector`, $post);
        //here's your new object
        print ("Imported: " + $importedObj[0] + "\n");
        $return = $importedObj[0];
```

```
        //delete intersector
        deleteUI $intersector;
    }
    else
        error "Please select a mayaAscii file";
    return $return;


}
```

5.7 The getNeedleAttr Procedure

5.7.1 Outline

This procedure is needed to get the height and radius values of the imported object (the needle). Height and radius are two attributes of the polyCylinder node.

Figure 5-2

To get the values we have to traverse over all nodes, find which one has the attributes we need (height and radius), and then get the value from those attributes. Since this workflow looked like something that might prove handy in other scenarios as well, I made it a generic procedure that takes the attribute and the node as arguments:

```
getAttribute (attributeWeNeed, Node)
```

Here is how it works:

1. Get the shape of the transform.
2. Traverse through all connected nodes.

Chapter 5

3. On all those nodes, look for the attribute specified in the argument of the procedure.

4. If you find that attribute, get its value.

5.7.2 New Commands

listHistory: This command traverses backward or forward in the graph from the specified node and returns all of the nodes whose construction history it passes through.

For example:

```
// create a sphere
polySphere;

// list history nodes
listHistory `ls -sl`;
// pSphereShape1 polySphere1 //

// list "future" nodes
listHistory -f 1 `ls -sl`;
// pSphereShape1 initialShadingGroup //
```

attributeExists: This command is pretty obvious. It checks to see if the named attribute exists in the given node.

For example:

```
string $shapeName[] = `cone`;

if (`attributeExists "scaleX" $shapeName[0]`)
    {
    print "Attribute exists\n";
    }
else
    {
    print "Attribute does not exist\n";
    }
```

5.7.3 Code and Comments

```
global proc float getNeedleAttr (string $attr, string $obj)
{
```

```
float $needleAttr;
//get the shape of the arg
string $shape[] = `listRelatives -s $obj`;
// traverse back through node
string $history[] = `listHistory $shape[0]`;
// look through all attr of all traversed nodes to find attr
for ($eachNode in $history)
// if the attr exists
if (`attributeExists $attr $eachNode`)
    {
    //print ($eachNode + " is the node we need \n") ;
    // get its value
    $needleAttr = `getAttr ($eachNode + "." + $attr )`;
    }
// return value
return $needleAttr;
}
```

5.8 The UI Procedure: km_debrisCreator

5.8.1 Outline

This procedure creates the main UI, which is mainly a column of intSliderGrp and floatSliderGrp controls. Although nothing spectacular, it is important to note that you should always use the correct type of slider or field to avoid user error. This means that if you want the user to input an integer in a field, you have to use intField and not textField. That way the user cannot put a letter where he should only be able to put numbers, and you won't have to debug your code because some procedure gets the wrong type of argument.

5.8.2 New Commands

menuBarLayout: Creates a layout containing a menu bar. You populate the menuBarLayout by parenting menuItems to it. I like to use menu bar layouts to make an Edit → Reset UI functionality, which enables the user to reset all the UI controls to their original state.

> **IMPORTANT:** Whenever there is a -parent flag in UI controls, use it to parent the control. This saves you (most of the time) from having to mess around with setParent.

For example:

```
if (`window -exists menuExWin`)
    deleteUI menuExWin;

window menuExWin;
    columnLayout -adjustableColumn true;

menuBarLayout mainBar;
    menu -p mainBar -label "Monday" monMenu;
    menuItem -p monMenu -label "Kate";
    menuItem -p monMenu -label "Rosa";
    menuItem -p monMenu -label "Vicky";

menu -p mainBar -label "Tuesday" TuMenu;
    menuItem -p TuMenu -label "Rosa";
    menuItem -p TuMenu -label "Rosario";
    menuItem -p TuMenu -label "Cindy";

showWindow menuExWin;
```

textFieldButtonGrp: By default this command creates some text, a text field, and a button next to each other. We use this command so the user can pick the needle geometry from an existing file. When he presses the button, a file chooser window opens (achieved by the browseNeedle procedure, explained later in this chapter), and the path of the selected file is placed in the text field.

For example:

```
string $window = `window`;
columnLayout -adj 1 mainCol;
textFieldButtonGrp -label "Path"
        -text "Here goes path"
        -buttonLabel "Browse"
```

```
        -cw3 60 165 10
        -ct3 "left" "both" "left"
browseTFG;
showWindow $window;
```

5.8.3 Code and Comments

> **Note:**   In some of the code, the formatting is a bit strange due to the limitations
> of the book's page width.

```
//===================================================================
// km_debrisCreator generates the UI
//===================================================================

global proc km_debrisCreator(){

string $path = `getSceneDir`;

if (`window -exists km_debrisCreatorUI`)
    deleteUI km_debrisCreatorUI;

window -wh 295 500 -mxb 0 -t "km_debrisCreator" -s 1 km_debrisCreatorUI;
menuBarLayout;
    menu -label "Edit";
        menuItem -l "Reset to defaults"
            -c "resetUI()"
            ;

columnLayout -adj 1 mainCol;

//########## FRAME ONE: Debris specs  ##########

frameLayout -l "Debris Specs "
    -collapsable 1
    -borderStyle "etchedIn"
    specsFrame;

    columnLayout -adj 1 specsCol;

        intSliderGrp -label "Amount"
                -ann "The number of pieces"
```

```
                    -cw3 60 50 10
                    -ct3 "left" "both" "left"
                    -field true
                    -minValue 1
                    -maxValue 100
                    -fieldMinValue 1
                    -fieldMaxValue 100
                    -value 10
                    numSlider;

floatSliderGrp -label "ScaleMin"
                    -ann "The scale of the smallest piece"
                    -cw3 60 50 10
                    -ct3 "left" "both" "left"
                    -field true
                    -minValue .1
                    -maxValue 100.0
                    -fieldMinValue .1
                    -fieldMaxValue 100.0
                    -value .5
                    scaleMinSlider;

floatSliderGrp -label "ScaleMax"
                    -ann "The scale of the largest piece"
                    -cw3 60 50 10
                    -ct3 "left" "both" "left"
                    -field true
                    -minValue .1
                    -maxValue 100.0
                    -fieldMinValue .1
                    -fieldMaxValue 100.0
                    -value 2
                    scaleMaxSlider;

floatSliderGrp -label "Spread"
                    -ann "The radius-based distance from the locator from
                    which pieces will be created. Only works when a
                    locator is selected"
                    -cw3 60 50 10
                    -ct3 "left" "both" "left"
                    -field true
```

```
                                -minValue 1
                                -maxValue 20
                                -fieldMinValue 1
                                -fieldMaxValue 20
                                -value 5
                                spreadSlider;


                floatSliderGrp -label "Smoothness"
                                -ann "Defines the edges of the pebbles"
                                -cw3 60 50 10
                                -ct3 "left" "both" "left"
                                -field true
                                -minValue 0.10
                                -maxValue 1
                                -fieldMinValue .10
                                -fieldMaxValue 1
                                -value 0.75
                                coarseSlider;

        frameLayout -l "Grouping" -collapsable 0 -borderStyle "etchedIn"
                groupFrame;
            columnLayout -adj 1 groupCol;
                checkBox -label "Create Group"
                                -align "left"
                                -value 1
                                //-onc `textField -e -en 1 groupNameField`
                                -cc "groupOnOff()"
                                groupChkBox;


                textField //-label "GroupName"
                                -en 1
                                -tx "DebrisGroup"
                                groupNameField;


                button -l "Create Debris"
                    -c "debrisCmd ()"
                                createButton;


        setParent mainCol;

        //########### FRAME TWO: Needle specs  ###########
```

Chapter 5

```
frameLayout -l "Needle Specs " -collapsable 1 -borderStyle "etchedIn"
        needlesFrame;
    columnLayout -adj 1 needlesCol;
        textFieldButtonGrp -label "Geo"
                -text $path
                -buttonLabel "Browse"
                -bc "browseNeedle()"
                -cw3 60 165 10
                -ct3 "left" "both" "left"
                browseTFG;


        intSliderGrp -label "Amount"
                -ann "The number of pieces"
                -cw3 60 50 10
                -ct3 "left" "both" "left"
                -field true
                -minValue 1
                -maxValue 1000
                -fieldMinValue 1
                -fieldMaxValue 1000
                -value 10
                needlesAmountSlider;

// float $amountSlider = `floatSliderGrp -q -v needlesAmountSlider`;

        floatSliderGrp -label "Spread"
                -ann "The radius-based distance from the locator from
                which pieces will be created. Only works when a
                locator is selected"
                -cw3 60 50 10
                -ct3 "left" "both" "left"
                -field true
                -minValue 1
                -maxValue 50
                -fieldMinValue 1
                -fieldMaxValue 50
                -value 10
                needlesSpreadSlider;

// float $spreadSlider = `floatSliderGrp -q -v needlesSpreadSlider`;
```

```
        floatSliderGrp -label "lengthOffset"
                -ann "min = (original length - lengthOffset) and max
                = (original length + lengthOffset)"
                -cw3 60 50 10
                -ct3 "left" "both" "left"
                -field true
                -minValue .1
                -maxValue 50
                -fieldMinValue .1
                -fieldMaxValue 50
                -value 5
                needlesLengthSlider;

// float $lengthSlider = `floatSliderGrp -q -v needlesLengthSlider`;

        floatSliderGrp -label "radiusOffset"
                -cw3 60 50 10
                -ct3 "left" "both" "left"
                -field true
                -minValue .001
                -maxValue 5
                -fieldMinValue .001
                -fieldMaxValue 5
                -value .3
                needlesRadiusSlider;

// float $radiusSLider = `floatSliderGrp -q -v needlesRadiusSlider`;

        floatSliderGrp -label "curveMin"
                -ann "The min curvature of the needle"
                -cw3 60 50 10
                -ct3 "left" "both" "left"
                -field true
                -minValue .1
                -maxValue 5
                -fieldMinValue .1
                -fieldMaxValue 5
                -value .1
                needlesCurvatureMinSlider;
```

Chapter 5

```
// float $curvatureMinSlider = `floatSliderGrp -q -v
// needlesCurvatureMinSlider`;

        floatSliderGrp -label "curveMax"
                -cw3 60 50 10
                -ct3 "left" "both" "left"
                -field true
                -minValue .1
                -maxValue 1
                -fieldMinValue .1
                -fieldMaxValue 1
                -value .3
                needlesCurvatureMaxSlider;

        button -l "Create Needles"
            -c "needleCmd ()"
                createNeedlesButton;

setParent mainCol;
showWindow km_debrisCreatorUI;

}
```

5.9 **The UI Procedure: getSceneDir**

5.9.1 **Outline**

getSceneDir returns the scene directory of the current project. It gets passed to the browseNeedle procedure so the latter procedure can open the file chooser window at that location.

By the way, getSceneDir and browseNeedle are textbook examples of our guidelines about procedures (discussed in section 5.3.2): Ideally, procedures should be small, simple, layered, and built on other procedures. It is advisable (although sometimes not practical) to make a procedure do only one clearly identifiable thing.

5.9.2 **New Commands**

workspace: Create, open, or edit a workspace associated with a given workspace file. What is a workspace? It is a project, as in setProject. Why did they call it "workspace" and not "project"? Because that would be logical.

For example:

```
// Set the current workspace to "MH_0560"
workspace -openWorkspace "MH_0560";

//get the root directory of the current project
workspace -q -rootDirectory

//list all projects in your project dir
workspace -lw
```

5.9.3 **Code and Comments**

```
global proc string getSceneDir (){
    //check the current project and add "scenes" to it
    string $sceneDir=(`workspace -q -rootDirectory` + "scenes/");
    // return the above concatenation
    return $sceneDir;
}
```

5.10 **The UI Procedure: browseNeedle**

5.10.1 **Outline**

The browseNeedle procedure opens a file chooser window so the user can browse for the scene that has the needle geo.

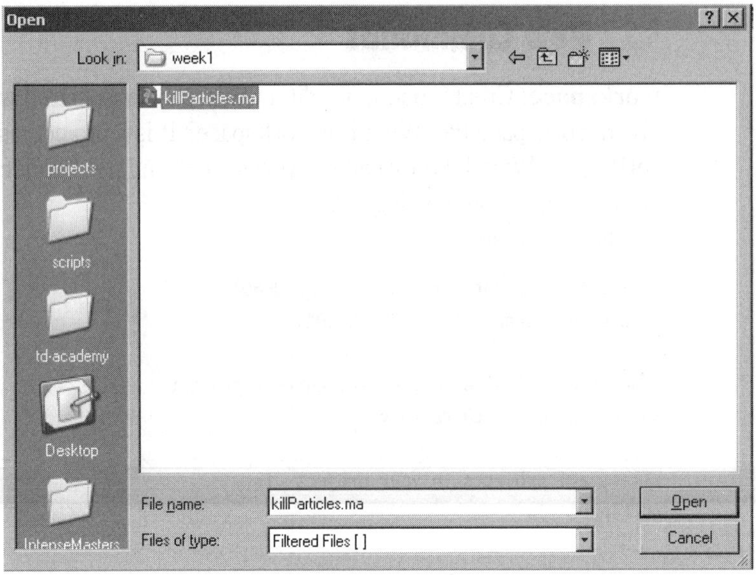

Figure 5-3

5.10.2 **New Commands**

fileDialog: Displays a file chooser window and returns the name of the file that the user picked. If the user picked no file, then an empty string is returned. We use the -directoryMask flag and pass this flag the result of the getSceneDir procedure. That way the file browser will open at that location.

5.10.3 **Code and Comments**

```
global proc string browseNeedle(){
    //string $path=(`workspace -q -rootDirectory` + "scenes/");
    string $path = `getSceneDir`;
    string $needleFile = `fileDialog -directoryMask $path`;
    // update the textField with the selected path + file
    textFieldButtonGrp -e -text $needleFile browseTFG;
    return $needleFile;
}
```

5.11 The UI "Suckers": needleCmd and debrisCmd

5.11.1 Outline

As you probably won't remember, I started this chapter by prosely-tizing about good coding techniques. One of those is to use model-view-controller (MVC) architecture, which is a fancy way of saying keep your UI procedures and work procedures separate. km_debrisCreator is an example of how to separate your UI procedures from your work procedures. km_needleCreator and debrisCreator are stand-alone procedures (i.e., executable from the command line) and do not rely on the UI.

Now the question arises: How do we connect these two types of procedures? In other words, how do we feed the values from the UI into the arguments of the work procedures?

Our knights in concatenated armor are the UI "suckers." These are procedures that query the UI controls, concatenate them to the command, and then execute that command.

This sounds scarier than it is. Say we have a procedure called createCurve, which has one argument that defines the length of the curve. This is the work procedure. We also have a UI that has a float slider, which defines the length of the curve. All a UI sucker does is:

1. Get the value from the UI (`floatSliderGrp -q -value`).
2. Concatenate this value into the command: `createCurve (10)`.
3. Execute the command (`eval (createCurve (10))`).
4. Attach this command to a button so it gets executed when pressed.

The only thing that will need a bit of thought and attention is the actual syntax of the concatenation. The result of the concatenation will be the command (the procedure) with all its arguments:

```
km_needleCreator("10" ,"10" ,"5" ,"0.3" ,"0.1" ,"0.3" );
```

The trick is to use the `print` command often to check if your concatenation looks correct.

5.11.2 **New Commands**

eval: The purpose of the `eval` command is to provide a way for the user to execute a MEL command or procedure that can only be determined at run time. Any valid MEL statement can be passed as the string argument to `eval`. For those familiar with C, this provides functionality akin to function pointers.

+=: The `+=` combination is not a command, but shorthand for adding a value to the first element in the equation. This is mainly used in expressions to add numbers, but it works for strings as well.

For example:

```
// simple example
string $b;
string $z;
// full out
$b = $b + $z
// in shorthand
$b += $z

//Example with words

string $attr = "This attr ";
string $fab = " is fab";
//normal concatenation
$attr = $attr + $fab;

// shorthand
$attr += $fab;
$attr += " innit";
$attr += "says AliG";
```

5.11.3 **Code and Comments**

```
//============================================================
// needleCmd assembles the main needle command
// of the UI input
//============================================================

global proc needleCmd ()
{

    string $cmd = "km_needleCreator";
    $cmd += ("(");
    $cmd += ("\"" + (string)`intSliderGrp -q -v needlesAmountSlider` +
    "\" ");
    $cmd += ",";
    $cmd += ("\"" + (string)`floatSliderGrp -q -v needlesSpreadSlider`
        + "\" ");
    $cmd += ",";
    $cmd += ("\"" + (string)`floatSliderGrp -q -v needlesLengthSlider`
        + "\" ");
    $cmd += ",";
    $cmd += ("\"" + (string)`floatSliderGrp -q -v needlesRadiusSlider`
        + "\" ");
    $cmd += ",";
    $cmd += ("\"" + (string)`floatSliderGrp -q -v
        needlesCurvatureMinSlider` + "\" ");
    $cmd += ",";
    $cmd += ("\"" + (string)`floatSliderGrp -q -v
        needlesCurvatureMaxSlider` + "\" ");
    $cmd+=(");");
    print $cmd;
    eval($cmd);
}

// km_needleCreator("10" ,"10" ,"5" ,"0.3" ,"0.1" ,"0.3" );

//============================================================
// debrisCmd assembles the main debris command
// of the UI input
//============================================================
```

Chapter 5

```
global proc debrisCmd ()
{

    string $cmd = "debrisCreator";
    $cmd += ("(");
    $cmd += ("\"" + (string)`intSliderGrp -q -value numSlider` +
        "\" ");
    $cmd += ",";
    $cmd += ("\"" + (string)`floatSliderGrp -q -v scaleMinSlider` +
        "\" ");
    $cmd += ",";
    $cmd += ("\"" + (string)`floatSliderGrp -q -v scaleMaxSlider` +
        "\" ");
    $cmd += ",";
    $cmd += ("\"" + (string)`floatSliderGrp -q -v spreadSlider` +
        "\" ");
    $cmd += ",";
    $cmd += ("\"" + (string)`floatSliderGrp -q -v coarseSlider` +
        "\" ");
    $cmd += ",";
    $cmd += ("\"" + (string)`checkBox -q -v groupChkBox` + "\" ");
    $cmd += ",";
    $cmd += ("\"" + (string)`textField -q -text groupNameField` +
        "\" ");
    $cmd+=(");");
    print $cmd;
    eval($cmd);

}
```

Chapter 6

Scene Management with ewc_extendedLayerManager

Note from Kevin Mannens: This chapter is written by fellow melophiliac Ed Caspersen and deals with the development of his extremely useful script Extended Layer Manager. The purpose of this chapter is not only to guide you through the process of writing this script, but also to provide you with a slightly different approach to concepts and techniques we already covered in previous chapters. After all, even using good coding practices, no two programmers will ever tackle the same problem in exactly the same way. It's like your mother's mashed potatoes and my mother's mashed potatoes. I am sure both are delicious, yet both are created using slightly different techniques that our mums have perfected over the years. Each will have its own secret ingredient and hence specific flavor. It is up to you to try them both out and immerse yourself in each specific aroma.

The purpose of Extended Layer Manager 2.1 is to provide users with an efficient interface that allows for extended control over the layers within Maya. The default layer editor in Maya is suitable for basic layer management, but is somewhat cumbersome (if not unusable) when dealing with more complex scenes that contain a large (i.e., more realistic) number of objects.

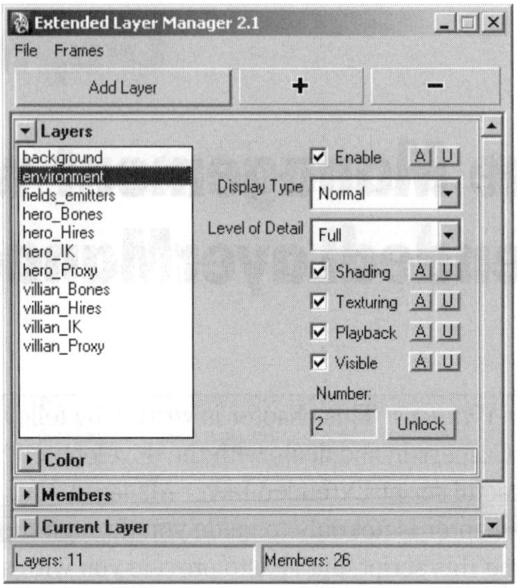

Figure 6-1

6.1 **Introduction and Preparation**

6.1.1 **The Inspiration to Build a Layer Manager**

I suggest you start this section by watching a video I made that explains the idea behind and the usage of ELM. You can find the video on the companion disc and at **http://mel4prod.mayawiki.com/**.

This script was the accumulation of many other small scripts and shelf buttons from past projects of mine.

Most users are familiar with the default layer editor in Maya:

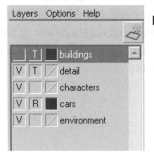

Figure 6-2

To the left of the layer names are three boxes. The first box (from the left) toggles visibility of the members of a particular layer, the middle toggles the display type (normal, template, and reference), and the third is a color swatch that displays the wireframe color of the members if the viewport shading is toggled off.

Note: Before we move on, I want to clarify what I am referring to as a member. Maya refers to the relationship between objects and layers as memberships. You can think of a layer as a club, and the objects that are assigned to the layer are the members of that club. That is why I use the term "member." When I refer to a highlighted member, I am referring to the highlighted item in a text list. Later on we will use the command textScrollList to create a text list that can hold string values representing the members. By default, when you highlight a name in the list it does not actually create a selection in the viewport, though we can add that option later, so the members are actually only highlighted and not really selected.

Double-clicking a layer name opens the Edit Layer dialog. The visibility and display type options are once again available, but from here a user can change the name and the wireframe color.

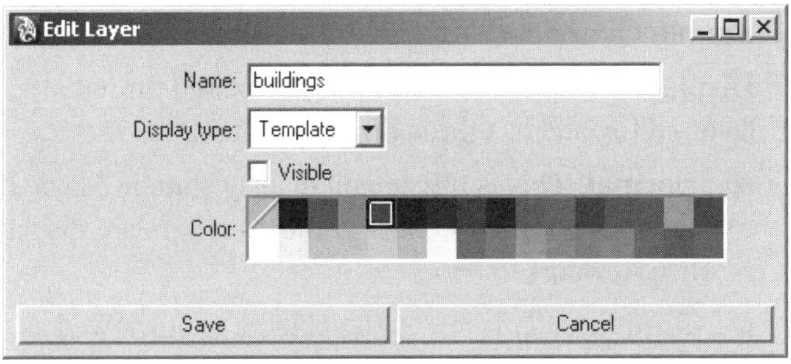

Figure 6-3

This is most likely common knowledge to anyone reading this book. However, you may not be familiar with the other drawing properties of layers that I am about to cover.

Several years back I started looking at the drawing options of display layers in Maya. I discovered a number of drawing options that are available through the Attribute Editor in addition to those displayed in the default layer editor. These options are shown in the Drawing Override Options section of the Attribute Editor, as shown in Figure 6-4.

Chapter 6

Attribute Editor: buildings

List   Selected   Focus   Attributes   Help

buildings | layerManager

displayLayer: buildings   [Focus]
                                           [Presets]

▼ Drawing Override Options
                    ☑ Enable Overrides
    Display Type   Template ▼
    Level of Detail Full ▼
                    ☑ Shading
                    ☑ Texturing
                    ☑ Playback
                    ☐ Visible
           Color   ▬▬▬▬▬——|——————— Index
          Number   5

▶ Node Behavior
▶ Extra Attributes

Notes: buildings

[Select]   [Load Attributes]   [Copy Tab]   [Close]

Figure 6-4

Let's look at these options more closely.

- **Enable Overrides:** Toggles drawing states all at once.

- **Display Type:** This attribute can be edited through the default layer editor, and has three drawing states.

  - **Normal:** This is the default display state in Maya. It changes nothing about how the members are displayed in the viewport.

  - **Template:** This forces the objects to be viewed as wireframe (even if viewport shading is on) and prevents the members from being directly selected in the viewport.

  - **Reference:** The members are viewed normally (like the Normal state), but cannot be directly selected in the viewport.

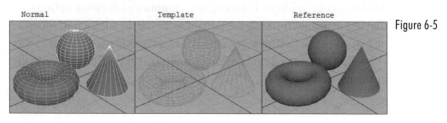

Normal   Template   Reference

Figure 6-5

- **Level of Detail:** This attribute has two drawing states.
  - **Full:** Displays the geometry of the members. This is the default.
  - **Bounding Box:** Draws the bounding box of the members.

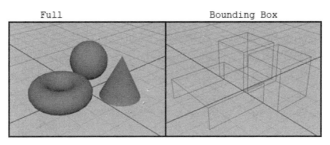

Figure 6-6

- **Shading:** This attribute toggles the shading state of the members, even if the viewport shading is toggled on. This attribute has no effect if the viewport shading is toggled off.
- **Texturing:** This attribute toggles the texture drawing state of the members. The attribute has no effect unless texture display is toggled on in the viewport by pressing 6 on the keyboard.
- **Playback:** This attribute toggles the playback state of animated members. This only affects the actual playback. When the playback is stopped, the animated members assume their correct transformations as they relate to the current frame.
- **Visible:** This attribute can be toggled through the default layer editor. It controls the visibility state of the members.
- **Color:** This attribute controls the displayed wireframe color of the members.

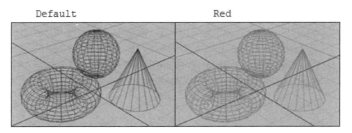

Figure 6-7

Chapter 6

- **Number:** This attribute identifies the layer.

Many of these I would find to be quite useful in my own work, but I did not find the current interface to be very efficient. Even though the additional drawing options are available as submenus of the right-click menus in the display layers, I still found this to be a cumbersome workflow. I also wanted an easier way to control the additional drawing attributes. Early on I began creating shelves and shelf buttons for each project file to modify a specific drawing state of a layer. A common shelf button to modify shading would look like this:

```
if (`getAttr layer1.shading`)
    setAttr layer1.shading 0;
else
    setAttr layer1.shading 1;
```

Using shelf buttons would suffice on smaller projects, but in time I recognized that I needed something more functional and efficient. This inspired me to sit down and start outlining exactly what I needed in a layer manager.

6.1.2 Outlining the Functionality of ewc_extendedLayerManager

The Importance of Pen and Paper

For me the planning process starts away from the computer. I don't need the distractions of updating RSS feeds, screen savers, instant messages, or anything else that interrupts my concentration. Also, I learned early on that I am too tempted to open Maya and start experimenting with ideas before planning is even done, so not being near a computer removes that temptation. All the tools I need are a legal pad, pens, and sticky notes. I then find somewhere quiet and comfortable and get to work. While I'm on the road I use a micro recorder to record everything that I can't write down, so if I have made some notes on the recorder I get that out as well. (I used to get weird looks on the road, but nowadays with Bluetooth and other hands-free technology, I don't get as many strange looks as I did just a few years ago.)

Core Functionality of the Layer Manager

So the first question is this: What am I looking for in a layer manager? I think this should be an important question for anyone building tools and utilities for production purposes. I need a compact utility that allows me to:

▪ Create a layer with a prompt to name the layer; this prompt can be toggled off.

▪ Display the layers in a list.

▪ Add selected objects to a newly created layer.

▪ Use large buttons to add or remove selected objects to and from a specific layer.

▪ Control all drawing states for a layer in one window.

▪ Use a color palette to change the wireframe color of a layer.

▪ Change the number (identification attribute) of a layer.

To see what this means, take a look at the Maya preferences. A display layer can be merged with another display layer with a matching ID when importing files into one another. Actually, other than this importing option, the layer ID doesn't do much. I left it in the main layers frame for three reasons: to emulate the Attribute Editor better, to show how to deal with connected attributes (which were a real pain to debug), and finally, to keep it accessible on the off chance it was needed.

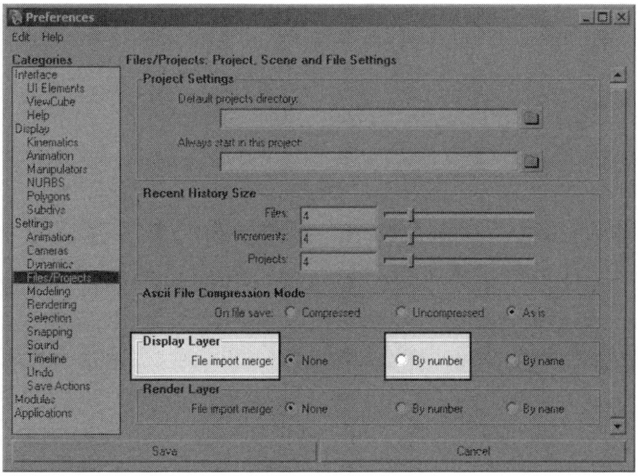

Figure 6-8

- Change the current layer, which is the default layer that new objects are assigned to when created.

    Whenever an object is created and displayed in the viewport, it is automatically assigned to a layer called "defaultLayer" that exists in all scenes. By default this layer is the current layer; however, any layer can be set as the current layer in a scene.

- Easily rename or remove layers directly through the list.

Member Functionality of the Layer Manager

In planning I decided that I wanted to implement another list to display the members (objects) of the currently selected layer. The functions I want to include are:

- **Rename a highlighted member.** This feature will allow a user to conveniently rename any member of a layer without having to select it in the viewport. Even if hidden, an object can be renamed.

- **Select all members in the list.** This feature would allow for a selection to be created of all members assigned to a specific layer. This could be useful if the members need to be deleted from the scene or assigned to another layer.

- **Create a selection out of the highlighted members.** When clicking on a member's name in the list no selection actually takes place in the viewport. This will allow items that are highlighted in a list to be created into an actual selection.

- **Remove highlighted members.** This will remove the highlighted members from a layer, assigning them back to the defaultLayer.

- **Open the Attribute Editor for a member.** This feature will allow a user to open the attribute of a member directly from the member without having to locate and select it in a viewport.

- **Launch the Relationship Editor.** The Relationship Editor in Maya provides additional options and controls for handling layers and their members. This editor is used for additional control of various other scene elements.

Further Tweaks to the Layer Manager

Lastly, I want some options that a user can modify to change the behavior of several of the features while the script is running. These options are:

- Toggle active selection of members from a list.
- Default layer naming convention.
- Toggle input prompt for a layer name.
- Toggle that adds selected objects to a new layer.

I want to take all the parts (layers, members, options) that were outlined above and turn them into controls that will be nested into collapsible frames that are contained within a scrolling frame. This means that the layer manager UI will be very similar to what you see in the Attribute Editor and other Maya windows. Figure 6-9 shows what these elements look like.

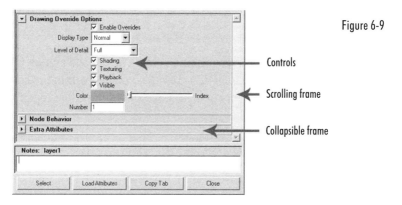

Figure 6-9

Controls

Scrolling frame

Collapsible frame

At the bottom of the interface, a toolbar similar to the Help Line in Maya should be created to display the count of layers and members. This feature will serve as a visual aid for the user.

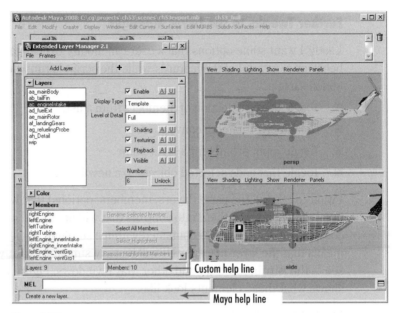

Figure 6-10

Some of the common controls to create layers and edit memberships should be buttons that are not contained within the scrolling frame; a good spot for them is above the frame at the top of the interface.

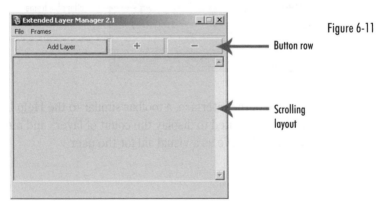

Figure 6-11

There should be a way for a user to permanently (and easily) change the default settings of the four user options previously outlined. We will do this code based and not UI based, just because we can. See section 6.4, "Creating the Functionality — Part I," for an in-depth explanation of this.

The Menus of the Layer Manager

Some other common functions will be included in a File menu located in the main menu bar:

- Add a new layer.
- Rename an existing layer.
- Remove a layer from the scene.
- View the Attribute Editor for a layer.
- Open the Relationship Editor.
- Refresh the layer and member lists.

Finally, a Frames menu should be added to toggle layout presets of the collapsible frames.

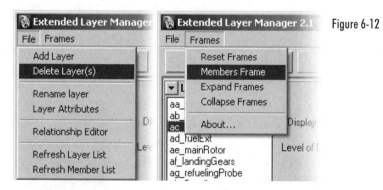

Figure 6-12

6.1.3 Attributes: Queries and Assignments

Attributes are properties, or parameters, of nodes within Maya. The dot syntax for attributes in MEL is:

```
node.attribute
```

Attributes can be queried and modified through the use of MEL. Earlier, I showed you an example script for toggling the shading attribute of a layer:

```
if (`getAttr layer1.shading`)
    setAttr layer1.shading 0;
else
    setAttr layer1.shading 1;
```

This code contains two commands that call the shading attribute (getAttr and setAttr).

- **getAttr:** Retrieves the current value of an attribute. This particular attribute returns a Boolean value (1 or 0) as an integer. Other data types that can be returned can be floats, strings, and vectors.

- **setAttr:** Sets a new value to the attribute, in this case a Boolean (1 or 0).

Placing the getAttr command inside back quotes allows a test to be performed directly through the command. Alternatively, this command could be queried and stored in a variable before being tested. For example:

```
int $v = `getAttr layer1.shading`;
if ($v)
    setAttr layer1.shading 0;
else
    setAttr layer1.shading 1;
```

The back quote is on the same key as the tilde (on most keyboards, this is the leftmost key on the row of numbers).

Figure 6-13

Forgetting a back quote is a common mistake and will generate an error. If back quotes are omitted, like this:

```
int $v = getAttr layer1.shading;
```

Maya will respond with an error:

```
// Error: Line 1.27: Invalid use of Maya object "getAttr". //
```

Other errors may occur when trying to assign a value that is out of range for a Boolean, which only takes a 1 or 0. For example:

```
setAttr layer1.shading 2;
```

Produces this error message:

```
// Error: line 1: Cannot set the attribute 'layer1.shading' past
its maximum value of 1. //
```

So knowing all this we can return to the toggle statement and begin to analyze the first line, which reads:

```
if (`getAttr layer1.shading`).
```

What this literally is saying is that if the tested value is anything but 0, it is returned as true and the nested commands under the if statement will be executed. To illustrate this better, experiment with the following conditional test in Maya:

```
int $test = 1;
if ($test)
    print "true";
else
    print "false";
```

Running this script will print "true". Change the value of $test to any number but 0 (even negative values like –1) and it will still print true. To print false, set the initial value to 0. The condition only contains the $test variable within the parentheses, which is a shorthand method:

```
if ($test)
```

If the condition is written in full (using an operator), it would look like this:

```
if ($test == 1)    // $test exactly equal to 1
```

So let's go through the toggle script once more, step-by-step with the added comments, because you will see this again and again.

```
// Query the current shading state of layer1
if (`getAttr layer1.shading`)
    // If the layer is not 0 (shading is on) turn off shading
    setAttr layer1.shading 0;
// If the query returns 0
else
    // Layer shading is off, turn it on
    setAttr layer1.shading 1;
```

Chapter 6

6.1.4 **Booleans**

Boolean values are commonly set with integer values of 1 and 0. Booleans can also be set literally using true and false or yes and no, and it is important to note that these literal alternatives are case sensitive. If you try using True instead of true, you will get an error. If you would like to experiment with these values, you can take the previous conditional examples and swap the integer values out for the literal values.

Assign a literal to an integer variable:

```
int $bool = true;
```

Now a value of 1 is stored in the variable $bool.

The next print statement merely concatenates two string values called "true" and "false". Proper capitalization is used, but enclosing the literals in quotes turns them into strings.

```
print ("true" + "false");
truefalse
```

The next two examples return integer results. The first print command is taking the literals, which are not enclosed in quotes, and converting them to their integer equivalents of 1 and 0 and adding them together.

```
print (true + false);
1
```

The next print statement is literally adding 1 and 1 after interpreting the literal equivalents:

```
print (true + yes);
2
```

Two different operations occurred although the same basic structure exists. The + operator can perform more than one operation based on the data types it exists between. If used between two strings, or a string and integer (or float), it combines them into one string. If used between any combination of floats and integers, it performs a mathematical addition. This behavior is sometimes referred to as *polymorphism*.

6.1.5 **Bracket Delimiters**

You may have noticed that in most if statements there are curly brackets ({ }) surrounding the nested commands. These are also referred to as *bracket delimiters*, or just *delimiters*. When there is only one line to be executed, the delimiters may be omitted; they are only required when a condition will have more than one command being executed. In fact, we could place the commands on the same line as the conditions.

Below is a shortened version of the previous shading toggle with the commands on the same line as the condition. This is not a recommended method.

```
if (`getAttr layer1.shading`)setAttr layer1.shading 0;
else setAttr layer1.shading 1;
```

And the cleaner version:

```
if (`getAttr layer1.shading`)
    setAttr layer1.shading 0;
else
    setAttr layer1.shading 1;
```

Finally, a clean version including delimiters (curly brackets) that group blocks of code under the parent statement:

```
if (`getAttr layer1.shading`)
    {
    setAttr layer1.shading 0;
    }
else
    {
    setAttr layer1.shading 1;
    }
```

A comment is not considered a line of code, so a delimiter would not be necessary.

```
if (`getAttr layer1.shading`)
    // I am ignored at run time, no delimiter needed
    setAttr layer1.shading 0;
else
    setAttr layer1.shading 1;
```

Chapter 6

6.1.6 **Procedures and Arguments**

Procedures and arguments have been explained and used in previous chapters, but just to make sure it has sunk in, here is a brief summary.

Local and global procedures, which we will obviously be using throughout the actual layer manager, are declared by simply typing the following:

```
// This is a local procedure declaration
proc myProcedureName()
{
    command -flags;
    command -flags;
}

// or

// This is a global procedure declaration
global proc myProcedureName()
{
    command -flags;
    command -flags;
}
```

Defining a procedure as global means it can be called from anywhere within Maya and from different scripts. Local procedures can only be used in the script that is running that procedure.

Procedures can take arguments that are passed through parentheses. In the example below, the procedure is declaring an integer variable called $case as its argument:

```
proc ewc_toggle(int $case){}
```

When a procedure takes an argument, a value must be contained within the parentheses when calling the procedure. The example below is not passing an argument; therefore it will create an error.

```
ewc_toggle()        // No argument, this will cause an error
```

```
// Error: ewc_toggle(); //
// Error: Line 1.12: Wrong number of arguments on call to ewc_toggle. //
```

Now try to pass the string "apple":

```
ewc_toggle("apple");
```

A warning is printed that Maya has converted the string to an integer value of 0. This is because the procedure was declared with an integer argument. Maya does not know how to interpret a string as an integer and automatically passes it a value of 0.

```
// Warning: ewc_toggle("apple"); //
// Warning: Line 1.20: Converting string "apple" to an int value of 0.//
```

The value passed must match the data type that was originally declared.

```
ewc_toggle(2)              // This works as intended
```

More than one argument can be declared and passed, and the data types of the arguments may be different from one another.

```
// declare the procedure with two arguments
proc ewc_procedure(int $arg1, string $arg2)
{
    print ($arg2 + $arg1);
}
```

If you attempt to pass a single argument, like this:

```
ewc_procedure(2)
```

Maya returns an error because the first argument is an integer but the string argument is missing.

```
// Error: Line 1.17: Wrong number of arguments on call to ewc_
procedure.//
```

Ensure that the order of arguments being passed matches the order of data types declared in the procedure argument (first an integer, then a string).

```
ewc_procedure(2, "apple")
```

Maya prints the concatenation of the value passed to $arg2 with the value passed to $arg1:

```
apple2
```

Chapter 6

6.1.7 **Switch Statements**

When writing the procedures for the functionality of the layer manager, I keep smaller and related commands under one procedure and assign them to individual case statements based on the control that will be calling them. Using switch statements and if statements, we can define exactly which part of the procedure is going to be used by a specific control by passing a unique argument from each control. Since most of the arguments being tested in section 6.3 will be tested through switch statements, I want to take a moment to review the fundamentals of a switch statement.

General Usage

A switch statement evaluates a variable and then matches the value in the variable to a case statement that has the corresponding value and executes the block of code inside the case statement. Your head just exploded, so let me rephrase that. *Switch statements* take a value and test it against predefined case statements for a match to determine which block of code will be executed.

In the example below, the string "hello" is cast in the variable held by $s and the variable itself is placed in the parentheses of the switch statement. The switch statement then compares the value being held in $s for a matching string that follows each case statement. The first case statement contains the matching string, so the print command under the case statement is executed.

```
string $s = "hello";
switch ($s)
{
    case "hello":
        print "Nice to meet you!";
        break;
    case "bye":
        print "Take care...";
        break;
    default:
        print "Excuse me?";
        break;
}
```

The default statement is optional and is similar to the else statement used with if statements. I normally implement a switch statement when I know that a procedure will be passed only pre-specified values through arguments. I normally reserve if statements for performing tests, especially when the value tested could be an unknown value. This is, however, a matter of personal choice and a subject of heated discussion amongst nerds.

Lastly, remember to include the break command to avoid falling. "Falling" occurs when the break command is left out, which causes MEL to continue on and evaluate the next case statement (and so on) until reaching either a break command or the end of the switch statement altogether. Omit the break command and the case statement that is called will continue on to the next case statement under it.

```
string $s = "bye";
switch ($s)
{
    case "hello":
        print "Nice to meet you!";
        break;
    case "bye":
        print "Take care...";
    default:
        print "Excuse me?";
}
```

The Script Editor prints back:

```
Take care...Excuse me?
```

Maya doesn't know when to stop after the second case statement and falls right through to the default statement, executing it as well. The last condition in a switch statement, whether it is a case or default statement, doesn't require a break command, but it is good practice to add one anyway.

Pitfalls when Using Switch Statements

One of the most common problems I see when people first use switch statements is that they forget to add a colon after a case value.

```
case value    // This will create an error
case value:   // Remembering the colon up front will avoid many problems
```

A second common problem is forgetting the `break` command at the end of a case statement. Since a case statement does not use delimiters (curly brackets), something must be in place to tell Maya when the case statement ends. This is why a `break` command is used.

Try the next example and see what is printed.

```
int $v = 1;
switch ($v)
{
    case 1:
        print "Looks like ";
    case 2:
        print "someone forgot ";
    case 3:
        print "to add a break command!";
}
```

The bottom line of the Script Editor will read:

```
Looks like someone forgot to add a break command!
```

If you can remember these two important features of a switch statement, then you are set.

6.1.8 If Statements

Earlier in this chapter I briefly covered if statements. Now I am going to address them again, and in more detail. The if statement takes a value and tests it to determine if the block of code will be executed. Earlier, we used a simple if statement to create a shading toggle for a layer:

```
if (`getAttr layer1.shading`)
    setAttr layer1.shading 0;
else
```

```
setAttr layer1.shading 1;
```

The if statement tested a value that was directly inserted into the condition using the getAttr command.

```
if (`getAttr layer1.shading`)
```

When a condition or variable is inside the parentheses without any operators (covered next), then the if statement returns true as long as the getAttr query returns any value except 0. If 0 is returned, it jumps to the else statement and runs the block underneath it.

Implementing operators in the statement increases the range of possibilities to return true.

Comparison Operators

== is equal to   If the value that is being tested (on the left of the operator) exactly matches the value on the right side of the operator, then it returns true.

```
int $v = 5;
if ($v == 5)
    print "Is true";
```

!= is not equal to   If the value that is being tested (on the left of the operator) does not match the value on the right side of the operator, then it returns true. The example below is commonly used to check if a string is empty.

```
string $v = "apple";
if ($v != "")
    print "String is not empty.";
```

< is less than   If the value that is being tested (on the left of the operator) is less than the value on the right side of the operator, then it returns true.

```
int $v = 5;
if ($v < 6)
    print "Variable $v is less than 6";
```

> is greater than   If the value that is being tested (on the left of the operator) is greater than the value on the right side of the operator, then it returns true.

Chapter 6

```
int $v = 7;
if ($v < 6)
    print "Variable $v is greater than 6";
```

<= is less than or equal to If the value that is being tested is less than or equal to the value on the right side of the operator, then it returns true.

```
int $v = 6;
if ($v <= 6)
    print "Variable $v is equal to or less than 6";
```

```
int $v = 5;
if ($v <= 6)
    print "Variable $v is equal to or less than 6";
```

>= is greater than or equal to If the value that is being tested is greater than or equal to the value on the right side of the operator, then it returns true.

```
int $v = 6;
if ($v >= 6)
    print "Variable $v is equal to or greater than 6";
```

```
int $v = 7;
if ($v >= 6)
    print "Variable $v is equal to or greater than 6";
```

Logical Operators

|| (or) either left or right is true If either of the values being tested returns true, the entire if statement will return true.

```
int $x = 1;
string $y = "apple";
if ($x == 1 || $y == "peach")
    print "At least one condition tested true";
```

&& (and) both sides are true Both of the values being tested must return true for the if statement to return true.

```
int $x = 1;
string $y = "apple";
if ($x == 1 && $y == "apple")
    print "Both conditions returned true";
```

! (not) condition is false   Unlike the previous logical operators, the not operator only tests one condition and only returns true if the test returns false (0).

```
int $x = 0;
if (! $x)
    print "The value is 0.";
```

The not operator is the opposite of:

```
if ($x)
```

which tests true if the value is anything but 0. To best demonstrate how this works, take another look at the toggle for the shading state of a layer.

Toggle with not operator	Original toggle

if (!`getAttr layer1.shading`)
    setAttr layer1.shading 1;
else
    setAttr layer1.shading 0;
	if (`getAttr layer1.shading`)
	    setAttr layer1.shading 0;
	else
	    setAttr layer1.shading 1;

Switch Statements or If Statements

An if statement with else if conditions could be used to simulate a switch statement. The else if will test for additional conditions before reaching the else statement. More than one else if can be added to test for multiple conditions.

This if statement will toggle through the various display types of a layer (there are three of them). Both the if statement and switch statement toggles work identically.

(Make sure you actually have a layer1 in your scene if you want to test this code in Maya.)

```
if(`getAttr layer1.displayType` == 0)
    {
    setAttr layer1.displayType 1;
    print "Template\n";
    }
else if(`getAttr layer1.displayType` == 1)
    {
```

Chapter 6

```
    setAttr layer1.displayType 2;
    print "Reference\n";
    }
else
    {
    setAttr layer1.displayType 0;
    print "Normal\n";
    }
```

The switch statement for the exact same toggle would look like this:

```
int $disp = `getAttr layer1.displayType`;
switch($disp)
{
    case 0:
        setAttr layer1.displayType 1;
        print "Template\n";
        break;
    case 1:
        setAttr layer1.displayType 2;
        print "Reference\n";
        break;
    case 2:
        setAttr layer1.displayType 0;
        print "Normal\n";
        break;
}
```

The upside to if statements is that you don't have to remember the colon like with the case condition or use a break command to end each block. If statements are ideal for simple toggles, like the layer shading states and performing tests on data input by a user. And lastly, a command can be directly tested within the parentheses of an if statement.

```
if (`getAttr layer1.shading`)
```

Switch statements do not accept commands, and values must be queried outside the scope of the switch statement and passed through a variable.

```
switch(`getAttr layer1.displayType`)
{
```

```
case 0:
    setAttr layer1.displayType 1;
    print "Template\n";
    break;
case 1:
    setAttr layer1.displayType 2;
    print "Reference\n";
    break;
case 2:
    setAttr layer1.displayType 0;
    print "Normal\n";
    break;
}
```

```
// Error: switch(`getAttr layer1.displayType`)
//
// Error: Line 1.36: undefined is an invalid type for a switch
    expression. //
```

The upside of switch statements is there is only one set of delimiters (curly brackets) used to contain the case statements. If statements require delimiters for each condition (else if, and else) being tested. Switch statements are best used in a situation when known values are going to be used.

6.2 Early Interface of the Layer Manager

In this section I will illustrate the evolution of the early version of the script to briefly demonstrate good coding techniques.

The earliest version of the layer manager was an interface that was called from a shelf button that consisted of a floating window containing multiple buttons. The buttons toggled the drawing states of specific layers. This was rather cumbersome, as I had to write a new script for each scene, but it did clean up my shelf (compared to the earlier all-shelf version of my technique), leaving room for other buttons.

Here is an early example of the system I was using. It is a simple window containing eight buttons to edit specific drawing states

Chapter 6

of layers in a scene. There are five layers in this example, three of which I need to be able to quickly toggle two attributes of.

Layer name	First attribute	Second attribute
cars	shading	levelOfDetail
characters	shading	playback
buildings	shading	levelOfDetail
environment	shading	
detail	levelOfDetail	

My earliest scripts looked similar to this:

```
if (`window -ex layerDisplayUI`)
    deleteUI layerDisplayUI;
window -t "Layers" layerDisplayUI;
gridLayout -nc 2 -cw 85;
button -l "Cars - Shading" -c("if (`getAttr cars.shading`)"
                    +"setAttr cars.shading 0;"
                    +"else setAttr cars.shading 1;");
button -l "Cars - LOD" -c("if (`getAttr cars.levelOfDetail`)"
                    +"setAttr cars.levelOfDetail 0;"
                    +"else setAttr cars.levelOfDetail 1;");
button -l "Char - Shading" -c("if (`getAttr characters.shading`)"
                    +"setAttr characters.shading 0;"
                    +"else setAttr characters.shading 1;");
button -l "Char - Playback" -c("if (`getAttr characters.playback`)"
                    +"setAttr characters.playback 0;"
                    +"else setAttr characters.playback 1;");
button -l "Bld - Shading" -c("if (`getAttr buildings.shading`)"
                    +"setAttr buildings.shading 0;"
                    +"else setAttr buildings.shading 1;");
button -l "Bld - LOD" -c("if (`getAttr buildings.levelOfDetail`)"
                    +"setAttr buildings.levelOfDetail 0;"
                    +"else setAttr buildings.levelOfDetail 1;");
button -l "Env - Shading" -c("if (`getAttr environment.shading`)"
                    +"setAttr environment.shading 0;"
                    +"else setAttr environment.shading 1;");
button -l "Detail - LOD" -c("if (`getAttr detail.levelOfDetail`)"
                    +"setAttr detail.levelOfDetail 0;"
                    +"else setAttr detail.levelOfDetail 1;");
showWindow layerDisplayUI;
```

This script creates a small window with eight buttons arranged in two columns.

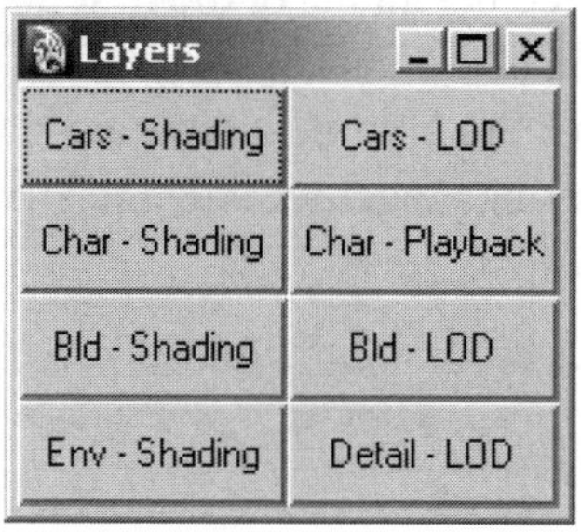

Figure 6-14

The first line is a common conditional statement used in interface development. If you try to open a window that is already open, Maya will print an error. This statement tests if a specific window exists with the -ex flag (short name for -exists). If it does, then delete the window. Note the back quotes in the if statement.

```
if (`window -ex layerDisplayUI`)
    deleteUI layerDisplayUI;
```

Next, create a window using the window command and assign it the title "Layers" using the -t flag. Note that running this command alone won't display the window.

```
window -t "Layers" layerDisplayUI;
```

Before adding controls to an interface, some form of layout has to be created first. In this example, a gridLayout is used. The number of columns is defined with the -nc flag and the pixel width of each column is declared using the -cw flag.

```
gridLayout -nc 2 -cw 85;
```

Now create the eight buttons needed with the following two flags:

- **-l**: Shorthand for -label. Adds a label to the button.

- **-c**: Shorthand for -command. Stores a string that will be executed as a command. This may be an actual command or (more commonly) a procedure name.

Chapter 6

A string can span multiple lines with the use of concatenation and parentheses. The entire string must be enclosed in parentheses, with the opening parenthesis at the beginning of the first line and the closing parenthesis at the end of the final line. Each line requires its own quotes, and each line after the first must have a concatenation character (+) to stitch the strings together into one string to be stored in the –c flag.

```
button -l "Cars - Shading" -c("if (`getAttr cars.shading`)"
                           +"setAttr cars.shading 0;"
                           +"else setAttr cars.shading 1;");
```

Due to the page width limitations in this book, I will show the code using multiple-line concatenation. If the string were to exist on one line, it would look like this:

```
"if(`getAttr cars.shading`)setAttr cars.shading 0;else setAttr cars.shading 1;"
```

Seven more buttons are created using the same method. The final line containing the showWindow command does what you think it does: It displays the window to the user.

```
showWindow layerDisplayUI;
```

The name layerDisplayUI is used in the first conditional statement, the deleteUI command, the window command, and the showWindow command. In order for Maya to know which window is being queried, deleted, or displayed, the window needs to be named. This is done by assigning the name at the end of the window command right before the semicolon. (We will discuss naming conventions for windows and controls in section 6.3.)

6.2.1 **Comments**

This window serves its purpose but just wasn't quite enough for what I needed later. There are also a few problems here I want to point out as well. The script runs without errors, but there is more to a good script than just having it work.

The first thing to point out is that there are no comments whatsoever. Even in small scripts like this, inserting some comments is a good practice. I should have a comment at the top of the script, at the very least, that reads something like:

```
// Display layer control for the
// scene simple_example01.mb
```

Later on you will see how I use comments to talk through procedures before actually writing any code. This is a stage of planning known as *pseudocoding*.

Comments have been covered before, but since they are so vital, I will repeat some of that information. In-line comments are identified with two forward slashes (//), and Maya ignores everything that is written after them for the rest of the line that the comment is on.

```
// Everything after me on this line will be ignored.
```

The second type of comment is the block comment, which starts with a forward slash and asterisk (/*). Everything after that will be commented out and ignored by Maya until it reaches an asterisk and forward slash (*/), which closes the block comment. Block comments are flexible because they can span multiple lines.

```
/*
This will be ignored.
And so will this.
Until the block comment is closed.
*/
```

A block comment can also be placed the middle of a command and its arguments.

```
print /* ignore me */ "Print Me!";
```

In this example, Maya ignores the block comment but still prints the string.

Any programmer will tell you that commenting and documentation is crucial. On a production pipeline or even an independent group project, you can bet commenting will be a requirement.

6.2.2 **Structure and Readability**

Flag Names

Using short names for flags is quite common; however, their use makes the code much more difficult to read.

Here is an example of code using short flag names:

```
if (`window -ex layerDisplayUI`)
    deleteUI layerDisplayUI;
window -t "Layers" layerDisplayUI;
gridLayout -nc 2 -cw 85;
```

In the MEL documentation you will notice that flags have a long name and a short name next to them in parentheses.

```
-exists (-ex)
```

When I first started out, I thought I would save myself a lot of time and headaches by using the short names. And at the time it did seem to go faster. Version 1.0 to 1.5 of ewc_extendedLayerManager was written like this. Not even half a year later, when I decided to rewrite the script to fix some bugs and incorporate a redesign of the interface, I would be regretting that decision. The time I initially saved was made up for by having to dig back through the MEL documentation to find out what those short names meant.

Examine the previous block again, but this time with long names. It is much easier to interpret what is going on (without constantly referring to the documentation) when long names are used.

```
if (`window -exists layerDisplayUI`)
    deleteUI layerDisplayUI;
window -title "Layers" layerDisplayUI;
gridLayout -numberOfColumns 2 -cellWidth 85;
```

There are a few command flags that are so commonly used that most people use the short names anyway. Probably one of the most commonly used is the ls -sl command, which is the command that builds an array out of selected items. The long name is ls -selected.

You will see short names used again in section 6.3 when I use formLayout to edit the position of controls in the interface of the layer manager. The flag names are really quite long and are repeated so many times that I feel it is actually more efficient to use the short names.

Indenting

The next thing I want to point out is the importance of indentation. Indenting makes for very readable code and just looks more professional overall.

```
// A Window
    // A button
    // A button
    // Input field
// Show window
// Global procedure
    // If condition
        // first command
        // second command
    // Else
        // first command
        // second command
// End procedure
```

Lastly, avoid placing all the commands in the command strings. For example, my strings for the buttons looked like this:

```
-c("if (`getAttr detail.levelOfDetail`)"
            +"setAttr detail.levelOfDetail 0;"
            +"else setAttr detail.levelOfDetail 1;");
```

This is not the recommended method nor is it good practice for assigning commands to a control. It is hard to read and not a very clean and professional way to work. When writing scripts and interfaces, the normal practice is to create procedures to perform custom tasks and commands. A procedure name should be stored in a -command string instead of the entire if statement.

Cleaning House

The following is essentially the same script as far as how it functions, but it is laid out much cleaner and is easier to edit and read.

Chapter 6

```
// Display layer control for the
// scene simple_example01.mb

if (`window -exists layerDisplayUI`)
// Query if the window currently exists
    deleteUI layerDisplayUI;              // Delete it if it does

// Create the main window
window -title "Layers" layerDisplayUI;
    // Create a layout to hold the controls
    gridLayout -numberOfColumns 2 -cellWidth 85;
        // Create the buttons
        button -label "Cars - Shading"  -command "ewc_toggle(1)";
        button -label "Cars - LOD"      -command "ewc_toggle(2)";
        button -label "Char - Shading"  -command "ewc_toggle(3)";
        button -label "Char - Playback" -command "ewc_toggle(4)";
        button -label "Bld - Shading"   -command "ewc_toggle(5)";
        button -label "Bld - LOD"       -command "ewc_toggle(6)";
        button -label "Env - Shading"   -command "ewc_toggle(7)";
        button -label "Detail - LOD"    -command "ewc_toggle(8)";
// Show the window
showWindow layerDisplayUI;

// Procedure to toggle drawing states
proc ewc_toggle(int $case)
{
    switch ($case)
    {
        case 1: // Toggle shading of cars layer
            if (`getAttr cars.shading`)
                setAttr cars.shading 0;
            else
                setAttr cars.shading 1;
            break;
        case 2: // Toggle level of detail of cars layer
            if (`getAttr cars.levelOfDetail`)
                setAttr cars.levelOfDetail 0;
            else
                setAttr cars.levelOfDetail 1;
            break;
        case 3: // Toggle shading of characters layer
```

```
        if (`getAttr characters.shading`)
            setAttr characters.shading 0;
        else
            setAttr characters.shading 1;
        break;
    case 4: // Toggle playback of characters layer
        if (`getAttr characters.playback`)
            setAttr characters.playback 0;
        else
            setAttr characters.playback 1;
        break;
    case 5: // Toggle shading of buildings layer
        if (`getAttr buildings.shading`)
            setAttr buildings.shading 0;
        else
            setAttr buildings.shading 1;
        break;
    case 6: // Toggle level of detail of buildings layer
        if (`getAttr buildings.levelOfDetail`)
            setAttr buildings.levelOfDetail 0;
        else
            setAttr buildings.levelOfDetail 1;
        break;
    case 7: // Toggle shading of environment layer
        if (`getAttr environment.shading`)
            setAttr environment.shading 0;
        else
            setAttr environment.shading 1;
        break;
    case 8: // Toggle level of detail of detail layer
            if (`getAttr detail.levelOfDetail`)
                setAttr detail.levelOfDetail 0;
            else
                setAttr detail.levelOfDetail 1;
    } // End switch
} // End ewc_toggle()
```

Throughout the script, comments are used to indicate the purpose of each case statement. Comments are also used to indicate whether a delimiter is closing the switch statement or the procedure itself.

Chapter 6

The buttons have also had the conditional statements removed from the -command flag and replaced with a call to the procedure found just below the showWindow command. This is much easier to read than the previous version, and is the recommended workflow when attaching commands to controls.

Each command has the same procedure name, but each has a unique number enclosed in parentheses. This is an argument that was covered earlier. If you are confused at this point, I suggest reviewing section 6.1.6, "Procedures and Arguments," before moving on.

6.2.3 **Functions**

A *function* is a procedure that returns a value to where it was called from.

Do you remember your trigonometry? Probably about as much as I do. So let's write a script that converts degrees to radians. Start by declaring a procedure, with one difference: A data type must be declared in the procedure before the procedure name.

```
proc float degtorad(int $d)
{
    float $pi = 3.14159;
    return ($d * ($pi / 180));
}
```

This procedure uses the word float right after proc and before the procedure name to define the data type that will be returned. The procedure also takes an integer argument named $d. It is necessary to declare a data type. Maya cannot determine on its own what the data type must be for the return. In fact, if you attempt to declare the procedure without a specific data type, Maya will return an error.

```
proc degtorad(int $d)
{
    float $pi = 3.14159;
    return ($d * ($pi / 180));
}
```

Maya will detect a procedure that contains a `return` command with no data type declared and display an error message like this:

```
// Error: return ($d * ($pi / 180)); //
// Error: Line 3.27: This procedure has no return value. //
```

The second line tells us exactly what is wrong: The procedure has no return value. Maya will not allow you to forget a data type when declaring a procedure containing a return value.

Enter the following correct function to continue with the example:

```
proc float degtorad(int $d)
{
    float $pi = 3.14159;
    return ($d * ($pi / 180));
}
```

A variable for pi is created and stored in a float called `$pi`. The second line holds the return statement. This statement will return the result of multiplying the argument by `$pi` and dividing it by 180. The result will be the conversion to radians.

To demonstrate how a return works, enter the following `print` command:

```
print ("Question: What is 90 degrees in radians? "
    + "Answer: " + degtorad(90));
```

and Maya prints back:

```
Question: What is 90 degrees in radians? Answer: 1.570795
```

What is happening here is when the `print` command executes, it concatenates the strings with the returned result. The `degtorad(90)` sends the integer 90 to the procedure. The math conversion then takes place, converting degrees to radians. The result of 1.570795 is returned to the `print` command and then concatenated with the string.

It is important that the data type of the procedure is declared correctly, especially when doing mathematical conversions. For example, change the data type in the procedure from float to int, and declare the procedure again. Ignore the warning from Maya about the changed definition, then enter:

```
degtorad(90);
```

Maya returns:

```
// Result: 1 //
```

Since we changed the procedure data type to integer, the return shaved off the remainder and returned a whole number for the result. This would not be the correct answer when converting to radians.

About Naming Conventions for Functions and Procedures

Many programming languages such as Pascal, FORTRAN, and Ada distinguish between functions or function subprograms, which return values (via a return statement), and subroutines or procedures, which do not. Some languages such as C and MEL do not make this distinction, and treat those terms as synonymous. However, to conform to the other chapters in this book, I will use the term procedure, regardless of whether or not the procedure returns a value.

6.2.4 Getting Creative with Functions... er... Procedures

In the next section we build the interface for the layer manager. This is a fairly lengthy process and the final global procedure will be very long. It would be incredibly inconvenient for someone to dig through the code to locate the actual chunk that creates the controls to change the default values for the four user options covered in section 6.1.2, "Outlining the Functionality of ewc_extendedLayerManager."

Below I will introduce what is in my opinion an easier method to change these defaults; easier because there is no need to dig around in the interface procedure.

Before moving on I want to clarify why I chose this method. In earlier beta tests I had experimented with using a binary file to write and store user settings. I posted the layer manager in a zip file with the binary file and a text file explaining that both files needed to be placed in the user scripts directory. As a technical director (TD) this seems straightforward, but TDs don't think like everyone else. At least 400 users downloaded the zip file, and within a 24-hour period I received 380 e-mails complaining that the script wasn't working. As it turned out, in every case the binary file was *not* placed into the user scripts directory. After this I decided to use procedures with returns (covered in a bit) that were stored in the script itself. If a user was so inclined to change the defaults, then it was up to him to manually modify the script.

Since only four controls will have their initial states controlled through this method, the actual code (which you will see in section 6.3) really will be quite simple and easy to edit. The controls are:

- Actively Select Members (check box)
- Add Selected to New Layer (check box)
- Input Prompt for New Layers (check box)
- Default Layer Name (text field)

Global Variables

In earlier releases of the layer manager, global variables were used to hold the default states for the user options. The example below illustrates how this would be done.

First declare the global variables:

```
global int $firstCheckBox = 1;
global int $secondCheckBox = 0;
```

Create a simple window with two check boxes. The –value flags of the check boxes will use the names of the global variables as arguments.

```
proc checkboxWindow()
{
    // import the global variables
    global int $firstCheckBox;
    global int $secondCheckBox;
    // Create the window with a layout
    string $testwin = `window`;
```

```
        columnLayout -rowSpacing 10;
            checkBox
                -label "First Checkbox"
                // Use $firstCheckBox to load the starting value
                -value $firstCheckBox;
            checkBox
                -label "Second Checkbox"
                // Use $secondCheckBox to load the starting value
                -value $secondCheckBox;
            showWindow $testwin;
}
checkboxWindow();
```

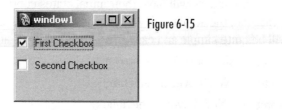

Figure 6-15

Before moving on I want to point out an important fact concerning global variables. When you want to use a global variable in a procedure, it first needs to be declared (without assigning a value) in that procedure. Look again at the procedure and note the global variables are declared (just declared; no values are being assigned) before the window is created.

```
// import the global variables
global int $firstCheckBox;
global int $secondCheckBox;
// Create the window with a layout
```

The issue (and danger) with global variables is that they can easily be changed from anywhere in Maya by simply assigning new values. In other words, global variables don't have scope like local variables. This will only last until Maya is restarted or the script holding the original global variable declaration is executed again.

```
$firstCheckBox = 3;   // a new value easily assigned
// Result: 3 //
```

If your script attempts to declare a global variable of a matching data type that already exists in another script, whether that script is a Maya default or another custom user script, the original global variable could be overwritten. This can create serious problems for other scripts and tools within Maya. If the data types don't match, you will get an error.

Try redeclaring the first global procedure as a string:

```
global string $firstCheckBox = "Make me a global string";
```

This will cause an error.

```
// Error: global string $firstCheckBox = "Make me a global string"; //
// Error: Line 1.30: Invalid redeclaration of variable "$firstCheckBox"
   as a different type. //
```

There is no way to lock a variable so it can't have a new value assigned. In this case an alternative is needed, one that can hold the default value and cannot be edited unless the script itself is manually changed.

As an alternative, a procedure with a return function can be used to perform exactly the same task but without the drawbacks of a global variable. A switch statement is used to hold values for multiple controls as long as the controls take the same data type.

```
proc checkboxWindow()
{
    // Create the window with a layout
    string $testwin = `window`;
        columnLayout -rowSpacing 10;
            checkBox
                -label "First Checkbox"
                // Use cbval(1) to load the starting value
                -value (cbval(1));
            checkBox
                -label "Second Checkbox"
                // Use cbval(2) to load the starting value
                -value (cbval(2));
        showWindow $testwin;
}

proc int cbval(int $case)
```

```
{
    switch ($case)
    {
        case 1: // First check box
            return 1;
            break;
        case 2: // Second check box
            return 0;
            break;
    }
}
// Run the interface
checkboxWindow();
```

Note that when calling a function with the -value flag, the entire function must be within parentheses.

```
-value (cbval(1));
```

If the parentheses are omitted:

```
-value cbval(1);
```

Maya will return this error:

```
// Error: line 9: Error while parsing arguments. //
```

Now the only way a user can change the defaults is the way I intend them to, by opening the script and editing the return value.

As mentioned before, this application of global variables will be fleshed out in section 6.4, "Creating the Functionality — Part I," so don't call your mummy just yet.

6.3 **Designing the Interface**

Before I get started, I want to give you a little more background about the development process of the layer manager. Early on during the beta of the original layer manager I encountered an anomaly in creating utilities for other users. (It turned out that users depend on the blatantly obvious in order to correctly use the interface I had built. In fact, the blatantly obvious can be the key factor for competent user interaction with any interface you build. Needless to say, as a good TD your task is to make a UI as user friendly and dummy proof as possible.)

The first three buttons I had created in the first version of the layer manager UI were buttons to create a layer, add objects to a layer, and to remove objects from a layer. When I set up the buttons, I assumed that they were self-explanatory enough for anyone to interpret. My mistake.

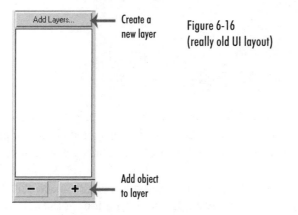

Figure 6-16
(really old UI layout)

So I get an e-mail from a modeler who says that the button to add a new layer isn't working. After going back and forth I realized the problem: He had been clicking on the + button the whole time. Despite the button at the top of the UI being labeled "Add Layers...", somehow there was a misinterpretation that both buttons would serve the same purpose. To remedy this, I began annotating the controls with tooltips that indicated the purpose of the controls

Chapter 6

to users. I also started disabling controls that could not yet perform their function. The screenshot below is an empty Attribute Editor; notice that several of the buttons and menu items are grayed out, indicating that they are disabled.

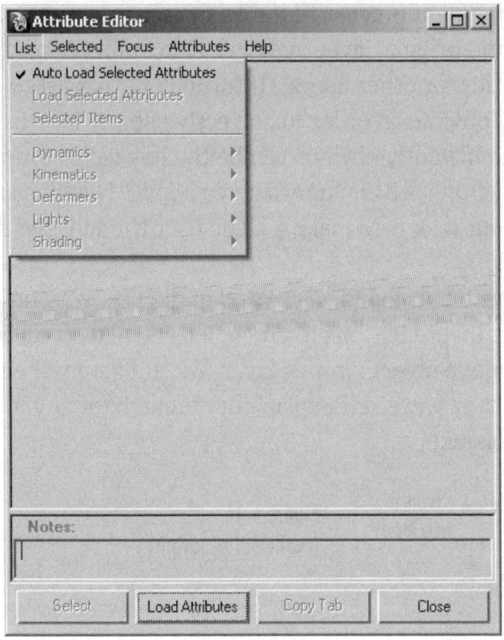

Figure 6-17

These controls will be enabled only when an object is selected and these controls can actually be used. This is incredibly common in commercial applications, but is rarely seen in small user-developed utilities.

In my layer manager, I use this philosophy to enable and disable controls in the UI. For example, the +/– buttons at the bottom of the UI will not be enabled until a layer is clicked in the list. Meaning that the buttons will only be enabled when they are actually usable. Between controlling the enable states of controls and using annotations, my users will find it easier to navigate the UI.

Figure 6-18 (disabled)

Figure 6-19 (controls enabled when a layer is highlighted)

This is probably something most people don't pay attention to when creating their own interfaces. It is easy, from a developer's standpoint, to forget that users will not have an intimate knowledge of the interface. To assist users in knowing when a control can and cannot be used, I will be writing the interface with most controls disabled. We will implement toggles in our procedures to enable controls that are ready to function as intended. This also means that sometimes more time will be spent developing the interface than the functionality.

In short, show your users that you are committed to writing the most thorough and user-friendly scripts they have ever seen, and you will be rewarded with bourbon and back rubs.

6.3.1 **Naming Conventions**

When beginning any type of UI building, it is a very good idea to establish a naming convention for the UI-related controls and procedures. If you are working with more than one person on a project, this step must be taken before the first variable is even declared. Everyone must be on the same page and have the same list to ensure continuity throughout the whole project.

Chapter 6

The prefixes I intend to use are my initials followed by an underscore: ewc_. For the sake of instruction I recommend using this prefix for the entire chapter. When you set out on your first MEL project you will want to set up a universal naming convention for all your procedures and controls. This is a sign of a consistent coder.

For the naming of controls and procedures we need a secondary prefix that comes after my initials and the underscore. Try to keep it simple, yet make sure you can identify the control type just by looking at the prefix. The table below is an example of the naming conventions I will be using here. You may even want to make a copy of the naming prefixes for reference.

Naming convention list for ewc_extendedLayerManager.mel			
Global procedures	ewc_gproc	Check boxes	ewc_cbox
Column layouts	ewc_col	Scroll layouts	ewc_scroll
Frame layouts	ewc_frame	Form layouts	ewc_form
Option menus	ewc_optmen	Input fields	ewc_fld
Buttons	ewc_btn	Text labels	ewc_txt
Text scroll lists	ewc_tsl	Color palette	ewc_palprt
Menu items	ewc_mi		

For this project there is only one main window: ewc_winExtendedLayerManager.

There will be one exception to the naming conventions for global procedures. When calling a script, the main (or default) procedure that executes, in this case the interface procedure, must have the same name as the script. In our case, the script name is ewc_extendedLayerManager.mel, so the interface procedure is named ewc_extendedLayerManager().

6.3.2 **Conceptualizing the Interface**

Before attempting to design an interface you should always sketch out a concept. These sketches are for your own personal benefit and are not meant to impress anyone. The point is just to get your idea on paper. If there is one advantage you will have over me, it is that you will probably never have to put your sketches into publication for the whole world to see.

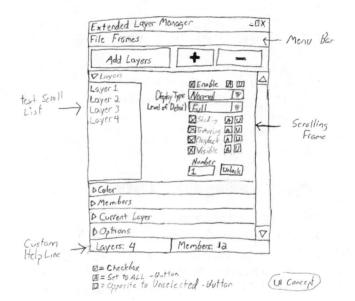

Figure 6-20

6.3.3 **Indenting By Hierarchy**

Using indentation helps create a visual outline and cues for the hier-archical structure of the layouts and controls. The following example shows the outline for the File menu. The full outline can be found on the companion disc, along with a list that contains the names of the controls. I recommend setting up a list of control names before tak-ing on a large interface project.

Chapter 6

Note that the code covered here and in section 6.4 have corresponding MEL files on the companion disc to compare your progress with.

```
>
Main Interface
    >>
    Menu Bar
        >>>
        File Menu
            >>>>
            Add Layer
            Delete Layer(s)
            Rename Layer
            Layer Attributes
            Relationship Editor
            Refresh Layer List
            Refresh Member List
            ...
```

6.3.4 **Pseudocoding the Interface**

Now that a visual outline has been established, it is time to declare the global procedure for the main interface. Using comments we will talk our way through the global procedure that creates the interface. I like to think of pseudocode as a road map. The following is a sample of the pseudocode for the hierarchical example shown earlier for the File menu.

```
//===========================
// MAIN INTERFACE PROCEDURE

global proc ewc_extendedLayerManager()
{
    // Test to see if main window exists
        // and if it does then delete it
    // Create the main window
        // Create the File menu
            // Menu Item: Add Layer
            // Menu Item: Delete Layer(s)
            // Menu Item: -divider-
```

```
// Menu Item: Rename Layer
// Menu Item: Layer Attributes
// Menu Item: -divider-
// Menu Item: Relationship Editor
// Menu Item: -divider-
// Menu Item: Refresh Layer List
// Menu Item: Refresh Member List
...
```

The full pseudocode can be found in ewc_extendedLayerMana-ger_01.mel on the companion disc. This is where you will want to start. I will be using the comments in that file as guides for you to follow.

Now that the entire interface has been pseudocoded, it will be easier to navigate through the structure of this interface. Nesting layout controls gets tricky, and without a solid structure to follow it is too easy to become lost in the procedure. Pseudocoding to this level of detail only comes in time with knowledge gained through experience and practice.

6.3.5 Creating the Window and Menus

The first step is to create the window and menus. We need two menus called File and Frames, which will contain the items outlined in the pseudocode.

Start with the condition to query if the window exists. If the condition returns true (window exists), then delete the queried window.

```
// Test to see if main window exists
if (`window -exists ewc_winExtendedLayerManager`)
    // and if it does then delete it
    deleteUI ewc_winExtendedLayerManager;
```

After the conditional test, create the window. Four flags will be used to create the window:

- **-title:** Creates the title that will be displayed at the top of the window.

- **-widthHeight:** Defines the initial width and height.

■ **-maximizeButton:** Disables the button to maximize the window.

■ **-menuBar:** By default windows don't have a menu bar; this flag enables the feature.

Complete the command by adding the name of the window, ewc_winExtendedLayerManager, before the semicolon:

```
// Create the main window
window
    -title "Extended Layer Manager 2.1"
    -widthHeight 380 315
    -maximizeButton 0
    -menuBar 1
    ewc_winExtendedLayerManager;
```

Now that a window has been established and the -menuBar flag is enabled, create the File menu using the menu command.

■ **-label:** Creates a title that is displayed on the menu bar.

■ **-parent:** Specifies the window that the menu belongs to.

```
// Create the File menu
menu -label "File" -parent ewc_winExtendedLayerManager;
```

Ensure that the commands are aligned (indented) with the original comments. This will make for a cleaner script when the code for the UI is completed.

Directly underneath the menu, use the menuItem command to create the items for the menu. These menuItem commands use the same -label flag as the menu command, along with the -command flag, which will be left blank by using empty quotes ("").

```
// Menu Item: Add Layer
menuItem
    -label "Add Layer"
    -command "";

// Menu Item: Delete Layer(s)
menuItem
    -label "Delete Layer(s)"
    -enable 0
```

```
        -command ""
    ewc_miDeleteLayer;

// Menu Item: -divider-
menuItem -divider 1;

// Menu Item: Rename Layer
menuItem
    -label "Rename Layer"
    -enable 0
    -command ""
    ewc_miRenameLayer;

// Menu Item: Layer Attributes
menuItem
    -label "Layer Attributes"
    -enable 0
    -command ""
    ewc_miLayerAttr;

// Menu Item: -divider-
menuItem -divider 1;

// Menu Item: Relationship Editor
menuItem
    -label "Relationship Editor"
    -command "";

// Menu Item: -divider-
menuItem -divider 1;

// Menu Item: Refresh Layer List
menuItem
    -label "Refresh Layer List"
    -command "";

// Menu Item: Refresh Member List
menuItem
    -label "Refresh Member List"
    -command "";
```

This defines the first menu for the window. All the -command flags have been left blank using empty quotes (""), which creates an empty string. This must be done since the flag requires a string value. An empty string is still a string and Maya will accept it as a valid argument for the flag.

The flags used here are:

- **-label:** The text displayed in the menu.

- **-command:** Holds a string of a command or procedure. This flag requires a string, even an empty one.

- **-divider:** Used alone, it creates a horizontal separator.

- **-enable:** Disables a control if set to 0.

Three items have their -enable flag set to 0, which means they are disabled. Most of the controls that will be added later will also be disabled. Ever notice in some applications that certain features are disabled until they have a purpose to be enabled? That is exactly what we will do here.

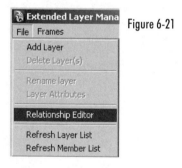

Figure 6-21

The three disabled menu items have also been named. In order to edit the -enable state, each control will need a unique name. Menus and menu items are normally left unnamed. Maya will assign them temporary names when the interface procedure is run.

Setting up the Frames menu is an identical process with slightly fewer items to add:

```
// Create the Frames menu
menu -label "Frames" -parent ewc_winExtendedLayerManager;
```

```
// Menu Item: Reset Frames
menuItem
    -label "Reset Frames"
    -command "";

// Menu Item: Members Frame
menuItem
    -label "Members Frame"
    -command "";

// Menu Item: Expand Frames
menuItem
    -label "Expand Frames"
    -command "";

// Menu Item: Collapse Frames
menuItem
    -label "Collapse Frames"
    -command "";

// Menu Item: -divider-
menuItem -divider 1;

// Menu Item: About...
menuItem
    -label "About..."
    -command "";
```

Before you can run this script there is one crucial command that must be added. At the bottom of the pseudocode file locate the `// Show the window` comment and under that add the `showWindow` command with the window name assigned earlier. The `window` command creates a window; to actually display it in a workspace the `showWindow` command must be used:

```
// Show the window
showWindow ewc_winExtendedLayerManager;
```

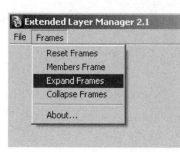

Figure 6-22:
ewc_extendedLayer
Manager_02.mel

6.3.6 Laying Out the First Level of Controls

The first controls to create are the three buttons across the top.

- **Add Layer:** Creates a new layer.

- **+ (Add Selected):** Adds selected objects to a layer.

- **– (Remove Selected):** Removes selected objects from a layer.

Later on, we'll add a scrolling layout, created with the `scrollLayout` command, to hold the collapsible frames. The first row of buttons that we create must be outside of the scrollLayout, so they must be created first before adding the scrollLayout.

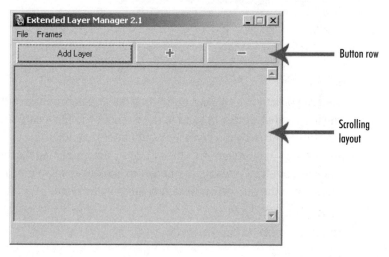

Figure 6-23

Before any objects can be created, however, a formLayout must be created. When any controls are added to a form, some sort of layout must be used (see the MEL documentation for a complete list).

```
// Form layout that will control the outer controls (main)
string $form1 = `formLayout ewc_formMainLayout`;
```

With a formLayout created, the next step is to create the buttons. Two types of buttons are going to be created.

- **button:** A standard button that displays a text label with the -label flag.

- **symbolButton:** This button functions the same as the standard button but displays an image as the label using the -image flag.

Add the button on the left first:

```
// Top Button row
// Button to add a layer
string $b1 = `button
            -label "Add Layer"
            -height 27
            -command ""
            -annotation "Create a new layer."
            ewc_btnCreateNewLayer`;
```

I will explain why these controls are assigned to variables when we edit the formLayout. Right now I want to describe the flags for the buttons. Remember to surround the command in back quotes to assign the control to a variable.

- **-label:** Text to be displayed on a button; this is only available with the button command.

- **-height:** Controls the height (in pixels) of the control.

- **-image:** Image displayed as the label; this is only available with the symbolButton command.

- **-enable:** Enables/disables the state of the control.

- **-command:** This will execute a command or procedure stored in a string.

- **-annotation:** When the mouse hovers over the control, a tooltip appears in the Maya Help line.

Chapter 6

The file used for the `-image` flag can be a user-supplied bitmap image or one of the .xpm image files that comes with Maya. Any custom images should be placed in the same directory as the script. For our example, we'll use two of Maya's images: setEdAddCmd.xpm and setEdRemoveCmd.xpm.

> **Note:** Probably the easiest tool for locating the appropriate .xpm file to use is a script called xpm2008.mel made by Han Jiang, which can be found at http://www.highend3d.com. The script will take about 30 to 40 seconds to load, but when it is completed it will generate a list of all the stock images that come with Maya. If you hold your mouse over an .xpm, the name is displayed in the Help line.

Figure 6-24

Continue by adding the other two buttons, which are created with the `symbolButton` command. Check to make sure that the `button` command, flags, and button names are surrounded with back quotes.

```
// Button to add selected to a layer
string $b2 = `symbolButton
            -image "setEdAddCmd.xpm"
            -enable 0
            -command ""
            -annotation "Assign selected objects to layer."
            ewc_btnAddSelectedObjects`;
// Button to remove selected from a layer
string $b3 = `symbolButton
            -image "setEdRemoveCmd.xpm"
            -enable 0
            -command ""
            -annotation "Remove selected objects from layer."
            ewc_btnRemoveSelectedObjects`;
```

When you run the script at this point you'll see that all the buttons are sitting on top of each other in the top-left corner. This is because the controls must be manually positioned when using a formLayout.

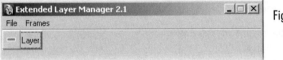

Figure 6-25

Editing the formLayout

The formLayout must be edited to define the exact position of its children (the controls; in our case the buttons and symbolButtons) within the window. At the bottom of the procedure, add the `// Edit Layouts` comment:

```
// Edit Layouts
    // Edit the layout of top level
```

The formLayout is called with the `-edit` flag, which permits the editing of the children. The formLayout was stored in a string variable called `$form1`. This variable is used to identify the specific formLayout that is being edited.

```
// Edit the layout of top level
formLayout -edit
    $form1;
```

Before the variable $form1 and after the formLayout command we add a line for each control position. Of all the various flags for attaching a control, only three will be used. This is the one exception I make concerning the short name rule for flags. Since these flags will be used over and over again, the use of short names for these flags is appropriate.

- **-attachForm** (-af): Attaches an edge of a control to the edge of the form with a pixel offset from the form that the edge is being attached to.

- **-attachControl** (-ac): Attaches an edge of a control to another control with a pixel offset from the control that the edge is being attached to.

- **-attachPosition** (-ap): Attaches an edge to the opposite side of a form with an offset and second integer that functions as a percentage of the form's width. This flag allows a control to scale uniformly with a window even if it only occupies a small part of the window.

```
// Edit the layout of top level
formLayout -edit
    // Add layer button
```

Attach the left edge of the button to the form with an offset of five pixels from the left side:

```
// attach at left edge with a 5 pixel offset
-af $b1    "left"    5
```

Attach the top edge of the button to the form with an offset of two pixels from the top side:

```
// attach at top edge with a 2 pixel offset
-af $b1    "top"    2
```

Attach the right edge of the button to a position relative to 45% of the window width, with an offset of zero pixels. This flag will retain its relative position if the window is resized.

```
// attach the right edge to the opposite side
// with a 0 pixel offset and at 45% of the window width
-ap $b1    "right"    0    45
```

```
// Add selected button
```

Attach the left edge of the button ($b2) to the right edge of the button stored in $b1 with an offset of five pixels:

```
// attach at the left edge to the add layer button
// while keeping a 5 pixel offset
-ac $b2     "left"      5       $b1
```

Attach the top edge of the button to the form with an offset of two pixels from the top side:

```
// attach at top edge with a 2 pixel offset
-af $b2     "top"       2
```

Attach the right edge of the button ($b2) to the left edge of the button stored in $b3 with an offset of five pixels:

```
// attach at the right edge to the remove selected button
// while keeping a 5 pixel offset
-ac $b2     "right"     5       $b3
// Remove selected button
```

Attach the left edge of the button to a position relative to 73% of the window width, with an offset of 0 pixels. This flag will retain the control's 73% relative position if the window is resized.

```
// attach the left edge to the opposite side
// with a 0 pixel offset and at 73% of the window width
-ap $b3     "left"      0       73
```

Attach the top edge of the button to the form with an offset of two pixels from the top side:

```
// attach at top edge with a 2 pixel offset
-af $b3     "top"       2
```

Attach the right edge of the button to the form with an offset of five pixels from the right side:

```
// attach at right edge with a 5 pixel offset
-af $b3     "right"     5
$form1;
```

If you run the script now you will see the three buttons are distributed across the top of the window. Try resizing the window, and

Chapter 6

notice the buttons retain their relative proportions to one another. Experiment with the offset values to see what they do. Experimentation is the best way to understand attaching controls. Since there will be at least two dozen more controls to edit I won't be commenting every single -attach* flag like I did above. However, I will, and suggest you do as well, comment each block for each control that is edited.

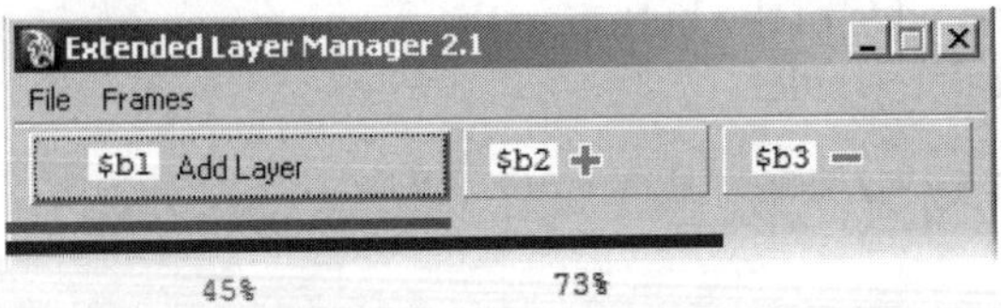

Figure 6-26

In my code I prefer to store the controls in variables because I use the variables to call the control that will have its position edited. Alternatively, the actual control names of the buttons (and the formLayout) could be called to edit the positions.

```
// Edit the layout of top level
formLayout -edit

    // Add layer button
    // attach at left edge with a 5 pixel offset
    -af ewc_btnCreateNewLayer        "left"    5
    // attach at top edge with a 2 pixel offset
    -af ewc_btnCreateNewLayer        "top"     2
    // attach the right edge to the opposite side
    // with a 0 pixel offset and at 45% of the window width
    -ap ewc_btnCreateNewLayer        "right"   0    45


    // Add selected button
    // attach at the left edge to the add layer button
    // while keeping a 5 pixel offset
    -ac ewc_btnAddSelectedObjects    "left"    5    $b1
    // attach at top edge with a 2 pixel offset
    -af ewc_btnAddSelectedObjects    "top"     2
    // attach at the right edge to the remove selected button
    // while keeping a 5 pixel offset
    -ac ewc_btnAddSelectedObjects    "right"   5    $b3
```

```
// Remove selected button
// attach the left edge to the opposite side
// with a 0 pixel offset and at 73% of the window width
-ap ewc_btnRemoveSelectedObjects  "left"     0     73
// attach at top edge with a 2 pixel offset
-af ewc_btnRemoveSelectedObjects  "top"      2
// attach at right edge with a 5 pixel offset
-af ewc_btnRemoveSelectedObjects  "right"    5

ewc_formMainLayout;
```

Both work equally well. However, an advantage to using the control names is that you will know exactly what control you are positioning simply by referring to the name. If you choose to use the variable method to position controls, be sure to meticulously comment.

6.3.7 The scrollLayout Control

This is the control that will enable a scroll bar when any of the window's children are not visible. By default a window does not scroll if a control is not in view. You must create a scrollLayout to enable this feature in a window.

```
// Scroll Layout
string $scroll1 = `scrollLayout
                   -horizontalScrollBarThickness 0
                   -childResizable 1
                   ewc_scrollFrameHolder`;
```

- ■ **-horizontalScrollBarThickness:** Sets the size of the horizontal bar. (There is a similar flag for the vertical bar; see the MEL documentation for more information.) To turn it off, set its size to 0.

- ■ **-childResizable:** Enabling this flag will force the children (specifically the underlying layouts) to scale with the scrollLayout.

Similar to the buttons added previously, the scrollLayout must have its position edited within the formLayout.

```
// Main scroll layout
-ac $scroll1    "top"    2    $b1
```

Chapter 6

```
-af $scroll1    "bottom"    25
-af $scroll1    "left"      0
-af $scroll1    "right"     0
$form1;
```

Run the script to see a scrolling layout that is centered in the window. The padding of 25 pixels at the bottom will leave the necessary space for the custom help line.

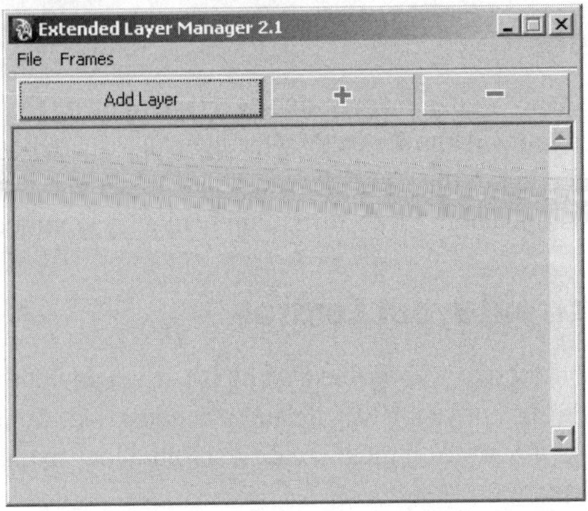

Figure 6-27:
ewc_extendedLayer
Manager_04.mel

6.3.8 Constructing a Custom Help Line

At the bottom of the window I want two interface elements that resemble a help line but only display the number of layers in a scene and the number of members in a highlighted layer.

Figure 6-28

Before this can be done the scope of the scrollLayout must be defined. If this is not done, the custom help line will become a child of the scrollLayout, meaning it will be located inside the scrollLayout. Add the associated comments from the following example and add the `setParent` command, which closes the scope of the scrollLayout. All controls added after this will be outside of the scrollLayout.

```
// Close the scope of the Scroll Layout
setParent ..;
// Layouts and controls to design a custom help line
```

The two periods (..) in the `setParent` command are shorthand for going up one level in an interface hierarchy. The actual flag is written as:

```
setParent -upLevel;
```

Another method you may use is the name of the parent layout:

```
setParent ewc_nameOfLayout;
```

All three methods are valid. If using the –upLevel flag or the .. shorthand, be sure to meticulously comment so you (and others) will never need to guess which layout the setParent is referring to.

Now it is safe to create the first frame for the layer count. The only control to create under the frameLayout is a text control. Close the scope of the frameLayout with the `setParent` command.

```
// Layouts and controls to design a custom help line
// Non-collapsing frame (Layer count)
string $helpLeft = `frameLayout -labelVisible 0 ewc_frameHelpLayer`;
    text -label "Layers:" ewc_txtLayerCount;

// Close scope of the Layer count frame
setParent ..;
```

Now create the second frame for the member count and the text control. Again, use the `setParent` command to close the scope of the frameLayout.

```
// Non-collapsing frame (Member count)
string $helpRight = `frameLayout -labelVisible 0 ewc_frameHelpMember`;
    text -label "Members:" ewc_txtMemberCount;

// Close scope of the Member count frame
setParent ..;
```

These frames work differently from the ones we create later on. The first difference is that these will not be collapsible; frames do not collapse by default. Second, there is only one flag being used; it turns off the label of the frame, leaving only the default border style.

■ **-labelVisible:** Toggles the label visibility state of a frame.

Now edit the position of the frames:

```
// Left help line
-ac $helpLeft    "top"      2    $scroll1
-af $helpLeft    "left"     2
-ap $helpLeft    "right"    2    50
-af $helpLeft    "bottom"   2


// Right help line
-ac $helpRight   "top"      2    $scroll1
-af $helpRight   "right"    2
-ap $helpRight   "left"     2    50
-af $helpRight   "bottom"   2

$form1;
```

Now run the script to see the custom help line positioned under the scrollLayout. Like the top row of buttons, the frames also retain their proportions when the window is resized.

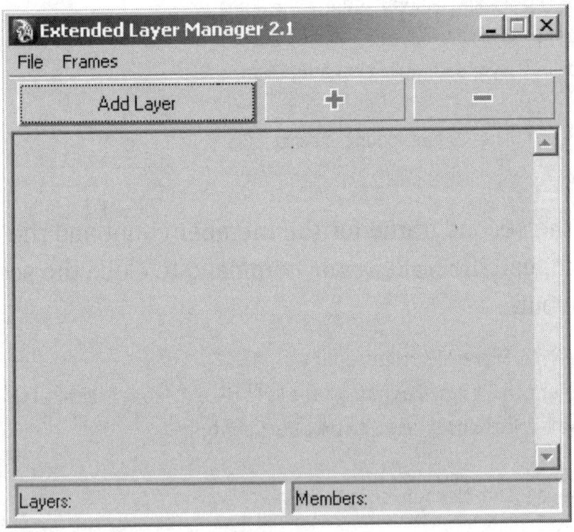

Figure 6-29:
ewc_extendedLayer
Manager_05.mel

This completes the first level of controls for the interface. From here on, the controls added will be children of the scrollLayout.

6.3.9 **Collapsing Frames with frameLayout**

Any Maya user is familiar with collapsing frames; they are most commonly seen in the Attribute Editor. Below is a screenshot of collapsible frames containing the attributes of a polyCube transform node. This is the style of interface that I want to reflect in the layer manager.

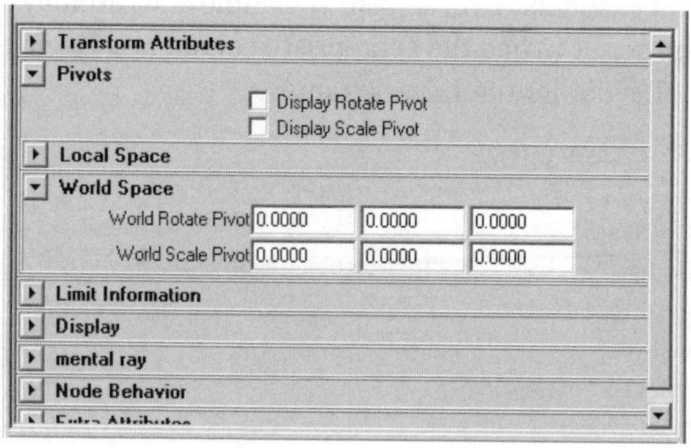

Figure 6-30

I want to keep some level of uniformity in the design so other Maya users will have a relatively familiar interface to work with. Start by adding a columnLayout. This control will arrange and hold the frames within the scrollLayout.

```
// Column layout to structure the collapsible frames
columnLayout -adjustableColumn 1 -rowSpacing 2 ewc_colFrameHolder;
```

- **-adjustableColumn:** This flag will force the collapsible frames to be attached to the entire width of the scrollLayout, even when the window is resized.

- **-rowSpacing:** This flag will create horizontal padding between each frame.

The following flags will be used when creating the frameLayout control:

- **-label:** The title of the frame.

- **-labelAlign:** The position of the label relative to the outline of the frame.

Chapter 6

- **-collapsable:** This flag must be enabled in order for a frame to be collapsible.
- **-collapse:** Indicates whether or not the frame is collapsed by default.
- **-borderStyle:** Indicates the type of drawing method that occurs around the boundary of a frameLayout.

Speed is not essential here, so take your time and carefully scroll through the script to find the appropriate comments. Begin by creating a frameLayout for the Layers frame:

```
// Collapsible Layers frame
frameLayout
    -label "Layers"
    -labelAlign "bottom"
    -collapsable 1
    -collapse 0
    -borderStyle "etchedIn"
    ewc_frameLayers;
```

Scroll down to close the scope of the Layers frame with the `setParent` command. Directly after that create a frameLayout for the Members frame.

```
// Close the scope of the Layers frame
setParent ..;

// Collapsible Members frame
frameLayout
    -label "Members"
    -labelAlign "bottom"
    -collapsable 1
    -collapse 1
    -borderStyle "etchedIn"
    ewc_frameMembers;
```

Scroll down to close the scope of the Members frame with the `setParent` command. Directly after that create a frameLayout for the Current Layer frame.

```
// Close the scope of the Members frame
setParent ..;
```

```
// Collapsible Current Layer frame
frameLayout
    -label "Current Layer"
    -labelAlign "bottom"
    -collapsable 1
    -collapse 1
    -borderStyle "etchedIn"
    ewc_frameCurrentLayer;
```

Scroll down to close the scope of the Current Layer frame with the
setParent command. Directly after that create a frameLayout for
the Options frame.

```
// Close the scope of the Current Layer frame
setParent ..;

// Collapsible Options frame
frameLayout
    -label "Options"
    -labelAlign "bottom"
    -collapsable 1
    -collapse 1
    -borderStyle "etchedIn"
    ewc_frameOptions;
```

Scroll down to close the scope of the Options frame:

```
// Close the scope of the Options frame
setParent ..;
```

Before running the script to see the new frames, the columnLayout
created at the beginning must be closed:

```
// Close the scope of the columnlayout
setParent ..;
// Close the scope of the Scroll Layout
```

Now the scrollLayout contains four collapsing frames that scale with
the window. If your script is not working and Maya is giving you
errors, you can open up the version provided on the companion disc
and compare it with yours. Layouts and setParent commands can
take a while for some people to understand, but if you step back and

Chapter 6

look through everything again a few more times, it all becomes quite logical.

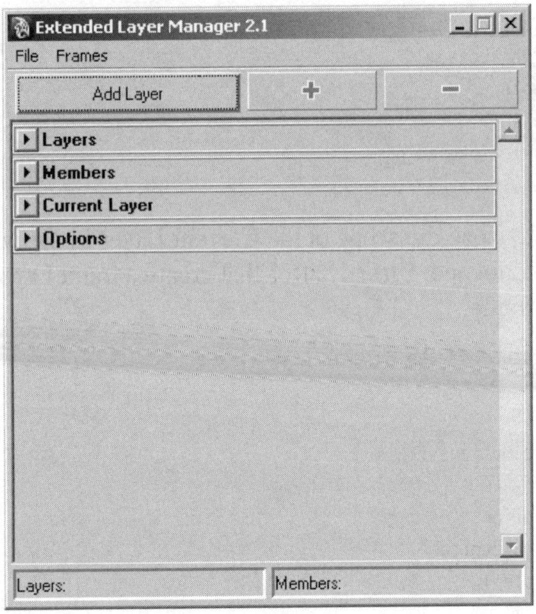

Figure 6-31: ewc_extendedLayer Manager_06.mel

6.3.10 Adding Controls to the Layers Frame

Now that the frames are defined we can start to include the controls necessary to select and edit the layers. First a columnLayout must be created to hold the formLayout. One flag is being called here.

- ■ **-adjustableColumn:** The children of the layout (in this case the formLayout) will be attached to both sides and scale in proportion with the parent.

```
// Form layout
columnLayout -adjustableColumn 1 ewc_colLayerControls;
```

Create a formLayout to hold the controls:

```
// Form layout
string $form2 = `formLayout ewc_formLayerControls`;
```

Close the scope of both layouts. You could consider the setParent command to be almost like a closing delimiter in a conditional statement when controlling the scope of a layout. The `setParent` commands shown in bold below are the ones that must be created.

```
    // Close the scope of the form layout
    setParent ..;

    // Collapsible Color frame
        // Layer color - color palette
    // Close the scope of the color frame

// Close the column layout
setParent ..;

// Close the scope of the layers frame
setParent ..;
```

Create the Layer List

Return to where the formLayout was created and create a textScrollList directly below it. Assign the textScrollList to a string variable called $tslLayer. The flags used are as follows:

- **-height**: Sets the height of the control.
- **-width**: Sets the width of the control.
- **-allowMultiSelection**: Allows a user to select multiple items in a list.
- **-annotation**: Prints a tooltip in the Maya Help line when the mouse is over the control.

```
// Text scroll list for layer names
string $tslLayer = `textScrollList
                -height 202
                -width 125
                -allowMultiSelection 1
                -annotation "Double-click to rename a layer. Del or
                Backspace to delete. RMB to refresh list."
                ewc_tslLayerList`;
```

I want to point out in the above example that the `-annotation` string is supposed to be all on one line. Line wrapping will occur from time to time for the rest of the chapter on other `-annotation`

Chapter 6

flags due to the page width restrictions of the book. If it must extend to more than one line, then it must be formatted like this:

```
-annotation ("Double-click to rename a layer. Del or "
+"Backspace to delete. RMB to refresh list.")
```

Locate the formLayout that was edited earlier for the main interface, and directly below that set up the formLayout for editing:

```
// Edit the layout of the layer controls
formLayout -edit
    $form2;
```

Once that has been defined, edit the position of the textScrollList:

```
// layer list
-af $tslLayer      "top"      2
-af $tslLayer      "left"     2
-af $tslLayer      "bottom"   5
$form2;
```

For each control or set of controls I will be editing the formLayout before moving on. Working like this I can run the script at its current state to check that each control is positioned properly before creating more.

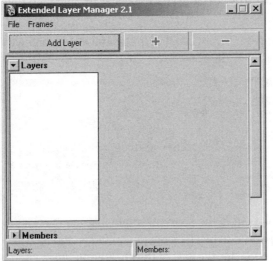

Figure 6-32

Creating the Drawing Controls

Continue adding the five check boxes and two option menus that will eventually be used to control the drawing states. These controls are created by using the `checkBox` and `optionMenu` commands. These commands share the same flags.

- **-label**: The name of the control that will be displayed to the user.

- **-changeCommand**: The command string executed when the state of the control has been changed.

- **-enable**: Enables/disables the control.

- **-annotation**: Prints a tooltip in the Maya Help line when the mouse is over the control.

```
// Enable override check box
string $cb1 = `checkBox
          -label "Enable"
          -changeCommand ""
          -enable 0
          -annotation "Enable/Disable all drawing overrides on
              current layer."
          ewc_cboxEnableToggle`;

// Shading check box
string $cb2 = `checkBox
          -label "Shading"
          -changeCommand ""
          -enable 0
          -annotation "Toggle shading on all members."
          ewc_cboxShadingToggle`;

// Texturing check box
string $cb3 = `checkBox
          -label "Texturing"
          -changeCommand ""
          -enable 0
          -annotation "Toggle texturing on all members."
          ewc_cboxTexturingToggle`;

// Playback check box
```

```
string $cb4 = `checkBox
        -label "Playback"
        -changeCommand ""
        -enable 0
        -annotation "Toggle playback on all members."
        ewc_cboxPlaybackToggle`;

// Visible check box
string $cb5 = `checkBox
        -label "Visible"
        -changeCommand ""
        -enable 0
        -annotation "Toggle visibility on all members."
        ewc_cboxVisibilityToggle`;
```

An option menu itself does not actually have a flag to hold items.
The menu items must be created using the `menuItem` command.
These do not use a `-command` flag. The `-changeCommand` flag of the
optionMenu is the command that calls the procedure that we will
write in section 6.4, "Creating the Functionality — Part I."

```
// Display Type option menu
string $opt1 = `optionMenu
            -label "Display Type"
            -enable 0
            -changeCommand ""
            -annotation "Set the Display Type."
            ewc_optmenDisplayType`;
                menuItem -label "Normal";
                menuItem -label "Template";
                menuItem -label "Reference";
                menuItem -divider 1;
                menuItem -label "Set to all...";
                menuItem -divider 1;
                menuItem -label "-Set Unselected-";
                menuItem -label "Normal";
                menuItem -label "Template";
                menuItem -label "Reference";

// Level of Detail option menu
string $opt2 = `optionMenu
            -label "Level of Detail"
```

```
        -enable 0
        -changeCommand ""
        -annotation "Set the Level of Detail."
        ewc_optmenLevelOfDetail`;
            menuItem -label "Full";
            menuItem -label "Bounding Box";
            menuItem -divider 1;
            menuItem -label "Set to all...";
            menuItem -divider 1 ;
            menuItem -label "-Set Unselected-";
            menuItem -label "Full";
            menuItem -label "Bounding Box";
```

Be sure to follow the example above exactly for the option menus. The procedures will be dependent on the order of the `menuItem` commands.

Now we need to position the newly created controls. When editing a formLayout, the order in which each control is positioned does not have to match the order in which they were created. After the first checkBox, referred to by `$cb1`, the two optionMenu controls are positioned before positioning the remaining checkBox controls.

```
// enable toggle
-af $cb1    "top"     2
-ac $cb1    "left"    83    $tslLayer

// display type
-ac $opt1   "top"     5     $cb1
-ac $opt1   "left"    17    $tslLayer

// level of detail
-ac $opt2   "top"     5     $opt1
-ac $opt2   "left"    10    $tslLayer

// shading toggle
-ac $cb2    "top"     5     $opt2
-ac $cb2    "left"    83    $tslLayer

// texturing toggle
-ac $cb3    "top"     5     $cb2
-ac $cb3    "left"    83    $tslLayer
```

```
// playback toggle
-ac $cb4     "top"      5     $cb3
-ac $cb4     "left"    83     $tslLayer

// visibility toggle
-ac $cb5     "top"      5     $cb4
-ac $cb5     "left"    83     $tslLayer

$form2;
```

Because of how the labeling occurs on the left side of an option menu, using the same offset values when editing the position won't work. The left edge that the formLayout reads is based on the first letter of the label, which explains why we use different values to position the option menus. (See Figure 6-33.) There is no real fancy trick when editing the placement; it literally boils down to trial and error and single-digit adjustments in offsets.

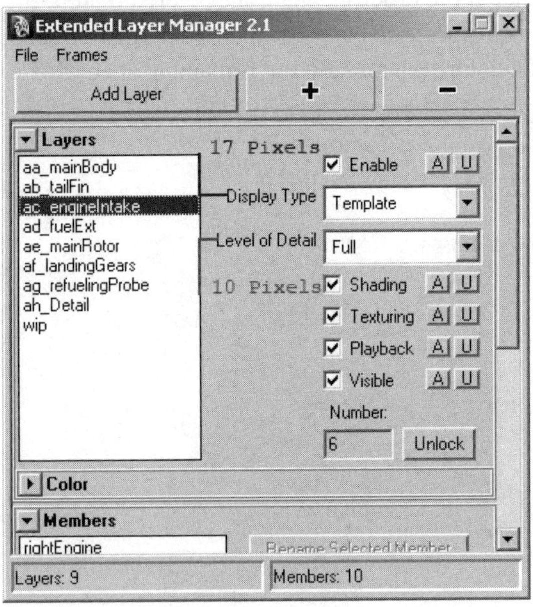

Figure 6-33

Run the script to see that the Layers frame is starting to look quite a bit like the Attribute Editor for a layer, with the obvious exception of the textScrollList.

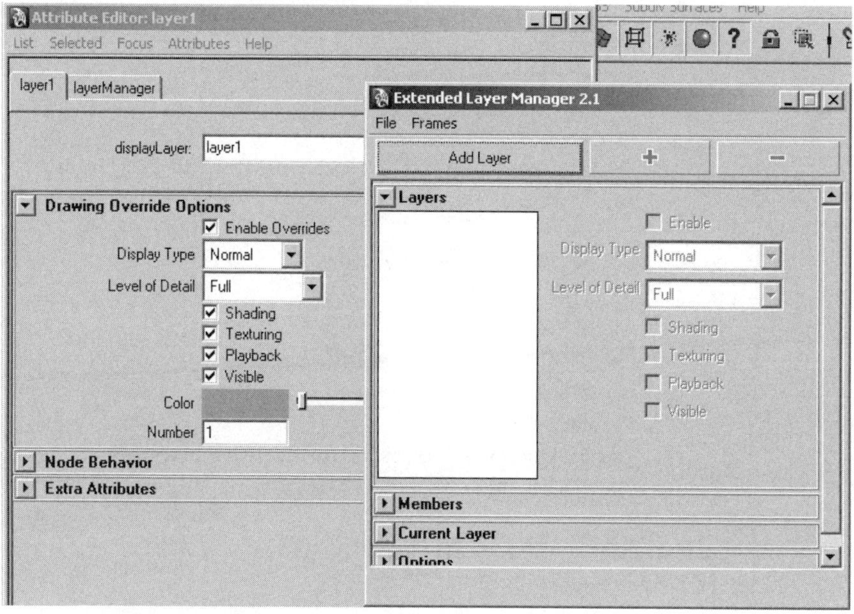

Figure 6-34: ewc_extendedLayerManager_07.mel

6.3.11 **Bonus Drawing Controls**

The first bonus feature of the layer manager is the set of controls that allow the user to send the current drawing state of a layer to all layers. A second set of controls allows the assignment of the opposite drawing state of a highlighted layer to those that are not highlighted in the textScrollList.

We add ten buttons in two columns to the right side of the check boxes that will be used for the bonus features. The labels of the buttons will be single letters only: A for the "apply to all" buttons and U for the "apply opposite to unselected" buttons. Doing this keeps everything compact in size. Utilizing the -annotation flag for every button will provide a way to communicate a more accurate

Chapter 6

description of the purpose of each button to a user through the Help
line.

```
// Current enable state to all
string $b4 = `button
        -label "A"
        -height 14
        -enable 0
        -command ""
        -annotation "Apply current override state to all layers."
        ewc_btnBonusDrawing1`;

// Opposite enable state to unselected
string $b5 = `button
        -label "U"
        -height 14
        -enable 0
        -command ""
        -annotation "Apply opposite to unselected layers."
        ewc_btnBonusDrawing2`;

// Current shading state to all
string $b6 = `button
        -label "A"
        -height 14
        -enable 0
        -command ""
        -annotation "Apply current shading state to all layers."
        ewc_btnBonusDrawing3`;

// Opposite shading state to unselected
string $b7 = `button
        -label "U"
        -height 14
        -enable 0
        -command ""
        -annotation "Apply opposite to unselected layers."
        ewc_btnBonusDrawing4`;

// Current texturing state to all
string $b8 = `button
        -label "A"
```

```
                -height 14
                -enable 0
                -command ""
                -annotation "Apply current texture state to all layers."
                ewc_btnBonusDrawing5`;

// Opposite texturing state to unselected
string $b9 = `button
                -label "U"
                -height 14
                -enable 0
                -command ""
                -annotation "Apply opposite to unselected layers."
                ewc_btnBonusDrawing6`;

// Current playback state to all
string $b10 = `button
                -label "A"
                -height 14
                -enable 0
                -command ""
                -annotation "Apply current playback state to all layers."
                ewc_btnBonusDrawing7`;

// Opposite playback state to unselected
string $b11 = `button
                -label "U"
                -height 14
                -enable 0
                -command ""
                -annotation "Apply opposite to unselected layers."
                ewc_btnBonusDrawing8`;

// Current visibility state to all
string $b12 = `button
                -label "A"
                -height 14
                -enable 0
                -command ""
                -annotation "Apply current visibility state to all layers."
                ewc_btnBonusDrawing9`;
```

Chapter 6

```
// Opposite visibility state to unselected
string $b13 = `button
        -label "U"
        -height 14
        -enable 0
        -command ""
        -annotation "Apply opposite to unselected layers."
        ewc_btnBonusDrawing10`;
```

Now edit the positions of the buttons:

```
// enable to all
-af $b4    "top"     2
-ac $b4    "left"    153   $tslLayer

// enable opposite to unselected
-af $b5    "top"     2
-ac $b5    "left"    2     $b4

// shading to all
-ac $b6    "top"     5     $opt2
-ac $b6    "left"    153   $tslLayer

// shading opposite to unselected
-ac $b7    "top"     5     $opt2
-ac $b7    "left"    2     $b6

// texturing to all
-ac $b8    "top"     5     $cb2
-ac $b8    "left"    153   $tslLayer

// texturing opposite to unselected
-ac $b9    "top"     5     $cb2
-ac $b9    "left"    2     $b8

// playback to all
-ac $b10   "top"     5     $cb3
-ac $b10   "left"    153   $tslLayer

// playback opposite to unselected
-ac $b11   "top"     5     $cb3
```

```
-ac $b11      "left"    2      $b10

// visibility to all
-ac $b12      "top"     5      $cb4
-ac $b12      "left"    153    $tslLayer

// visibility opposite to unselected
-ac $b13      "top"     5      $cb4
-ac $b13      "left"    2      $b12


$form2;
```

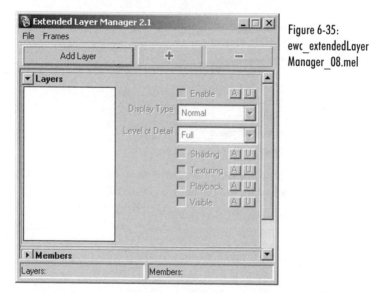

Figure 6-35:
ewc_extendedLayer
Manager_08.mel

6.3.12 Layer Identification Controls

The next three controls we add are a text control, an integer field, and a button. The text control is simply for labeling purposes. The only flag used is the -label flag.

```
// Layer identification field
string $txt1 = `text -label "Number:" ewc_txtLayerIdLabel`;
```

The integer field will hold the identification number of a highlighted layer. Since editing the identification attribute of a layer is not a common practice, the integer field will be disabled and, unlike the other controls, will not be enabled when a layer is highlighted.

- **-editable:** Determines whether the value is read-only or editable.

- **-value:** The initial value of the field. Must be at least equal to the value in the -minValue flag.

- **-minValue:** The lowest number that the field accepts. This is an early form of error checking. The layer identification only takes positive numbers. Setting this flag to a value of 1 will prevent users from entering a negative value.

- **-changeCommand:** Command executed when the value is changed.

```
string $intFld1 = `intField
            -editable 0
            -value 1
            -minValue 1
            -changeCommand ""
            ewc_fldLayerID`;
```

When the identification number needs to be edited, the integer field will be unlocked by the button we create next.

```
// Layer ID lock/unlock button
string $b14 = `button
            -label "Unlock"
            -width 50
            -enable 0
            -command ""
            -annotation "Lock/unlock layer number field."
            ewc_btnToggleLayerID`;
```

The button calls a -width flag. This is important because later on, when the button toggles the enable state of the integer field, the label of the button itself will be changed to reflect its purpose (i.e., lock or unlock). When the -width flag is not set, the button scales to fit the characters being held in the -label flag.

Figure 6-36

I want the button to retain a uniform width inside the interface at all times, like this:

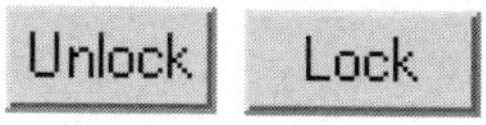

| Unlock | Lock | Figure 6-37

Edit the positions of the layer identification controls.

```
// layer id label
-ac $txt1      "top"      5      $cb5
-ac $txt1      "left"     87     $tslLayer

// integer field for layer id
-ac $intFld1   "top"      2      $txt1
-ac $intFld1   "left"     82     $tslLayer

// button to unlock/lock the id field
-ac $b14       "top"      2      $txt1
-ac $b14       "left"     5      $intFld1

$form2;
```

This will end the positioning of controls for the formLayout being stored in $form2.

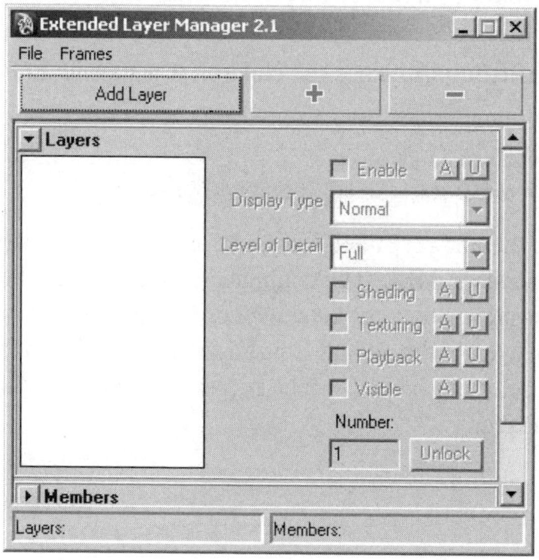

Figure 6-38:
ewc_extendedLayer
Manager_09.mel

Chapter 6

6.3.13 **Creating a Color Palette**

The last control we add to the Layers frame is a color palette for changing the wireframe color of one or more layers. A color palette is a fairly large control in comparison to check boxes and buttons. To keep the interface compact, I will nest another collapsible frame to hold the palette control.

Create a new frameLayout control. Since this control is after the `setParent` command for the formLayout and before the `setParent` command for the columnLayout, it will be nested within the Layers frame, and positioned directly under the controls contained within the previous formLayout.

```
// Collapsible Color frame
frameLayout
        -label "Color"
        -labelAlign "bottom"
        -collapsable 1
        -collapse 1
        -borderStyle "etchedIn"
        ewc_frameColor;
```

Another columnLayout must be added to hold the palettePort control.

■ **-columnAttach:** Attaches the children to a specific side with an offset.

```
// Column layout for color palette
columnLayout -columnAttach "left" 2 ewc_colColorPalette;
```

The flags for the `palettePort` command are unique compared to the other controls in MEL. The command creates a control that displays color swatches that can be selected. The palettePort is the same control used in the default Edit Layer dialog in Maya that changes the color of a layer. I will be recreating this exact control in the layer manager.

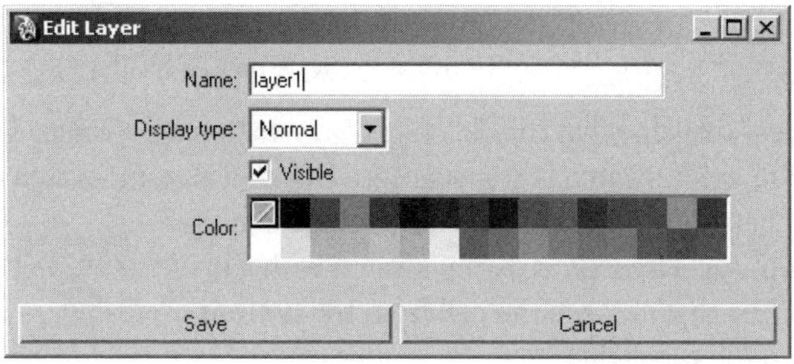

Figure 6-39

- **-dimensions:** This flag takes two integers; the first is the number of columns and the second is the number of rows. Since the palette contains 32 colors (cell count goes from 0 to 31), setting the value to 16 2 will create two rows of cells.

- **-actualTotal:** This flag must match the actual number of color cells that will be displayed in the palette.

- **-topDown:** This flag must be set to 1 for the cell count to start at the top-left corner cell; the default is the bottom-right corner if this flag is not edited.

- **-colorEditable:** Disables the editing for the color index through the palettePort.

- **-transparent:** This flag identifies which cell will be transparent.

```
// Layer color - color palette
palettePort
          -dimensions 16 2
          -width 320
          -height 40
          -actualTotal 32
          -topDown 1
          -colorEditable 0
          -transparent 0
          -enable 0
          -changeCommand ""
          ewc_palprtLayerColor;
```

Assign the transparent swatch to the transparent cell:

Chapter 6

```
//set the transparent swatch
palettePort -edit -rgb 0 0.6 0.6 0.6 ewc_palprtLayerColor;
```

To best explain what this is, open Maya and create a layer. The
default color swatch is transparent. The transparent swatch does
not change the wireframe color of objects in the
viewports. The icon is a gray swatch with a diagonal line that crosses the cell from the bottom
left to the top right.

 Figure 6-40

The −rgb flag take one integer value and three floats. The integer is the index number of the transparent swatch and the three
floats represent the RGB values. The index number for the transparent cell is 0, and it is being assigned 0.6 0.6 0.6, which returns
the transparent icon for the cell.

What needs to happen now is for the color palette to represent
the colorIndex in Maya. The colorIndex is actually a MEL command that can be used to query and edit the color palette in Maya.
There are a handful of flags available for this command, but we will
only be using colorIndex to query RGB values. The palette can
also be changed on a per-user basis using the colorIndex command, but that is beyond the scope of this chapter. To extract the
correct colors from the colorIndex, a loop statement will loop
through the colorIndex (which only holds 31 colors):

```
// loop the color palette and assign the color cells
// the appropriate RGB values from the color index.
for ($i = 1; $i < 32; $i++)
{
```

Query each color index for the RGB value and store the result in a
float array:

```
float $indexArray[] = `colorIndex -query $i`;
```

The individual elements of the array are called to edit the RGB
value of each cell to properly represent the colorIndex. The loop is
set with the initialization value at 1 ($i = 1). Doing this skips over
the first cell that is assigned to index 0, which is the transparent
value, leaving 31 cells corresponding to the 31 swatches of the
colorIndex.

```
palettePort -edit
    -rgb $i
    $indexArray[0]
    $indexArray[1]
    $indexArray[2]
    ewc_palprtLayerColor;
}
```

Since a columnLayout was used to hold the color palette, a setParent command will have to be added to close the layout:

```
// Close the scope of the column layout
setParent ..;
```

Close the frameLayout for the Color frame:

```
// Close the scope of the color frame
setParent ..;
```

There should now be four setParent commands closing all the layouts:

```
            // Close the scope of the column layout
            setParent ..;
        // Close the scope of the Color frame
        setParent ..;
    // Close the column layout
    setParent ..;
// Close the scope of the Layers frame
setParent ..;
```

There is a lot to digest here concerning interface scripting. The good news is that the Layers frame was the hardest part of the interface. If you hung on this far, you have done quite well and are more than ready to continue.

Chapter 6

241

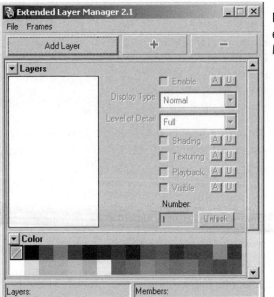

Figure 6-41:
ewc_extendedLayer
Manager_10.mel

6.3.14 **Adding Controls to the Members Frame**

Locate the `frameLayout` command for the Members frame.
Underneath it, create a formLayout to hold the controls:

```
// Form layout
string $form3 = `formLayout ewc_formMemberControls`;
```

Scroll down and close the formLayout:

```
    // Close the scope of the form layout
    setParent ..;
// Close the scope of the Members frame
```

The first control will be a textScrollList. This will use exactly the
same flags as the layer list created earlier. (Remember to keep the
annotation string on one line.)

```
// Text scroll list for members names
string $tslMember = `textScrollList
             -height 205
             -width 125
```

```
            -allowMultiSelection 1
            -annotation "Double-click to rename a member.
             Del or Backspace to remove member(s).
             RMB to refresh list."
            ewc_tslMemberList`;
```

Set up the formLayout for editing and position the textScrollList:

```
// Edit the layout of the member controls
formLayout -edit
    // member list
    -af $tslMember    "top"      2
    -af $tslMember    "left"     2
    -af $tslMember    "bottom"   5
    $form3;
```

Next create seven buttons and one check box:

```
// Rename highlighted button
string $b15 = `button
              -label "Rename Selected Member"
              -enable 0
              -command ""
              -width 150
              ewc_btnMemberEdit1`;

// Select all button
string $b16 = `button
              -label "Select All Members"
              -enable 0
              -command ""
              -width 150
              ewc_btnMemberEdit2`;

// Select highlighted button
string $b17 = `button
              -label "Select Highlighted"
              -enable 0
              -command ""
              -width 150
              ewc_btnMemberEdit3`;

// Remove highlighted button
```

Chapter 6

```
string $b18 = `button
            -label "Remove Highlighted Members"
            -enable 0
            -command ""
            -width 150
            ewc_btnMemberEdit4`;


// Remove all button
string $b19 = `button
            -label "Remove All Members"
            -enable 0
            -command ""
            -width 150
            ewc_btnMemberEdit5`;


// Member attributes button
string $b20 = `button
            -label "Member Attributes"
            -enable 0
            -command ""
            -width 150
            ewc_btnMemberEdit6`;


// Relationship Editor button
string $b21 = `button
            -label "Relationship Editor"
            -command ""
            -width 150
            ewc_btnRelationshipEditor`;


// Check box to toggle active selection of members
string $cb6 = `checkBox
            -label "Actively Select Members"
            -changeCommand ""
            -enable 0
            ewc_cboxActiveSelect`;
```

All buttons have had their –width flag set to 150. This will create a uniform display of the controls in the interface. The Relationship Editor button is enabled because this control does not depend on a list member to be highlighted. It simply opens the default Relationship Editor in Maya, which offers additional functionality.

The last step is to edit the positions of the controls.

```
// rename button
-af $b15     "top"     2
-ac $b15     "left"    15    $tslMember

// select all button
-ac $b16     "left"    15    $tslMember
-ac $b16     "top"     5     $b15

// select highlighted
-ac $b17     "left"    15    $tslMember
-ac $b17     "top"     5     $b16

// remove highlighted
-ac $b18     "left"    15    $tslMember
-ac $b18     "top"     5     $b17

// remove all
-ac $b19     "left"    15    $tslMember
-ac $b19     "top"     5     $b18

// member attributes
-ac $b20     "left"    15    $tslMember
-ac $b20     "top"     5     $b19

// toggle active selection
-ac $cb6     "left"    15    $tslMember
-ac $cb6     "top"     5     $b20

// relationship editor
-ac $b21     "left"    15    $tslMember
-ac $b21     "top"     5     $cb6

$form3;
```

This will complete the Members frame.

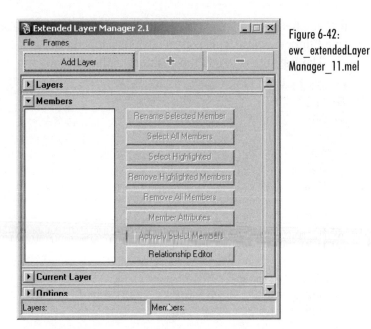

Figure 6-42:
ewc_extendedLayer
Manager_11.mel

6.3.15 **Adding Controls to the Current Layer Frame**

As with previous frames, a formLayout must be created first:

```
// Form layout
string $form4 = `formLayout ewc_formCurrentControls`;
```

Scroll down a few comments and add the command to close the formLayout:

```
    // Close the scope of the form layout
    setParent ..;
// Close the scope of the Current Layer frame
```

Only three controls will be created: a text control and two buttons. The text control will be used in section 6.4 to hold the name of the current layer in a scene.

```
// Text control to display name of current layer
string $txt2 = `text -label "Current: " ewc_txtCurrentLayer`;
```

```
// Assign button to assign the highlighted layer as current
string $btn22 = `button
            -label "Set Current"
            -command ""
            -enable 0
            -width 75
            ewc_btnSetCurrentLayer`;

// Reset button to set defaultLayer as current
string $btn23 = `button
            -label "Reset Default"
            -command ""
            -width 75
            ewc_btnResetDefaultLayer`;
```

Edit the position of the controls:

```
// Edit layout for Current Layer frame
formLayout -edit
    // text label for displaying current layer
    -af $txt2    "top"     2
    -af $txt2    "left"    5
    -af $txt2    "bottom"  2

    // set current layer button
    -af $btn22   "top"     2
    -af $btn22   "left"    150
    -af $btn22   "bottom"  5

    // reset current layer button
    -af $btn23   "top"     2
    -ac $btn23   "left"    5      $btn22
    -af $btn23   "bottom"  5

    $form4;
```

The Reset Default button is enabled (unlike most of the controls) because no highlighted item is required in either of the text lists to reset to the defaultLayer (this layer exists by default in all scenes).

Figure 6-43:
ewc_extendedLayer
Manager_12.mel

6.3.16 Adding Controls to the Options Frame

This frame holds several options that the user can change to modify
the behavior of the layer manager. We create four controls: a text
control, a text field, and two check boxes. A nested frame will hold a
text control that will contain general information about the layer
manager.

Create a columnLayout with the -adjustableColumn flag:

```
// options columnLayout
columnLayout -adjustableColumn 1 ewc_colOptionsColumn;
```

Create a formLayout to hold the controls:

```
// options formLayout
string $form5 = `formLayout ewc_formOptionControls`;
```

Create the four controls for the user options:

```
// Text control for labeling purposes
string $txt3 = `text -label "Default Layer Name:" ewc_txtDefLayerName`;

// Input field for default layer naming
string $txtFld1 = `textField
            -width 100
            ewc_fldDefaultLayerName`;

// Check box to toggle selected objects added to the new layer
string $cb7 = `checkBox
            -label "Add Selected to New Layer"
            ewc_cboxAddSelected`;

// Check box to toggle the input prompt for naming a new layer
string $cb8 = `checkBox
            -label "Input Prompt for New Layers"
            ewc_cboxInputPrompt`;
```

Close the formLayout before creating the nested frame:

```
// Close the scope of the form layout
setParent ..;
```

The next control to create is a frameLayout, which is nested inside the Options frame:

```
// Collapsible About frame
frameLayout
        -label "About..."
        -labelAlign "bottom"
        -collapsable 1
        -collapse 1
        -borderStyle "etchedIn"
        ewc_frameAbout;
```

Create a scrollLayout that will be nested inside of the About... frame:

```
// Scroll layout for about info
scrollLayout -horizontalScrollBarThickness 0 -height 100
        ewc_scrollAboutInfo;
```

Last is the text control that holds general information. You may write whatever you want or just copy this block from the completed script on the companion disc. This is a prime example of concatenation of a single string spanning multiple lines. I highly suggest taking the time and trying this with either the information below or your own.

```
// text control to display general info
text -label
("About Extended Layer Manager v2.1.0\n"
    +"Author: Ed Caspersen\n"
    +"Contact: ed.caspersen (at) gmail dot com\n"
    +"==================================================\n"
    +"\n"
    +"Version 2.1: This release revolved heavily around the\n"
    +"redesign of the interface. All the pop-up windows have\n"
    +"been removed and packed into collapsable frames all under\n"
    +"one interface to reduce screen clutter.\n"
    +"\n"
```

Chapter 6

```
+"The Options frame will reset each time this script is run.\n"
+"To permanently change the default state you will need to\n"
+"edit the global variables, which are found at the top of\n"
+"the script before the procedures, after editing resource\n"
+"the script using the command:\n"
+"source \"ewc_extendedLayerManager.mel\";\n"
+"\n"
+"Any and all feedback is welcome to improve future releases\n"
+"of this script.\n") ewc_txtAboutDetails;
```

Two more layouts have been created (frameLayout and scrollLayout) and they need to be closed, as well as the columnLayout, before running the script. The `setParent` commands shown in bold below are the commands that must be added.

```
        // Close the scope of the About scroll layout
        setParent ..;
    // Close the scope of the About frame
    setParent ..;
// Close the scope of the columnLayout
setParent ..;
// Close the scope of the Options frame
setParent ..;
```

Set up the formLayout for editing and position the controls:

```
formLayout -edit
// label
-af $txt3        "top"     2
-af $txt3        "left"    5

// default layer name
-ac $txtFld1     "top"     2      $txt3
-af $txtFld1     "left"    5

// add selected toggle
-af $cb7         "top"     2
-af $cb7         "left"    150

// input toggle
-ac $cb8         "top"     5      $cb7
-af $cb8         "left"    150
```

```
$form5;
```

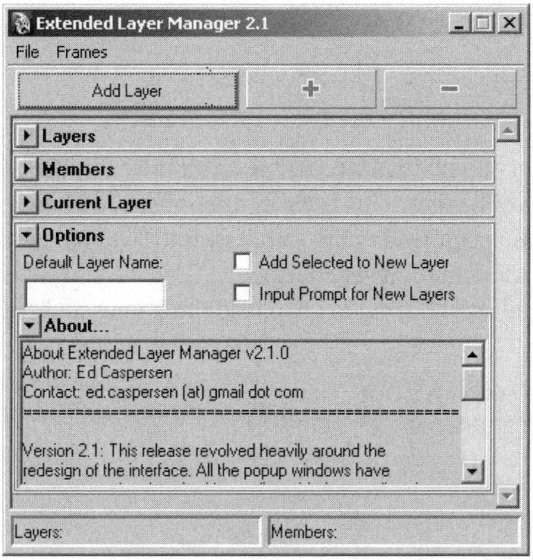

Figure 6-44:
ewc_extendedLayer
Manager_13.mel

6.3.17 **Pop-up Menus**

The last features I want to add are several pop-up menus. I want a
pop-up menu for each textScrollList to refresh the lists. The third is
a pop-up menu that can be accessed within the main scrollLayout
and contains exactly the same options as the Frames menu.

Start with the layer list and create a popupMenu:

```
ewc_tslLayerList˜;
// refresh popup menu
popupMenu -parent ewc_tslLayerList;
    menuItem
            -label "Refresh"
            -command "";
```

> **Tip:** Most editors have an option to find a specific string of text. Using the string
> "ewc_tslLayerList" in the search will save you a lot of time.

Next, locate the member list and add a popupMenu:

```
ewc_tslMemberList˜;
// refresh popup menu
popupMenu -parent ewc_tslMemberList;
    menuItem
            -label "Refresh"
            -command "";
```

I want the last pop-up to be accessible on all the collapsible frames within the scrollLayout. This is easily accomplished by parenting the popupMenu command to the scrollLayout. The pop-up will be inherited by the frameLayout controls.

Locate the scrollLayout used to hold the frames and create a popupMenu:

```
ewc_scrollFrameHolder˜;
// frame display popup menu
popupMenu -parent ewc_scrollFrameHolder;
    menuItem
            -label "Reset Frames"
            -command "";
    menuItem
            -label "Members Frame"
            -command "";
    menuItem
            -label "Expand Frames"
            -command "";
    menuItem
            -label "Collapse Frames"
            -command "";
    menuItem -divider 1;
    menuItem
            -label "About..."
            -command "";
```

Now a right-click pop-up menu is available on all the frames and text lists.

If you are getting errors or your pop-up menus are not accessible, you can check the finished version of the script up to this point on the companion disc (ewc_extendedLayerManager_14.mel) and compare it with your script.

6.4 **Creating the Functionality — Part I**

In this section we cover the procedures used to define the functionality of the main controls for layer management and editing.

- User options
- Creating a new layer
- Populating the layers list
- Enabling and updating the controls
- Populating the members list
- Layer drawing states using check boxes
- Layer drawing states using option menus
- Layer identification (working with connected attributes)
- Editing layers (renaming, deleting)

None of these procedures were written to save space or time. I am aware that some people who are new to MEL may be overwhelmed by the amount of material in this section and the next one (6.5, "Creating the Functionality — Part II"). I have taken care to break up long procedures into smaller blocks to address each one individually. The comments in this book are the same as those found in the scripts on the companion disc. These are not just for show-and-tell. I encourage you to include them in your own scripts so you become more attuned to commenting.

Blindly entering commands into your editor is not the best way to learn programming. Comments help you talk yourself through every step to clearly define every step of every procedure. The two most effective methods of learning are through commenting and repetition.

6.4.1 **Why Switches?**

One thing people often notice about my code is the heavy use of switch statements. In the first section I discussed the differences between switch statements and case statements. Now let me explain why I favor switch statements.

First off, I lean toward switch statements when blocks of code will be associated with the controls of an interface. Think of light switches or toggle switches; these are all real-world controls, and like the buttons or check boxes in an interface, they will only perform a specific number of predefined tasks, similar to case statements. The comparison I make is that the UI elements (buttons, check boxes, etc.) are my virtual switches and therefore I prefer controlling them through a switch statement.

The second reason I prefer switch statements is that I try to avoid using delimiters ({}) unless absolutely necessary because, quite frankly, delimiters annoy me sometimes. Using a switch statement requires only one set of delimiters. If these statements were to be written as if statements and else if conditions, then there would need to be five to eight sets of delimiters (10 to 16 curly brackets).

However, if I have to query anything or evaluate user input, then I prefer an if statement, even if I query an attribute that only returns two possible values (a Boolean). As you will see, my switch statements are written when a predefined argument is being passed from a control, not when there is any querying taking place.

I truly don't think that either way is better; it's just a matter of personal choice. I think that most people prefer if statements because they learn those way before switch statements (I know I did). Then, by the time they learn switch statements, they have become totally indoctrinated by the way of the "if". I forced myself to sit down and really use switch statements. In doing so, I have really grown quite fond of them and found them extremely useful in writing clean blocks of code.

I know that there are people out there who will initially not be comfortable with the idea of using switch statements. I ask that you keep an open mind to what I am about to show you. Maybe you too will in the end be persuaded to come over to the switch side.

6.4.2 **Procedures for User Options**

The first two procedures that we write will contain values for the controls contained within the Options frame and the check box control inside the Members frame.

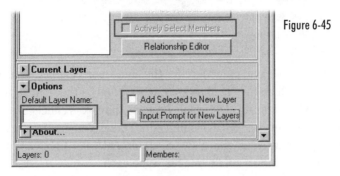

Figure 6-45

These controls were created without initial values. These are options a user can modify while the script is running to alter the behavior of several of the features. The values held in these procedures are default values that the controls will reset themselves to each time the script is run.

The values exist inside the procedures, and not as arguments for the controls, to allow a user to open the script and easily locate and edit the default values. This is much easier than going back through the interface procedure (from section 6.3) and editing flags every time a value needs to be changed.

Creating ewc_gprocDefaultLayerName

Place your cursor at the very first line in the script and hit Enter a few times to add some space between the interface procedure and the top of the script. Placing procedures at the very top makes them easier for a user to locate and edit. The first procedure holds the string for the default layer name. When this procedure is called, it will return the string "layer1" to a control (in this case the text field in the Options frame) to be used as an argument for the -text flag.

Chapter 6

```
//===========================
// USER OPTION PROCEDURES
// Function that holds the default layer name
global proc string ewc_gprocDefaultLayerName()
{    // To edit the default layer naming convention
     // simply change the text below, make sure that
     // you keep the name in quotes so it works properly
     return "layer1";
}    // End ewc_gprocDefaultLayerName()
```

Create the second procedure for the check box defaults. The defaults will be the checked state (controlled by the -value flag) of a checkBox control. The value 1 means the box is checked; a value of 0 means unchecked. This procedure takes one integer argument. This procedure contains a switch statement with three case statements returning a single integer value each.

```
// Function that returns the values to be used
// as defaults for the checkBox controls in the
// Options and Members frames. These values will
// determine whether or not the check boxes are
// checked when the script is run.
global proc int ewc_gprocDefaultToggleStates(int $case)
{
    switch($case)
    {
        case 1: // Active selection (Members frame)
            return 0;
            break;
        case 2: // Add selected to new layer toggle
            return 1;
            break;
        case 3: // Input prompt for new layer name
            return 1;
            break;
    }
}    // End ewc_gprocDefaultToggleStates()
```

Since these procedures return values (and should hence strictly speaking be called functions), remember to include a data type when declaring the arguments.

Assigning Procedures to the Controls

In order for these procedures to perform the way I intend, they will need to be inserted as arguments in the correct controls. When using a procedure with a return function, the procedure name *must* be inside parentheses in order for it to work.

Locate the textField control in the Options frame and add a -text flag. For the argument, use the ewc_gprocDefault-LayerName() function enclosed in parentheses:

```
// Input field for default layer naming
string $txtFld1 = `textField
            -width 100
            -text (ewc_gprocDefaultLayerName())
            ewc_fldDefaultLayerName`;
```

Just below the textField, locate the check box controls. Add a -value flag to each and assign the corresponding functions and arguments (2 and 3):

```
// Check box to toggle selected objects added to the new layer
string $cb7 = `checkBox
            -label "Add Selected to New Layer"
            -value (ewc_gprocDefaultToggleStates(2))
            ewc_cboxAddSelected`;
// Check box to toggle the input prompt for naming a new layer
string $cb8 = `checkBox
            -label "Input Prompt for New Layers"
            -value (ewc_gprocDefaultToggleStates(3))
            ewc_cboxInputPrompt`;
```

Locate the Actively Select Members check box in the Members frame. Add a -value flag with the correct function, passing the argument of 1:

```
// Check box to toggle active selection of members
string $cb6 = `checkBox
            -label "Actively Select Members"
            -changeCommand ""
            -enable 0
            -value (ewc_gprocDefaultToggleStates(1))
            ewc_memberEditOption7`;
```

Now when the script runs, the check boxes will call the function and pass it an integer argument. The function then evaluates the argument using a switch statement. The case statement that matches the argument will return the correct value to the check box. The check box for Actively Select Members has been disabled by default so the value won't initially be visible, but it is working.

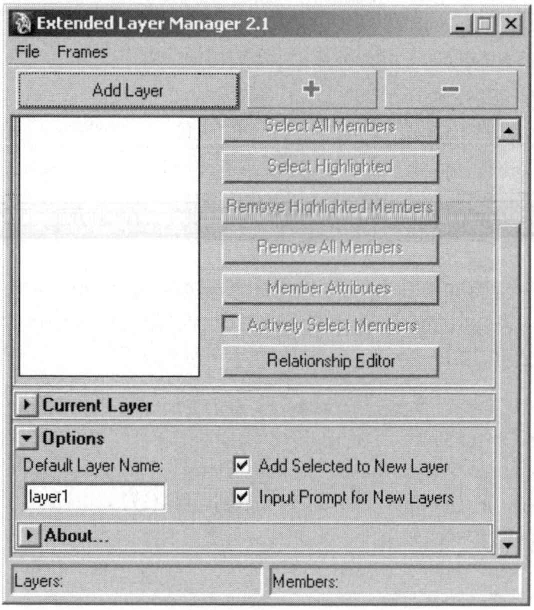

Figure 6-46:
ewc_extendedLayer
Manager_15.mel

Isn't This the Hard Way?

You may wonder why I didn't just use global variables. In my workflow, I try to avoid global variables wherever possible. The reason for this is that the data being held in a global variable can be replaced at any time from anywhere in Maya. Global variables are like that in any language, not just MEL.

A Word about Global Variables

Global variables are useful, and sometimes (in MEL at least) they're your only option. The main reason global variables are less desirable is because they make the code harder to understand and debug. Any piece of code anywhere in Maya can potentially change a global variable's value or influence its behavior. This can make it tricky to figure out what chunk of code is doing what. As such, it's generally a good idea to limit their use. Ideally, functions/procedures should be small and simple, layered, and built on other procedures, *not* relying on global variables. This keeps everything more localized. But it doesn't always work out that way in practice.

When I use global variables I try to keep them in the same file as the code that manipulates/requires them (when I'm writing something that spans multiple files). Avoiding duplication is always nice, so if you need to change the value, then it's only in one place. This way you can't forget to change it elsewhere and get out of sync.

Naming Convention for Global Variables

MEL has no concept of namespaces like some other languages, so all global variables and global procedures share the same namespace. This means they can stamp over each other if you're not careful about how you name things. As such, it is a very good idea to prefix global variables and stick with that convention.

I normally use a "g" (for global) as a prefix:

```
global float $gAnnoMinSize;
global float $gAnnoLockTolerance;
```

This way you can immediately recognize a global variable without having to trace through the code.

Another common convention is to group all the global variables together at the top of the file so you can see them all in one place without hunting through the code to find them.

The Global Variable Twilight Zone

Let's demonstrate the issue with a default global variable called $gMainWindow:

```
print $gMainWindow;
MayaWindow
```

As you probably guessed $gMainWindow is the name assigned to the main window of the Maya interface that other interface elements are parented under. To demonstrate the potential problem, I will assign a new string called WrongName to $gMainWindow:

Chapter 6

```
$gMainWindow = "WrongName";
// Result: WrongName //
```

I have now assigned a new string to a global variable that is used by many UI controls in Maya. Currently my menu panel is set to Polygons.

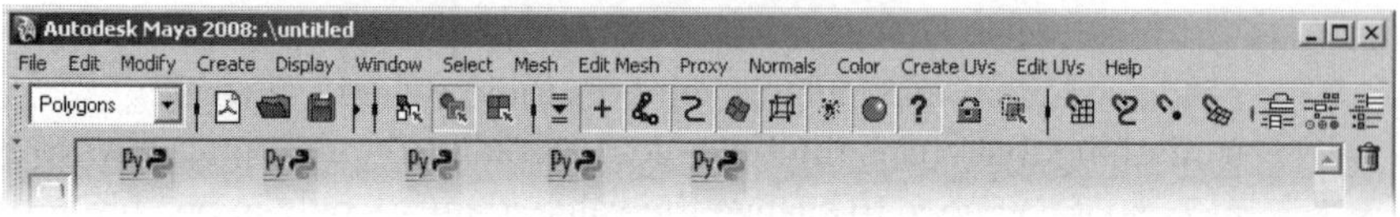

Figure 6-47

If I try to change it to Animation, not only will I get an error but the menus for the Animation module do not load.

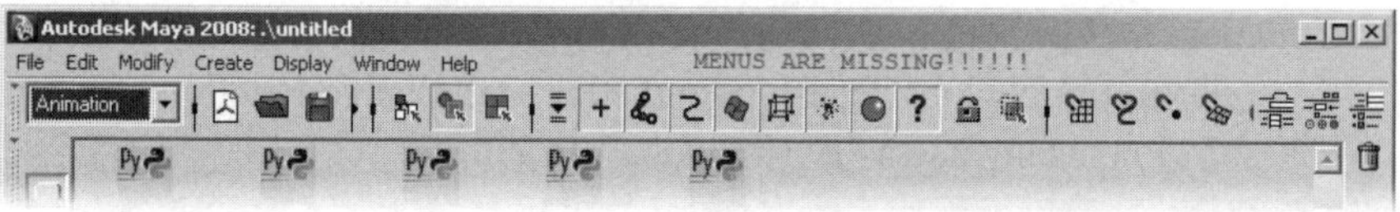

Figure 6-48

```
// Error: file: C:/Program Files/Autodesk/Maya2008/scripts/startup/
initMainMenuBar.mel line 251: Object not found: WrongName //
```

A possible workaround for this specific issue would be to hold the string MayaWindow in a procedure to be passed as a return value:

```
global proc string gMainWindow()
{
return "MayaWindow";
}
```

Needless to say, when using Maya's global variables you have to be very careful that you don't change their values unless you know exactly what you're doing. That means you need to read and understand the MEL that uses that variable.

6.4.3 **Creating a New Layer:**
ewc_gprocCreateLayer()

This procedure will do more than just create a new layer. First of all, it will check that the name entered doesn't already exist. It will also check that the name is valid; this means the name starts with a letter, and the remaining characters are any combination of letters, numbers, or underscores with no white space. This procedure will take one integer argument.

Pseudocoding the Procedure

A new procedure must be created below the interface procedure. What we want is two case statements with the values of 1 and 2.

```
//============================
// CREATE A NEW LAYER
global proc ewc_gprocCreateLayer(int $case)
{
    switch ($case)
    {
        case 1: // Create a new layer
            break;
        case 2: // Create a layer with default name
            break;
    } // End switch
} // End ewc_gprocCreateLayer()
```

Case 1: Create a New Layer

The first step is to pseudocode the entire block in case 1. Not only is this a recommended workflow, but the pseudocode will serve as a road map for you to follow along with. Due to page width limitations in this book, the proper indentation is not reflected correctly in the following samples. On the companion disc is a file named ewc_extendedLayerManager_16_pseudo.mel that is indented correctly.

Chapter 6

```
case 1: // Create a new layer
    // Query if the input prompt toggle is checked
        // Toggle is checked, open a prompt
            // If the Create button was pressed
                // If the $name variable isn't empty
                // Test if name is valid
                    // Make sure the name is not already in use
                        // If the name is in use warn the user
                            // User has elected to try again
                        // Query the add selected toggle
                        // Create the layer with the user-defined name
                        // and add the selected objects to the layer
                        // The query returns 0
                        // Create the layer with the user-defined name
                        // and leave the layer empty
                    // Name is invalid, warn the user
                // User has elected to try again
            // No name was entered, create layer with default name
    // If input prompt is toggled off
    break;
```

To begin, query the toggle state of the Input Prompt for New Layers check box from the Options frame. Remember to enclose the query in back quotes.

```
// Query if the input prompt toggle is checked
if (`checkBox -query -value ewc_cboxInputPrompt`)
{
```

If the query returns true, open an input prompt to name the new layer:

```
// Toggle is checked, open a prompt
string $result = `promptDialog
                -title          "Create New Layer"
                -message        "New layer name:"
                -button         "Create"
                -button         "Cancel"
                -defaultButton  "Create"
                -cancelButton   "Cancel"
                -dismissString  "Cancel"`;
```

The `$result` variable will store a string of the button that is pressed. The next if statement tests whether or not the Create button was pressed. If this was the case, then store the user input into a variable called `$name`. Then test that the variable `$name` is not empty.

```
// If the Create button was pressed
if ($result == "Create")
{
    string $name = `promptDialog -query -text`;
    // If the $name variable isn't empty
    if ($name != "")
    {
```

Test that the name is valid using the `isValidObjectName` command. This command tests a string to ensure that it is a valid object name. This means that the name begins with a letter and is followed by any combination of letters, numbers, and underscores and does not contain any white space.

```
// Test if name is valid
if (isValidObjectName ($name))
{
```

The `isValidObjectName` command performs a test on a variable enclosed in parentheses. When written like this, no back quotes are required:

```
command(argument)
```

Alternatively, it could be written like this and still work the same:

```
if (`isValidObjectName $name`)
```

When using commands that are directly testing variables and not using flags, I prefer to write the argument in parentheses and omit the back quotes.

If the test returns true, check that the name isn't already assigned to another node by using the `objExists` command, which only returns true if the name is in use. If the name is in use, warn the user with a prompt.

```
// Make sure the name is not already in use
```

```
if (objExists($name))
   {
   // If the name is in use warn the user
   string $confirm = `confirmDialog
                  -title "Warning"
                  -message "Name is not unique. Try again?"
                  -button "OK"
                  -button "Cancel"
                  -defaultButton "OK"
                  -cancelButton "Cancel"
                  -dismissString "Cancel"`;
```

If the user clicks the OK button, then recall the procedure passing an argument of 1. This will start the input prompt all over again.

```
If ($confirm    "OK")
   // User has elected to try again
   ewc_gprocCreateLayer(1);
}
```

If the name isn't in use, create the layer using the name entered into the input prompt. The first if statement tests the value of the Add Selected to New Layer check box. If it returns true (the check box is checked), then create the layer with the selected objects added. Two flags are being called when creating this layer:

- **-name**: Assign a name to the new layer. In this case, that's the name being held in the string variable called $name.

- **-noRecurse**: If set, then only add selected objects to the display layer. Otherwise, all descendants of the selected objects will also be added. This flag takes no arguments.

```
else
   {
   // Query the add selected toggle
   if (`checkBox -query -value ewc_cboxAddSelected`)
      // Create the layer with the user-defined name
      // and add the selected objects to the layer
      createDisplayLayer -name $name -noRecurse;
```

If the Add Selected to New Layer check box query returns false, the layer is still created with the name the user entered but without the selected objects, leaving the layer empty.

- **-name:** Assign a name to the new layer. In this case, that's the name being held in the string variable called $name.

- **-empty:** Creates an empty layer. Ignores selections made in the viewport. This flag takes no arguments.

```
// The query returns 0
else
    // Create the layer with the user-defined name
    // and leave the layer empty
    createDisplayLayer -name $name -empty;
}
```

If the isValidObjectName command returns false, a dialog will open that warns the user that the name is invalid and gives the option to start over or cancel.

```
}
else
    {
    // Name is invalid, warn the user
    string $confirm = `confirmDialog
                -title "Warning"
                -message
                    ("The name \"" + $name + "\" is invalid."
                    +"Valid names only contain alphanumeric\n"
                    +"characters. The name may not start "
                    +"with a digit.\n"
                    + "Whitespace characters are not allowed.")
                -button "OK"
                -button "Cancel"
                -defaultButton "OK"
                -cancelButton "Cancel"
                -dismissString "Cancel"`;
```

Pay close attention to the -message flag; there is a lot of concatenation taking place. The $name variable is being concatenated on the first line. To include quotes in a string, they must be escaped using \". Inserting \n creates a new line for the following characters.

The confirmDialog that was just created will look similar to the warning prompt that appears when an invalid name is entered when renaming a layer through Maya's default layering workflow.

Chapter 6

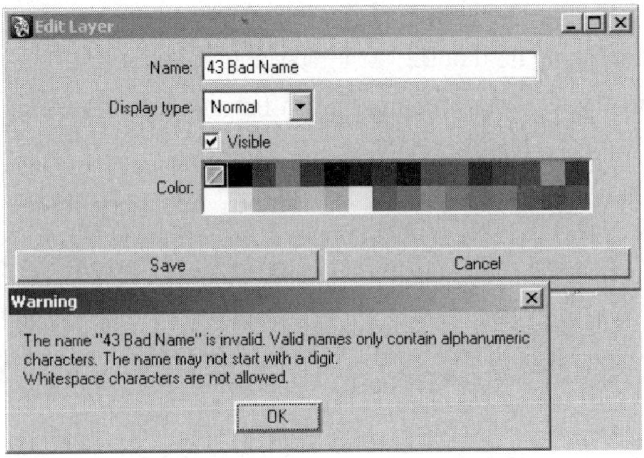

Figure 6-49

Here an invalid name is entered into the input prompt that was created in the beginning of case 1.

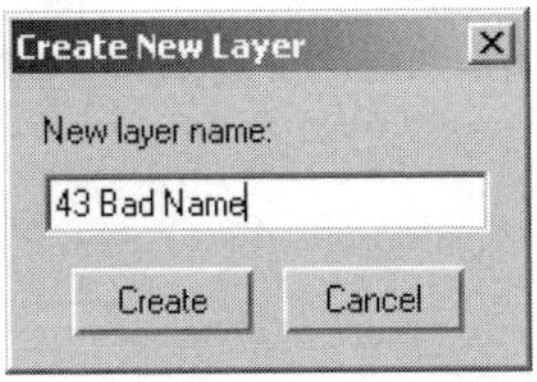

Figure 6-50

The confirmDialog that was just created reflects the default dialog from Maya, with the additional option for a user to cancel the entire operation.

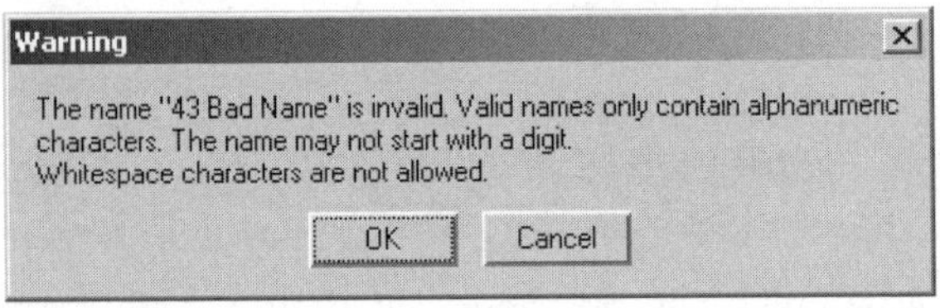

Figure 6-51

Returning to the procedure, if the user clicks OK, call the procedure with an argument of 1 to start the input prompt over again.

```
if ($c == "OK")
    // User has elected to try again
    ewc_gprocCreateLayer(1);
}
```

If a name was not entered ($name was left blank), then the second case statement is called by passing an argument of 2, which will create a layer with the default naming convention.

```
// No name was entered, create layer with default name
}
else
    ewc_gprocCreateLayer(2);
```

At the very beginning of case 1 was the if statement to query the value of the Input Prompt for New Layers check box:

```
// Query if the input prompt toggle is checked
if (`checkBox -query -value ewc_cboxInputPrompt`)
{
```

The first curly bracket above the comment is necessary to close the scope of the if statement that verifies whether the Create button was pressed when creating a new layer. The next else statement is the condition that the previous if statement will jump to if the Input Prompt for New Layers check box query returns false.

```
    }
// If input prompt is toggled off
}
else
    ewc_gprocCreateLayer(2);
break;
```

Case 2: Create a Layer with the Default Name

The next block will create a layer using the default naming convention.

```
case 2: // Create a layer with default name
    // If add selected is toggled on
        // Create a layer with default name
        // add selected objects to the layer
    // If add selected is toggled off
        // Create a layer with default name and leave it empty
break;
```

Query the Add Selected to New Layer check box to obtain its current state. If the state is true (checked), create the layer with the

default layer name and add the selected objects by adding the
-noRecurse flag. The argument for the -name flag is querying the
textField directly. This is a shortcut and only works when the query
is surrounded by back quotes.

```
// If add selected is toggled on
if (`checkBox -query -value ewc_cboxAddSelected`)
    // Create a layer with default name
    // add selected objects to the layer
    createDisplayLayer
        -name (`textField -query -text ewc_fldDefaultLayerName`)
        -noRecurse;
```

If the query returns false (unchecked), create a layer with the
default layer name, excluding the selected objects with the -empty
flag.

```
// If add selected is toggled off
else
    // Create a layer with default name and leave it empty
    createDisplayLayer
        -name (`textField -query -text ewc_fldDefaultLayerName`)
        -empty;
break;
```

Even though the createDisplayLayer command extends over
more than one line, it is still one command and it reads as one line of
code. Delimiters are not required.

Locate the Add Layer menuItem for the File menu and edit the
-command flag.

```
// Menu Item: Add Layer
menuItem
    -label "Add Layer"
    -command "ewc_gprocCreateLayer(1)";
```

Locate the command that creates the Add Layer button at the top of
the interface and edit the -command flag.

```
string $b1 = `button
    -command "ewc_gprocCreateLayer(1)"
    ewc_btnCreateNewLayer`;
```

You may want to refer to the ewc_extendedLayerManager_16.mel file on the companion disc to view the finished script with the proper indentation.

6.4.4 Populating the Layer List: ewc_gprocLoadCurrentLayers()

The layer manager can now create layers, but nothing is being displayed in the layer list. A procedure must be set up to query the layers in a scene and load them into the textScrollList. This same procedure will be called from the interface procedure when the script is run. It can also be called from the Refresh Layer List menuItem in the File menu, and from the pop-up menu assigned to the layer textScrollList. This procedure will not take any arguments.

Start with the pseudocode to outline the flow of the procedure:

```
//=========================
// PROCEDURE TO LOAD THE LAYERS
global proc ewc_gprocLoadCurrentLayers()
{
    // Query the layers in a scene
    // Create an array to hold defaultLayer
    // Remove defaultLayer from the array
    // Alphabetically sort the array
    // Get the total count of items currently in the list
    // If the list isn't empty, clear it
    // Loop through the array and add each item to the list
        // Attach commands to each item
    // Update the custom help line
} // End ewc_gprocLoadCurrentLayers()
```

First, an array must be created that holds the names of the layers in the scene. Use the `ls` command (enclosed in back quotes) with the `-exactType` flag. The arguments string is `displayLayer`, which queries all the nodes that match the specified type and creates an array called `$allLayers`.

```
// Query the layers in a scene
string    $allLayers[] = `ls -exactType "displayLayer"`;
```

Another array needs to be created. This array will be declared with the string defaultLayer.

```
// Create an array to hold defaultLayer
string    $defaultLayer[] = {"defaultLayer"};
```

The defaultLayer exists in all scenes. This layer cannot be edited and isn't even accessible in the default layer editor in Maya. The next step is to remove the defaultLayer from the $allLayers array. The stringArrayRemove command will test the two arrays. Any strings in $allLayers that match any of the strings in $defaultLayer will be removed. The result is stored in a new array.

```
// Remove defaultLayer from the array
string    $layers[] = stringArrayRemove($defaultLayer, $allLayers);
```

I want the layers to be listed alphabetically in the layer list. This means the array must be sorted before the elements are individually assigned to the layer list.

```
// Alphabetically sort the array
sort($layers);
```

The next step is crucial. A textScrollList does not automatically clear itself when it refreshes. If this procedure were being called to refresh the list, it would add the layers to the existing names (even if they are matching), displaying duplicates in the list. The thing to do is edit the textScrollList using the -removeAll flag, which removes all the items.

```
// Clear the textScrollList of all items
textScrollList -edit -removeAll ewc_tslLayerList;
```

An array has been created without the defaultLayer and is alphabetically sorted. Now a loop will iterate through each element and append it to the textScrollList.

Iterations

■ The loop starts the count at 0. This value is stored in a variable called $i.

■ It will cycle while the count ($i) is less than the actual size of the array. Array elements start their count at 0. The size command starts the count at 1. What will happen is that if an array has five elements, the actual count of the elements goes from 0 to 4 ($layers[0], $layers[1], and so on). The size command will return 5. This iteration will cover all elements in the array because the actual element ID will end at 4, even though it is the fifth element. (It's normal if images of Milla Jovovich pop in your head now.)

■ The $i++ will add a value of 1 each time the loop iterates.

```
// Loop through the array and add each item to the list
for ($i = 0; $i < size($layers); $i++)
{
```

The textScrollList appends each element of the array using the –append flag on each iteration of the loop. Three new flags are attached to the list items.

■ **-doubleClickCommand**: Executes a command string when the textScrollList is double-clicked.

■ **-deleteKeyCommand**: Executes a command string when the Delete or Backspace keys are pressed.

■ **-selectCommand**: Executes a command string when an item is clicked in the textScrollList.

Right now the command strings will be left empty until the procedures are written.

```
textScrollList
    -edit
    -append $layers[$i]
    // Attach commands to each item
    -doubleClickCommand ""
    -deleteKeyCommand ""
    -selectCommand ""
```

Chapter 6

```
        ewc_tslLayerList;
}
```

The final step in the procedure is to update the -label flag of the text control in the custom help line. The string "Layers: " is concatenated with the value returned from the size command.

```
// Update the custom help line
text    -edit
        -label ("Layers: " + size($layers))
        ewc_txtLayerCount;
```

Now return to the interface procedure, scroll to the comment at the bottom (// Update the layer list), and create a call to the new procedure. This will automatically load the layers into the textScrollList when the interface opens.

```
// Update the layer list
ewc_gprocLoadCurrentLayers();
```

scriptJob

The scriptJob command tests for certain events in Maya. In our case, if a layer was deleted how would the textScrollList know to refresh the list? The answer is "It doesn't." For this to happen, a scriptJob command has to be attached to the main interface of the layer manager.

Using the -event flag we can specify what event will trigger the scriptJob and hence refresh the layer list. When an event is detected, the second argument of the scriptJob (which holds a procedure) will be executed.

> **Note:** The MEL documentation shows the entire list of flags for scriptJob as well as all the events a scriptJob can check for.

The -parent flag will connect the scriptJob to a control; in this case the main window of the layer manager. This means that the scriptJob will only be active while the window is open, and is killed when the window is closed. It is crucial to close a scriptJob when it is not in use. If it is not killed, the scriptJob will continue to run; in the case of refreshing the layer list, this could generate errors.

ScriptJobs do require their own system resources to run, and making sure that they only run when necessary is recommended.

Create two `scriptJob` commands to detect the creation and deletion of layers and update the list accordingly:

```
// Event detection for when a layer is added
scriptJob
    -parent ewc_winExtendedLayerManager
    -event    "displayLayerAdded"    "ewc_gprocLoadCurrentLayers()";
// Event detection for when a layer is deleted
scriptJob
    -parent ewc_winExtendedLayerManager
    -event    "displayLayerDeleted"    "ewc_gprocLoadCurrentLayers()";
```

Locate the Refresh Layer List menuItem toward the top of the UI procedure. It will be under the command to create the File menu. Edit the –command flag with the new global procedure:

```
// Menu Item: Refresh Layer List
menuItem
    -label "Refresh Layer List"
    -command "ewc_gprocLoadCurrentLayers()"
```

Locate the Refresh pop-up for the layer textScrollList. Edit the string for the –command flag to hold the procedure name:

```
...
ewc_tslLayerList `;
// refresh popup menu
popupMenu -parent ewc_tslLayerList;;
    menuItem
        -label "Refresh"
        -command "ewc_gprocLoadCurrentLayers()";
```

Figure 6-52 demonstrates layers being displayed in the text list.

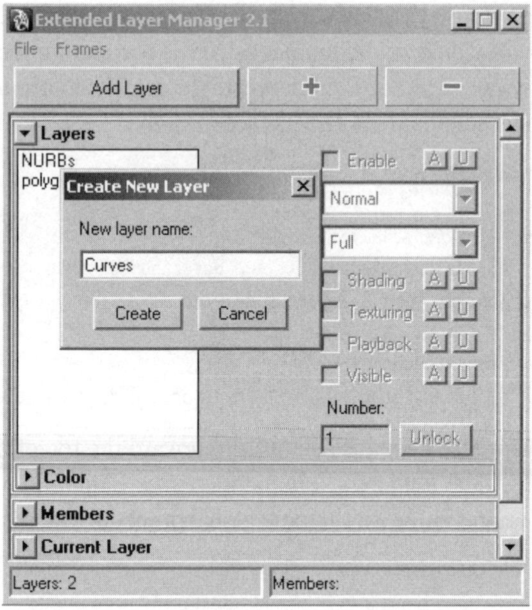

Figure 6-52:
ewc_extendedLayer
Manager_17.mel

6.4.5 **Enabling and Updating Controls: ewc_gprocQueryDrawingOptions()**

Now that the list is being populated with layers, it is time to start enabling controls and updating the drawing states when a layer is selected. This procedure will not take any arguments.

Start with the pseudocode:

```
//==========================
// CONTROL ENABLE STATES
global proc ewc_gprocQueryDrawingOptions()
{
    // Get currently selected layer
    // Test the first array element
        // Query the enable state of the drawing override option
        // The state will be used to enable/disable drawing controls
        // Enable toggle, and value state the Enable check box
        // Enable toggle, and value state the Shading check box
        // Enable toggle, and value state the Texturing check box
        // Enable toggle, and value state the Playback check box
```

```
        // Enable toggle, and value state the Visibility check box
        // Enable toggle, and select the appropriate
        // menu item for the Display Type optionMenu
        // Enable toggle, and select the appropriate
        // menu item for the Level of Detail optionMenu
        // Enable the add selected button
        // Enable the remove selected button
        // Enable bonus controls for Enable check box
        // Enable toggle on all bonus drawing controls
        // Update the layer identification field
        // Enable toggle for the lock/unlock button
        // Update color index
        // Enable set current layer button located in the
        // Current Layer frame
    // End if
} // End ewc_gprocQueryDrawingOptions()
```

Query the currently highlighted layer. The -selectItem flag only
returns a string array of all items in the list. Even if there is only
one item highlighted in the list, an array is still required.

```
string    $layer[] = `textScrollList -query -selectItem
    ewc_displayLayersTSL`;
```

Verify the first element of the array is not empty:

```
// Test the first array element
if ($layer[0] != "")
{
```

Query the .enabled attribute of the highlighted layer. The -enable
flags of the drawing controls will inherit the state of the .enabled
attribute.

```
// Query the enable state of the drawing override option
// The state will be used to enable/disable drawing controls
int $en = `getAttr ($layer[0] + ".enabled")`;
```

The Enable check box control itself is not disabled when toggled off;
set the -enable flag to 1. The -value flag directly queries the
enabled attribute for the initial value. In parentheses, enter the first
index of the $layer array, which is the currently highlighted layer,

Chapter 6

and concatenate it with an attribute, which in this case is the .enabled attribute.

This technique will be used on the rest of the check boxes for the -value flags.

```
// Enable toggle, and value state the Enable check box
checkBox
    -edit
    -enable 1
    -value `getAttr ($layer[0] + ".enabled")`
    ewc_cboxEnableToggle;
```

Use the getAttr command directly in the value field to query and assign the actual attribute value. The argument being passed to the -enable flag is the $en variable, which holds the value returned from querying the .enabled attribute.

```
// Enable toggle, and value state the Shading check box
checkBox
    -edit
    -enable $en
    -value `getAttr ($layer[0] + ".shading")`
    ewc_cboxShadingToggle;
// Enable toggle, and value state the Texturing check box
checkBox
    -edit
    -enable $en
    -value `getAttr ($layer[0] + ".texturing")`
    ewc_cboxTexturingToggle;
// Enable toggle, and value state the Playback check box
checkBox
    -edit
    -enable $en
    -value `getAttr ($layer[0] + ".playback")`
    ewc_cboxPlaybackToggle;
// Enable toggle, and value state the Visibility check box
checkBox
    -edit
    -enable $en
    -value `getAttr ($layer[0] + ".visibility")`
    ewc_cboxVisibilityToggle;
```

Option menus work a bit differently. Instead of a `-value` flag, a `-select` flag is used to select a menuItem based on its index order. The `getAttr` command used here differs from the previous one in that it uses the + operator to add 1 to the returned value.

```
// Enable toggle, and select the appropriate
// menu item for the Display Type optionMenu
optionMenu
    -edit
    -enable $en
    -select ((`getAttr ($layer[0] + ".displayType")`) + 1)
    ewc_optmenDisplayType;
// Enable toggle, and select the appropriate
// menu item for the Level of Detail optionMenu
optionMenu
    -edit
    -enable $en
    -select ((`getAttr ($layer[0] + ".levelOfDetail")`) + 1)
    ewc_optmenLevelOfDetail;
```

Querying the display states returns integer values with an index count that starts at 0:

```
layer[0].levelOfDetail 0 = Normal
layer[0].levelOfDetail 1 = Template
layer[0].levelOfDetail 2 = Reference
```

The optionMenu counts the items in the list with a starting index of 1.

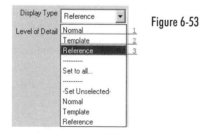 Figure 6-53

What is happening is that the query occurs first within the nested parentheses and the returned value has the value of 1 added to it. This will select the appropriate menuItem within the list.

The parentheses are arranged to define an order of operations, like this:

```
((do this first) do this second)
```

Enable the two symbol buttons for adding and removing selections from a layer:

```
// Enable the add selected button
symbolButton    -edit    -enable 1    ewc_btnAddSelectedObjects;
// Enable the remove selected button
symbolButton    -edit    -enable 1    ewc_btnRemoveSelectedObjects;
```

Enable the two bonus drawing buttons next to the Enable check box:

```
// Enable bonus controls for Enable check box
button          -edit    -enable 1    ewc_btnBonusDrawing1;
button          -edit    -enable 1    ewc_btnBonusDrawing2;
```

Loop through the remaining eight bonus buttons, setting the initialization to 3 since the first two buttons have already been enabled. The $en variable is again passed as the argument for the -enable flag. The $i variable is being concatenated with the string ewc_btnBonusDrawing, which will match it, one at a time, to the rest of the control names for the bonus drawing buttons.

```
// Enable toggle on all bonus drawing controls
for ($i = 3; $i < 11; $i++)
    button -edit -enable $en ("ewc_btnBonusDrawing" + $i);
```

Like an if statement, a for loop that only has one of line code does not require delimiters.

Update the layer identification integer field and enable its unlock/lock toggle button:

```
// Update the layer identification field
intField
    -edit
    -value (`getAttr ($layer[0] + ".identification")`)
    ewc_fldLayerID;
// Enable toggle for the lock/unlock button
button          -edit    -enable 1    ewc_btnToggleLayerID;
```

Update the color palette with the correct color index and pass the $en variable as the argument for the −enable flag:

```
// Update color index
palettePort -edit -setCurCell (`getAttr ($layer[0]+".color")`) -enable
    $en ewc_palprtLayerColor;
```

Enable the button that will set a new current layer in the Current Layer frame.

```
// Enable set current layer button located in the
// in the Current Layer frame
button          -edit    -enable 1    ewc_btnSetCurrentLayer;
```

Activate the disabled menu items from the File menu:

```
// Enable the menu items
menuItem        -edit    -enable 1    ewc_menuDeleteLayer;
menuItem        -edit    -enable 1    ewc_menuRenameLayer;
menuItem        -edit    -enable 1    ewc_menuLayerAttr;
```

Close the if statement:

```
} // End if
```

With the procedure completed, the last step is to edit the −selectCommand flag of the textScrollList located in the ewc_gprocLoadCurrentLayers() procedure. Now clicking a layer in the list will update the drawing options to reflect the drawing attributes of a layer.

```
textScrollList
    -edit
    -append $layers[$i]
    // Attach commands to each item
    -doubleClickCommand ""
    -deleteKeyCommand ""
    -selectCommand "ewc_gprocQueryDrawingOptions();"
    ewc_tslLayerList;
```

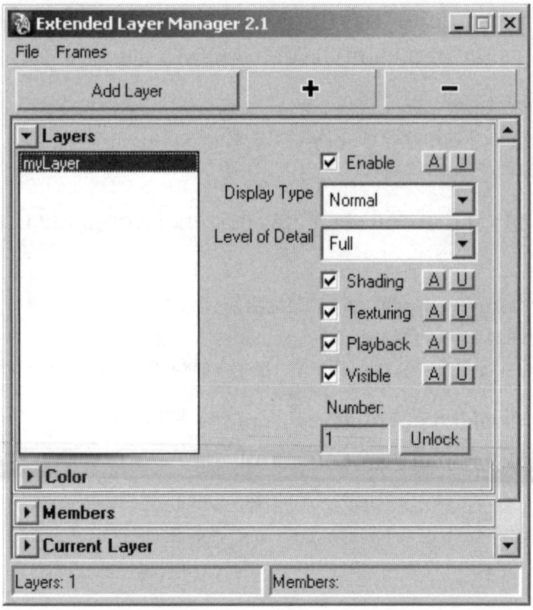

Figure 6-54:
ewc_extendedLayer
Manager_18.mel

6.4.6 Updating the Members List: ewc_gprocUpdateMemberList()

Next, a procedure will be created that queries the members of a layer and displays them in the textScrollList in the Members frame. This procedure will take no arguments. It will be executed when a layer is clicked, and will also be available through the Refresh Member List option in the File menu and as a pop-up from the textScrollList in the Members frame.

Create the procedure and write the pseudocode.

```
//===========================
// PROCEDURE TO LOAD THE MEMBERS
global proc ewc_gprocUpdateMemberList()
{
    // Query the selected layer
    // Check to make sure that there is a selection
        // If there is a selection then make an array of the members
        // Sort it alphabetically
        // Get the total count of items currently in the list
```

```
        // If the list isn't empty, clear it
        // Loop through the array appending the new members
        // Update the Members help line
    // Get a count of the members in the list
    //If there are no members toggle off controls
    //If there are, then toggle on the general controls
} // End ewc_gprocUpdateMemberList()
```

Before the if statement, query the highlighted layer and store it in the $layer string array:

```
// Query the selected layer
string    $layer[] = `textScrollList -query -selectItem
    ewc_tslLayerList`;
```

Next, a condition tests that the first element of the array is not empty:

```
// Check to make sure that there is a selection
if ($layer[0] != "")
{
```

Query the members of the highlighted display layer using the editDisplayLayerMembers command. The members will then be stored in the $mem string array.

```
// If there is a selection then make an array of the members
string    $mem[] = `editDisplayLayerMembers -query $layer[0]`;
```

Alphabetically sort the array:

```
// Sort it alphabetically
sort($mem);
```

As with the textScrollList in the Layers frame, this list must be cleared before populating it with new items.

```
// Clear the member list
textScrollList -edit -removeAll ewc_tslMemberList;
```

Loop through the array and append the items to the textScrollList. As with the layer list, the three command flags will be created with empty strings.

```
// Loop through the array appending the new members
```

Chapter 6

```
for ($i = 0; $i < size($mem); $i++)
    {
    textScrollList
        -edit
        -append $mem[$i]
        // Attach commands to each item
        -doubleClickCommand ""
        -deleteKeyCommand ""
        -selectCommand ""
        ewc_tslMemberList;
    }
```

Update the custom help line with the member count of the high-lighted layer by using the `size` command on the `$mem` array. Add the closing delimiter to finish the if statement.

```
// Update the Members help line
text    -edit
    -label ("Members: " + size($mem))
    ewc_txtMemberCount;
}
```

The last few comments won't be filled in just yet. The procedure needed for this section to work has not been written yet. Leave the comments as is for right now; I will be returning to them later.

```
// Get a count of the members in the list
// If there are no members toggle off controls
// If there are, then toggle on all controls
```

Before the members can be displayed in the textScrollList, the ewc_gprocLoadCurrentLayers() procedure will have to be edited. Locate the `-selectCommand` flag within the loop that edits the textScrollList. Edit the `-command` flag as shown below so that the string now holds two procedures. When more than one procedure (or command) exists within a string, a semicolon must be used to separate them.

```
textScrollList
    -selectCommand ("ewc_gprocQueryDrawingOptions();"
            + "ewc_gprocUpdateMemberList();")
    ewc_tslLayerList;
```

In the File menu locate the `menuItem` command for the Refresh
Member List item. Update the `-command` flag string:

```
// Menu Item: Refresh Member List
menuItem
    -command "ewc_gprocUpdateMemberList()"
    -label "Refresh Member List";
```

Locate and edit the `-command` flag for the Member list pop-up
menu:

```
...
ewc_tslMemberList`;
// refresh popup menu
popupMenu -parent ewc_tslMemberList;
    menuItem
        -label "Refresh"
        -command "ewc_gprocUpdateMemberList()";
```

Now the textScrollList in the Members frame displays a list of all
the members for a highlighted layer. The count of the members is
also displayed in the custom help line.

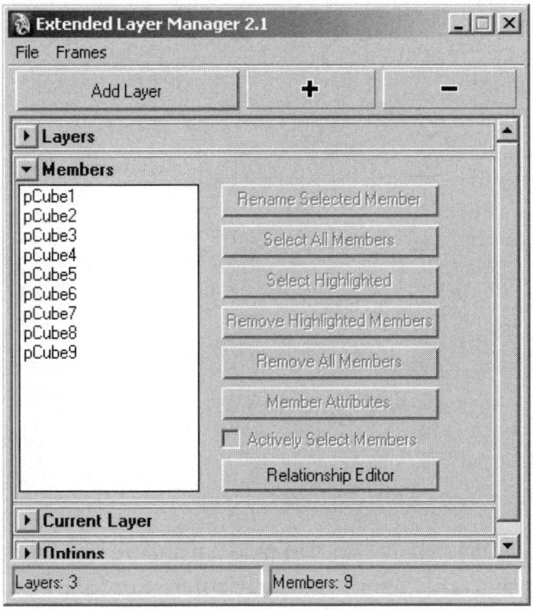

Figure 6-55:
ewc_extendedLayer
Manager_19.mel

6.4.7 **Layer Drawing Control: ewc_gprocLayerDrawingStates()**

This procedure will toggle the drawing states of layers. It will handle the functionality of the checkBox controls and the palettePort only. The procedure takes one integer argument.

Pseudocode the procedure with the switch statement.

```
//==========================
// DRAWING CONTROLS
global proc ewc_gprocLayerDrawingStates(int $case)
{
    // Selected layers
    // Evaluate and match the attribute
    switch ($case)
    {
        case 1: // Enable toggle
                // Store the current checkBox state
                // Apply state to highlighted layers
                // Toggle check boxes
                // Toggle option menus
                // Toggle bonus buttons
                // Toggle color palette
                break;
        case 2: // Shading toggle
                break;
        case 3: // Texturing toggle
                break;
        case 4: // Playback toggle
                break;
        case 5: // Visibility toggle
                break;
        case 6: // Color
                break;

    } // End switch
} // End ewc_gprocLayerDrawingStates()
```

First, create a string array that will hold a list of all highlighted layers. Creating this array above the switch statement allows all case statements to use the array.

```
// Selected layers
string $layer[] = `textScrollList -query -selectItem
    ewc_displayLayersTSL`;
```

Case 1: Enable Toggle

This block will have a unique function in that it toggles the enable state of the drawing controls on and off.

Get the value stored in the check box and store it in the variable $val:

```
// Store the current checkBox state
int $val = `checkBox -query -value ewc_cboxEnableToggle`;
```

Loop through each element in the $layer array and set the .enabled attribute with the value being held in $val:

```
// Apply state to highlighted layers
for ($i in $layer)
    setAttr ($i + ".enabled") $val;
```

Assign the value held in $val as the argument for the -enable flags:

```
// Toggle check boxes
checkBox      -edit    -enable $val    ewc_cboxShadingToggle;
checkBox      -edit    -enable $val    ewc_cboxTexturingToggle;
checkBox      -edit    -enable $val    ewc_cboxPlaybackToggle;
checkBox      -edit    -enable $val    ewc_cboxVisibilityToggle;
// Toggle option menus
optionMenu    -edit    -enable $val    ewc_optmenDisplayType;
optionMenu    -edit    -enable $val    ewc_optmenLevelOfDetail;
```

Loop through the bonus drawing buttons to assign the $val variable to the -enable flags. Since $i was used on the previous loop, it is now a string and can't be used as an integer within this case statement. Instead, use the variable $j for the iteration count.

```
// Toggle bonus buttons
for ($j = 3; $j < 11; $j++ )
    button    -edit    -enable $val    ("ewc_btnBonusDrawing" + $j);
```

Complete the case statement by assigning $val to the -enable flag of the palettePort:

```
// Toggle color palette
palettePort    -edit    -enable $val    ewc_palprtLayerColor;
```

Case 2: Shading Toggle

Loop through each element in the $layer array and assign the shading check box state to the .shading attribute of each layer:

```
case 2: // Shading toggle
    for ($i in $layer)
        setAttr ($i + ".shading")
        (`checkBox -query -value ewc_cboxShadingToggle`);
    break;
```

The first argument in the setAttr command will concatenate the array element temporarily assigned to $i with the string .shading. The second argument for the value is obtained by directly querying the state of the check box. Because there is concatenation and an in-line query being performed, each argument must be surrounded by parentheses.

A simple setAttr command like this would not need parentheses:

```
setAttr object.attribute 1;
```

When building custom production tools you will most likely be using some hybrid version with concatenations and in-line queries. Seeing a setAttr command formatted like this will be a common occurrence:

```
setAttr (argument 1) (argument 2);
```

Case 3: Texturing Toggle

Loop through each element in the $layer array and assign the texturing check box state to the .texturing attribute of each layer:

```
case 3: // Texturing toggle
    for ($i in $layer)
        setAttr ($i + ".texturing")
        (`checkBox -query -value ewc_cboxTexturingToggle`);
    break;
```

Case 4: Playback Toggle

Loop through each element in the $layer array and assign the playback check box state to the .playback attribute of each layer:

```
case 4: // Playback toggle
    for ($i in $layer)
        setAttr ($i + ".playback")
        (`checkBox -query -value ewc_cboxPlaybackToggle`);
    break;
```

Case 5: Visibility Toggle

Loop through each element in the $layer array and assign the visible check box state to the .visibility attribute of each layer:

```
case 5: // Visibility toggle
    for ($i in $layer)
        setAttr ($i + ".visibility")
        (`checkBox -query -value ewc_cboxVisibilityToggle`);
    break;
```

Case 6: Color

Loop through each element in the $layer array and assign the currently selected cell (which represents the color index) to the .color attribute of each layer:

```
case 6: // Color
    for ($i in $layer)
        setAttr ($i + ".color")
        (`palettePort -query -setCurCell ewc_palprtLayerColor`);
    break;
```

Before testing the script the interface procedure will need to be updated. Locate and update the -changeCommand flags of the five check boxes and the palettePort in the Layers frame.

Use the example below to ensure that each control is passing the correct argument.

```
string $cb1 = `checkBox
    -changeCommand "ewc_gprocLayerDrawingStates(1)"
    ewc_cboxEnableToggle`;
```

```
string $cb2 = `checkBox
    -changeCommand "ewc_gprocLayerDrawingStates(2)"
    ewc_cboxShadingToggle`;

string $cb3 = `checkBox
    -changeCommand "ewc_gprocLayerDrawingStates(3)"
    ewc_cboxTexturingToggle`;

string $cb4 = `checkBox
    -changeCommand "ewc_gprocLayerDrawingStates(4)"
    ewc_cboxPlaybackToggle`;

string $cb5 = `checkBox
    -changeCommand "ewc_gprocLayerDrawingStates(5)"
    ewc_cboxVisibilityToggle`;


palettePort
    -changeCommand "ewc_gprocLayerDrawingStates(6)"
    ewc_palprtLayerColor;
```

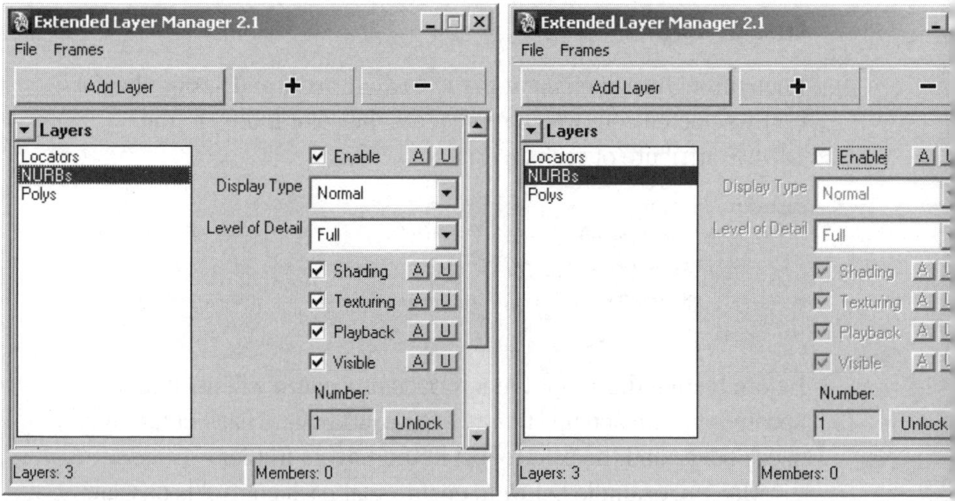

Figure 6-56

The ewc_extendedLayerManager_20.mel file on the companion disc shows the current progress.

6.4.8 **Bonus Drawing Controls: ewc_gprocBonusDrawing()**

This procedure will enable the bonus drawing control features of the layer manager. The default layer editor in Maya has a right-click menu for each layer. From this menu a feature is available that will apply the drawing state of one layer to all layers. The first bonus drawing feature of our layer manager emulates this. The second feature will apply the opposite drawing state of a highlighted layer to all layers not highlighted in the list. So, if the highlighted layer is visible, the layers not highlighted will have their visibility property turned off. This was an experiment that actually turned out to be useful in managing scenes.

This procedure takes two integer arguments. The first will match the attribute type being changed, which is determined through the $type variable. The second, $attr, will determine if the specific attribute is applied to all layers or just the unselected layers. This will occur in a nested switch statement inside each case statement.

Begin with the pseudocode and the switch statement to evaluate $type.

```
//=============================
// DRAWING CONTROLS
global proc ewc_gprocBonusDrawing(int $case, int $attr)
{
    // Get selected layer
    // Get all layers
    // Evaluate and match the attribute
    switch ($case)
    {
        case 1: // Enable
            break;
        case 2: // Shading
            break;
        case 3: // Texturing
            break;
        case 4: // Playback
            break;
```

Chapter 6

```
    case 5: // Visibility
        break;
    } // End switch
} // End ewc_gprocBonusDrawing()
```

Above the switch statement, create a string array of the highlighted layers in the textScrollList:

```
// Get selected layer
string   $sel[] = `textScrollList -query -selectItem ewc_tslLayerList`;
```

Directly beneath, create another string array that contains all layers listed in the textScrollList. This is done by querying the list with the -allItems flag.

```
// Get all layers
string   $all[] = `textScrollList -query -allItems ewc_tslLayerList`;
```

Case 1: Enable

Pseudocode the first case statement. A second switch statement is nested and evaluates the second argument of $attr.

```
case 1: // Enable
    switch($attr)
    {
        case 1: // To all
            break;
        case 2: // To unselected
            // Remove selected layers, create new array
            // If the box is checked (true) toggle unselected off
            // If the box is not checked (false) toggle unselected on
            break;
    }
    break;
```

The first case statement loops through each element in the $all array. It then sets the .enabled attribute with the value that is obtained directly from the getAttr command, querying the .enabled attribute of the highlighted layer in the textScrollList. The getAttr command can be called within a setAttr as long as back quotes are surrounding the entire query.

```
// To all
for ($i in $all)
    setAttr ($i + ".enabled") (`getAttr ($sel[0] + ".enabled")`);
```

In the second case statement, create a new array by removing the highlighted layers ($sel) from the $all array. This will create an array of layer names that are not highlighted.

```
// To unselected
// Remove selected layers, create new array
string $unSel[] = stringArrayRemove($sel,$all);
```

Query the state of the Enable check box. If the box is checked (returns true), then turn off the .enabled attribute on all the layers in the $unSel array:

```
// If the box is checked (true) toggle unselected off
if (`checkBox -query -value ewc_cboxEnableToggle`)
    {
    for ($i in $unSel)
        setAttr ($i + ".enabled") 0;
    }
```

If the check box is not checked (returns false), turn on the .enabled attribute for all the layers in the $unSel array:

```
// If the box is not checked (false) toggle unselected on
else
    {
    for ($i in $unSel)
        setAttr ($i + ".enabled") 1;
    }
```

The four remaining case statements will have an identical block structure.

Case 2: Shading

Ensure that the attribute is changed to .shading:

```
case 2: // Shading
    switch($attr)
    {
        case 1: // To all
```

```
        for ($i in $all)
            setAttr ($i + ".shading")
            (`getAttr ($sel[0] + ".shading")`);
        break;
    case 2: // To unselected
        // Remove selected layers, create new array
        string $unSel[] = stringArrayRemove($sel,$all);
        // If the box is checked (true) toggle unselected off
        if (`checkBox -query -value ewc_cboxShadingToggle`)
            {
            for ($i in $unSel)
                setAttr ($i + ".shading") 0;
            }
        // If the box is not checked (false) toggle unselected on
        else
            {
            for ($i in $unSel)
                setAttr ($i + ".shading") 1;
            }
        break;
    }
break;
```

Case 3: Texturing

Ensure that the attribute is changed to .texturing:

```
case 3: // Texturing
    switch($attr)
    {
        case 1: // To all
            for ($i in $all)
                setAttr ($i + ".texturing")
                (`getAttr ($sel[0] + ".texturing")`);
            break;
        case 2: // To unselected
            // Remove selected layers, create new array
            string $unSel[] = stringArrayRemove($sel,$all);
            // If the box is checked (true) toggle unselected off
            if (`checkBox -query -value ewc_cboxTexturingToggle`)
                {
                for ($i in $unSel)
```

```
                    setAttr ($i + ".texturing") 0;
                }
        // If the box is not checked (false) toggle unselected on
        else
                {
                for ($i in $unSel)
                    setAttr ($i + ".texturing") 1;
                }
            break;
        }
    break;
```

Case 4: Playback

Ensure that the attribute is changed to .playback:

```
case 4: // Playback
    switch($attr)
    {
        case 1: // To all
            for ($i in $all)
                setAttr ($i + ".playback")
                (`getAttr ($sel[0] + ".playback")`);
            break;
        case 2: // To unselected
            // Remove selected layers, create new array
            string $unSel[] = stringArrayRemove($sel,$all);
            // If the box is checked (true) toggle unselected off
            if (`checkBox -query -value ewc_cboxPlaybackToggle`)
                {
                for ($i in $unSel)
                    setAttr ($i + ".playback") 0;
                }
            // If the box is not checked (false) toggle unselected on
            else
                {
                for ($i in $unSel)
                    setAttr ($i + ".playback") 1;
                }
            break;
        }
    break;
```

Case 5: Visibility

Ensure that the attribute is changed to `.visibility`:

```
case 5: // Visibility
    switch($attr)
    {
        case 1: // To all
            for ($i in $all)
                setAttr ($i + ".visibility")
                (`getAttr ($sel[0] + ".visibility")`);
            break;
        case 2: // To unselected
            // Remove selected layers, create new array
            string $unSel[] = stringArrayRemove($sel,$all);
            // If the box is checked (true) toggle unselected off
            if (`checkBox -query -value ewc_cboxVisibilityToggle`)
                {
                for ($i in $unSel)
                    setAttr ($i + ".visibility") 0;
                }
            // If the box is not checked (false) toggle unselected on
            else
                {
                for ($i in $unSel)
                    setAttr ($i + ".visibility") 1;
                }
            break;
    }
    break;
```

Before the script can be tested we need to return to the interface
procedure and locate the buttons for the bonus drawing controls.
Edit the -command flags with the corresponding arguments:

```
string $b4 = `button
    -command "ewc_gprocBonusDrawing(1,1)"
    ewc_btnBonusDrawing1`;

string $b5 = `button
    -command "ewc_gprocBonusDrawing(1,2)"
    ewc_btnBonusDrawing2`;
```

```
string $b6 = `button
    -command "ewc_gprocBonusDrawing(2,1)"
    ewc_btnBonusDrawing3`;

string $b7 = `button
    -command "ewc_gprocBonusDrawing(2,2)"
    ewc_btnBonusDrawing4`;

string $b8 = `button
    -command "ewc_gprocBonusDrawing(3,1)"
    ewc_btnBonusDrawing5`;

string $b9 = `button
    -command "ewc_gprocBonusDrawing(3,2)"
    ewc_btnBonusDrawing6`;

string $b10 = `button
    -command "ewc_gprocBonusDrawing(4,1)"
    ewc_btnBonusDrawing7`;

string $b11 = `button
    -command "ewc_gprocBonusDrawing(4,2)"
    ewc_btnBonusDrawing8`;

string $b12 = `button
    -command "ewc_gprocBonusDrawing(5,1)"
    ewc_btnBonusDrawing9`;

string $b13 = `button
    -command "ewc_gprocBonusDrawing(5,2)"
    ewc_btnBonusDrawing10`;
```

The ewc_extendedLayerManager_21.mel file on the companion disc shows the current progress.

6.4.9 Display Type Option Menu: ewc_gprocDisplayType()

This procedure will control the DisplayType toggle as well as the bonus features similar to what was created earlier for the other drawing attributes. This procedure takes no arguments.

Chapter 6

The case statement values will reflect the index order of items in the optionMenu. The -select flag will be used to query which item in the optionMenu is selected.

```
int $sel = `optionMenu -query -select ewc_optmenDisplayType`;
```

Following is the index of the menu items:

- 1 = Normal
- 2 = Template
- 3 = Reference
- 4 = -Divider- (even dividers are counted)
- 5 = Set to all...
- 6 = -Divider-
- 7 = -Set Unselected- (only a label but still counted)
- 8 = Normal
- 9 = Template
- 10 = Reference

Pseudocode the procedure and the switch statement. Menu items 4, 6, and 7 are omitted since 4 and 6 are dividers and 7 only serves as a label. The default statement will be used to collect 4, 6, and 7 if they are clicked.

```
//===========================
// DISPLAY TYPE
global proc ewc_gprocDisplayType()
{
    // Query the highlighted layer
    // Query the selected menu item
    // Evaluate and match the menu item
    switch($dispType)
    {
        case 1: // Normal
            break;
        case 2: // Template
            break;
        case 3: // Reference
            break;
        case 5: // Set to all...
```

```
            break;
      case 8: // Unselected - Normal
            break;
      case 9: // Unselected - Template
            break;
      case 10:// Unselected - Reference
            break;
      default:// Reset the optionMenu
            break;
   } // End switch
} // End ewc_gprocDisplayType()
```

Above the switch statement, query the highlighted layers in the textScrollList:

```
// Query the highlighted layer
string $layer[] = `textScrollList -query -selectItem
   ewc_tslLayerList`;
```

Next, query the menuItem selected by the user:

```
// Query the selected menu item
int $dispType = `optionMenu -query -select ewc_optmenDisplayType`;
```

Case 1, 2, and 3: Normal, Template, and Reference

The first three case statements (1 to 3) will loop through the high-lighted layers and assign a value that corresponds with the display type.

Loop through the array of highlighted layers and change their .displayType attribute to 0 (Normal):

```
case 1:// Normal
   for ($i in $layer)
      setAttr ($i + ".displayType") 0;
```

Loop through the array of highlighted layers and change their .displayType attribute to 1 (Template):

```
case 2:// Template
   for ($i in $layer)
      setAttr ($i + ".displayType") 1;
   break;
```

Loop through the array of highlighted layers and change their
`.displayType` attribute to 2 (Reference):

```
case 3:// Reference
    for ($i in $layer)
        setAttr ($i + ".displayType") 2;
```

Case 5: Set to All...

This case assigns the current displayType to all layers in the list. To
build an array of all items in a list, use the `-allItems` flag when performing the query.

```
case 5:// Set to all...
    // Get all items
    string $all[] = `textScrollList -query -allItems ewc_tslLayerList`;
```

Loop through the array and assign each layer to the same state as
the highlighted layer. Remember to use back quotes to hold the
`getAttr` query.

```
// Loop the array and set the .displayType attribute on all
for ($i in $all)
setAttr ($i + ".displayType") (`getAttr ($layer[0] + ".displayType")`);
```

The optionMenu will remain on "Set to all..." after this block executes. The menu must be edited to list the correct attribute state.
The argument for the `-select` flag holds the `getAttr` command,
which retrieves the attribute value. Since the attribute value has a
starting index of 0 (and the optionMenu starts at 1), a value of 1
must be added to the returned value to select the correct
menuItem.

```
// Reset the optionMenu
optionMenu
    -edit
    -select ((`getAttr ($layer[0] + ".displayType")`) + 1)
    ewc_optmenDisplayType;
break;
```

Case 8: Unselected - Normal

This feature will assign a displayType to the layers that are not high-lighted in the textScrollList. Start by creating an array of all the items in the list:

```
case 8:// Unselected - Normal
    // Get all items
    string $all[] = `textScrollList -query -allItems ewc_tslLayerList`;
```

Remove the highlighted layers ($layer) from the $all array and store the new array in $unSel:

```
    // Remove highlighted items
    string $unSel[] = stringArrayRemove($layer,$all);
```

Loop through the $unSel array and set the .displayType attribute to 0:

```
    // Loop unselected items
    for ($i in $unSel)
        setAttr ($i + ".displayType") 0;
```

Reset the optionMenu to display the correct attribute state:

```
    // Reset the optionMenu
    optionMenu
        -edit
        -select ((`getAttr ($layer[0] + ".displayType")`) + 1)
        ewc_optmenDisplayType
    break;
```

Case 9 and 10: Unselected - Template/Reference

The next two case statements are structured identically; only the value being set is changed.

```
case 9:// Unselected - Template
    // Get all items
    string $all[] = `textScrollList -query -allItems ewc_tslLayerList`;
    // Remove highlighted items
    string $unSel[] = stringArrayRemove($layer,$all);
    // Loop unselected items
    for ($i in $unSel)
        setAttr ($i + ".displayType") 1;
```

Chapter 6

```
    // Reset the optionMenu
    optionMenu
        -edit
        -select ((`getAttr ($layer[0] + ".displayType")`) + 1)
        ewc_optmenDisplayType
    break;
case 10:// Unselected - Reference
    // Get all items
    string $all[] = `textScrollList -query -allItems ewc_tslLayerList`;
    // Remove highlighted items
    string $unSel[] = stringArrayRemove($layer,$all);
    // Loop unselected items
    for ($i in $unSel)
        setAttr ($i + ".displayType") 2;
    // Reset the optionMenu
    optionMenu
        -edit
        -select ((`getAttr ($layer[0] + ".displayType")`) + 1)
        ewc_optmenDisplayType
    break;
```

If either of the two dividers (or the -Set Unselected- label) is clicked, the divider will take focus in the optionMenu. This is not a recommended behavior for an optionMenu.

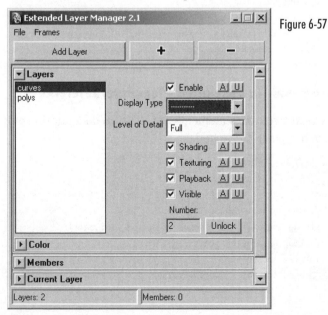

Figure 6-57

The default statement will catch this and reset the optionMenu to display the correct attribute state:

```
default://  Reset the optionMenu
    optionMenu
        -edit
        -select ((`getAttr ($layer[0] + ".displayType")`) + 1)
        ewc_optmenDisplayType;
    break;
```

Locate and edit the `-changeCommand` flag for the DisplayType optionMenu in the interface procedure.

```
string $opt1 = `optionMenu
    -changeCommand "ewc_gprocDisplayType()"
    ewc_optmenDisplayType`;
```

The ewc_extendedLayerManager_22.mel file on the companion disc shows the current progress.

6.4.10 Level of Detail Toggle: ewc_gprocLevelOfDetail()

This procedure is nearly identical to the previous one as far as functionality is concerned. The only difference is the number of case statements that will be created and the attribute type being edited. This procedure will not take any arguments.

Following is the index order of the menu items:

- 1 = Full
- 2 = Bounding Box
- 3 = -Divider-
- 4 = Set to all...
- 5 = -Divider-
- 6 = -Set Unselected-
- 7 = Full
- 8 = Bounding Box

Begin with the pseudocode for the procedure:

Chapter 6

```
//============================
// LEVEL OF DETAIL
global proc ewc_gprocLevelOfDetail()
{
    // Query the highlighted layer
    // Query the selected menu item
    // Evaluate and match the menu item
    switch($levelOfDetail)
    {
        case 1: // Full
            break;
        case 2: // Bounding Box
            break;
        case 4: // Set to all...
            // Get all items
            // Loop the array and set the .levelOfDetail attribute
            // on all
            // Reset the optionMenu
            break;
        case 7: // Unselected - Full
            // Get all items
            // Remove highlighted items
            // Loop unselected items
            // Reset the optionMenu
            break;
        case 8: // Unselected - Bounding Box
            // Get all items
            // Remove highlighted items
            // Loop unselected items
            // Reset the optionMenu
            break;
        default:// Reset the optionMenu
            break;
    } // End switch
} //End ewc_gprocLevelOfDetail()
```

Query the highlighted layers in the textScrollList:

```
// Query the highlighted layers
string    $layer[] = `textScrollList -query -selectItem
    ewc_tslLayerList`;
```

Query the optionMenu for the selected item:

```
// Query the selected menu item
int $levelOfDetail = `optionMenu -query -select
    ewc_optmenLevelOfDetail`;
```

The standard toggles are assigned to case 1 (Full) and case 2 (Bounding Box):

```
case 1:// Full
    for ($i in $layer)
        setAttr ($i + ".levelOfDetail") 0;
    break;
case 2:// Bounding Box
    for ($i in $layer)
        setAttr ($i + ".levelOfDetail") 1;
    break;
```

The bonus feature to assign the current drawing type to all layers is assigned to case 4:

```
case 4:// Set to all...
    // Get all items
    string $all[] = `textScrollList -query -allItems ewc_tslLayerList`;
    // Loop the array and set the .levelOfDetail attribute on all
    for ($i in $all)
        setAttr ($i + ".levelOfDetail")
        (`getAttr ($layer[0] + ".levelOfDetail")`);
    // Reset the optionMenu
    optionMenu
        -edit
        -select ((`getAttr ($layer[0] + ".levelOfDetail")`) + 1)
        ewc_optmenLevelOfDetail;
    break;
```

The bonus feature of assigning a specific state to unselected layers is directed to case 7 (Unselected - Full) and case 8 (Unselected - Bounding Box):

```
case 7:// Unselected - Full
    // Get all items
    string $all[] = `textScrollList -query -allItems ewc_tslLayerList`;
    // Remove highlighted items
    string $unSel[] = stringArrayRemove($layer,$all);
    // Loop unselected items
```

```
    for ($i in $unSel)
        setAttr ($i + ".levelOfDetail") 0;
    // Reset the optionMenu
    optionMenu
        -edit
        -select ((`getAttr ($layer[0] + ".levelOfDetail")`) + 1)
        ewc_optmenLevelOfDetail;
    break;
case 8:// Unselected - Bounding Box
    // Get all items
    string $all[] = `textScrollList -query -allItems ewc_tslLayerList`;
    // Remove highlighted items
    string $unSel[] = stringArrayRemove($layer,$all);
    // Loop unselected items
    for ($i in $unSel)
        setAttr ($i + ".levelOfDetail") 1;
    // Reset the optionMenu
    optionMenu
        -edit
        -select ((`getAttr ($layer[0] + ".levelOfDetail")`) + 1)
        ewc_optmenLevelOfDetail;
    break;
```

End with the default statement to catch items 3, 5, and 6 if they are clicked:

```
default:// Reset the optionMenu
    optionMenu
        -edit
        -select ((`getAttr ($layer[0] + ".levelOfDetail")`) + 1)
        ewc_optmenLevelOfDetail;
    break;
```

Locate the optionMenu in the interface procedure and edit the -changeCommand flag:

```
string $opt2 = `optionMenu
    -changeCommand "ewc_gprocLevelOfDetail()"
    ewc_optmenLevelOfDetail`;
```

The ewc_extendedLayerManager_23.mel file on the companion disc shows the current progress.

6.4.11 Layer Identification: ewc_gprocEditLayerID()

The last set of controls in the Layers frame is the layer identification field and the unlock/lock button next to it. The button will
unlock the field for editing the identification number of a layer. The
layer identification number can be used to merge layers with matching identifications when importing one scene into another. This is an
advanced feature and one that is not commonly used. This is why
the field is locked by default.

The procedure being created takes one integer argument.

```
//==========================
// LAYER IDENTIFICATION
global proc ewc_gprocEditLayerID(int $case)
{
    switch ($case)
    {
        case 1: // Lock/unlock the integer field
            break;
        case 2: // Edit layer identification
            break;
    } // End switch
} // End ewc_gprocEditLayerID()
```

Case 1: Lock/Unlock the Integer Field

The first case statement will be used to toggle the -editable flag
for the intField control. The current -editable state will be
directly queried to determine which block of code to run.

If the test returns true (1), then the field is locked. The label of
the button is changed to Unlock.

```
// If the field is editable lock the field
// and set the button -label flag to read "Unlock"
if (`intField -query -editable ewc_fldLayerID`)
    {
    // lock the field from editing
    intField
        -edit
        -editable 0
```

```
        ewc_fldLayerID;
    // change the button label
    button
        -edit
        -label "Unlock"
        -width 50
        ewc_btnToggleLayerID;
    }
```

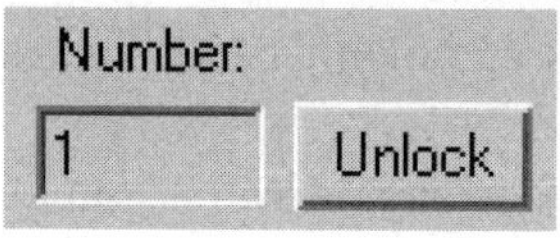

Figure 6-58

If the test returns false (0), then the field is unlocked. The label of
the button is changed to Lock.

```
// If the field is not editable unlock the field
// and set the button -label flag to read "Lock"
else
    {
    // unlock the field for editing
    intField
        -edit
        -editable 1
        ewc_fldLayerID;
    // change the button label
    button
        -edit
        -label "Lock"
        -width 50
        ewc_btnToggleLayerID;
    }
```

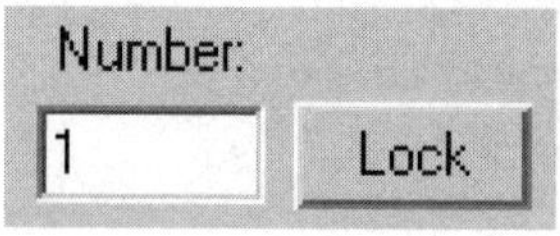

Figure 6-59

Case 2: Edit Layer Identification

The next task is to change the `.identification` attribute of a layer. This is harder than you might think. Create a layer and try changing its `.identification` attribute through the normal method by using the `setAttr` command.

```
setAttr layer1.identification 2;
```

Maya will return this error:

```
// Error: line 1: The attribute 'layer1.identification' is locked or
connected and cannot be modified. //
```

If an attribute of an object is connected, then the connecting node can be queried using the `listConnections` command.

Write out the pseudocode for case 2:

```
case 2: // Edit layer identification
    // Query the highlighted layer in the textScrollList
    // Get the input value
    // Convert it to a string
    // Create an array of all display layers
    // Create two empty arrays needed for the next loop
    // Loop through each layer and get the ID of each
        // Then take each index in the integer array
        // and place it into a string array
    // Test to see if the string in $inputStr
    // matches any of the elements in $stringID
    // and evaluate the test result in the if statement
    // If the test returns 1 (true))
        // Warn user if the number is not unique
        // intField must lose focus so the field can be reset
        // Reset the intField
    // If the test returns 0 (false)
        // Query the highlighted layer in the textScrollList
        // Store the listConnection concatenated with the
        // layer as a string to be evaluated.
        // Use the eval command to run the listConnections and
        // store the results
        // Assign the first element of the $eval array as
        // the target attribute to receive the user input value
    break;
```

Chapter 6

307

Query the highlighted layer:

```
// Query the highlighted layer in the textScrollList
string $layer[] = `textScrollList -query -selectItem ewc_tslLayerList`;
```

Query the value that is being held in the intField control:

```
// Get the input value
int $inputInt    = `intField -query -value ewc_fldLayerID`;
```

Now convert the integer to a string by assigning it to a string variable:

```
// Convert it to a string
string    $inputStr = $inputInt;
```

Query all the display layers and store them into the $layers array.

```
// Create an array of all display layers
string    $layers[] = `ls -exactType "displayLayer"`;
```

Create two blank arrays to be used in the next for loop:

```
// Create two empty arrays needed for the next loop
int $layerID[];
string    $stringID[];
```

The loop repeats while the iteration count is less than the size of the $layers array.

```
// Loop through each layer and get the ID of each
for ($i = 0; $i < size($layers); $i++)
{
```

Loop through all the layers and get the identification value. For the stringArrayContains command to work, the ID array (which is an integer data type) must be converted to a string array. The second line assigns each element of the int array to a corresponding element of the string array.

```
    $layerID[$i]    = `getAttr ($layers[$i] + ".identification")`;
    // Then take each index in the integer array
    // and place it into a string array
    $stringID[$i]    = $layerID[$i];
}
```

With the identifications stored in a string array, the stringArrayContains command can be used to test if the string value in $inputStr exactly matches any of the values being held in $stringID.

Now test the integer from the stringArrayContains command to see if the number the user entered is already in use. If it is, then print a warning and reset the field. The displayed number won't reset if the intField retains the focus. The setFocus command changes the focus to a different control.

```
// Test to see if the string in $inputStr
// matches any of the elements in $stringID
// and evaluate the test result in the if statement
// If the test returns 1 (true)
if (stringArrayContains($inputStr,$stringID))
    {
    // Warn user if the number is not unique
    warning "A layer has already been assigned to this number.
        Operation cancelled.";
    // intField must lose focus so the field can be reset
    setFocus ewc_btnCreateNewLayer;
    // Reset the intField
    intField
        -edit
        -value (`getAttr ($layer[0] + ".identification")`)
        ewc_fldLayerID;
    }
```

The listConnections command must be used to extract the correct object and attribute to change the identification. The listConnections command returns a list of connected objects of a specific object based on the flags used.

- **-destination:** This is a default flag that returns the connected objects that are output connections, or simply the "destination" of the specified object.

- **-plugs:** When this flag is included it returns the connected attributes of the connected objects returned from the -destination flag.

To demonstrate these flags, create an empty layer with the default name of layer1. Run the listConnections command with the two flags discussed above:

```
listConnections -destination 1 -plugs 1 layer1;
```

This is the actual object and attribute that must be called to change the value. The object name will always be layerManager (-destination), but the attribute (-plugs) will always have a different ID number in the brackets. That is why the listConnections command must be run each time to query the appropriate attribute ID.

```
// Result: layerManager.displayLayerId[1] //
```

If the test returns false, then the number is not in use:

```
// If the test returns 0 (false)
else
{
```

Test that the first element in the array is not empty. Run the listConnections command with the correct flags using the first element in $layer. The result is stored in the $lmid array.

```
if ($layer[0] != "")
    {
    // Concatenate the highlighted layer and store the results
    string $lmid[] = `listConnections -destination 1 -plugs 1 $layer[0]`;
```

The first element of the array (no matter how many results are returned) will always hold the correct destination and plug. This is the object and attribute that will receive the new identification value.

```
    // Assign the first element of the $lmid array as
    // the target attribute to receive the user input value
    setAttr $lmid[0] $inputInt;
    }
```

The listConnections command can return more than one connection if the layer has members. Create another layer, add a polyCube to the layer, and then run the listConnections command again:

```
listConnections -destination 1 -plugs 1 layer2;
// Result: layerManager.displayLayerId[2] pCube1.drawOverride
    pCubeShape1.drawOverride //
```

Display layers control the display of objects through the
.drawOverride attribute. Now that you know why and how a
listConnections query on a layer will return an array, it should be
clear why a setAttr command should not be used like this:

```
setAttr (`listConnections -destination 1 -plugs 1 $layer[0]`) $inputInt;
```

What is literally being interpreted and executed in the setAttr
command would resemble this:

```
setAttr layerManager.displayLayerId[1] 1;
```

Due to the nature of how some of these commands work, the extra
steps are necessary to avoid potential problems that can, and will,
show up during production.

Finally, edit the -changeCommand flag for the intField and the
-command flag for the button.

```
string $intFld1 = `intField
    -changeCommand "ewc_gprocEditLayerID(2)"
    ewc_fldLayerID`;

string $b14 = `button
    -command "ewc_gprocEditLayerID(1)"
    ewc_btnToggleLayerID`;
```

The ewc_extendedLayerManager_24.mel file on the companion
disc shows the current progress.

6.4.12 Additional Layer Editing:
ewc_gprocLayerEditing()

A procedure will be needed to rename layers, delete layers, and
open the Attribute Editor for a specific layer. This procedure will
take one integer argument. This procedure will be called from the
File menu, or by double-clicking on the layer list, or by pressing the
Delete or Backspace keys on the keyboard with a list item
highlighted.

Chapter 6

Create the procedure and the switch statements:

```
//===========================
// PROCEDURES FOR LAYER EDITING
global proc ewc_gprocLayerEditing(int $case)
{
    // Query highlighted layers
    switch ($case)
    {
        case 1: // Delete layers
            break;
        case 2: // Rename a layer
            break;
        case 3: // Attribute Editor
            break;
    } // End switch
} // End ewc_gprocLayerEditing()
```

At the top of the procedure, create an array to hold the highlighted layers:

```
// Query highlighted layers
string    $layer[] = `textScrollList -query -selectItem
    ewc_tslLayerList`;
```

Case 1: Delete Layers

The next block will be used to delete layers from a scene. It will be accessible through the File menu or by using the Delete or Backspace keys on the keyboard.

Pseudocode the case statement:

```
case 1: // Delete layers
    // Check that there is a selection
    // Delete all elements in the array
    // Disable the controls
    // Empty the member list
    // Reset the custom help line
    // Loop through the array
        // Check to see if the layer being deleted is the current layer
            // Current layer procedure
    break;
```

Verify that a layer has been highlighted:

```
// Check that there is a selection
if ($layer[0] != "")
{
```

Delete all objects held in the $layer array:

```
// Delete all elements in the array
delete $layer;
```

The procedure for disabling the controls has not been written yet. Leave the comment as is.

```
// Disable the controls
```

When a layer is deleted there will not be a selection in the textScrollList. Therefore, the member list must be cleared and the custom help line reset to its default state:

```
// Empty the member list
textScrollList -edit -removeAll ewc_tslMemberList;
// Reset the custom help line
text -edit -label "Members:" ewc_txtMemberCount;
```

The last few comments will be left empty for now. The procedure required has not been written yet, but in the next section we create the loop that is commented below.

```
// Loop through the array
    // Check to see if the layer being deleted is the current layer
        // Current layer procedure
```

Case 2: Rename a Layer

In section 6.5, "Creating the Functionality — Part II," a procedure will be created to handle the renaming of both layers and members. The reason is that the procedure will be almost as long as the one written earlier to create a layer. Since exactly the same format to rename members and layers is going to be used, it is pointless to write it out twice. For now, just write out the comments and leave them as is until the next section.

```
case 2: // Rename a layer
    // Verify the first array element is not empty
        // Call the renaming procedure and pass the
        // string "Layer" and the highlighted layer
```

Chapter 6

Case 3: Attribute Editor

This command will be run from the File menu and will open the Attribute Editor for a layer.

```
case 3: // Attribute Editor
    // Select the highlighted layer
    select $layer[0];
    // Open the Attribute Editor
    openAEWindow;
    break;
```

That's it! Now all that is left is to add the procedures to the right controls.

Locate the File menu within the interface procedure and edit the -command flags of the corresponding menuItem commands.

```
menuItem
    -command "ewc_gprocLayerEditing(1)"
    ewc_miDeleteLayer;

menuItem
    -command "ewc_gprocLayerEditing(2)"
    ewc_miRenameLayer;

menuItem
    -command "ewc_gprocLayerEditing(3)"
    ewc_miLayerAttr;
```

Locate the ewc_gprocLoadCurrentLayers() procedure. Inside the loop that appends layers to the textScrollList, locate and edit the -doubleClickCommand and -deleteKeyCommand flags. The functionality to rename layers has not been written yet. However, since the procedure and case statement have been set up, it is safe to edit the -doubleClickCommand.

```
textScrollList
    -doubleClickCommand "ewc_gprocLayerEditing(2)"
    -deleteKeyCommand "ewc_gprocLayerEditing(1)"
    ewc_tslLayerList;
```

You can check your progress with the ewc_extendedLayer-Manager_25.mel file on the companion disc.

6.5 Creating the Functionality — Part II

6.5.1 Adding and Removing Selected Objects: ewc_gprocEditLayerMemberships()

This procedure creates the functionality for the top two buttons that add and remove objects selected in a viewport from a specific layer. The procedure takes one integer argument.

```
//===========================
// LAYER MEMBERSHIPS
global proc ewc_gprocEditLayerMemberships(int $case)
{
    // Create an array of the selections

    switch ($case)
    {
        case 1: // Add selected
            break;

        case 2: // Remove selected - sends to defaultLayer
            break;

    } // End switch

    // Reload member list
    // Update member frame
} // End ewc_gprocEditLayerMemberships()
```

Create the array that holds the selected objects:

```
// Create an array of the selections
string    $sel[]    = `ls -selection -flatten`;
```

The first line of case 1 will test for a selection. The highlighted layer is queried and stored in the $layer array. The next line adds the selected objects to the layer name stored in $layer[0]. The −noRecurse flag ensures that only the selected nodes, and not their children, are added to the layer.

```
// Add selected
if ($sel[0] != "")
    {
    // Get the selected layer
    string $layer[] = `textScrollList -query -selectItem
        ewc_tslLayerList`;
    editDisplayLayerMembers -noRecurse $layer[0] $sel;
    }
```

The second case statement will perform the same test (check that there is a selection) and then remove the selected objects. It isn't technically a remove command as the selected objects are just being assigned to the defaultLayer.

```
// Remove selected - sends to defaultLayer
if ($sel[0] != "")
    editDisplayLayerMembers -noRecurse "defaultLayer" $sel;
```

Call the procedure that populates the member list to refresh the list and update the custom help line with the new member count:

```
// Reload member list
ewc_gprocUpdateMemberList();
```

The last comment is for a procedure that will be written next:

```
// Update member frame
```

In the interface procedure, locate the symbolButton commands used to create the two buttons and edit the -command flags:

```
string $b2 = `symbolButton
    -command "ewc_gprocEditLayerMemberships(1)"
    ewc_btnAddSelectedObjects`;

string $b3 = `symbolButton
    -command "ewc_gprocEditLayerMemberships(2)"
    ewc_btnRemoveSelectedObjects`;
```

The ewc_extendedLayerManager_26.mel file on the companion disc shows the current progress.

6.5.2 **Toggling the Enable State of the Controls: ewc_gprocControlStates()**

This procedure will manage the enabling and disabling of the appropriate controls in the layer manager. The procedure will take one integer argument. Note that the functionality of the Members frame has not been created yet.

Declare the procedure and create a switch statement:

```
//===========================
// TOGGLE ENABLE STATES OF CONTROLS
global proc ewc_gprocControlStates(int $case)
{
    switch ($case)
    {
        case 1: // Disable all controls in the Layers frame
            break;

        case 2: // Enable specific member buttons
            break;

        case 3: // All member controls off
            break;

        case 4: // Toggle member -enable states
            break;

    } // End switch
} // End ewc_gprocControlStates()
```

Case 1

Turn off all controls in the Layers frame as well as the Add Selected and Remove Selected buttons.

Chapter 6

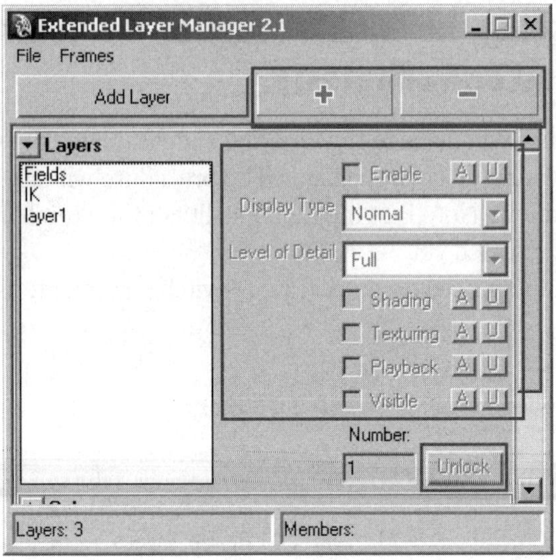

Figure 6-60

The intField for the layer identification will have its -value flag set to 1:

```
// Check boxes
checkBox    -edit    -enable 0    -value 0    ewc_cboxEnableToggle;
checkBox    -edit    -enable 0    -value 0    ewc_cboxShadingToggle;
checkBox    -edit    -enable 0    -value 0    ewc_cboxTexturingToggle;
checkBox    -edit    -enable 0    -value 0    ewc_cboxPlaybackToggle;
checkBox    -edit    -enable 0    -value 0    ewc_cboxVisibilityToggle;

// Option Menus
optionMenu  -edit    -enable 0    ewc_optmenDisplayType;
optionMenu  -edit    -enable 0    ewc_optmenLevelOfDetail;

// Buttons
symbolButton    -edit    -enable 0    ewc_btnAddSelectedObjects;
symbolButton    -edit    -enable 0    ewc_btnRemoveSelectedObjects;

for ($i = 1; $i < 11; $i++)
    button    -edit    -enable 0    ("ewc_btnBonusDrawing" + $i);

    button    -edit    -enable 0    ewc_btnToggleLayerID;

// The set current button in the Current Layer frame
```

```
button        -edit    -enable 0    ewc_btnSetCurrentLayer;

// Integer Field
intField      -edit    -value 1     ewc_fldLayerID;

// Color palette
palettePort   -edit    -enable 0    ewc_palprtLayerColor;

// File menu items that require an active layer to be selected
menuItem      -edit    -enable 0    ewc_menuDeleteLayer;
menuItem      -edit    -enable 0    ewc_menuRenameLayer;
menuItem      -edit    -enable 0    ewc_menuLayerAttr;
```

Case 2

Enable member-specific editing buttons.

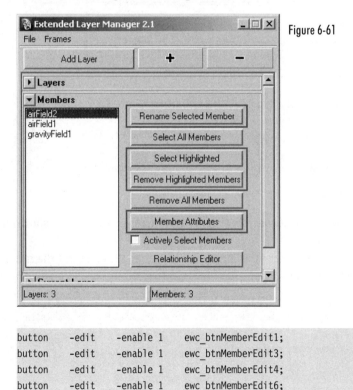

Figure 6-61

```
button    -edit    -enable 1    ewc_btnMemberEdit1;
button    -edit    -enable 1    ewc_btnMemberEdit3;
button    -edit    -enable 1    ewc_btnMemberEdit4;
button    -edit    -enable 1    ewc_btnMemberEdit6;
```

Chapter 6

Case 3

Loop through the member controls and disable them all.

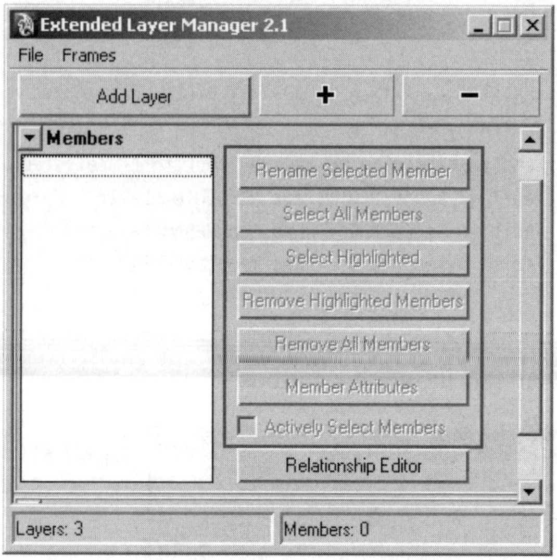

Figure 6-62

```
// Loop through all buttons and disable them
for ($i = 1; $i < 7; $i++)
    button    -edit -enable 0   ("ewc_memberEditOption" + $i);

    checkBox  -edit -enable 0   ewc_memberEditOption7;
```

Case 4

Toggle on all controls that are not member-specific, as shown in Figure 6-63.

First, query the highlighted layer and then query the members of the layer:

```
// Query the highlighted layer
string $layer[] = `textScrollList -query -selectItem ewc_tslLayerList`;

// Query the members of a layer
if($layer[0] != "")
    {
    string $mem[] = `editDisplayLayerMembers -query $layer[0]`;
```

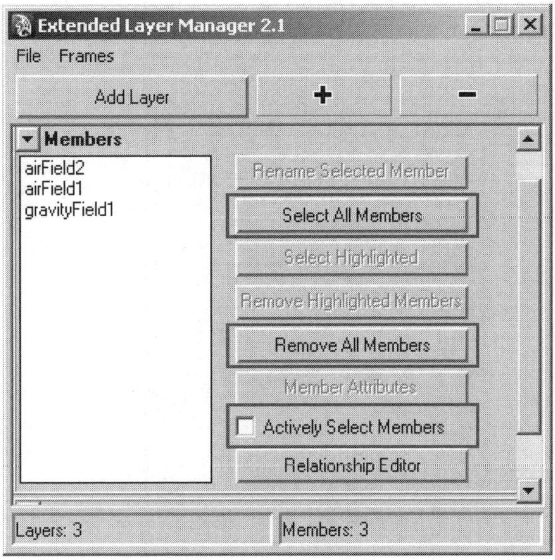

Figure 6-63

Test the size of the array with the `size` command. If the query returns true, enable buttons that only require a layer to have members and do not depend on a member being highlighted in the textScrollList:

```
// If the array is not empty
if (size($mem))
    {
    // Partially enable the member controls
    button     -edit     -enable 1     ewc_btnMemberEdit2;
    button     -edit     -enable 1     ewc_btnMemberEdit5;
    checkBox   -edit     -enable 1     ewc_cboxActiveSelect;
    }
```

If the query returns false, then there are no members. Call this procedure again with an argument of 3 to disable all the member controls:

```
// If it is, then disable all controls
else
    ewc_gprocControlStates(3);
    }
```

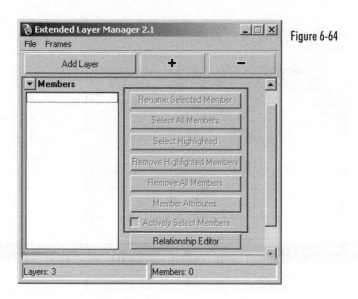

Figure 6-64

Implementing the Functionality

Locate the ewc_gprocLoadCurrentLayers() procedure. Inside the loop that appends layers to the textScrollList, edit the -selectCommand flag to hold three procedures:

```
textScrollList
    -selectCommand ("ewc_gprocQueryDrawingOptions();"
        + "ewc_gprocUpdateMemberList();"
        + "ewc_gprocControlStates(4)")
    ewc_tslLayerList;
```

When a user highlights a layer, the case statement will query that layer to determine if it has any members. If there are, then enable the three controls that are not member-specific; if not, then make sure all controls are disabled in the Members frame. Figure 6-65 shows layer1 as the highlighted layer. It contains two members (pCube2 and pCube1); therefore the Select All Members and Remove All Members buttons have been enabled. Also, the Actively Select Members check box has been enabled.

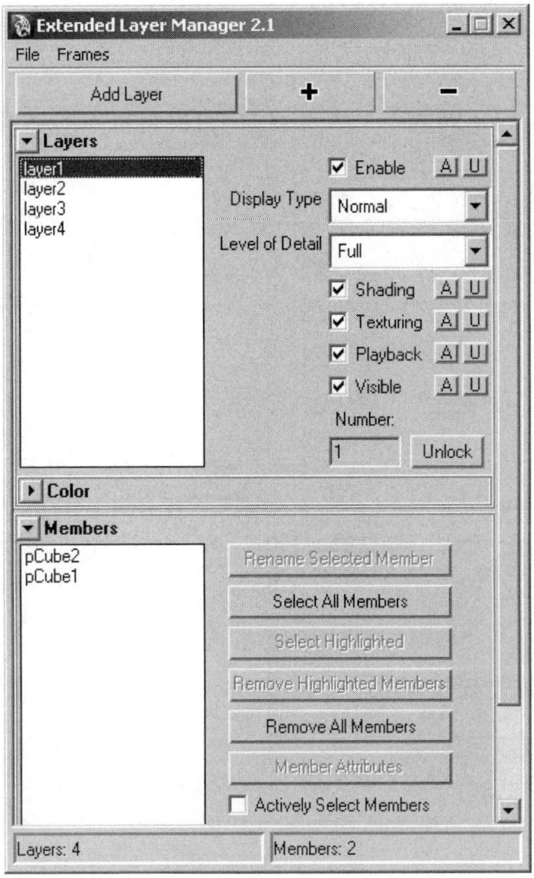

Figure 6-65

Locate the ewc_gprocLayerEditing() procedure. In case 1, which is the condition that deletes layers, identify the corresponding comment, and add two calls to the procedure, passing the arguments of 1 and 3.

```
// Disable the controls
ewc_gprocControlStates(1);
ewc_gprocControlStates(3);
```

When a layer is deleted, the textScrollList will lose focus and no items will be selected. When this happens, the controls on both the Layers and Members frames must be disabled until another layer is highlighted.

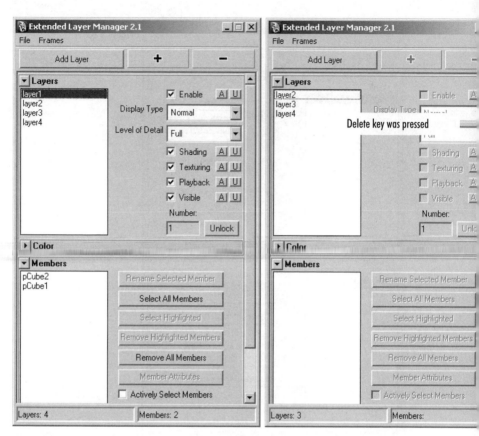

Figure 6-66

The remaining buttons will be enabled when a member is high-lighted. Locate the ewc_gprocUpdateMemberList() procedure. Inside the loop that appends members to the textScrollList, edit the -selectCommand flag:

```
textScrollList
    -selectCommand "ewc_gprocControlStates(2)"
    ewc_tslMemberList;
```

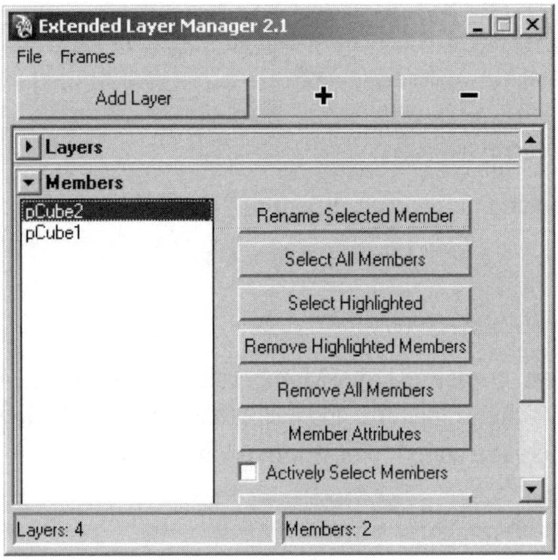

Figure 6-67

In the same procedure, add the next block of code below the if statement. This is a backup conditional test in case the member list is refreshed from either the File menu or the right-click pop-up.

If a query of the number of items in the textScrollList returns true, pass an argument of 4 to enable controls that are not member-specific.

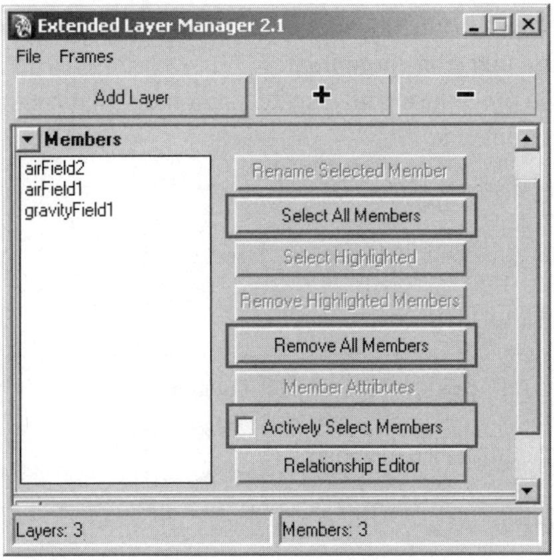

Figure 6-68

```
// Get a count of the members in the list
//If there are any then toggle on the general controls
if (`textScrollList -query -numberOfItems ewc_tslMemberList`)
    ewc_gprocControlStates(3);
    ewc_gprocControlStates(4);
```

If false is returned, pass an argument of 3 to disable all controls:

```
//If there are no members toggle off controls
else
    ewc_gprocControlStates(3);
```

Locate the ewc_gprocEditLayerMemberships() procedure. At the very bottom of the procedure, add a call that will run whenever selected objects are added to or removed from a layer:

```
// Update member frame
ewc_gprocControlStates(4);
```

You can open ewc_extendedLayerManager_27.mel to compare your progress so far.

6.5.3 Member Editing: ewc_gprocMemberEditing()

Now that the buttons in the Members frame are enabled, the procedure that defines the functionality of the controls can be created. This procedure takes one argument.

Create the procedure with a switch statement that contains seven case statements:

```
//===========================
// MEMBER EDITING
global proc ewc_gprocMemberEditing(int $case)
{
    // Query the highlighted layer

    // Get the full names of the layers' members

    // Query the highlighted members

    switch ($case)
```

```
{
    case 1: // Rename member
        break;

    case 2: // Select all members
        break;

    case 3: // Select highlighted
        break;

    case 4: // Remove highlighted members
        break;

    case 5: // Remove all members
        break;

    case 6: // Member attributes
        break;

    case 7: // Interactive selection
        break;

    } // End switch
} // End ewc_gprocMemberEditing()
```

Full DAG Paths

The full path to a DAG object lists all parenting nodes of the DAG object:

```
parent|parent|object
```

To retrieve the full path, the -fullNames flag will be used when querying objects. In Maya, objects can share the same name in situations where they do not share the same parent. In Figure 6-69, both group1 and group2 contain an object named pCube1.

Chapter 6

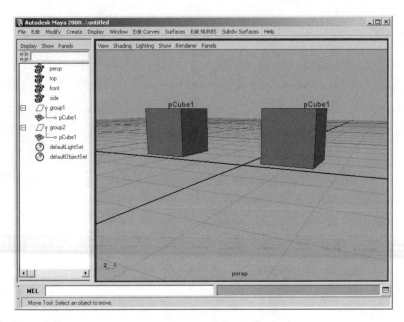

Figure 6-69

This can create selection problems when trying to script a selection:

```
select "pCube1";
```

```
// Error: line 1: More than one object matches name: pCube1 //
```

To select the cube in the first group, I will need to select it through its parent node. This is done by using a pipe (|) between the parent and the object:

```
select "group1|pCube1";
```

If the cube in group1 were on a layer called cubeLayer and needed to be selected, the full path would need to be returned. This is why the -fullNames flag must be used since it returns the full path to the object.

```
editDisplayLayerMembers -query -fullNames cubeLayer;
// Result: |group1|pCube1 //
```

Now that you are aware of potential selection errors that could occur, it is obvious why the -fullNames flag must be used.

Create the Arrays

Before the switch statement, create three arrays:

```
// Query the highlighted layer
string $layer[] = `textScrollList -query -selectItem ewc_tslLayerList`;

// Get the full names of the layers
string $fullNames[] = `editDisplayLayerMembers -query -fullNames
   $layer[0]`;

// Query the highlighted members
string $memberItems[] = `textScrollList -query -selectItem
   ewc_tslMemberList`;
```

Case1: Rename Member

In section 6.4, "Creating the Functionality — Part I," I left a case statement empty for renaming layers. Do the same here. The procedure that will handle the actual renaming of both layers and members will be written next.

```
case 1: // Rename highlighted

   // Verify the first array element is not empty
   // Create variables to be used in the loop

   // Loop through the array of actual members
      // Separate the full names using the bar

      // Test the array
         // Call the renaming procedure and pass the
         // string "Member" and the highlighted member

   break;
```

Case 2: Select All Members

This block will select all members of the current layer.

The first command will clear any current selections that are active in the viewport. Next, use the `select` command with the `-replace` flag, which will replace the current selection with the objects held in the `$fullNames` array:

```
case 2: // Select all members
    select -replace $fullNames;
    break;
```

Case 3: Select Highlighted

Clicking on items in a list does not create a selection in the viewport. This case statement will take the highlighted items in the textScrollList and create an actual selection out of them.

The first step is to clear the current selection, then query the actual members and store them in an array:

```
case 3: // Select highlighted

    // Clear any current selection
    select -clear;
```

Create an empty string array and an integer variable to be used inside the next loop:

```
    // Create variables to be used in the loop
    string $fullPath[];
    int $pathSize;

    // Loop through the array of actual members
    for ($i = 0; $i < size($fullNames); $i++)
    {
```

The `tokenize` command can be used to separate the strings based on characters. When querying full names of objects, a string similar to the following will be returned:

```
|group2|group1|pCube1
```

The string to be split up is the first argument in a `tokenize` command. The second is a string that will be the split character that separates the nodes and objects into individual strings; in this case, it is the pipe character (|). The third argument is the array that will be holding the separated strings. The `tokenize` command itself returns the total number of strings generated as an integer value and stores it in `$pathSize`.

```
// Separate the full names using the bar
$pathSize = `tokenize $fullNames[$i] "|" $fullPath`;
```

Remember that an array starts its index at 0, so if `tokenize` returns a value of 3 (meaning there were three strings), then subtract 1 to test if it exists in the `$memberItems` array. The final element will hold the object that needs to be selected. If the separated string matches one of the highlighted items from the list, then use the full path to the object to add it to the selection:

```
// Test the array.
if(stringArrayContains($fullPath[$pathSize - 1], $memberItems))
    select -add $fullNames[$i];
}
break;
```

Case 4: Remove Highlighted Members

This block will remove the highlighted members from the current layer. This differs from the Remove Selected button at the top of the layer manager in that this command does not require a selection to be active in the viewport.

```
case 4: // Remove highlighted members

    // Create variables to be used in the loop
    string $fullPath[];
    int $pathSize;

    // Loop through the array of actual members
    for ($i = 0; $i < size($fullNames); $i++)
    {
        // Separate the full names using the bar
        $pathSize = `tokenize $fullNames[$i] "|" $fullPath`;
```

This time each element of the `$memberItems` array (which is the array of highlighted list items) will be compared to the last element of the `$fullPath` array. If there is a match, use the path string held in the corresponding element `$fullNames` in the `editDisplayMembers` command to send the target object to the defaultLayer:

Chapter 6

```
// Test the array
if($memberItems[$i] == $fullPath[$pathSize - 1])
editDisplayLayerMembers -noRecurse "defaultLayer"
    $fullNames[$i];
}

// Update member list
ewc_gprocUpdateMemberList();
break;
```

Case 5: Remove All Members

This block will remove all members from the current layer:

```
case 5: // Remove all members
editDisplayLayerMembers -noRecurse "defaultLayer" $fullNames;
// Update member list
ewc_gprocUpdateMemberList();
break;
```

Case 6: Member Attributes

Launch the Attribute Editor for the specific member. Select the member in the first element of the array. Use the openAEWindow procedure that already exists by default in Maya.

```
case 6: // Member attributes

    // Verify the first array element is not empty
    // Create variables to be used in the loop
    string $fullPath[];
    int $pathSize;

    // Loop through the array of actual members
    for ($i = 0; $i < size($fullNames); $i++)
    {
        // Separate the full names using the bar
        $pathSize = `tokenize $fullNames[$i] "|" $fullPath`;
```

In this case, select the object when a match is made and open the Attribute Editor:

```
// Test the array
if($memberItems[0] == $fullPath[$pathSize - 1])
```

```
        {
            select $fullNames[$i];
            // Open the Attribute Editor, this will either
            // open the shape or transform node.
            openAEWindow;
        }
    }
break;
```

Case 7: Interactive Selection

This feature will enable the interactive selection of items in the textScrollList, thus allowing a user to click and drag in the list to create selections in the viewport. The first step is to query the state of the Actively Select Members check box in the Members frame. If the test returns true, simply call the third case statement, which selects the highlighted members.

```
case 7: // Interactive selection
    // Query the state of the check box
    // If it is checked then call the procedure
    // with an argument of 3 to select highlighted
    if(`checkBox -query -value ewc_cboxActiveSelect`)
        ewc_gprocMemberEditing(3);
    break;
```

Assignments and Arguments

In the procedure that creates the interface, locate the block that creates the buttons for the Members frame. Use the list below for the correct arguments when editing the -command flags. The last control is a check box that uses a -changeCommand flag instead.

```
string $b15 = `button
    -command "ewc_gprocMemberEditing(1)"
    ewc_btnMemberEdit1`;

string $b16 = `button
    -command "ewc_gprocMemberEditing(2)"
    ewc_btnMemberEdit2`;

string $b17 = `button
```

```
    -command "ewc_gprocMemberEditing(3)"
ewc_btnMemberEdit3`;

string $b18 = `button
    -command "ewc_gprocMemberEditing(4)"
ewc_btnMemberEdit4`;

string $b19 = `button
    -command "ewc_gprocMemberEditing(5)"
ewc_btnMemberEdit5`;

string $b20 = `button
    -command "ewc_gprocMemberEditing(6)"
ewc_btnMemberEdit6`;

string $cb6 = `checkBox
    -changeCommand "ewc_gprocMemberEditing(7)"
ewc_cboxActiveSelect`;
```

Locate the ewc_gprocUpdateMemberList() procedure. In the loop
that appends members to the textScrollList, locate and edit the
arguments for -selectCommand, -deleteKeyCommand, and
-doubleClickCommand:

```
textScrollList
    -doubleClickCommand "ewc_gprocMemberEditing(1)"
    -deleteKeyCommand "ewc_gprocMemberEditing(4)"
    -selectCommand ("ewc_gprocControlStates(2);"
                  +"ewc_gprocMemberEditing(7)")
ewc_tslMemberList;
```

You can open ewc_extendedLayerManager_28.mel on the companion disc to compare your progress so far.

6.5.4 Renaming Procedure: ewc_gprocRenamingPrompt()

Now a procedure will be created to rename layers and members.
This procedure will take two string arguments. The first string will
be used to identify what is being renamed (layer or member). The
second string is the name of the item that is being renamed.

Pseudocode the procedure. Due to page width limitations, the proper indentation cannot be printed accurately in this book. On the companion disc, locate the ewc_extendedLayerManager_29_ pseudo.mel file to view the comments with proper indentation.

```
//===========================
// RENAME OBJECTS/LAYERS
global proc ewc_gprocRenamingPrompt(string $type, string $orig)
{
    // If renaming object extract the name
    // from the paths. First store original path

        // Separate the object from the path

        // Return the original object name to the $orig variable

        // Open an input prompt
        // If OK button was clicked
            // Store the name entered
            // Check that the variable isn't empty
                // Check that the name was actually changed
                // Test if name is valid
                // Test if the name is already in use
                // Warn the user if it does
                // User has elected to try again
            // Rename the objects
            // Evaluate which list is refreshed
                // Update the layer list
                // Select the renamed layer
                // Update the member list
                // Select the renamed member
            // Name is invalid, warn the user
            // User has elected to try again
} //End ewc_gprocRenamingPrompt()
```

The first step is to query if the object being renamed is an object (member) and not a layer. Store the original string (containing the full path) in a new variable. Use the `tokenize` command to separate the object from the parent nodes. Store the object name back into the `$orig` variable.

Chapter 6

```
// If renaming object extract the name
// from the paths. First store original path
string $originalArgument = $orig;

if ($type == "Member")
    {
    // Separate the object from the path
    string $object[];
    int $element = `tokenize $orig "|" $object`;

    // Return the original object name to the $orig variable
    $orig = $object[$element - 1];
    }
```

Create an input prompt for the new name. The -title flag contains a concatenation of the argument being passed to the $type variable. The -text flag will print the original name of the item being renamed. This is useful if a user just needs to correct a misspelled name.

```
// Open an input prompt
string $prompt = `promptDialog
            -title ("Rename " + $type)
            -message "Enter new name:"
            -button "OK"
            -button "Cancel"
            -defaultButton "OK"
            -cancelButton "Cancel"
            -dismissString "Cancel"
            -text $orig`;
```

Test if the OK button was clicked. If it was, store the input from the user into the variable $name by querying the text field of the promptDialog.

```
// If the OK button was clicked
if ($prompt == "OK")
    {
    // Store the name entered
    string $name = `promptDialog -query -text`;
```

Test that the input field wasn't left empty. Then test that the user actually changed the name before clicking OK.

```
// Check that the variable isn't empty
if ($name != "")
    {
    // Check that the name was actually changed
    if ($name != $orig)
        {
```

Test that the name the user entered is valid; a valid name starts with a letter and is followed by any combination of letters, numbers, and underscores with no white space.

```
// Test if name is valid
if (isValidObjectName($name))
    {
```

Test that the user input is a unique name and not already in use:

```
// Test if the name is already in use
if (objExists($name))
    {
```

If the name is in use, warn the user:

```
// Warn the user if it does
string $confirm = `confirmDialog
            -title "WARNING"
            -message "Name is not unique. Try again?"
            -button "OK"
            -button "Cancel"
            -defaultButton "OK"
            -cancelButton "Cancel"
            -dismissString "Cancel"`;
```

If the user clicks OK, restart the procedure and pass the same arguments that were passed to the procedure in the first place. This will restart the whole procedure with the original arguments.

```
if ($confirm == "OK")
// User has elected to try again
ewc_gprocRenamingPrompt($type, $originalArgument);
```

If the `objExists` command returns false, then the name is not in use. Use the `rename` command to rename the object stored (with its full path) in `$originalArgument` with the string value held in

$name. Next, the switch statement tests the argument held in
$type. Only two possible values will be passed to $type. Depending on which procedure the argument is passed from, either the
string "Layer" or the string "Member" will be passed. The matching case statement will update the correct textScrollList and
highlight the renamed member or layer.

```
else
    {
    // Rename the objects
    rename $originalArgument $name;

    // Evaluate which list is refreshed
    switch($type)
        {
        case "Layer":
            // Update the layer list
            ewc_gprocLoadCurrentLayers();
            // Select the renamed layer
            textScrollList -edit -selectItem $name ewc_tslLayerList;
            break;
        case "Member":
            // Update the member list
            ewc_gprocUpdateMemberList();
            // Select the renamed member
            textScrollList -edit -selectItem $name ewc_tslMemberList;
            break;
        }
    }
```

If the isValidObjectName command returns false, warn the user
that the name is invalid. The user input being held in $name will be
concatenated in the -message flag to display what the invalid string
was. If the user clicks OK, restart the procedure and pass the original arguments.

```
    }
else
    {
    // Name is invalid, warn the user
    string $confirm = `confirmDialog
```

```
                    -title "Warning"
                    -message ("The name \"" + $name + "\" is invalid. "
                        + "Valid names only contain alphanumeric\n"
                        + "characters. The name may not start with a"
                        + " digit.\n"
                        + "Whitespace characters are not allowed.")
                    -button "OK"
                    -button "Cancel"
                    -defaultButton "OK"
                    -cancelButton "Cancel"
                    -dismissString "Cancel"`;
        if ($confirm == "OK")
            // User has elected to try again
            ewc_gprocRenamingPrompt($type, $originalArgument);
    }
```

To close all the if statements, three delimiters must be added before the final delimiter that ends the procedure itself. Your script should reflect the example below:

```
            }
        }
    }
} //End ewc_gprocRenamingPrompt()
```

Assignments and Arguments

Locate the ewc_gprocLayerEditing() procedure. In the second case statement, edit the block to pass the correct arguments:

```
case 2: // Rename a layer
    // Verify the first array element is not empty
    if ($layer[0] != "")
        // Call the renaming procedure and pass the
        // string "Layer" and the highlighted layer
        ewc_gprocRenamingPrompt("Layer", $layer[0]);
    break;
```

Now locate the ewc_gprocMemberEditing() procedure. In the first case statement, create a query that will match the item in the list to the actual object assigned to the layer. When a match is made between the strings tested in the if statement, pass the full path to the object as an argument to the rename procedure.

```
case 1: // Rename member

    // Verify the first array element is not empty
    // Create variables to be used in the loop
    string $fullPath[];
    int $pathSize;

    // Loop through the array of actual members
    for ($i = 0; $i < size($fullNames); $i++)
        {
        // Separate the full names using the bar
        $pathSize = `tokenize $fullNames[$i] "|" $fullPath`;

        // Test the array
        if($memberItems[0] == $fullPath[$pathSize - 1])
            // Call the renaming procedure and pass the
            // string "Member" and the highlighted member
            ewc_gprocRenamingPrompt("Member", $fullNames[$i]);
        }

    break;
```

Now when the procedure is called it will function according to the arguments being passed. The first argument will name the title correctly on the input prompt and will be used to refresh the correct list after the item has been renamed.

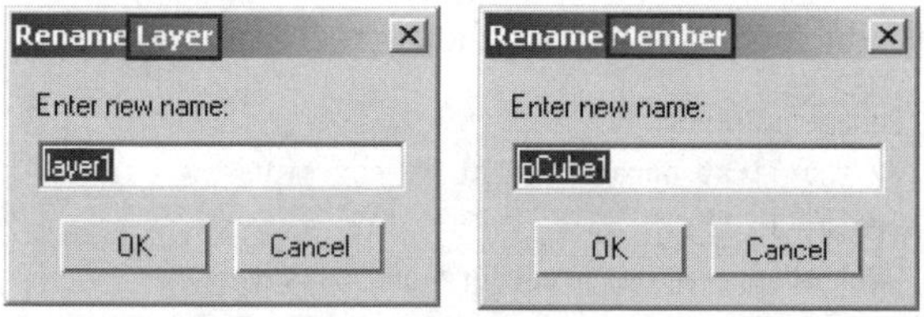

Figure 6-70

The second argument being passed is holding the original name of either the layer or member, which is used for display in the renaming prompt (see the screenshot above). If you are having problems, please refer to ewc_extendedLayerManager_29.mel on the companion disc.

6.5.5 The Current Layer: ewc_gprocEditCurrentLayer()

In the default layer editor in Maya, highlighting a layer makes it the current layer. Since the layer manager itself requires a layer to be highlighted to change its attributes, I felt that another system should be in place to control which layer is assigned as the current one.

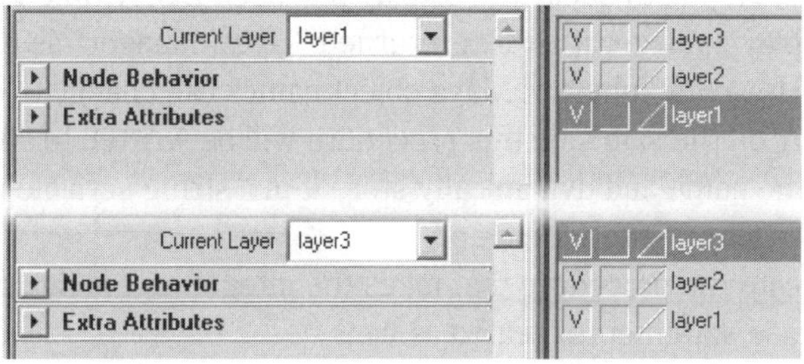

Figure 6-71

I wanted a unique but simple form of functionality in the layer manager I was building. This feature should be straightforward and use only the necessary number of controls to edit the current layer.

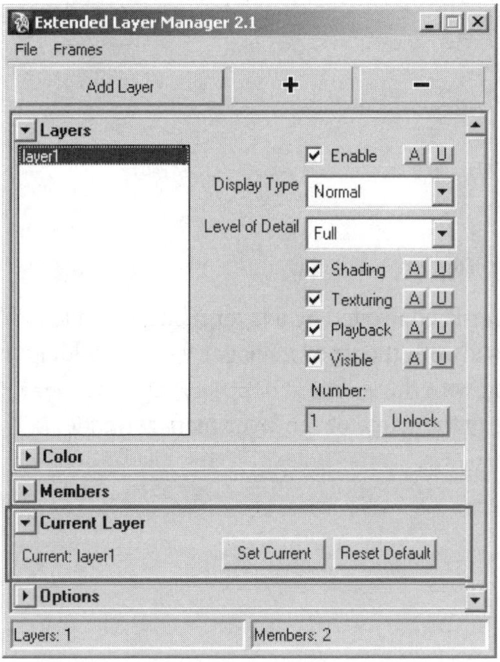

Figure 6-72

Chapter 6

341

The current layer is the layer that all newly created objects are assigned to. This procedure will take one integer argument. There will be three case statements:

■ Two for the Current Layer frame

■ One that will be called from within the interface procedure to update the text control in the Current Layer frame

The first step is to query the display manager. Every time I queried the display manager it always returned "layerManager" as the name. However, inherent Maya object names can change over time, so to err on the safe side this procedure will be written to always query the name and dynamically store it in a string variable instead of hard-coding "layerManager."

Create the procedure that takes the integer argument. We need three case statements created as well.

```
global proc ewc_gprocEditCurrentLayer(int $case)
{
    // Get the layer manager
    switch ($case)
    {
        case 1: // Set the current layer
            break;
        case 2: // Reset to default
            break;
        case 3: // Query current layer (UI loading)
            break;
    } // End switch
} // End ewc_gprocEditCurrentLayer()
```

The current layer is controlled by a layer manager node in Maya, not to be confused with the layer manager we are building. By using the `ls` command with the `-type "displayLayerManager"` flag, we can directly query the name of the layer manager node.

```
// Get the layer manager
string    $lm[]    = `ls -type "displayLayerManager"`;
```

Case 1: Set the Current Layer

This block will take the currently highlighted layer in the textScrollList and make it the current layer in the scene.

Query the highlighted layer that will become the current layer:

```
case 1: // Set the current layer
    // Query for the selected layer
    string $layer[] = `textScrollList -query -selectItem
        ewc_tslLayerList`;
```

Get the identification number of the highlighted layer:

```
    // Query and store the identification of the selected layer
    int $val = `getAttr ($layer[0]+".identification")`;
```

To determine the current layer for new objects, Maya reads identification numbers, not names. This is why the `setAttr` command is using the value being held in `$val` as the argument. The attribute of the layerManager that is being changed is `.cdl` (current display layer).

```
    // Assign the layer as current by passing the layer
    // manager handler concatenated with ".cdl" attributes
    // and the identification value of the selected layer
    setAttr ($lm[0] + ".cdl") $val;
```

The next command will force new objects into the current layer:

```
    // Force newly created objects to be created in the current layer
    editDisplayLayerGlobals -useCurrent 1;
```

Finally, update the text control in the Current Layer frame to reflect the correct layer:

```
    // Update the text field
    text -edit -label ("Current: " + $sel[0]) ewc_txtCurrentLayer;
    break;
```

Chapter 6

Case 2: Reset to Default

Reset the scene to use the defaultLayer as the current layer:

```
case 2: // Reset to default
    // Get the defaultLayer identification number
    int $val = `getAttr "defaultLayer.identification"`;
    // Assign defautlLayer as current layer
    setAttr ($lm[0]+".cdl") $val;
    // Update the text field to display defaultLayer
    text -edit -label ("Current: defaultLayer") ewc_txtCurrentLayer;
    break;
```

Case 3: Query Current Layer (UI Loading)

When the interface loads, this block will be called to update the text control to properly reflect the current layer in the scene.

Create an array of the layers in the scene:

```
case 3: // Query current layer (UI loading)
    // Create array of scene layers
    string $layers[] = `ls -exactType "displayLayer"`;
```

Querying the current layer of a scene returns only the identification number:

```
    // Query the identification of the current
    // layer through the layer manager
    int $val = `getAttr ($lm[0]+".cdl")`;
```

Loop through each element in the $layers array to query the identification attribute and test the returned value against the value being stored in $val for a match. When a match is found, update the text control to reflect the current layer.

```
    // Loop through all the layers to query identifications
    for ($i in $layers)
    {
        int $id = `getAttr ($i + ".identification")`;
        // Compare identifications
        if ($id == $val)
            // Edit the text field by concatenating the name
            text -edit -label ("Current: " + $i) ewc_txtCurrentLayer;
    }
    break;
```

Assignments and Arguments

At the very bottom of the interface procedure, right above the showWindow command, add a call to the third case statement to load the current layer name into the -label flag of the text control. This way the correct default layer will be displayed when the UI gets created.

```
// Update current layer display
ewc_gprocEditCurrentLayer(3);
```

Go up further in the procedure, to locate the buttons in the Current Layer frame and edit the -command flags:

```
button
    -command "ewc_gprocEditCurrentLayer(1)"
    ewc_btnSetCurrentLayer;

button
    -command "ewc_gprocEditCurrentLayer(2)"
    ewc_btnResetDefaultLayer;
```

Locate the ewc_gprocLayerEditing() procedure and edit the first case statement to include an if statement that will test if the layer being deleted is the current layer. A shortcut is to concatenate the name being held in $i with the string "Current: ". Then compare it to the string being held in the label of the text control for an exact match.

```
if (("Current: " + $i) == `text -query -label    ewc_txtCurrentLayer`)
```

If a match is made, then one of the layers being deleted is the current layer. Calling the second case statement will reset the scene back to using the defaultLayer.

```
case 1: // Delete layers
    // Check that there is a selection
    if ($layer[0] != "")
    {
        // Delete all elements in the array
        delete $layer;
        // Disable the controls
        ewc_gprocControlStates(1);
```

```
ewc_gprocControlStates(3);
// Empty the member list
textScrollList -edit -removeAll ewc_tslMemberList;
// Reset the custom help line
text -edit -label "Members:" ewc_txtMemberCount;
// Loop Through the array
for ($i in $layer)
    {
    // Check to see if the layer being deleted is the
    // current layer
    if (("Current: " + $i) == `text -query -label
        ewc_txtCurrentLayer`)
        // Current layer procedure
        ewc_gprocEditCurrentLayer(2);
    }
}
break;
```

You can open ewc_extendedLayerManager_30.mel to compare your progress so far.

6.5.6 More scriptJob Commands: ewc_gprocELMScriptJobs()

In section 6.4.4 two scriptJobs were created to detect when a layer was created or deleted. Three more will have to be set up here, but first a procedure must be created. The procedure will take one integer argument.

Create the procedure with a switch statement:

```
//===========================
// SCRIPT JOBS
global proc ewc_gprocELMScriptJobs(int $case)
{
    // Query the highlighted layer
    switch ($case)
    {
        case 1: // Dag object created
            break;
        case 2: // Undo/Redo query
            break;
```

```
        case 3: // New scene - Open a scene
            break;
    } // End switch
} // End ewc_gprocElmScriptJobs()
```

Query the highlighted layer above the switch statement:

```
// Query the highlighted layer
string $layer[] = `textScrollList -query -selectItem ewc_tslLayerList`;
```

Case 1: DAG Object Created

A scriptJob will be created that detects when a new object is created in the viewport. It will call to case 1, which will check if the highlighted layer is the current layer. If it is, the member list must be updated. Use a shortcut that will concatenate "Current: " with the name of the layer. If it matches the -label query of the text control, then the member list must be updated to display the new members.

```
case 1: // Dag object created
// If the concatenated selection doesn't match the current layer
if (("Current: " + $layer[0]) == `text -query -label
    ewc_txtCurrentLayer`)
    ewc_gprocUpdateMemberList();
break;
```

Case 2: Undo/Redo Query

Whenever an Undo and Redo operation occurs, the layer manager will test that the contents of the layer and member lists still match the actual data in the scene.

This case statement will be longer than the previous one, so we will start with the pseudocode:

```
case 2: // Undo/Redo query
    // Test that the first element is not empty
    if ($layer[0] != "")
        // Get a list of all layers and the default layer
        // Omit the defaultLayer
        // Create an array from the text list
        // Compare the display layers to the layer list
            // If a layer is not in the list
        // Compare the layer list to the display layers
```

Chapter 6

```
        // If a list item is not a display layer
        // Create an array from the member list
        // Create an array of the actual members
        // Compare the actual members with the member list
            // If a layer is not in the list
        // Compare the list with the actual members
            // If a list item is not an actual member
    }
    break;
```

The entire block needs to be contained within the if statement that tests for an empty string in the first array element. This is important because whenever the layerManager is running, it will detect any Undo/Redo operations, regardless of whether there is a highlighted item in the layer list, and attempt to execute this case statement. This will prevent potential errors.

Create an array of all the display layers. Create another array that only holds the defaultLayer. Then use the `stringArrayRemove` command to omit the default layer from the other display layers.

```
// Get a list of all layers and the default layer
string $allLayers[] = `ls -exactType "displayLayer"`;
string $defaultLayer [] = {"defaultLayer"};
// Omit the defaultLayer
string $layers[] = stringArrayRemove($b, $a);
```

Create an array containing all items in the layer list:

```
// Create an array from the text list
string $listLayers[] = `textScrollList -query -allItems
    ewc_tslLayerList`;
```

Loop through each element of the `$layers` array and use the not operator (`!`) to test if any element of `$layers` does not match any of the elements in `$listLayers`. If no match is made, the textScrollList must be refreshed. The `break` command will break out of the loop since it no longer needs to run.

```
// Compare the display layers to the layer list
for ($i in $layers)
    {
    // If a layer is not in the list
```

- DagObjectCreated
- Undo
- Redo
- NewSceneOpened
- SceneOpened

```
// Event detection for when new objects are created
scriptJob
    -parent   ewc_winExtendedLayerManager
    -event    "DagObjectCreated"    "ewc_gprocELMScriptJobs(1)";
// Event detection for undo
scriptJob
    -parent   ewc_winExtendedLayerManager
    -event    "Undo"                "ewc_gprocELMScriptJobs(2)";
// Event detection for redo
scriptJob
    -parent   ewc_winExtendedLayerManager
    -event    "Redo"                "ewc_gprocELMScriptJobs(2)";
// Event for new scene
scriptJob
    -parent   ewc_winExtendedLayerManager
    -event    "NewSceneOpened"      "ewc_gprocELMScriptJobs(3)";
// Event for opened scene
scriptJob
    -parent   ewc_winExtendedLayerManager
    -event    "SceneOpened"         "ewc_gprocELMScriptJobs(3)";
```

You can open ewc_extendedLayerManager_31.mel to compare your progress so far.

6.5.7 Addressing Itchy Behavior

When a layer is set as the current layer, it will receive *all* new objects, including shapes. This is not the desired behavior I want in the layer manager. It can quickly clutter the member list with unnecessary nodes. Child nodes inherit the drawing states of the parent node. When you add a group node to a layer, only the group node exists in the list, but the children of the group node will still inherit the drawing states. The same goes for transform and shape nodes. Since shapes will inherit the drawing states, and display

Chapter 6

layers simply exist to control object displays in a viewport, it is not of any real benefit to assign a shape to a layer.

The following screenshot is relatively simple, but consider a larger project with hundreds, if not thousands, of objects. This can quickly clutter the textScrollList.

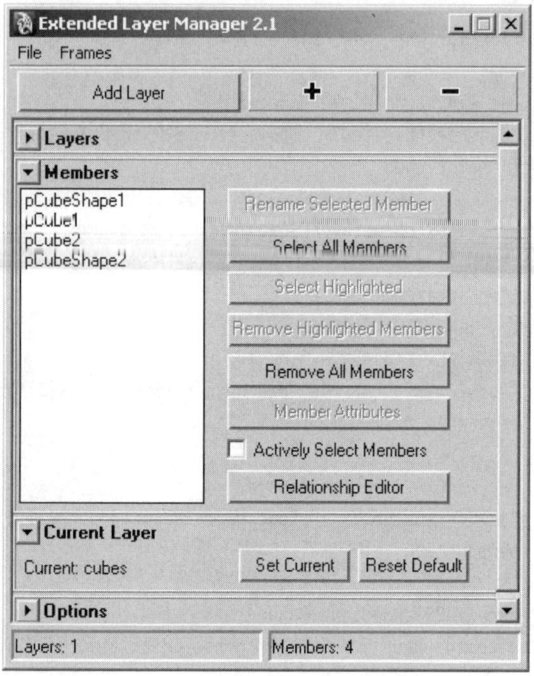

Figure 6-73

Locate the ewc_gprocUpdateMemberList() procedure because several commands will need to be added and changed. This was not done in section 6.4 because it would have been difficult to demonstrate and rationalize without the scriptJobs and current layer editing functionality.

Locate the line that is in bold in the example below and start from here:

```
// If there is a selection then make an array of the members
string    $mem[] = `editDisplayLayerMembers -query $layer[0]`;

// Sort it alphabetically
sort($mem);
```

Change the name of the array to $fullNames and add the
-fullNames flag:

```
// If there is a selection then make an array of the members
string $fullNames[] = `editDisplayLayerMembers -query -fullNames
    $layer[0]`;
```

Create another array using the ls command with the -shapes flag
to query the $fullNames array. This is why the -fullNames query
was necessary. If two transforms shared the same name, so could
their shape nodes.

```
// Extract a list of the shape nodes
string $shapes[] = `ls -shapes $fullNames`;
```

Use the size command to test if there are any shapes present in the
array. If there are, assign all elements of the $shapes array to the
defaultLayer.

```
// If there are shape nodes present (array does not equal 0)
if (size($shapes))
    editDisplayLayerMembers -noRecurse "defaultLayer" $shapes;
```

Create a new array that removes all shapes from the members list,
and name the array $noShapes, which is the original array that is
still being used for the rest of the procedure.

```
// Create a new array without the shapes
string $noShapes[] = stringArrayRemove($shapes,$fullNames);
```

The next loop will require two arrays. Create them now:

```
// Create arrays to avoid scope problems
string $mem[];
string $paths[];
```

Loop through each element in the $noShapes array and split the
strings using the pipe character. Take the final element of the
$paths array, created by the tokenize command, and store it in the
$mem array.

```
for ($i = 0; $i < size($noShapes); $i++)
    {
    // Separate the object from the paths
    int $pathSize = `tokenize $noShapes[$i] "|" $paths`;
```

```
// Store the object into the array
$mem[$i] = $paths[$pathSize - 1];
}
```

The lines in bold reflect the edits required to properly remove shapes before populating the member list:

```
// If there is a selection then make an array of the members
string $fullNames[] = `editDisplayLayerMembers -query -fullNames
    $layer[0]`;

// Extract a list of the shape nodes
string $shapes[] = `ls -shapes $allMem`;

// If there are shape nodes present (array does not equal 0)
if (size($shapes))
    editDisplayLayerMembers -noRecurse "defaultLayer" $shapes;

// Create a new array without the shapes
string $noShapes[] = stringArrayRemove($shapes,$fullNames);

// Create arrays to avoid scope problems
string $mem[];
string $paths[];

for ($i = 0; $i < size($noShapes); $i++)
    {
    // Separate the object from the paths
    int $pathSize = `tokenize $noShapes[$i] "|" $paths`;
    // Store the object into the array
    $mem[$i] = $paths[$pathSize - 1];
    }

// Sort it alphabetically
sort($mem);
```

You can open ewc_extendedLayerManager_32.mel to compare your progress so far.

6.5.8 **Frames Menu: ewc_gprocFrameToggle()**

Figure 6-74

The functionality of the Frames menu and the right-click pop-up clone that appears if you RMB anywhere in the UI will create a list of preset collapse states of the frames. This is a simple procedure that simply edits the –collapse flag of a frameLayout. This procedure takes one integer argument.

```
//===========================
// FRAME CONTROL
global proc ewc_gprocFrameToggle(int $case)
{
    switch ($case)
    {
        case 1: // Reset frames
            break;

        case 2: // Members frame
            break;

        case 3: // Expand all frames
            break;

        case 4: // Collapse all frames
            break;

        case 5: // About...
            break;

    } // End switch
} // End ewc_gprocFrameToggle()
```

Case 1: Reset Frames

Restore the collapsible frames to the default state. Only the Layers frame is opened:

```
case 1: // Reset frames
    frameLayout -edit -collapse 0 ewc_frameLayers;
    frameLayout -edit -collapse 1 ewc_frameColor;
    frameLayout -edit -collapse 1 ewc_frameMembers;
    frameLayout -edit -collapse 1 ewc_frameCurrentLayer;
    frameLayout -edit -collapse 1 ewc_frameOptions;
    frameLayout -edit -collapse 1 ewc_frameAbout;
    break;
```

Case 2: Members Frame

Only the Members frame is opened:

```
case 2: // Members frame
    frameLayout -edit -collapse 1 ewc_frameLayers;
    frameLayout -edit -collapse 1 ewc_frameColor;
    frameLayout -edit -collapse 0 ewc_frameMembers;
    frameLayout -edit -collapse 1 ewc_frameCurrentLayer;
    frameLayout -edit -collapse 1 ewc_frameOptions;
    frameLayout -edit -collapse 1 ewc_frameAbout;
    break;
```

Case 3: Expand All Frames

Open all frames, including the two nested frames, of the interface:

```
case 3: // Expand all frames
    frameLayout -edit -collapse 0 ewc_frameLayers;
    frameLayout -edit -collapse 0 ewc_frameColor;
    frameLayout -edit -collapse 0 ewc_frameMembers;
    frameLayout -edit -collapse 0 ewc_frameCurrentLayer;
    frameLayout -edit -collapse 0 ewc_frameOptions;
    frameLayout -edit -collapse 0 ewc_frameAbout;
    break;
```

Case 4: Collapse All Frames

Close all frames of the interface:

```
case 4: // Collapse all frames
    frameLayout -edit -collapse 1 ewc_frameLayers;
    frameLayout -edit -collapse 1 ewc_frameColor;
    frameLayout -edit -collapse 1 ewc_frameMembers;
    frameLayout -edit -collapse 1 ewc_frameCurrentLayer;
    frameLayout -edit -collapse 1 ewc_frameOptions;
    frameLayout -edit -collapse 1 ewc_frameAbout;
    break;
```

Case 5: About...

Collapse all frames except the Options and About... frames:

```
case 5: // About...
    frameLayout -edit -collapse 1 ewc_frameLayers;
    frameLayout -edit -collapse 1 ewc_frameColor;
    frameLayout -edit -collapse 1 ewc_frameMembers;
    frameLayout -edit -collapse 1 ewc_frameCurrentLayer;
    frameLayout -edit -collapse 0 ewc_frameOptions;
    frameLayout -edit -collapse 0 ewc_frameAbout;
    break;
```

Assignments and Arguments

Locate the `menuItem` commands created under the Frames menu
and edit the `-command` flags:

```
menu -label "Frames" ewc_menuFramesMainWindow;

    // Menu Item: Reset Frames
    menuItem
        -label "Reset Frames"
        -command "ewc_gprocFrameToggle(1)";

    // Menu Item: Member Frame
    menuItem
        -label "Members Frame"
        -command "ewc_gprocFrameToggle(2)";

    // Menu Item: Expand Frames
```

Chapter 6

```
menuItem
    -label "Expand Frames"
    -command "ewc_gprocFrameToggle(3)";

// Menu Item: Collapse Frames
menuItem
    -label "Collapse Frames"
    -command "ewc_gprocFrameToggle(4)";

// Menu Item: -divider-
menuItem -divider 1;

// Menu Item: About...
menuItem
    -label "About..."
    -command "ewc_gprocFrameToggle(5)";
```

Locate the `menuItem` commands created under the pop-up menu under the scrollLayout and edit the `-command` flags:

```
popupMenu -parent ewc_scrollFrameHolder;

    menuItem
        -label "Reset Frames"
        -command "ewc_gprocFrameToggle(1)";

    menuItem
        -label "Members Frame"
        -command "ewc_gprocFrameToggle(2)";

    menuItem
        -label "Expand Frames"
        -command "ewc_gprocFrameToggle(3)";

    menuItem
        -label "Collapse Frames"
        -command "ewc_gprocFrameToggle(4)";

    menuItem -divider 1;
```

```
menuItem
    -label "About..."
    -command "ewc_gprocFrameToggle(5)";
```

This is an easy procedure to set up and even modify with your own layout presets.

You can open ewc_extendedLayerManager_33.mel to compare your progress so far.

6.5.9 **Relationship Editor**

The File menu and the Members frame both contain a control to open the Relationship Editor. This is a default editor in Maya with considerably more member functionality. The File menu item and Members frame button give the user quick access to this editor. The procedure to launch the editor already exists by default in Maya.

Locate the `menuItem` command in the File menu and edit the `-command` flag:

```
// Menu Item: Relationship Editor
menuItem
    -label "Relationship Editor"
    -command "LayerRelationshipEditor";
```

Locate the button for the Relationship Editor (the last one created) and edit the `-command` flag:

```
button
    -command "LayerRelationshipEditor"
    ewc_btnRelationshipEditor`;
```

Now a user can quickly access the Relationship Editor.

Chapter 6

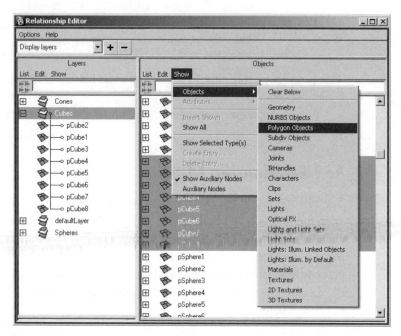

Figure 6-75

You can open ewc_extendedLayerManager_34.mel to compare your progress so far.

6.5.10 **Autographing Your Work**

The last thing you will want to do with your script is create a block comment at the top of the script. This comment should contain information about the author, date of last revision, contact information, and any other additional data you want to share with the user.

```
/*********************************************
:: Author:    Ed Caspersen
:: Script:    ewc_extendedLayerManager.mel
:: Version:   2.1
:: Email:     ed.caspersen (at) gmail dot com
:: Date:      July 16, 2008
-------------------------------------------------
:: Description:    This script gives a user a
:: floating interface that allows for additional
```

```
:: control over layer management and editing.
*********************************************/
```

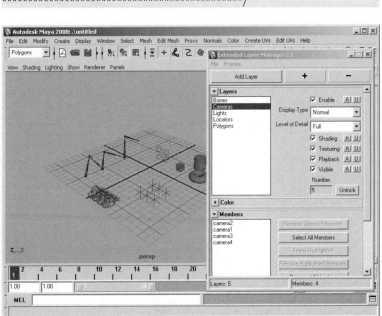

Figure 6-76

You can use ELM_example_scene.mb on the companion disc to give the ELM a test run.

Enjoy!

Chapter 7

Recursion

> **Note:** This chapter is based on the wonderful and inspiring work of Malcolm Kesson. Kudos to Malcolm for letting us use his excellent example of recursion. You can find Malcom's extremely informative site at: http://www.fundza.com/.

I would also like to explicitly thank Craig "bring on the radians" Davies for his invaluable input on this chapter.

7.1 Introduction

This chapter is fairly heavy stuff. If the previous chapters were strong, dark Belgian ale, then this chapter is a 30-year-old, single-barrel malt whiskey. It takes a refined, educated, and well-traveled man with a good palate to appreciate all the nuances of such fine liquor. This chapter, well, requires none of those characteristics, but a background in trigonometry (or at least a willingness to refresh) will come in handy.

7.1.1 What Is Recursion?

For more information about recursion, see the chapter about recursion.

You are probably wondering what that was all about. This is the chapter about recursion, yet I am referring to it for information about recursion. This geeky little joke illustrates exactly what recursion is. Recursion is a slightly more advanced programming technique that we will use in this and the later chapters to do a variety of things. As such, it is a good idea to clearly understand what recursion is and how it can be used.

In terms of MEL, recursion is when a function directly (or indirectly) calls itself, as in the following:

```
global proc int factorial(int $n)
{
    if ($n <= 1)
        return 1;

    return $n*factorial($n-1);
}
```

In the example above, you can clearly see (in bold) that the procedure is calling itself in the procedure.

In Plain English

(Borrowing from http://en.wikipedia.org/wiki/Recursion here):

Recursion is the process a procedure goes through when one of the steps of the procedure involves rerunning the procedure. A procedure that goes through recursion is said to be recursive. Something is also said to be recursive when it is the result of a recursive procedure.

An everyday example would be shampoo directions:

1. Lather
2. Rinse
3. Repeat

To understand recursion, one must recognize the distinction between a procedure and the running of a procedure. A *procedure* is a set of steps that are to be taken based on a set of rules. The *running of a procedure* involves actually following the rules and performing the steps. An analogy might be that a procedure is like a restaurant menu because the procedure lists all possible steps, while running a procedure is actually choosing the steps (or courses for the meal) from the menu.

A procedure is recursive if one of the steps that makes up the procedure calls for a new running of the procedure. Therefore, a recursive four-course meal would be a meal in which one of the choices of appetizer, salad, entrée, or dessert was an entire meal unto itself. So a recursive meal might be potato skins, baby greens salad, chicken Parmesan, and for dessert, a four-course meal consisting of crab cakes, Caesar salad, a four-course meal, and chocolate cake for dessert. And so on until each of the meals within the meals is completed.

Recursions as Loops

Throughout this book you have been introduced to various examples and uses of loops. What separates recursion from other loops is that an entire procedure is being looped. Like loops, there is an inherent danger to recursive procedures: triggering an infinite loop. You may have seen examples in the past of for loops that looked like the following one.

Warning: Maya will crash if you try the code below!

```
for ( $i = 0; $i >= 0; )
    print "oops\n";
```

If you were to run this, you would get an infinite loop because $i will always be at least equal to (at least on the first iteration) and greater than 0. If you were to run this script with the script editor open, you might see an infinite printing of the word "oops" before Maya locks up (a.k.a. "hangs").

```
oops
oops
oops
oops
oops
// and so on!!!!
```

A technique I use to demonstrate why loops, even ones that only print strings, can quickly crash Maya is to have people repeat the same word over and over until they begin to run out of breath. Infinite loops essentially suck the "breath" out of Maya until no air is left.

The same mistake can be made with recursions. For example, the following procedure would infinitely loop over and over again, creating one NURBs sphere after another on top of each other. It is doing this because the procedure calls its own name after the sphere command.

```
proc foo()
{
    sphere; // make a sphere
    foo();
}
```

Like with loops, using a recursive procedure can be incredibly powerful, and in *most* situations it is a better choice for optimizing your scripts; you just have to make sure you control the depth of the recursion. (Sometimes a recursion can be less optimal than a loop because of the overhead of making a procedure call.)

Recursive procedures also make code more elegant and intuitive. Some might even say that recursions make code beautiful and desirable. Those people need to get out more.

7.1.2 Terminating Recursions

We looked at two ways to successfully crash Maya. Now let's look at how to stop the recursion process. This is done through the use of arguments. Passing an integer value through an argument is probably the most efficient way to generate a condition that is tested before the procedures calls itself again.

```
proc foo(int $depth)
{
    // test to terminate the recursion
    if ($depth == 0)
        return;
    // make a sphere
    sphere;
    // call foo again and subtract 1 from the argument
    foo($depth - 1);
}
```

Now if we execute the command:

```
foo(5)
```

Five spheres will be created on top of each other in the viewport.

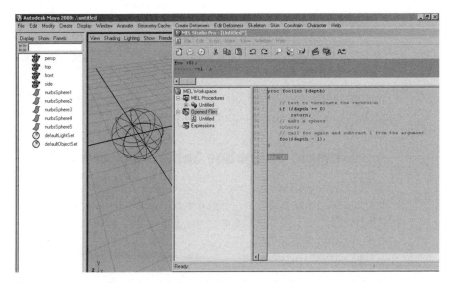

Figure 7-1

First I want you to look at the previous recursion example again. Notice any problems? I do, and a big one at that. We have not completely secured the procedure from an infinite loop. When writing scripts for production, you have to take into consideration everyone working on the pipeline. You know how the script works and how to use it correctly, but your users might not. If someone were to accidentally enter a negative value like this:

```
foo(-3)
```

Then Maya would do what it was told to do: Continue subtracting 1 from the current value, which will actually be taking our variable further away from 0. This creates, you guessed it, another infinite loop and Maya will crash. By using the abs command (returns an absolute value) on the variable $depth you can ensure that whatever value you are testing is positive:

```
proc foo(int $depth)
{
    // test to terminate the recursion
    if (abs($depth) == 0)
        return;
    // make a sphere
```

```
sphere;
// call foo again and subtract 1 from the argument
foo(abs($depth) - 1);
}
```

Small additions to your scripts like this will go a long way in improving the workflow of a production pipeline.

7.1.3 Example 1: Knobby Sphere (sphere.mel)

Using recursions you can create a preset of parameters to incrementally size and position geometry. This example uses NURBs spheres. All that the user needs to enter is the initial count, pivot position, and radius.

Declare the procedure:

```
proc spheres(int $depth, vector $pnt, float $rad)
{
```

Perform the termination test:

```
// test $depth
if (abs($depth) == 0)
    return;
```

If no termination happens, create a sphere. The flags for -pivot and -radius will have their values influenced by the arguments sent to the procedure.

```
// creates a sphere
sphere
    // argument $pnt used to change the pivot
    -pivot   ($pnt.x) 0 ($pnt.z)
    // $rad sets the radius value.
    -radius $rad
    // The end sweep will create a hemisphere
    -endSweep 180;
```

The .x and .z extensions on the $pnt variable extract individual components: the X and Z components of the vector. The $pnt is a vector, meaning it contains three float values, such as $<<24, 32, 55>>$. In this example, .x returns 24, .y returns 32 (although we aren't using .y in this particular procedure), and .z returns 55. This procedure will place the new sphere in a new location on the XZ-plane while staying flush with the y-axis.

The next chunk of code has an order of operations. By reading the parentheses, starting with the innermost operation, you can see the order of the calculation.

■ First is `sphrand`, which will generate a random vector coordinate based on the radius provided in the parentheses.

■ Then the `unit` command will take that vector and create another vector that points to the same point in space but with a length of 1.

■ This vector is then multiplied by the radius of the most recent sphere.

■ Finally, this vector will be passed in the next recursion for placing the next sphere in a relative offset to the radius of the sphere that was just created, and the final vector is stored in `$pnt`.

```
// find a random location on the surface of the sphere
$pnt = unit(sphrand(1)) * $rad;
```

To control the recursion, subtract 1 from the value in `$depth` before passing it as an argument:

```
// control the recursion by subtracting the depth by 1
// and reducing the radius by 25 percent
spheres(abs($depth) - 1, $pnt, $rad * 0.75);
}
```

The full script looks like this:

```
proc spheres(int $depth, vector $pnt, float $rad)
{
    // test $depth
    if (abs($depth) == 0)
        return;
    // creates a sphere
    sphere
        // argument $pnt used to change the pivot
        -pivot    ($pnt.x) 0 ($pnt.z)
        // $rad sets the radius value.
        -radius $rad
```

```
// Setting the endsweep flag to 180
// will create the hemisphere
-endSweep 180;
// find a random location on the surface of the sphere
$pnt = unit(sphrand(1)) * $rad;
// control the recursion by subtracting the depth by 1
// and reducing the radius by 25 percent
spheres(abs($depth) - 1, $pnt, $rad * 0.75);
}
```

To see what it does, enter this:

```
spheres(10, <<5,0,5>>, 4);
```

You should see something similar to the following:

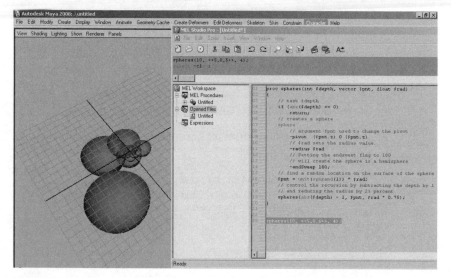

Figure 7-2

Unit Command

The unit command, used above and again in the example below, might need some further elaboration. I will assume that not everyone reading this book is proficient in (or remembers) their trigonometry, so I am going to attempt to illustrate exactly how the unit command works.

In Maya, create a locator in the center of the scene by entering the following:

```
spaceLocator -position 0 0 0;
```

Create a second locator using the following command. This will create a second locator in an obscure position in the viewport.

```
float $x = 3.496;
float $y = 5.729;
float $z = -3.954;
spaceLocator -position $x $y $z;
```

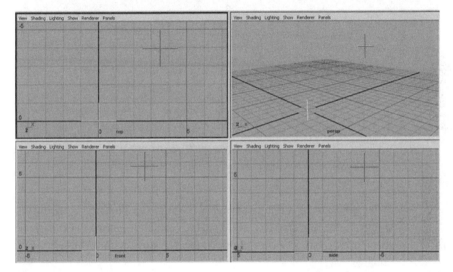

Figure 7-3

Now take the values used to position the second locator and plug them into the `unit` command:

```
vector $newVec = 'unit <<$x, $y, $z >>';
```

The returned result should be something like this:

```
// Result: <<0.448805, 0.73547, -0.507601>> //
```

The position flag requires float values. To use a vector index in place of float values, surround the variable with parentheses.

```
spaceLocator -position ($newVec.x) ($newVec.y) ($newVec.z);
```

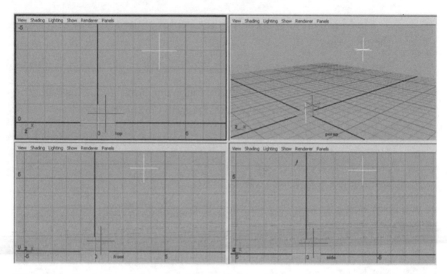

Figure 7-4

The MEL documentation states:

"This command returns the normalized vector — a vector pointing in the same direction as the argument but with a length of one."

What is meant by a length of one is that the third locator is within the first grid unit of 0 0 0 world space. Notice in Figure 7-4 that in all three orthographic views the third locator stays within the first grid squares.

Now create a 1 degree curve that starts at the first locator and ends at the third locator:

```
curve -degree 1 -point 0 0 0 -point ($newVec.x) ($newVec.y) ($newVec.z);
```

at the top of the sphere, in a cluster around the north pole, the size of which is roughly controlled by the multiplier *2 on the first line. Then you add on $pnt, the center of the sphere you just made, and recurse. In doing so, it's picking random points on the tops of the previous spheres.

```
$p = unit($p)*$rad + $pnt;
```

We then control the recursion by subtracting 1 from the depth and reducing the radius by 40 percent. (To write percentages, we use float values ranging from 1.0 (100%) to 0.0 (0%). To reduce by 40 percent, subtract 0.4 from 1.0 to get 0.6.)

```
spheres($depth - 1, $p, $rad * 0.6);
}
```

The full script looks like this:

```
global proc bubbleTree(int $depth, vector $pnt, float $rad)
{
// reduce the depth and check if it drops to zero or less (then stop)
if ($depth <= 0)
return;
// creates a sphere
sphere
    // argument $pnt used to change the pivot
    -pivot ($pnt.x) ($pnt.y) ($pnt.z)
    // $rad sets the radius value.
    -radius $rad
    //-endSweep 180;
    ;
for ($i=0;$i<4;$i++)
    {
    // find a random vector in a sphere
    vector $p = sphrand($rad*2);
    // keep XZ components
    // then translate the point up from the XZ-plane
    // to a height of $radius
    $p = <<$p.x,$rad,$p.y>>;
    // project that point on the surface of a unit sphere
    $p = unit($p)*$rad + $pnt;
    // control the recursion by subtracting the depth by 1
    // and reducing the radius by 40 percent
```

```
    bubbleTree($depth - 1, $p, $rad * 0.6);
    }
}
```

To try the script, source the procedure and then type:

```
bubbleTree (5, <<0,0,0>>, 1);
```

If you always want the same tree, you can use the seed command:

```
// use seed so it gives the same tree each time
seed 56789;
bubbleTree (5, <<0,0,0>>, 1);
```

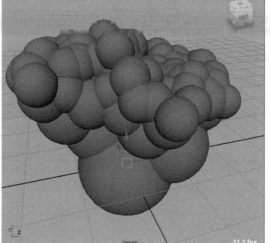

Figure 7-7

7.2 Recursion and Branching (tree.mel)

This next script will introduce a practical example, on a larger scale, of how recursion would be useful in a production environment. This script will generate curves that resemble a branch-like structure (like a tree or coral) by utilizing an algorithm that locates the endpoint of a curve and then uses that endpoint to extend additional curves. By recursing over this method, we will be able to create branches.

Figure 7-8

This script is rather involved and requires some trigonometry. We will start by briefly outlining and illustrating what the script will do in sections 7.2.1 and 7.2.2. Then we will review some trigonometry and vector math (sections 7.2.3 to 7.2.6), and finally we will go through each procedure of the script line by line (starting with section 7.2.7 and continuing to the end of the chapter). The entire script can be found on the companion disc.

7.2.1 Finding the First Branch: Workflow

Step 1: Calculate a circle representing the branch radius.

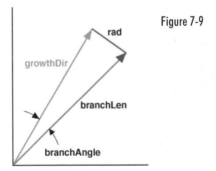

Figure 7-9

Step 2: Find a random vector on the circle. This is done with the vectorOnCircle() procedure.

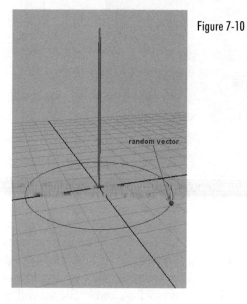

Figure 7-10

Step 3: Translate the vector up the y-axis by branch length units ($branchLen in the tree procedure).

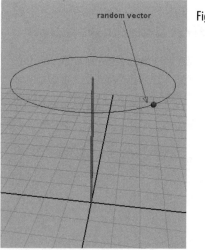

Figure 7-11

Step 4: Rotate the vector by the branch angle to find the end of a branch ($branchAngle in the tree procedure).

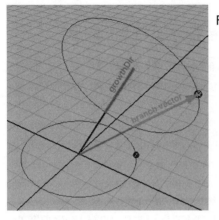

Figure 7-12

Step 5: Draw a line between the base ($base) of the branch and the (relative) end of the branch. To do this, we will need to compute the angles needed to rotate a vector to align to the y-axis in such a way that it aims along a particular vector — in this case, the growth direction ($growthDir). The aimY procedure, explained in depth in section 7.2.7, will be written for this purpose.

Step 6: Draw a curve that represents the first branch.

Step 7: Recurse.

7.2.2 Finding the Second Branch: Workflow

Step 1: Define the second branch as if it were a reflection of the first branch about the $growthDir vector. This is done with the reflect procedure.

Step 2: Move the end of the second branch relative to the base point. (This is the $end2 vector in the tree procedure.)

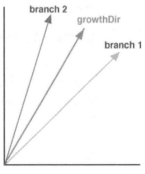

Figure 7-13

Step 3: Draw the second branch.

Step 4: Recurse.

7.2.3 Aligning the Y-axis to a Vector

> **Note:** The inspiration for this text can be found at
> http://www.fundza.com/mel/axis_to_vector/align_axis_to_vector.html.

The Challenge

Step 5 of finding the first branch calls for something that is a bit challenging. We need to compute the angles needed to rotate a vector to align to the y-axis in such a way that it aims along a particular vector — in this case, the growth direction ($growthDir). In other words, we need to apply a series of rotations to a coordinate system so that one of its axes points in a specific direction.

Visualizing Vectors

A good way to visually follow and/or calculate vector rotations is using your hand. Make your right hand a fist and extend your index finger and thumb to make a "pistol." Now point your index finger toward the ceiling and lift your middle finger until it is perpendicular to your index finger. You are now representing the right-handed Cartesian coordinate system with your hand. Your thumb is the x-axis, your middle finger is the y-axis, and your index finger is the z-axis. Using this technique, it should be fairly straightforward to follow things like: "the xAngle rotation will swing from the y-axis toward the z-axis."

Vectors: A Short Recap

As you know, aside from being a data type in MEL, a *vector* is mainly a mathematical representation of a point in the Cartesian three-dimensional coordinate system.

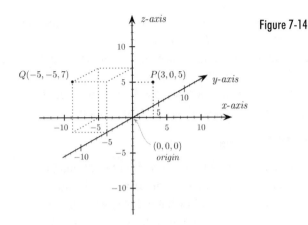

Figure 7-14

In the image from Wikipedia above, you can clearly see Q, P, and the origin as vectors, represented as three numbers in XYZ. By the way, the three components of a vector (represented in MEL code as <<1,2,3>>) are called *scalars*, or *scalar components*.

In addition to a point in space, a vector also has a length, which is called the *magnitude* of the vector. Using the magnitude of a vector, we can represent things like the distance between two points, the speed/velocity of a particle, or the intensity of a physical force (such as the magnitude of a turbulence field).

Free and Fixed Vectors

So, we have seen that vectors are entities that have direction and length (magnitude) and are typically defined by two or three values. Part of the confusion in dealing with vectors is the way they are represented in illustrations. Often they are represented as *free vectors* that can be moved to arbitrary locations depending on the concept that is being explained.

However, when it comes to performing certain mathematical operations on vectors it is essential to be aware that vectors are not "free" but are fixed at the origin of a coordinate system. For example, although it makes visual sense to show a surface normal (a type of vector) extending directly from a polygon, the normal is, in fact, not located at the surface of "its" polygon. It is located at the origin of the coordinate system in which the polygon is defined and as such must be treated as a *fixed* (or *bound*) *vector.*

So, bound or fixed vectors are vectors whose initial point is the *origin*. This is in contrast with free vectors, which are vectors whose initial point is not necessarily the origin. Keep this in the back of your head when reading the next section.

Back to the Challenge

Our initial challenge was to find a series of rotations for a coordinate system so that one of its axes points in a specific direction, specifically the growth direction. In what follows, we will attempt to show how the y-axis of a coordinate system can be aligned to a direction specified by a vector.

The illustration below shows a vector with coordinates $<<-2,2,1>>$. The gray diagonal lines show the vector projected onto the XY-plane, the XZ-plane, and the YZ-plane.

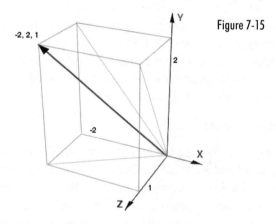

Figure 7-15

The easiest way of figuring out how to rotate the coordinate system so that the y-axis points in the direction of the vector is to think about the problem in reverse. The reverse of the problem would be: How can the vector be aligned to the current y-axis?

The Rotations

Step 1: Figure 7-16 shows that the vector forms the hypotenuse of a right-angled triangle.

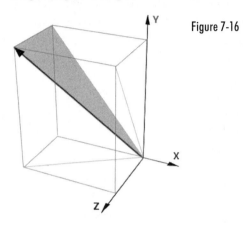

Figure 7-16

I know high school was probably a long time ago, so maybe a little refresher is appropriate.

A *hypotenuse* is the longest side of a right triangle; that is, the side opposite the right angle. The length of the hypotenuse of a right triangle can be found using the Pythagorean theorem, which states that the square of the length of the hypotenuse equals the sum of the squares of the lengths of the other two sides.

In other words, in any right triangle, the area of the square whose side is the hypotenuse (the side opposite the right angle) is equal to the sum of the areas of the squares whose sides are the two legs (the two sides that meet at a right angle).

For example:

(straight from http://en.wikipedia.org/wiki/Pythagorean_theorem)

If we let c be the *length* of the hypotenuse and a and b be the lengths of the other two sides, the theorem can be expressed as the equation:

$$a^2 + b^2 = c^2$$

or, solved for c:

$$c = \sqrt{a^2 + b^2}$$

Step 2: Figure 7-17 shows how the triangle can be aligned to the YZ-plane by applying a suitable rotation around the z-axis.

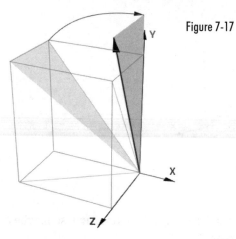

Figure 7-17

Step 3: Figure 7-18 shows that a rotation around the x-axis will align the vector to the y-axis of the coordinate system.

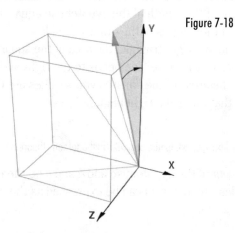

Figure 7-18

Figure 7-19 shows the (desired) result of all the rotations: the vector aligned with the y-axis.

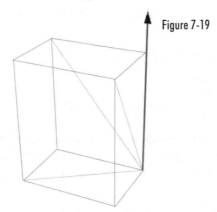

Figure 7-19

7.2.4 **The Calculations**

Section 7.2.3 showed how to rotate a coordinate system so that one of its axes points in a specific direction. Now all we have to do is create the calculations so we can put them in a MEL procedure.

Figure 7-20 shows the two angles that must be calculated in order to perform steps 2 and 3. To find the Z angle (shown in light gray) we must first calculate the length of the line xyLength on the XY-plane.

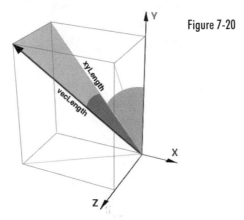

Figure 7-20

Given our original vector of $<<-2,2,1>>$, let's calculate xyLength:

```
$xyLength = sqrt(x * x + y * y);    // Pythagorean theorem
$xyLength = sqrt(-2 * -2 + 2 * 2);  //our values filled in formula
$xyLength = 2.83;                   //result
```

After which the angle shown in light gray can be found:

```
$zAngle = acos(y / xyLength);
$zAngle = acos(2.0 / 2.83);
$zAngle = 0.785; /* acos returns angle in radians */
```

Before we continue with the calculations, I think it is a good idea to briefly go over concepts like acos, cosine, and radian. This will enable us to more clearly grasp what happens in our code on a mathematical level.

7.2.5 Acos and Cosine

Strangely enough, the `acos` command does not appear in the actual MEL command reference in Maya 2008.

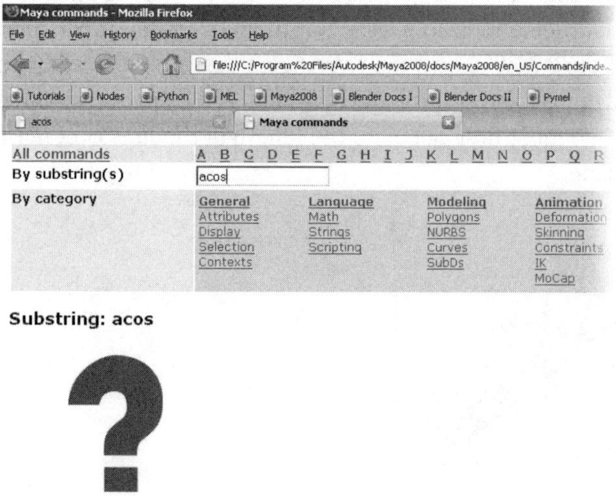

Substring: acos

Figure 7-21

It can, however, be found in the Maya documentation, and ironically, it is classified under MEL and Expressions.

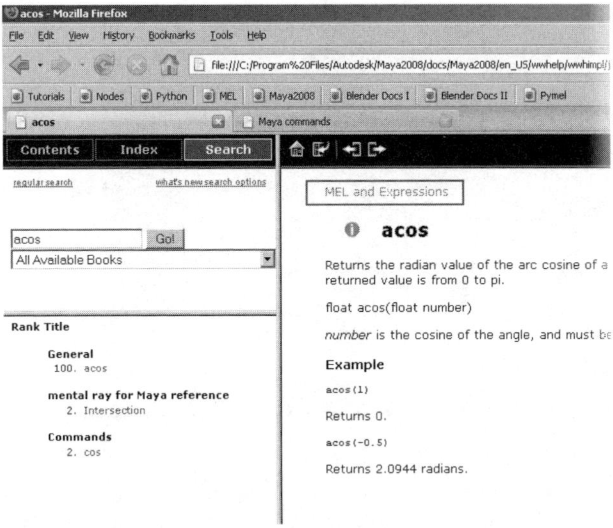

Figure 7-22

The `acos` command will return an angle (measured in radians) whose cosine is the input value to the command. Instead of digging too far into the actual formulas behind this, I will demonstrate this command in Maya by using curves.

Start by creating two curves:

```
curve
    -name "adjacent"
    -degree 1
    -point 0 0 0
    -point 5 0 0;
curve
    -name "hypotenuse"
    -degree 1
    -point 0 0 0
    -point 5 7 0;
```

Looking through the front viewport you should now see something like this:

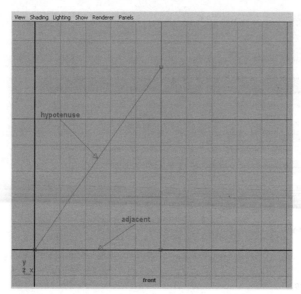

Figure 7-23

Now measure the distance that each curve spans using the distanceDimension command:

```
distanceDimension
    -startPoint 0 0 0
    -endPoint 5 0 0;
distanceDimension
    -startPoint 0 0 0
    -endPoint 5 7 0;
```

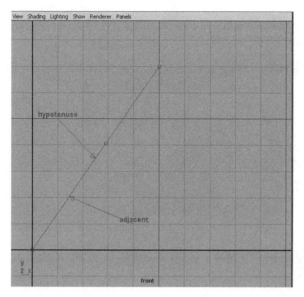

Figure 7-25

The adjacent curve has been rotated to lay exactly on the hypotenuse curve. The formula we will be writing requires a radian value so the `acos` command must be used; if you needed to obtain a result in degrees, the `acosd` command would be more suitable:

```
acosd($cosine);
// Result: 54.462321 //
```

Before moving on, there needs to be some clarification on radians and degrees.

7.2.6 Radian

A *radian* is a unit of measurement of an angle based on the radius, as opposed to degrees, which are based on the arbitrary division of a circle into 360 units. Radians are the standard unit of angular measurement in all areas of mathematics beyond the elementary level. This is because radians have a mathematical "naturalness" that leads to a more elegant formulation of a number of important results.

The pure definition of a radian (from http://en.wikipedia.org/wiki/Radian) is as follows:

One radian is the angle subtended at the center of a circle by an arc that is equal in length to the radius of the circle.

Figure 7-26

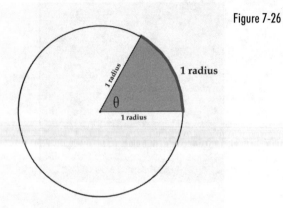

For a more visual explanation of radians, see http://www.wisc-online.com/objects/index_tj.asp?objID=TMH1301.

Now that we have a better insight into acos, cosine, and radians, we can return to the final part of our calculation.

To find the dark gray angle (shown in the figure below) and given our original vector of $<<-2,2,1>>$, the length of the vector must be found.

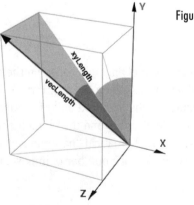

Figure 7-27

```
vecLength = sqrt(x * x + y * y + z * z);
vecLength = sqrt(-2 * -2 + 2 * 2 + 1 * 1);
vecLength = 3.0;
```

As with the light gray angle, the angle in dark gray is found from the cosine. I am referring to this angle as the xAngle because, as shown in the figure below, this angle will be used to define the rotation around the x-axis.

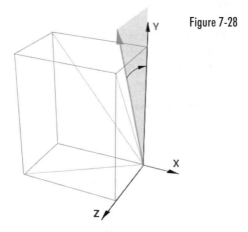

Figure 7-28

```
xAngle = acos(xyLength / vecLength);
xAngle = acos(2.83 / 3.0);
xAngle = 0.338;
```

If we convert back to degrees, we determine that the zAngle is 45.0 and the xAngle is 19.4.

Therefore, the rotations needed to orient the y-axis in the direction of the vector are:

1. First, a rotation around the x-axis of 19.4 degrees.

2. Then, a rotation around the z-axis of –45 degrees.

We are now ready to write the aimY() procedure in MEL.

7.2.7 **Create the aimY() Procedure**

As you might have gathered by now, the purpose of the aimY() procedure is to find the X/Z angles to rotate a vector aligned with the y-axis ($vec.y), in such a way that it aims along a particular vector (in this case, the growth direction).

```
proc float[] aimY(vector $vec)
{
```

First, create an array and the five variables that will be used throughout this procedure. The $out array is created with the number 2 in the brackets; this defines the scope (size) of the array upon creation.

```
// Create the variables
float $out[2];
float $xAngle;
float $zAngle;
float $xyLength;
float $yzLength;
float $vecLength;
```

sqrt

Although filling in the Pythagorean theorem would satisfy most people, it leaves us (real men) with a hollow feeling inside. We want more. We want to truly understand what a square root does. After all, a deep understanding of square root is a natural aphrodisiac.

In the following code, the value stored in $vec.y will be plugged into the acos command, which in turn will generate new angles from Z- and X-based coordinates. Using the sqrt command, we will generate a number that is the square root of the sum of squares of the two complementary coordinates.

I am going to step through this statement backward to break it down. We are going to create an angle for the x-axis ($xAngle). This angle will be obtained through the values in $vec.y and $vec.z, respectively.

As you probably know, a square is the result of multiplying a number by itself.

Chapter 7

```
print (4 * 4);
16
```

Create a vector variable with an obscure position in three-dimensional space:

```
vector $vec = <<10.009, 15.051, 10.28>>;
```

Use these coordinates to create a new curve:

```
curve
    -degree 1
    -point 0 0 0
    -point ($vec.x) ($vec.y) ($vec.z);
```

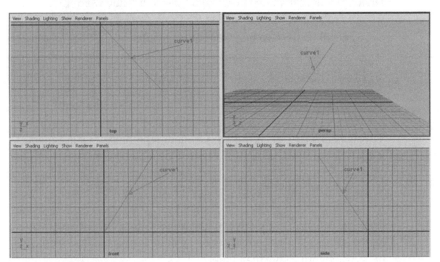

Figure 7-29

Multiply the .y and .z values with themselves to create the squares:

```
float $y = ($vec.y * $vec.y);
// Result: 226.532601 //
float $z = ($vec.z * $vec.z);
// Result: 105.6784 //
```

The "sum of squares" is obtained by adding the values in $y and $z together:

```
float $sum = ($y + $z);
// Result: 332.211001 //
```

Use the `sqrt` command to find the square root of the sum:

```
float $sqrt = sqrt($sum);
// Result: 18.226656 //
```

The value returned from the `sqrt` command is the value that must be multiplied with itself to match the value stored in `$sum`:

```
print ($sqrt * $sqrt);
332.211001
```

Divide the height value (`$vec.y`) by the root value (`$sqrt`). Since we are creating rotational angles for the XZ-plane, the coordinate in `$vec.y` will be used to help generate the angle.

```
float $quotient = ($vec.y / $sqrt);
// Result: 0.825769 //
```

The value in `$vec.y` (15.051) is less than the value in `$sqrt` (18.227), so a number within the range of –1 to 1 will be returned. This is necessary since the `acos` command requires a valid cosine angle.

```
float $xAngle = acos($quotient);
// Result: 0.599233 //
```

Now we will perform the same function for the z-axis. To save time, and since this is how the procedure will be formatted, the steps will be written with a shorthand method.

```
$sqrt = sqrt(($vec.x) * ($vec.x) + ($vec.y) * ($vec.y));
float $zAngle = acos($vec.y / $sqrt);
// Result: 0.586852 //
```

Now duplicate the curve and rotate it on the x-axis and z-axis:

```
duplicate curve1;
setAttr "curve2.rotateX" (rad_to_deg($xAngle));
setAttr "curve2.rotateZ" (rad_to_deg($zAngle));
```

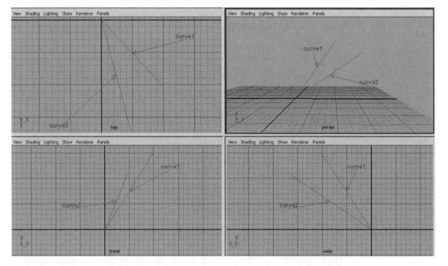

Figure 7-30

This may seem like a lot of steps when you could have easily rotated this curve yourself. However, we are building a recursion that will perform these steps for us while building the branches of the tree.

Returning to the aimY() procedure, create a square root of the sum of the squares for the .x and .y components and store them in $xyLength:

```
// Create a square root of the x and y values squared to find the
// length of the projection of $vec onto the XY-plane
$xyLength = sqrt(($vec.x) * ($vec.x) +
        ($vec.y) * ($vec.y));
```

Finally, create a square root for all components of $vec:

```
// Create a square root for the
// (x,y,z) values that have been added
$vecLength = sqrt(($vec.x) * ($vec.x) +
        ($vec.y) * ($vec.y) +
        ($vec.z) * ($vec.z));
```

7.2.8 **Ternary Operation**

This next block of code introduces a *ternary operator,* which is identified by a question mark (?) and colon (:), and is much easier to interpret than it seems. The structure of the operator is:

```
condition ? expression1 : expression2
```

This is the same as saying:

```
if (true)
expression1
else
expression2
```

So, first you declare a condition. The first value after the ? is the result if that condition is true, and the value after the : is the result if the condition is false.

In MEL, the following code will display "Big Man."

```
$i=10;
print($i>5 ? "Big Man!" : "Small Man!");
```

A ternary operation could be viewed as shorthand for an if-else statement. Some people (like my esteemed colleague Harry Mukhopadhyay) like to use them abundantly in particle expressions because it looks cleaner.

In all honesty, it is extremely nerdy and won't score you any points with the ladies, but it can — in some cases — make code more readable. Or, it can do your head in. The choice is yours.

Take, for example, the next block in our aimY() procedure. Using a traditional if-else statement, it would look like this:

```
if($xyLength == 0)
    {
    if($vec.x > 0)
        $zAngle = deg_to_rad(90);
    else
        $zAngle = deg_to_rad(-90);
    }
```

With ternary operators, it looks like this:

```
if($xyLength == 0)
    $zAngle = ($vec.x) > 0 ? deg_to_rad(90) : deg_to_rad(-90);
```

You could even go completely off and make the code even more compact by using the `sign` command:

```
if($xyLength == 0)
$zAngle = deg_to_rad(90)*sign($vec.x);
```

Call me old-fashioned, but I like the good old if-else statement best. But at least now you know what ternary statements are.

7.2.9 Catching the Division-by-zero

Now that you can tell your mum that you know what ternary operators do, we need to discuss the significance of this line (and how it relates to the rest of the code):

```
if($xyLength == 0)
```

This conditional is an attempt at avoiding a divide-by-zero (which, as you undoubtedly know, is very naughty), while maintaining a consistent direction to the Z rotation angle when the aim vector aligns with the z-axis. Division-by-zero would in this case be a miniscule possibility, occurring only if the vector aligns with Z, making `$xyLength` zero.

Allow me to elaborate.

`$xyLength` is the length of the projection of the aiming vector onto the XY-plane. The Z rotation angle normally comes from the `acos` after the else statement, but when the aim vector projects to a point on the XY-plane (i.e., it becomes aligned with the +/– z-axis), then `$xyLength` drops to zero. If this indeed happens, we need to catch the zero case so as not to divide by zero and pass a bogus value into the `acos` (or halt the script completely). After the whole procedure is explained, you can find a practical example of why this "catch" is needed.

The next part of the code requires a bit of mental acrobatics, so please bear with me. (Use the Cartesian hand trick to visualize!)

```
    $zAngle = ($vec.x) > 0 ? deg_to_rad(90) : deg_to_rad(-90);
else
    $zAngle = acos(($vec.y)/$xyLength);
```

So, if the value in $xyLength does not equal zero, divide the Y component of $vec by $xyLength, then find the arc cosine. The result of acos is an angle (measured in radians, not degrees) whose cosine equals the input argument (i.e., the inverse cos). The if statement avoids a divide-by-zero error.

As a simplified example, imagine the aim vector being positive in the X and Z components and zero in Y, so it lies in the XZ-plane. The xAngle rotation will swing from the y-axis toward the z-axis; then the zAngle rotation swings that result in the direction moving from Y to X toward the aim vector. So it moves 90 degrees from the YZ-plane over onto the XZ-plane.

These 90 degrees come from the following line of code. For clarity I added the actual calculation.

```
$zAngle = acos(($vec.y)/$xyLength);
//which is
acos(0);
// 1.570796 //
rad_to_deg (1.570796);
// 89.999982 //
```

In our example, that's 90 degrees clockwise though, so the last test of the proc flips it to be counterclockwise. This is because in a right-handed coordinate system, you typically measure angles counterclockwise, so in a rotation around Z, X moves toward Y; with a rotation around X, Y moves toward Z; with a rotation around Y, Z moves toward X. In our simplified example (where the aim vector lies in the XZ-plane), the Z-rotation would be 90 degrees clockwise, which is the same as –90 degrees counterclockwise.

After the conditional, we test the sign of $vec.z/$vec.x, and set the sign of the xAngle/zAngle (in our simplified example) to +/– 90 degrees so it matches what the code would produce. We have to do this because so far we have calculated all our angles without a sign. As such, we need to flip the signs so the rotations go in the correct direction. The results are then converted to degrees and stored in the $out variable, which the aimY() procedure returns in a float array.

(Note the ternary operators and their conditions in the second and fourth lines of the following block of code.)

```
$xAngle = acos($xyLength/$vecLength);
$xAngle = ($vec.z) > 0 ? $xAngle : -$xAngle;
$out[0] = rad_to_deg($xAngle);

$zAngle = ($vec.x) > 0 ? -$zAngle : $zAngle;
$out[1] = rad_to_deg($zAngle);
return $out;
}
```

To make sure everything has sunk in, let's look at the procedure in full and apply it to some vectors:

```
proc float[] aimY(vector $vec)
{

// Create the variables and set the scope of $out to 2.
float $out[2];
float $xAngle;
float $zAngle;
float $xyLength;
float $vecLength;

// Query and store the square root obtained through
// the sum of squares of the .x and .y components.
$xyLength = sqrt(($vec.x) * ($vec.x) + ($vec.y) * ($vec.y));

// Query and store the square root obtained through
// the sum of squares of all three of the components.
$vecLength = sqrt(($vec.x) * ($vec.x) + ($vec.y) * ($vec.y) +
    ($vec.z) * ($vec.z));

// Divide-by-zero error check. If the value is 0 test the value
// held in $vec.x and if it is greater than 0 store the radian
// equivalent of 90 degrees, if less than 0 store the negative
// equivalent of -90 degrees.
if($xyLength == 0)
    $zAngle = ($vec.x) > 0 ? deg_to_rad(90) : deg_to_rad(-90);
```

```
// If the value is not 0 then divide the $vec.y component by the
// $xyLength and convert the arc cosine value to a radian value.
else
    $zAngle = acos(($vec.y)/$xyLength);

// Create an arc cosine out of the $xyLength and $vecLength
// and convert to a radian value.
$xAngle = acos($xyLength/$vecLength);

// If the position of the $vec.z is positive use the current
// value in $xAngle, otherwise flip the value to orient
// to the negative value in $vec.z and store the conversion
// to degrees in the first element of $out[].
$xAngle = ($vec.z) > 0 ? $xAngle : -$xAngle;
$out[0] = rad_to_deg($xAngle);

// If the position of the $vec.x is positive invert the
// value in $zAngle, otherwise store the current value
// in $vec.z and store the conversion
// to degrees in the second element of $out[].
$zAngle = ($vec.x) > 0 ? -$zAngle : $zAngle;
$out[1] = rad_to_deg($zAngle);

// Return the new angles (in degrees)
return $out;
}
```

Practical Example of the Division-by-zero Catch

To use the aimY() procedure in a normal case, try this:

```
aimY(<<1,0,1>>);
// 45 -90.000001 //
```

However, now that we have a more complete grasp on the inner workings of the aimY() procedure, I can provide you with a more practical example of the aforementioned division-by-zero catch (which will also allow me to bring up floating-point errors. Oh, joy!). The block of code in question is of course this:

```
if($xyLength == 0)
    $zAngle = ($vec.x) > 0 ? deg_to_rad(90) : deg_to_rad(-90);
```

```
else
    $zAngle = acos(($vec.y)/$xyLength);
```

Assuming the aim vector aligns with the +/− z-axis (i.e., a positive or negative Z component, but the X/Y components are zero), the xAngle becomes +/− 90 degrees, and xyLength drops to zero (xyLength being the length of the projection of the aim vector onto the XY-plane). In this case, the code that computes the zAngle will fail; we test for `xyLength == 0` in order to avoid a divide-by-zero error, which would halt the script.

```
// the 'else' gets triggered with these vectors:
aimY(<<0.0001,0,1>>);
// Result: 89.994271 -90.000001 //
aimY(<<-0.0001,0,1>>);
// Result: 89.994271 90.000001 //

// the 'if' gets triggered here:
aimY(<<0,0,1>>);
// Result: 90.000001 -89.999988 //
```

7.2.10 Floating-point Errors

In the calculations above you might notice that you're not getting precisely 90 degrees because of the intermediate calculations involving pi. This brings us to the subject of *floating-point errors*, which, although quite rare in MEL, you should always keep in the back of your mind.

To illustrate what a floating-point error is, take out your phone and use its calculator to perform the following:

Divide 1.0 by 3.0.
The result is 0.33333333333.
Multiply that by 3.0 again.
You get 0.9999999 and not 1.0.

You can't you store the result 1/3 precisely because there are an infinite number of 3's after the decimal point and you have a finite number of bits in which to store the result. Because of this a small error has crept in. This small error could, however, cause large problems, depending on how you use the results of the calculation.

This illustrates that floating-point math is never 100% accurate. There are always slight numerical errors creeping in, because you can't calculate a result to infinite precision or store an infinite range of values within a finite number of bits.

Some of you have by now tried the aforementioned calculation in MEL and noticed that the floating-point error can't be reproduced:

```
float $a = 1.0;
float $b = 3.0;

float $div = $a/$b;
// 0.333333 //
float $mult = $div*3;
// 1 // Where is the float error?
```

The reason for this is a bit unclear. Some legends speak of hardware-dependent FPU rounding. (A floating-point unit is a part of a computer system specially designed to carry out operations on floating point numbers.) Most legends don't give a crap and get on with the job.

However, if you really want to impress that girl you've been dying to ask out, show her this:

```
float $multipliers = 1.000000100000001;
// 1 //
float $value = $multipliers * 1000000;
// 1000000.1 //
float $val2 = $value * 100000;
// 100000010000.00009 // A guaranteed panty dropper!!
```

Hordes of math nerds have written libraries full of books and papers about floating-point errors, so, if you were so inclined, there is a lot of reading up to do.

An Alternative to the Equality Conditional

While we are on the subject of effective pickup lines, it is worth mentioning that testing for equality like we do in the aimY() procedure can be problematic.

```
if($xyLength == 0)
```

This is because two computational sequences that are mathematically equal may well produce different floating-point values. As such, the use of the equality test (if($xyLength == 0)) is usually not recommended when expectations are based on results from pure mathematics. It would probably be better to write something like the following:

```
if (abs($xyLength)<1e-6)
```

That way you test for zero within a small tolerance, rather than zero itself (1e-6 is exponential shorthand for 0.000001).

7.2.11 Create the vectorOnCircle() Procedure

In order to sprout a new branch, an invisible circle is generated on the root branch and the new branch originates from a random position on that circle. The vectorOnCircle() procedure returns a vector value (the random position on the circle), and takes one float argument (the radius of the circle). In classic form I am going to demonstrate this using curves and locators in a manner that you can follow along with, because math and programming is not a spectator sport.

First, create a circle to provide a visual reference for the demonstration:

```
circle
    -radius 10
    -normal 0 1 0;
// Result: nurbsCircle1 makeNurbCircle1 //
```

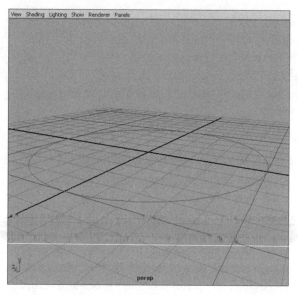

Figure 7-31

Query the radius of the circle and store the result in $rad:

```
float $rad = `getAttr "makeNurbCircle1.radius"`;
// Result: 10 //
```

In the next block, the rand command is used. This command takes two arguments — lower limit and upper limit — and generates a random number. In this case, the random number is between the radius and its negative equivalent (–10 to 10).

```
float $x = rand(-$rad,$rad);
// Result: 4.355326 //
```

Because this is a randomized result, your Script Editor will echo back different values. Since the circle is 2D and only spans the space of the XZ-plane, declare the $y variable with a value of 0:

```
float $y = 0;
// Result: 0 //
```

Like with the $x, randomize another value based on the queried radius and its negative equivalent and store it in $z:

```
float $z = rand(-$rad,$rad);
// Result: -3.512768 //
```

Now take the three values and combine them to create a new vector:

```
vector $vec = <<$x, $y, $z>>;
// Result: <<4.355326, 0, -3.512768>> //
```

We have a new and randomly generated position, but it does not correspond to any point along the original radius (the circle). Create a locator to see the current position we have created. Since we will be maneuvering this locator around with some vector math, let's annotate this first, original locator accordingly.

```
spaceLocator -position ($vec.x) ($vec.y) ($vec.z);
// Result: locator1 //
```

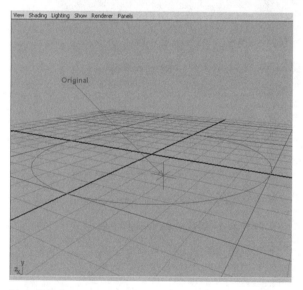

Figure 7-32

The first step in getting our new vector to be on the rim of the circle is to normalize the new vector with the `unit` command:

```
$vec = unit($vec);
// Result: <<0.778377, 0, -0.627797>> //
```

Create another locator to see the normalized position:

```
spaceLocator -position ($vec.x) ($vec.y) ($vec.z);
// Result: locator2 //
```

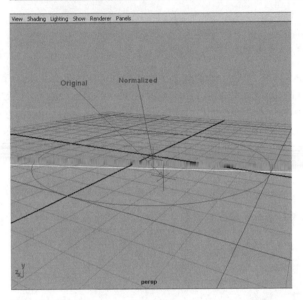

Figure 7-33

Multiply the vector, as a whole, by the radius to expand the point to meet the rim of the circle:

```
$vec = $vec * $rad;
// Result: <<7.78377, 0, -6.27797>> //
```

Create a locator using the newly created vector to visually display the new position:

```
spaceLocator -position ($vec.x) ($vec.y) ($vec.z);
// Result: locator3 //
```

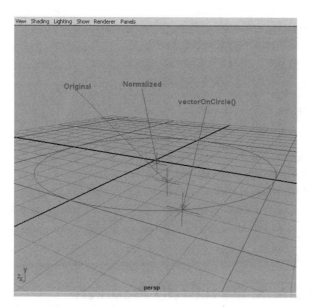

Figure 7-34

The vector (i.e., the random position on the circle) generated will be returned when this procedure is called from the tree() procedure during the recursion process. The vectorOnCircle() procedure returns a vector value (the random position on the circle), and takes one float argument (the radius of the circle):

```
proc vector vectorOnCircle(float $rad)
{
    // Using the argument passed from tree() create a
    // random float between the original value and its
    // negative equivalent
    float $x = rand(-$rad, $rad);

    // The y does not receive a randomized value
    float $y = 0;

    // Using the argument passed from tree() create a
    // random float between the original value and its
    // negative equivalent
    float $z = rand(-$rad, $rad);
```

```
// Take the previously generated values and
// store them into a vector
vector $vec = <<$x, $y, $z>>;

// Convert to a unit vector - this will place
// head of the vector on a circle of radius 1
$vec = unit($vec);

// Multiply the vector by the value
// held in $rad to scale the radius
$vec = $vec * $rad;

// Return the value to the tree() procedure
return $vec;
} // End vectorOnCircle()
```

7.2.12 Create the reflect() Procedure

If you remember correctly, the first step of finding the second branch (see section 7.2.2) required some sort of vector reflection. We need to define the second branch as if it were a reflection of the first branch about the $growthDir vector. This is done with the reflect procedure.

This procedure takes two arguments. The first is a vector position related to the end CV of a curve. The second is the direction of growth (X, Y, or Z). These values will be passed as arguments from the tree() procedure.

Allow me to illustrate the workflow with simple curves before we delve into the actual procedure.

Create two vectors and use them to create a new curve. The $base is for demonstration only and not part of the actual procedure, but $vec will be passed from the tree() procedure as the first argument. The vector values below are for illustration purposes only.

```
vector $base = <<1, 1, 1>>;
vector $vec = <<-4.5, 10, -2.75>>;

curve
    -degree 1
    -point ($base.x) ($base.y) ($base.z)
```

```
-point ($vec.x) ($vec.y) ($vec.z);
```

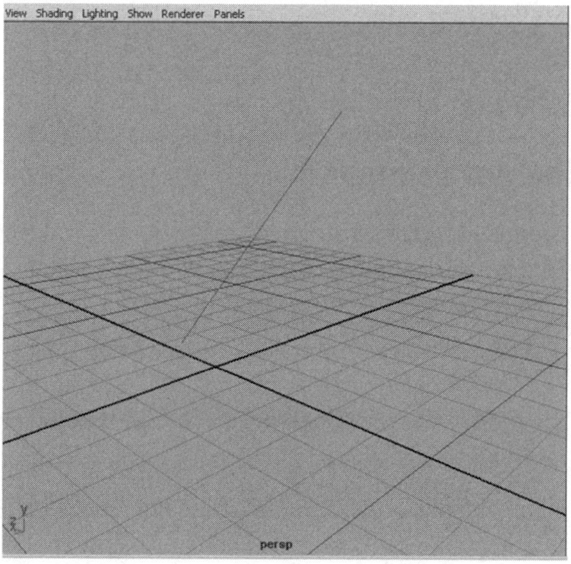

Figure 7-35

Create another vector, which is also passed from the tree() procedure, as the second argument. This is the direction of growth; in our
case, the Y direction.

```
vector $dir = <<0, 1, 0>>;
```

For demonstration purposes we need to reverse the value in $vec to
its negative equivalent. We do this simply by placing a "–" operator
at the beginning of the variable. During the recursion this will happen in the tree() procedure when the arguments are passed. Below
is a sample from the tree() procedure. The "–" operator at the
beginning of the variable reverses the value to its negative
equivalent.

```
$vec = reflect(-$vec, $growthDir);
```

In our simplified example, use the "–" operator and flip the current
value in $vec:

```
$vec = -$vec;
```

Normalize both of the new vectors:

```
$vec = unit($vec);
$dir = unit($dir);
```

Next, the dot product will be used.

7.2.13 **The dot Command**

The dot command returns a scalar value that is the product of two vectors. This is a verbatim definition, so I will quickly demonstrate the actual math that takes place to calculate a scalar value.

Multiply each component of each vector to one another, and add the products together:

```
print (($vec.x * $dir.x) + ($vec.y * $dir.y) + ($vec.z * $dir.z));
-0.884532
```

The dot command performs the exact same function, with less work:

```
dot($vec, $dir);
// Result: -0.884532 //
```

Now that I have covered exactly what the dot command does, let's return to our example. The reflect() procedure will return a calculation that looks as follows:

```
return $vec - 2 * dot($vec, $dir) * $dir;
```

To demonstrate this final step in the procedure, take the formula above and store it into a vector variable called $return:

```
vector $return = $vec - 2 * dot($vec,$dir) * $dir;
// Result: <<0.398039, 0.884532, 0.243246>> //
```

The next step is not part of the current procedure, and occurs later in the tree() procedure. Not to confuse you, but I do not want to end this demonstration without letting you see a final result. Add the two vectors in $return and $base together:

```
vector $end = $return + $base;
// Result: <<1.398039, 1.884532, 1.243246>> //
```

Now create another curve using the new vector values:

```
curve
    -degree 1
    -point ($base.x) ($base.y) ($base.z)
    -point ($end.x) ($end.y) ($end.z);
```

A shorter branch is positioned, reflecting the direction of the original branch.

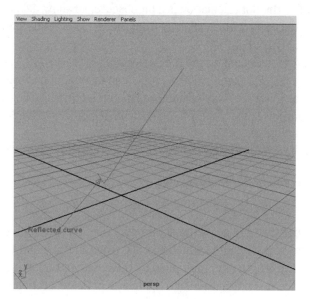

Figure 7-36

The final procedure returns a vector and takes two vectors as arguments:

```
proc vector reflect(vector $vec, vector $dir)
{
    // Create a normalized vector from the
    // first argument passed from tree()
    $vec = unit($vec);

    // Create a normalized vector from the
    // second argument passed from tree()
    $dir = unit($dir);
```

```
// Multiply the dot product of $vec and $dir
// by $dir and 2. Subtract the final product
// from the normalized vector in $vec
return $vec - 2 * dot($vec, $dir) * $dir;
} // End reflect()
```

7.2.14 **Analogy with Rays**

I do realize the dot calculation is a bit obscure, so allow me an attempt to clarify with an analogy from the world of rendering: reflected rays of light.

Imagine an incoming ray (i.e., a vector).

What the dot formula does is reflect an incoming, normalized vector **i** as if it were a ray striking a plane with normal **n**. For illustration purposes, we want **n** to be normalized for this to work.

Note: The code below is not MEL, just illustrative code/formulas.

Project **i** onto **n**, the length being:

```
dot(i,n)
```

Remember that `dot` gives the dot product (i.e., the scalar product) of two vectors, the result of which is scalar. You can think of `dot(i,n)` as being the length of **n**, multiplied by the length of the projection of **i** in **n**. Since **n** is normalized, it's the length of the projection of **i** onto/in **n**.

Because **i** points into the plane, this will be negative. Multiply by the normal to get a vector of that length, but opposite in direction to the normal:

```
dot(i,n)*n
```

Subtract this from **i** to give a vector that is parallel to the plane. You can imagine it starting at the "beginning" of **i** and ending above the normal to form a right-angled triangle. (Vectors don't actually have a beginning, but it's instructive to imagine that they do; see Figure 7-37.)

```
i-dot(i,n)*n
```

Now double that in length to take you across to the "end" of the reflected vector (which we're trying to compute):

```
2*(i-dot(i,n)*n)
```

Visualizing this as another triangle (not right-angled, though), subtract **i** to get the reflected vector, which we'll call **r**, then expand and simplify:

```
r = 2*(i-dot(i,n)*n)-i
r = 2*i-2*dot(i,n)*n-i
r = i-2*dot(i,n)*n
```

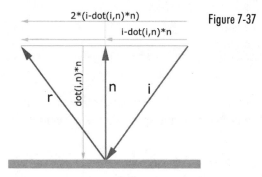

Figure 7-37

Now we are ready to move on to the actual procedure that will be performing the recursion. Take one more deep breath, pour a fresh coffee/whiskey, and get ready for the home stretch.

7.2.15 Create the tree() Procedure

This is the main procedure that will create the tree. This procedure contains the actual recursion and calls all the previously created procedures. The previous procedures each serve a function in performing mathematical calculations that will be needed by the tree() procedure to generate the branches of the tree.

Five arguments are needed:

- $depth: This is the depth of the recursion and essentially how complex the tree will be. More recursions mean more branches.

- $base: This is the position where the tree will start. For example, <<0,0,0>> would be the center of the world.

- $growthDir: This is the direction in which the branches will grow, and is the argument of the aimY() procedure.

- $branchAngle: This value controls the spread of the branching, similar to the cone angle of a spotlight.

- $branchLen: This value controls the overall length of the recurring branches.

```
proc tree(
    int      $depth,
    vector   $base,
    vector   $growthDir,
    float    $branchAngle,
    float    $branchLen)
{
```

Test that the first argument is not 0 or a negative value; if it is, cancel the procedure before attempting to run the remaining commands:

```
// If the value of depth is less than
// or equal to 0 use the return command
// to exit before running the commands
if($depth <= 0)
    return;
```

The sin command will return the sine of a given value. So if an angle value (in degrees) of 35 was passed as the fourth argument ($branchAngle), a sine of 0.573576 is returned.

```
sin(deg_to_rad(35));
// Result: 0.573576 //
```

This value will be multiplied by the fifth argument ($branchLen), passed to the tree() procedure, and stored in $rad. If the value were 2, for example, the float being passed as the radius to the vectorOnCircle() procedure would be 1.147153.

```
$rad = 2 * sin(deg_to_rad(35));
// Result: 1.147153 //
```

The new value in $rad is then passed as an argument for the vectorOnCircle() procedure, which returns a vector.

> **Note:** To facilitate the flow and understanding of the code, I will use the step-by-step breakdown used in sections 7.2.1 "Finding the First Branch" and 7.2.2 "Finding the Second Branch" as comments.

```
// Finding the first branch:
// STEP 1: Calculate a circle representing the branch radius.
$rad = $branchLen * sin(deg_to_rad($branchAngle));

// STEP 2: Find a random vector on the circle.
vector $vec = vectorOnCircle($rad);
```

In the next block, the rot command is used. Once again, for the sake of clarity, I will break away from the current procedure to demonstrate how this command works.

7.2.16 **The rot Command**

The rot command returns a vector position after rotating a point a given radian value around a specified axis in three-dimensional space. The docs describe it as follows: The rot command returns the position of the point after being rotated the number of radians about the axis.

This command requires three arguments:

- Position of a point in space to be rotated
- Axis (or the pivot point) of the rotation
- The amount of rotation to occur measured in radians

```
rot $point $axis $radian;
```

To illustrate this, create three variables. The first is a float that will hold the conversion of 90 degrees into radians:

```
float $rad = deg_to_rad(90);
```

The radian value stored is 1.570796. Since most people cannot visualize radian values easily, I performed the above conversion so you, the reader, will know we are working with a rotational equivalent of 90 degrees.

The next two variables are vectors that will be used to define a position in three-dimensional space:

```
vector $p1 = <<1, 0, 0>>;
vector $p2 = <<4, 5, 0>>;
```

The `rot` command can perform calculations on values without needing actual points in space (vertices or CVs) to refer to. To demonstrate this I will use a 1-degree curve with the CV display toggled on.

Create the curve using the vectors already created:

```
curve
    -degree 1
    -point ($p1.x) ($p1.y) ($p1.z)
    -point ($p2.x) ($p2.y) ($p2.z);
```

Toggle on the display of CVs for the curve:

```
toggle -controlVertex curve1;
```

The CV we will be rotating is circled in Figure 7-37.

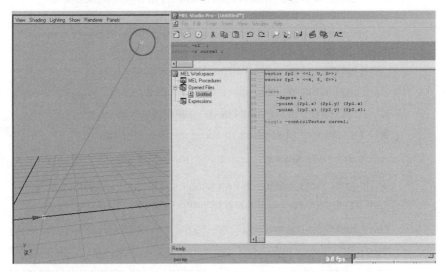

Figure 7-38

Chapter 7

Create a new vector variable containing the new position after being rotated by 90 degrees around the x-axis:

```
vector $newVec = `rot $p2 $p1 $rad`;
```

Apply the new position to the target CV:

```
xform -translation ($newVec.x) ($newVec.y) ($newVec.z) curve1.cv[1];
```

As you can now see, the CV has basically rotated around the x-axis and now lies on the XZ-plane of the grid. The x-axis was defined as the rotational axis from the vector value of <<1, 0, 0>> that is stored in the $p1 variable. The $p1 variable was the second argument (the axis) in the rot command.

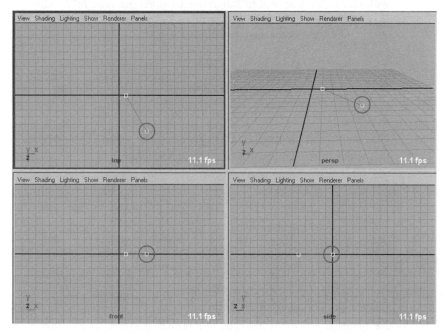

Figure 7-39

Getting Geeky with It

Let's turn up the geekiness a notch and link this to our previous exhilarating discussion about floating-point errors.

Select the CV that was just rotated:

```
select -replace curve1.cv[1];
```

In the Channel box, click to view the CV position attributes, as shown in Figure 7-40.

The number being held in the Y value is not 0; instead we see 1.13e-006. This is the (scientific) e notation, which indicates an extremely small number. The actual value is

Channels Object
curveShape1
CVs [click to hide]

	X	Y	Z
1	4	1.13e-	5

Figure 7-40

0.00000113, but the e-006 shifts the decimal to the right six places so it can be displayed. This is common in calculators and computer programs.

In fact, the value being stored in $newVec.y is an e notation as well (1.13397e-006) but prints in the smallest possible float value that MEL allows:

```
print ($newVec.y);
0.000001
```

Return the CV to its original position:

```
xform -translation ($p2.x) ($p2.y) ($p2.z) curve1.cv[1];
```

Now rotate the CV itself by 90 degrees on the x-axis. The -pivot flag will rotate from the position of the first CV.

```
rotate
    -relative
    -pivot 1 0 0
    -objectSpace 90 0 0
    curve1.cv[1];
```

Now the Channel box displays 0 for the Y value, indicating the rot command has flushed the CV approximately on the XZ-plane. If you undo/redo you will notice that there really isn't a visible difference between the two examples; in fact, you

Channels Object
curveShape1
CVs [click to hide]

	X	Y	Z
1	4	0	5

Figure 7-41

would probably have never even been aware of this if I hadn't geeked out just now.

The geekiness continues: MEL displays up to six decimal places and rounds off the rest. Python and high-end graphing calculators can display up to 11, which would have given us

1.57079632679 radians. The additional five decimal places are what we need to position the CV directly on 0 for the y-axis. MEL isn't inaccurate; this is simply a rounding error, which means that the results are not wrong, just varied in levels of accuracy.

Return the CV to its original position:

```
xform -translation ($p2.x) ($p2.y) ($p2.z) curve1.cv[1];
```

If you want to see this for yourself, click on the Python tab in the Script Editor and enter the following block of Python code. I won't explain each line since Python isn't the point of this book, but I left comments in place so you can interpret what is going on. In fact, I should clarify two things about Python to make this easier to follow:

- In Python, comments use # instead of //.

- Python uses no special characters (like $) for its variables, nor does it use data types like MEL does (int, string, float, vector).

Note: You must have Python installed for this to work! (http://www.python.org)

```
# Import modules
import maya.mel as mm
import maya.cmds as mc

# Convert 90 degrees to radians with a more precise decimal range
rad = math.radians(90)
import math

# Concatenate the rad variable (with the more precise decimal range)
# with the Maya rot command for a more accurate vector
vec = mm.eval("rot <<4, 5, 0>> <<1, 0, 0>> " + str(rad))

# Transform the CV
mc.xform('curve1.cv[1]', translation = [vec[0], vec[1], vec[2]])
```

Now if you check the CV in the Channel box you will see that its Y value is 0.

If you print the second index of the vec variable (in the Python tab) you will see that this number isn't 0; the e notation indicates a shift of 11 decimal places. This number is

Channels	Object		
curveShape1			
CVs [click to hide]			
	X	Y	Z
1	4	0	5

Figure 7-42

so small, however, that it goes beyond the range of how MEL calculates decimals and gets rounded off to 0:

```
print vec[1]
2.44829443007e-011
```

or

```
0.0000000000244829443007
```

7.2.17 Returning to the tree() Procedure

The first argument ($vec) is the point of the rotation. The second ($x_axis and $z_axis) is the axis of rotation. The third (deg_to_rad($angle[])) is the angle of rotation that will occur. The rot command requires radian values, which is why the deg_to_rad command must be used.

```
// STEP 3: Translate the vector up the y-axis by branch
// length units
vector $x_axis = <<1,0,0>>;
vector $y_axis = <<0,1,0>>;
vector $z_axis = <<0,0,1>>;
$vec = $vec + <<0, $branchLen, 0>>;

// STEP 4: Rotate the vector by the branch angle
// to find the end of a branch
// STEP 5: Draw a line between the base ($base) of the branch
// and the (relative) end of the branch.
// To do this, we will need to compute the angles needed to
// rotate a vector to align to the y-axis in such a way
// that it aims along a particular vector
// - in this case, the growth direction ($growthDir).
// The aimY procedure was written for this purpose
float $angle[2] = aimY($growthDir);
$vec = rot($vec, $x_axis, deg_to_rad($angle[0]));
$vec = rot($vec, $z_axis, deg_to_rad($angle[1]));

$vec = <<($vec.x), ($vec.y), ($vec.z)>>;

// Locate the end of the branch relative to the
```

```
// base of the branch.
vector $end1 = $base + $vec;
```

Draw the first curve using the calculated values as arguments for the -point flags:

```
// STEP 6: Draw a curve that represents the first branch
curve -degree 1
        -point ($base.x) ($base.y) ($base.z)
        -point ($end1.x) ($end1.y) ($end1.z);
```

Continue to create the reflected branch and perform recursions to generate the rest of the limbs:

```
// STEP 7: Recurse to the next branch
tree($depth - 1, $end1, $vec, $branchAngle, $branchLen * 0.6);

// Finding the second branch:
// STEP 1: Define the second branch as if it were a
// reflection of the first branch, first about the $growthDir
// vector
// The reflect procedure was written for this purpose.
$vec = reflect(-$vec, $growthDir);

$vec = <<($vec.x), ($vec.y), ($vec.z)>>;

// STEP 2: Locate the end of the branch relative to the
// base of the branch.
vector $end2 = $base + $vec;

// STEP 3: Draw the curve segment that represents
// the second branch.
curve -degree 1
        -point ($base.x) ($base.y) ($base.z)
        -point ($end2.x) ($end2.y) ($end2.z);

// STEP 4: Recurse to the next branch
tree($depth - 1, $end2, $vec, $branchAngle, $branchLen * 0.6);
}
```

To test out the script, enter the block of code that follows. When this many arguments need to be passed it can be easier to store the values in variables and pass the variables for the arguments.

Keep in mind the usages of the arguments:

- $depth: This is the depth of the recursion and essentially how complex the tree will be. More recursions mean more branches.

- $base: This is the position where the tree will start. For example, <<0,0,0>> would be the center of the world.

- $growthDir: This is the direction in which the branches will grow, which is the argument of the aimY() procedure.

- $branchAngle: This value controls the spread of the branching, similar to the cone angle of a spotlight.

- $branchLen: This value controls the overall length of the recurring branches.

```
vector $begin = <<0,0,0>>;
vector $dir = <<0,1,0>>;
float $spread = 15;
float $len = 2;
tree(7, $begin, $dir, $ spread, $len);
```

Figure 7-43

This is when you pop a cigar in your mouth, walk to the nearest beach, squat down, and say: "I love the smell of recursion in the morning. Smells like… victory."

MEL and Expressions

This chapter is dedicated to expressions, in particular to particle expressions. It is important to understand that there are differences between MEL and expressions.

I will start this chapter by explaining precisely what expressions are and how they differ from MEL. To illustrate how expressions are used in film production, I will use an FX rig originally conceptualized by John Cassella. Then, because I feel generous today and because I enjoy technical "spielrei," I will provide some rather techie examples of particle expressions.

Finally, I will show you how you can combine MEL and expressions to speed up workflow exponentially.

8.1 What Are Expressions and How Do They Differ from MEL?

8.1.1 Normal Expressions

Expressions are program-like instructions you create to control keyable attributes over time. Expressions can be comprised of mathematical equations, conditional statements, or MEL commands. Although you can create expressions to animate attributes for any purpose, they're ideal for attributes that you want to change incrementally, randomly, or rhythmically over time.

As an example, take the often used expression by FX TDs to animate the phase attributes of a turbulence field over time. Despite its name, turbulence is a static field; it has no direction as such.

Turbulence is in fact irregular in the force it perpetuates, but the perpetuation in itself is constant. You might have to read that sentence again and consult a dictionary. Frankly I am quite proud if it, so I am going to leave it there.

A common trick to have a turbulence field behave more like wind with a direction (in this case, we need a wind that blows in the X direction) is to write a little expression on the phase attribute (in this case, phaseX). Phase determines the direction of the disruption.

To write an expression on an attribute, you right-click on the attribute and choose "create new expression." Do this for phaseX.

In the Expression Editor, select turbulenceField1.phaseX in the Selected Object and Attribute field and drag it down to the Expression area.

Enter the following expression. (In doing so, you will already note a big difference between MEL and expressions, namely the direct access to attributes. More about this later.)

```
turbulenceField1.phaseX = time *4;
turbulenceField1.phaseY = time *2;
turbulenceField1.phaseZ = time *4;
```

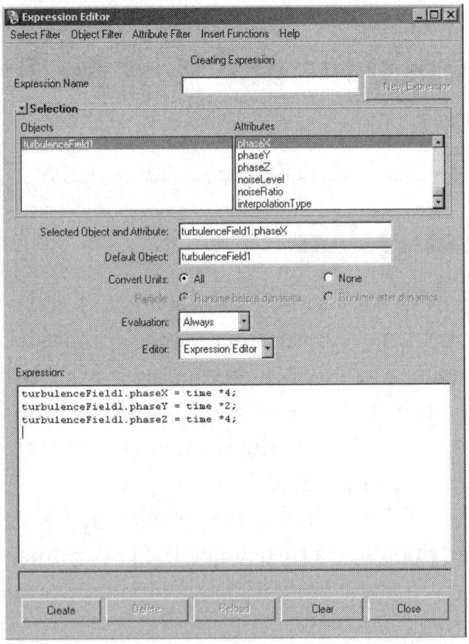

Figure 8-1

After you have entered the expression, click the Create button at the bottom of the Expression Editor.

This expression simply assigns the value of the timeline multiplied by 4 to the phaseX attribute.

As opposed to the `frame` command, however, time reflects the timeline in seconds, not in frames. So if you are working at 25 frames per second,

At frame 25 phaseX is 4,
at frame 50 phaseX is 8,
at frame 75 phaseX is 12,
at frame 100 phaseX is 16, and so on.

You get the idea.

A normal expression can be written on basically every attribute of every node. It does not have to be a dynamics related node.

8.1.2 Particle Expressions

As mentioned before, an expression is an instruction that controls a keyable attribute over time. No more, no less. When used on particles, there are two kinds of expressions: creation expressions and runtime expressions.

A creation expression gets executed *once* at the birth of each particle. A runtime expression gets executed for each particle, at every frame, except at the birth-frame of that particle.

To have particles behave, you generally write per-particle expressions for per-particle attributes (PPAs). On a plain-vanilla particle object, only the most basic PPAs are visible. If you want more, you have to add them yourself. To understand this better, create a particle object and open its Attribute Editor.

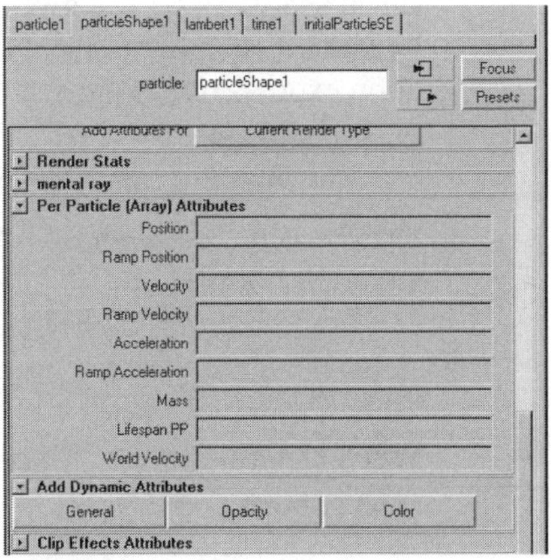

Figure 8-2

If you want to add more dynamic attributes, hit the General button in the Add Dynamic Attributes tab. You can use one of the pre-defined PPAs, as shown in Figure 8-3, or you can define your own attributes, as shown in Figure 8-4.

Figure 8-3 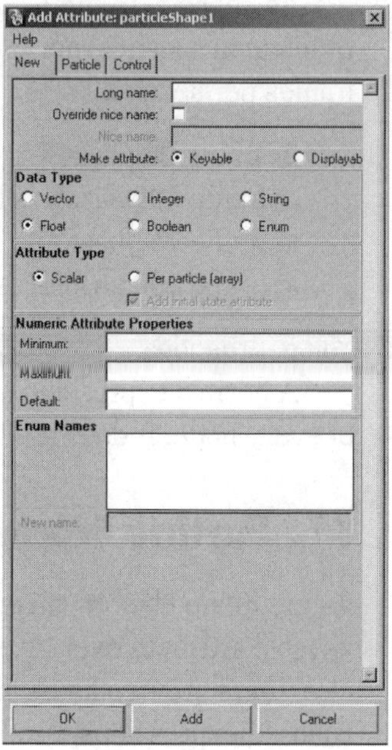   Figure 8-4

As an example, say we want each particle to have a different mass at its birth, so we need a per-particle (different for each particle) creation expression. To generate a random number, we will use the rand command.

Knowing this, open the AE of the particleShape and in the Per Particle Attributes tab, right-click on the Mass attribute and choose Creation Expression.

In the Expression Editor, type this:

```
particleShape1.mass = rand (1, 4);
```

Will it stay this simple? Of course not, your eyes will be bleeding soon enough.

8.1.3 **The Difference between Expressions and MEL**

Difference 1: Direct Access to Object Attributes

In an expression, you can directly access object attributes, whereas in MEL you must use the getAttr, setAttr, getParticleAttr, or setParticleAttr commands.

The following are some examples of expression syntax that directly access object attributes:

```
persp.translateX = 23.2;
float $perspRotX = persp.rotateX;
```

To do something like the above in MEL, you would have to use the setAttr and getAttr commands as the following example illustrates:

```
setAttr("persp.translateY", 23.2);
float $perspRotY = getAttr("persp.rotateY");
```

Execute the following command in the Script Editor to create a couple of particles:

```
particle -position 1 2 3 -position 2 1 3 -name dust;
```

Now you can use the following expression syntax for the particle shape:

```
vector $pos = position;
acceleration = <<2, 1, 0>>;
```

To do something like the above in MEL, you would have to use the setParticleAttr and getParticleAttr commands as the following example illustrates:

```
select dustShape.pt[0];
float $temp[] = getParticleAttr("-attribute", "position",
"dustShape.pt[0]");

vector $position = <<$temp[0], $temp[1], $temp[2]>>;
setParticleAttr("-attribute","velocity","-vectorValue",-3,0,0,
"dustShape.pt[0]");
```

The above MEL commands are only for the first particle in the particleShape.

Difference 2: Time and Frame Variables

In an expression, you can use the time and frame predefined variables. For example:

```
persp.translateY = frame;
persp.rotateY = time;
```

You can't use time and frame in MEL. To access time and frame information in MEL, you have to do something like the following:

```
float $frame = 'currentTime -q';
string $timeFormat = 'currentUnit -query -time';
currentUnit -time sec;
float $time = 'currentTime -q';
currentUnit -time $timeFormat;
```

Difference 3: Comments

You cannot use multi-line /* */ comments in expressions. You can only use // comments.

8.2 Procedural Dust with Expressions

8.2.1 Overview

This section deals with generating procedural dust using particle expressions for a simple scene that shows wood splintering. This will illustrate a practical application of expressions as well as the aforementioned differences between MEL and expressions.

We will set up a moderately complex rig that can be scaled for big shots in production. We will also add additional controls for the artists and animators to tweak the simulation, which in turn will affect the expressions internally. Although this example uses multiple particle systems, the core technique behind this effect is using one particle system as a seed that spawns other particle systems.

The beauty of doing this procedurally is that if the geometry were hand animated, the expressions would automatically pick up any new animation and update the effect accordingly. Finally, we will write a custom Z-depth pass for the particle systems using some more expressions and locators.

Thanks to Shiv Dholakia for the initial draft of this section.

8.2.2 **Outline**

1. Scene setup summary
2. Creating the particle systems
3. Setting up the expressions
4. Setting up the customized Z-depth pass for compositing
5. Particle disk cache

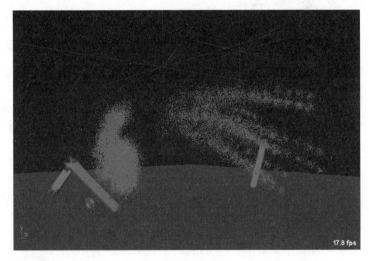

Figure 8-5

Chapter 8

8.2.3 **Scene Setup Summary**

Open up the WoodBreakingFXRig_start.ma file from the companion disc.

The scene has some basic geometry with dynamics simulated in Blast Code (http://www.blastcode.com/) that was baked onto keyframes for ease of use.

If you expand the origGeom group in the outliner, you will see four subgroups. These are, as shown in Figure 8-6, in the order of their hierarchy:

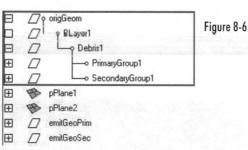

Figure 8-6

Since this example is primarily concerned with the expressions behind the dust rig, I will keep the BlastCode talk to a minimum. Basically, after shattering the geometry in Blast Code, I recorded it and baked the effect into keyframes. Then I deleted the BlastCode solver so that it could be ported to machines without the plug-in. What was left was the layer hierarchy shown above. The PrimaryGroup1 and SecondaryGroup1 layers contain the primary and secondary debris, respectively. If you play back the scene, you will see clearly that the wood breaks into a few large pieces (primary) and many small pieces (secondary).

I then duplicated those two groups with input connections so that the animation gets transferred. The reason behind this is that in a production pipeline, the original geometry/ animation would usually be referenced; and it is a bad idea to manipulate referenced geometry. Your outliner should show this:

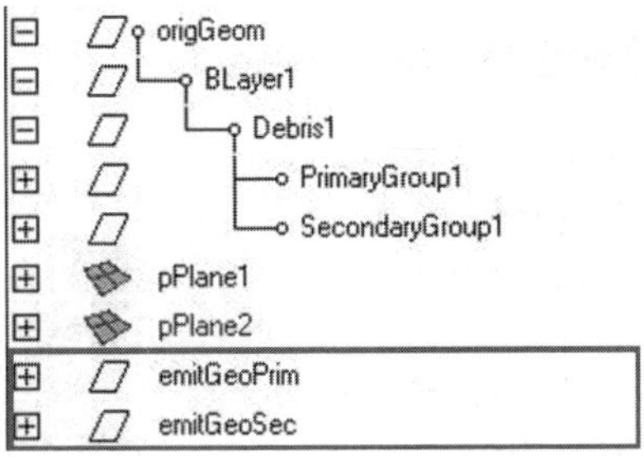

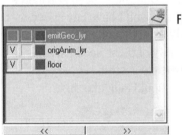

Figure 8-7

I have named the duplicates **emitGeoPrim** and **emitGeoSec**. I also assigned the objects to their respective layers for ease of use. The ground floor is in its own group called **floor**, the original geometry is in its own group called **origAnim_lyr**, and the duplicated geometry that will be used as particle emitters is in its own layer called **emitGeo_lyr**. Your layers should look like this:

Figure 8-8

Since you should never mess with the original referenced geometry, we set up the particle systems on the duplicated layer. The emitGeo_lyr layer is kept hidden because we don't want to see two copies of the same geometry. As we will see in the next section, the only purpose of the duplicated geometry is to set up the particle systems.

Now that we have everything set up in the scene, we are ready to design the particle systems.

8.2.4 **Creating the Particle Systems**

In this section we will be setting up the particle systems. Expand the emitGeoPrim group and select all the geometry in it in the outliner.

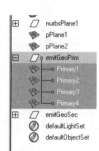

Once you have the geometry selected, go to the Dynamics menu set and choose **Particles > Emit from Object > Option Box**.

To be safe, be sure to reset any old settings that might be lingering in there.

Figure 8-9

For organizational purposes, let's name our particle objects and emitters consistently. Since we would be using the particles emitted from the geometry as seed to spawn other particle systems, type **seedEmittersPRim** in the Emitter name field. Change Emitter type to **Surface** and set Rate to **100** for now. Then in the Basic Emission Speed Attributes area, set Speed to **0**. These seed particles won't have any speed of their own; they will inherit their velocity from the falling debris. In turn, we will use the position and velocity of these seed particles to drive the emission of the actual dust particle system.

So your Emitter Options should look like this:

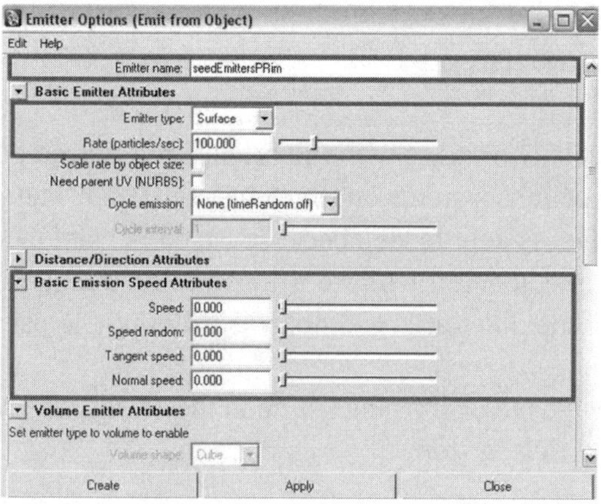

Figure 8-10

Set up the same options with the secondary geometry under the emitGeoSec and name it **seedEmittersSec**. Because we want each piece of debris to emit dust, each piece of geometry will have its own emitter and emit particles.

For both particle systems just created, set the Inherit Factor to 1 in the Channels box. This is a very important step, as this attribute basically controls the percentage of emitter velocity the particles emitted inherit. We set it to 1 so the particles will inherit 100% of the emitter's velocity. Do not forget this step, or the spawning will not work.

Rename the two particleShapes to **seedParticlesPrim** and **seedParticlesSec**, respectively.

Go to their particle shape nodes Attribute Editor, and in the Lifespan Attributes tab, set Lifespan Mode to **lifespanPP only**. Then in the Render Attributes tab, set Particle Render Type to **Points**.

In the Render Attributes tab, create per-object opacity and color attributes and set Opacity to **0** and the colors to whatever you want. For debugging purposes, I like to assign them a color even though I turned Opacity to 0.

Your setup should look like this:

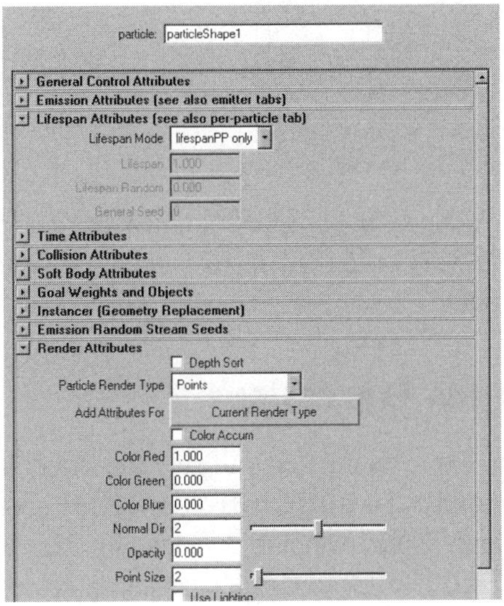

Figure 8-11

Next, create another particle emitter (doesn't matter which) and delete the emitter but keep the particle shape node and name this

dust. This particle object (dust) is what will get emitted from the seed particles based on expressions and conditions we will set up in the next section. (More precisely, we will use the `emit` command to emit *in* the dust particleShape.)

Go to the dust particle shape node, set its Lifespan Mode to **lifespanPP only** as well, change Particle Render Type to **MultiStreak**, and set the other options as shown below:

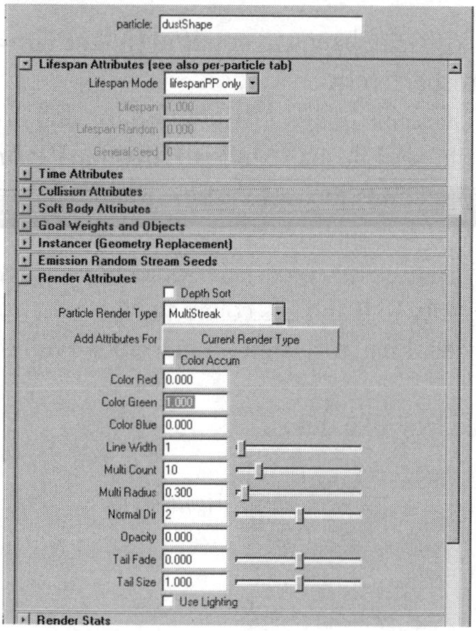

Figure 8-12

As you can see, I also added per-object color and opacity attributes. In the next section we will rig up the controls and write the expressions that drive this effect.

8.2.5 Setting up the Expressions

We will now write the expressions that will give this effect its soul. First, create a locator and call it **dustController.** Create an annotation and give it the same name. Annotations make for easier recognition in the scene. This locator will be an easily selectable control that will hold the main attributes for the user to tweak; a sort of FX-controller.

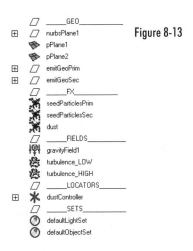

Figure 8-13

Next, select the locator and go the Channels box. We will add some custom attributes for it that will make it easier for the artist/animator to tweak the effect that will drive the expression underneath. From the Channels box choose **Channels > Attributes > Add Attribute** and add the following float attributes, leaving everything else as is:

Name	Data Type	Attribute Type
OrigVelMult	Float	Scalar
NoiseMult	Float	Scalar
VelThresh	Float	Scalar

Later, when you plug these attributes into the expression, make sure that you name them correctly. Remember that MEL is case sensitive.

The channel controls for the dust controller should look like those in Figure 8-14.

For now, these attributes are just empty strings for Maya because we

Channels Object

dustController
Translate X	11.928
Translate Y	15.509
Translate Z	0
Rotate X	0
Rotate Y	0
Rotate Z	0
Scale X	3.763
Scale Y	3.763
Scale Z	3.763
Visibility	on
Orig Vel Mult	0
Noise Mult	0
Vel Thresh	0

Figure 8-14

haven't connected them to our expressions yet. However, once we have plugged the attributes into our expression:

■ OrigVelMult will be a multiplier for the original velocity of the seed particles.

■ NoiseMult will be a multiplier for the 3D noise function, which we will discuss later.

■ VelThresh will be the velocity threshold that determines the minimum velocity of the seed particles for triggering dust emission.

These attributes will give the user external control over the amount of velocity and noise the particle will exhibit, without having to mess around in the expression.

Next, go to the seedParticlesPrim shape node, right-click on lifespanPP, and choose **Creation Expression**. As you know, the creation expression deals with the code executed at the birth time of the particles. Type the following line of code and click **Create**:

```
seedParticlesPrimShape.lifespanPP = .1;
```

Just as it says, this will set the lifespan per particle to 0.1 seconds. (Lifespan is in seconds, not in frames.) We basically want the seed particles (which will spawn the dust particles) to get born and then die very quickly. From then onward the runtime expressions will take over their behavior.

Next, go to the Runtime Before Dynamics Expression and type the following snippet of code in the Expression Editor, which will be explained below.

> **Note:** Some line wrapping has occurred due to the width of the pages in this book. You can find the original expression in WoodBreakingFXRig_final.ma.

```
// get length of velocity
float $mag = mag(seedParticlesPrimShape.velocity);

// store user input (from dyn control) in variable
// threshold determines the minimum velocity needed for triggering
// a dust emission.
```

```
float $threshold = dustController.velThresh;

// check if the magnitude of the seed particle's
// velocity is less than the threshold supplied
if($mag > $threshold)
    {
    // gets the seed particle's position
    vector $pos = seedParticlesPrimShape.position;
    // gets the seed particle's velocity
    vector $velo = seedParticlesPrimShape.velocity;

    // multiplies the velocity of the seed particles with the user
    // input in origVelMult
    $velo *= dustController.origVelMult;

    // add noise based on user input, velocity, position and frame
    vector $velNoise = (dustController.noiseMult) * dnoise($pos *
    ($mag * noise(frame + (seedParticlesPrimShape.particleId))));

    // adds the original velocity of the seed particles and the result
    // of $velNoise
    vector $newVelo = ($velo + $velNoise);

    // emit particles from seed particles
    emit -object "dust" -pos ($pos.x) ($pos.y) ($pos.z) -at velocity
    -vv ($newVelo.x) ($newVelo.y) ($newVelo.z);
    }
```

The runtime expression gets executed typically every frame of the animation. In our case we chose to update it before dynamics evaluation.

Let's go through the code line by line.

The first line gets the magnitude of the seed particle's velocity and stores it in the variable $mag:

```
float $mag = mag(seedParticlesPrimShape.velocity);
```

Since velocity is a vector, magnitude is defined as the length of that vector. As you know from previous chapters, it returns a floating-point number as the result. In this case, think of magnitude as the speed of the particle.

The threshold gets the velocity threshold from the user input in the dust controller's velThresh attribute. This is then stored in the $threshold variable for a conditional check in the next line. Threshold, as I explained before, determines the minimum velocity needed for triggering a dust emission.

```
float $threshold = dustController.VelThresh;
```

The if statement checks if the magnitude of the seed particle's velocity is less than the threshold supplied by the user. If affirmative, it executes the code in the braces.

```
if($mag > $threshold)
{
```

The first line inside the braces gets the seed particle's position in world space and stores it in a vector variable:

```
vector $pos = seedParticlesPrimShape.position;
```

The second line gets the seed particle's velocity and stores it in a vector variable:

```
vector $velo = seedParticlesPrimShape.velocity;
```

The third statement multiplies the velocity of the seed particles with the user input in origVelMult. This intensifies the velocity or decreases it, based on the user input.

```
$velo *= dustController.OrigVelMult;
// This is shorthand for $velo = $velo *dustController.OrigVelMult;
// This shorthand can be used for all operators.
```

The statement after that basically takes the user input from the noiseMult attribute and gives three-dimensional noise to it. To elaborate on the expression, it multiplies the noiseMult number with the dnoise function.

```
vector $velNoise = (dustController.noiseMult) * dnoise($pos * ($mag *
noise(frame + (seedParticlesPrimShape.particleId))));
```

In effect what this whole line of code is doing is applying a three-dimensional noise to every particle on every frame based on its position and velocity as input arguments. The result is the random scattering and distribution of the particle's position and velocity. The output of this whole line of code gets stored in the $velNoise variable.

The dnoise Command

The dnoise command, which is a variation of the noise command, returns a random number from –1 to 1. It works like the noise function except that dnoise takes and returns a vector. The result is a three-dimensional distribution of the noise.

The syntax is as follows:

```
vector dnoise(vector argument)
```

For example:

```
dnoise(<<5,12,-18>>) returns <<0.697768, 0.125272, 0.166748>>
```

The dnoise function is taking the position of the seed particle as an argument and multiplying it by the magnitude of the velocity of the same. The magnitude is then multiplied by the result of the noise function, which takes in the current frame number at run time and each particle's unique ID as an argument.

Since each particle has a different ID and the frame number is going to change every frame, the noise function will return a random number from –1 to 1 based on the result of the addition. Noise is one-dimensional. If you supply the same argument, noise returns the same value repeatedly.

Because the frame increases in larger increments, the values returned increase and decrease in much coarser patterns. Graphing the values, the noise frame looks like this:

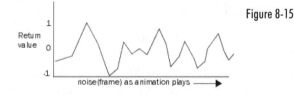

Figure 8-15

To simplify what I said above, the noise function returns a random number from –1 to 1 on every frame for each individual particle. A particle ID is a unique number assigned to each particle at birth. So each particle will have a separate resulting number.

The next line adds the original velocity of the seed particles and the result of the $velNoise variable. The output of this is stored in the $newVelo variable.

```
vector $newVelo = ($velo + $velNoise);
```

The emit Command

The last line deals with the main emission of the dust particles. The emit function adds particles to an existing particle object without the use of an emitter. It also lets you set any per-particle attribute for the newly created particles.

The syntax is:

```
emit [-attribute string] [-floatValue float] [-object string]
[-position float float float] [-vectorValue float float float]
```

Here the emit function adds the dust particles at the current position of the seed particles and the newly calculated velocity of the $newVelo variable discussed above:

```
emit -object "dust" -pos ($pos.x) ($pos.y) ($pos.z) -at velocity -vv
($newVelo.x) ($newVelo.y) ($newVelo.z);
}
```

Don't worry if the above seems a little difficult to understand. With time and practice it will become very clear.

After a little playing around, the dust controller values I found to work well are those shown in Figure 8-16.

Add Turbulence and Gravity

I also set up simple gravity and turbulence fields to give the dust some more

dustController	
Translate X	11.928
Translate Y	15.509
Translate Z	0
Rotate X	0
Rotate Y	0
Rotate Z	0
Scale X	3.763
Scale Y	3.763
Scale Z	3.763
Visibility	on
Orig Vel Mult	0.2
Noise Mult	5
Vel Thresh	0.5

Figure 8-16

variation and so that it falls down on the floor. The Regular Magnitude of 9.8 for gravity worked very well, and the Attenuation was set to 0 so the force of the field doesn't diminish with distance. For the Turbulence field, a Magnitude of 20 worked fine with a Frequency of 1.

Conserve

To simulate drag and air resistance, it is generally a good idea to set the Conserve attribute (at the top of the particles shape's Attribute Editor) to a value slightly less than 1, like 0.98 (although this is not physically correct). The Conserve value controls how much of a particle object's velocity is retained from frame to frame. Specifically, Conserve scales a particle's velocity attribute at the beginning of each frame's execution. After scaling the velocity, Maya applies any applicable dynamics to the particles to create the final positioning at the end of the frame.

If you set Conserve to 0, none of the velocity attribute value is retained. The velocity is reset to 0 before each frame. At the end of each frame, the velocity is entirely the result of dynamics applied during that frame.

If you set Conserve to 1, the entire velocity attribute value is retained. This is the real-world physical response.

If you set Conserve to a value between 0 and 1, a percentage of the velocity attribute value is retained. For example, if you set Conserve to 0.75, in each frame Maya first reduces the velocity attribute 25%, then it calculates any dynamic or expression effects on the object.

(Fixing) Collisions

To make the particles collide with the floor, select them and then the plane and choose **Particles > Make Collide**.

However, if some particles accidentally do end up going under the floor, you want them to die. To achieve this, simply go to the Runtime After Dynamics in the Expression Editor for the seedParticlesPrim shape and type the following:

```
vector $pos = chunkEmittersPrimShape.position;

if($pos.y <= 0)
chunkEmittersPrimShape.lifespanPP = 0;
```

The expression above is pretty straightforward. We get the particle's position at every frame and store it in a vector variable $pos. Then, in the if statement we check for the Y component of the position to see if it's less than or equal to 0. If it is, we simply set the lifespanPP to 0.

(You could do a similar thing where you have the particles die based on the y position of a locator instead of their position in the world.)

Lather. Rinse. Repeat.

Repeat the same steps of setting up the expressions above for the seedParticlesSec shape.

Hide the emitters for the seedParticlesPrim and seedParticlesSec shapes since we are only concerned with the dust. However, for debugging purposes it is always a good idea to add per-object color. You never know when you are in the mood for some bright green particles.

Dust Shape Expressions

We want the dust particles to all have a random lifespanPP (so they die at different times) and a random mass (so they don't all fall at the same rate). As you might have guessed, we will use the `rand` command to achieve this.

The `rand` command returns a random floating-point number or vector within a range you supply as an argument. Its syntax is:

```
float rand(float max)
float rand(float min, float max)
```

Executed at run time, a `rand` function will look somewhat like this:

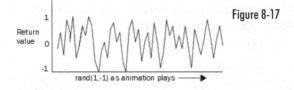

Figure 8-17

We will use the `rand` function in the creation expression as follows:

```
dustShape.lifespanPP = rand(4,6);
dustShape.mass = rand(1,2);
```

In the runtime, add the same die-if-you-go-below-zero expression to the dust particles:

```
vector $pos = dustShape.position;

if($pos.y <= 0)
dustShape.lifespanPP = 0;
```

8.2.6 Setting up a Customized Z-depth Pass for Compositing

In this section we're going to set up a customized Z-depth pass for compositing. We will first set up a few locators and position them for three different depth/color outputs:

- camLoc — (Foreground) Distance from camera to the frontmost locator

- midLoc — (Midground) Distance from frontmost locator to the midground locator

- farLoc — (Background) Distance from midground locator to the background locator

Figure 8-18

To get this to work, we will write an expression that evaluates a particle's position in relationship to the camera and locators, and sets the particle's color based on that data.

First create the three locators and name them camLoc, midLoc, and farLoc.

Then, point-snap camLoc to the camera's lens and parent constrain the locator to the camera. Next, position midLoc to where the stick is before it breaks away, and farLoc to where the pieces end up farthest in the positive x-axis after they have settled on the ground. The positioning of the locators obviously depends on the specific needs of the shot you are using them for. I also like to attach annotations to each locator so that the locators are clearly visible with titles hovering above them. I love annotations. Even more, I adore them. I take them out for dinner and write poems about them.

Figure 8-19

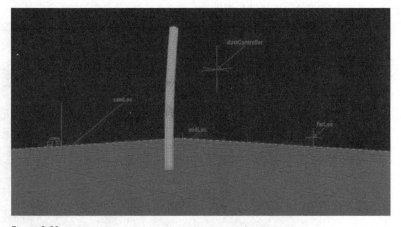

Figure 8-20

Now that we have the locators set up and positioned, let's proceed to writing the code for the customized Z-depth pass. Select the dust particle shape node, and using the Color button in the Add Dynamic Attributes, add a per-particle color attribute. This will add an

Chapter 8

attribute called `rgbPP` to the PPAs. Then, right-click on the `rgbPP` attribute field and choose Runtime Before Dynamics Expression. Type in the following code:

```
// -------- depth pass code -----------

// store position of locators
vector $camPos = <<camLoc.translateX, camLoc.translateY,
camLoc.translateZ>>;
vector $midPos = <<midLoc.translateX, midLoc.translateY,
midLoc.translateZ>>;
vector $farPos = <<farLoc.translateX, farLoc.translateY,
farLoc.translateZ>>;

//get the particles worldPosition
vector $partPos = worldPosition;

// calculate distances from particles
float $distToCamPP = mag ($partPos - $camPos);
float $distToMidPP = mag ($partPos - $midPos);

float $camDistToMidPos = mag ($camPos - $midPos);
float $midDistToFarPos = mag ($midPos - $farPos);

if ($distToCamPP < $camDistToMidPos)
    rgbPP = <<1, 0, 0>>;

else if ($distToMidPP < $midDistToFarPos)
    rgbPP = <<0, 1, 0>>;

else
    rgbPP = <<0,0,1>>;

// -------- depth pass code -----------
```

Set the render type of the particles to spheres so you can clearly see the colors. Hit Play.

You will notice that some particles are white during the first few frames. This is because we wrote this as a runtime expression. If you remember correctly, a runtime expression gets executed for each particle, at every frame — except at the birth-frame of that particle. We want our particles to adhere to this depth color scheme from when they are born. To achieve this, simply paste the expression above in the creation expression.

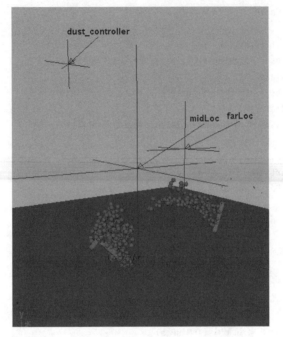

Figure 8-21

Let's now go through the code line by line.

The first three lines get the world space position of the three locators in vector variables:

```
vector $camPos = <<camLoc.translateX, camLoc.translateY,
camLoc.translateZ>>;
vector $midPos = <<midLoc.translateX, midLoc.translateY,
midLoc.translateZ>>;
vector $farPos = <<farLoc.translateX, farLoc.translateY,
farLoc.translateZ>>;
```

The line after that gets the particle's world position in a vector variable:

```
vector $partPos = worldPosition;
```

Then we get the distance between the different locators and the particle distance in relationship with the locators. Subtracting the world space between two different vectors is a good way to get the distance between them. Using the `mag` command, we calculate the magnitude or length of that vector. The `mag` command very conveniently converts a vector into a single float. I use `mag` to do conditional checking of the particle's position with respect to the distance between the locators.

```
// calculate distances between particles and locators
float $distToCamPP = mag ($partPos - $camPos);
float $distToMidPP = mag ($partPos - $midPos);

// calculate distances between locators
float $camDistToMidPos = mag ($camPos - $midPos);
float $midDistToFarPos = mag ($midPos - $farPos);
```

So, basically the first condition checks if the distance between the particle and camLoc is less than the distance between camLoc and midLoc. If the particle lies between those two locators, it is colored red by assigning a vector to them for R, G, and B.

```
if ($distToCamPP < $camDistToMidPos)
    rgbPP = <<1, 0, 0>>;
```

Similarly, if the distance between the particle and midLoc is less than the distance between midLoc and farLoc, it is colored green:

```
else if ($distToMidPP < $midDistToFarPos)
    rgbPP = <<0, 1, 0>>;
```

If none of the above two conditions are met, it is colored blue to indicate the farthest distance:

```
else
    rgbPP = <<0,0,1>>;
```

You can obviously position these locators according to your needs and it will update automatically. Since point particles are almost always colorized in compositing, this R, G, and B separation can be very useful to the compositor. He or she can, for example, use it as a Z-depth pass to control the number of particles in the final shot or to taper off opacity based on depth/color.

Chapter 8

8.2.7 **Particle Disk Cache**

What Is a PDC?

A particle disk cache (PDC) allows you to write a dynamic simulation to disk. This is mainly used for three purposes:

- It lets you play the scene faster and scrub in the time slider, and while doing so fine-tune and examine your simulation.

- Before you do a render of your simulation it is advisable to create a particle disk cache. This will not only speed up your render, it will make it much more reliable and predictable.

- If you render with a render farm, you *have* to create a PDC or the nights will be long and sleepless. This is because particle simulations are calculated on a frame-by-frame basis and each machine in the render farm grabbing frames to render needs to know where the particles were in the previous frame.

    For example, say you have machine1 rendering frames 1-10 and machine2 rendering frames 11-20. To render correctly, machine2 needs to know where the particles were at frame 10. Without creating a PDC, there is no way machine2 can know this.

File Format and Location of PDCs

Particle disk caches are written to the .pdc file format. By default, they are saved in the particles directory of the current project. For example: C:/000_Maya/projects/IntenseMasters/particles/dust-Particles. To keep things tidy, each time you create a PDC, a directory is made in the particles directory with the same name as the current scene file.

What Is Particle Startup Caching?

The particle startup cache lets you save files at frames greater than the start frame without doing a run-up. It saves a copy of the particle shape's attribute values in a different file from the particle disk cache files.

Using the startup cache lets you save and quickly reload scenes at frames greater than the start frames of your particle objects. If you always save your files at the particles' start frames, you can turn off Save Startup Cache for Particles to save disk space.

The disk space used for the particle cache is determined by how many particles are in your scene at the frame saved, and how many attributes they have. Likewise, the time savings at file load is determined by how heavy your scene is and how long it takes to play back. There is no simple formula — you must assess the trade-off between file size and time savings. Because of this, you can turn it on or off. It is turned on by default.

File Format and Location of Startup Caches

Like PDCs, startup caches are kept in a directory created by appending _startup to your scene name. For example, if your scene is called myScene, Maya puts the startup cache in a directory called myScene_startup.

Normally you never have to worry about startup caches.

Creating a PDC for Our Scene

To create a particle disk cache, select the particles and choose Solvers, then choose the Create Particle Disk Cache option box.

By default, particles will be cached in the current playback range.

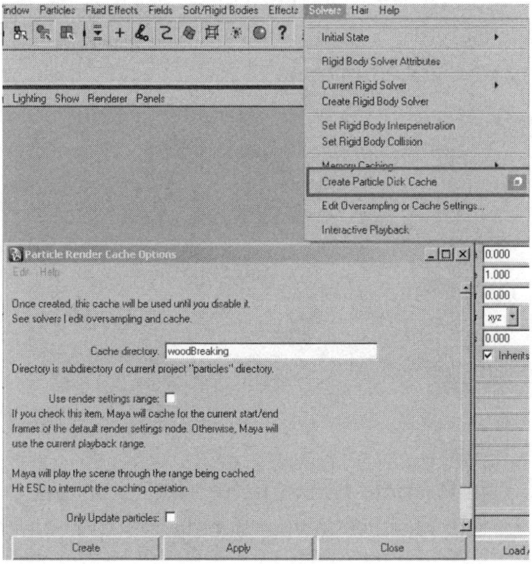

Figure 8-22

Normally you will just use the default settings, which use the current scene name to create the directory in which the PDC will be saved.

The first line in the PDC option box is of capital importance:

"Once created, this cache will be used until you disable it."

This means that after you create a PDC, changes to attributes on particles or fields will *not* work. In other words: Once you have created the cache, Maya uses that cache until you tell it not to. It ignores any changes in emission, forces, etc., on that particle object. You need to turn off the PDC before you will see the changes you made. This is something that you will easily forget.

Hit **Create** and watch the timeline run through the simulation. You will not see any updates in the viewport, but after Maya has run through the simulation, there will be a PDC file in the particles directory of the current project.

You can now scrub back and forth in the timeline and the particles will update correctly.

To turn off the PDC, or to load in a different one, go to **Solvers > Edit Oversampling or Cache Settings.**

Figure 8-23

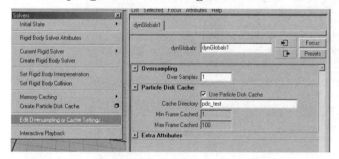

Figure 8-24

Then uncheck **Use Particle Disk Cache.** Once you have done that, you can make further changes to your simulation.

8.3 Annotating Collision Positions

8.3.1 Overview

Say you are working on a shot in a horror movie where snowflakes collide with the floor and morph into splats of blood. Now suppose you are having one of those days where nothing works. The collisions are all messed up and you need a tool that visually tells you exactly where every collision happens so you can debug your rig and go home. The expression explained in this section achieves this by placing a locator with an annotation at the exact position of each collision.

8.3.2 How Do I Get the Exact Position of a Collision?

I bet that is a question that keeps most people awake at night.

Using collisionWorldPosition and collisionTime

To get the exact position of a collision in world space, collisionWorldPosition is your friend. It's a PP attribute that is a bit hidden, and I couldn't find any docs on it, but it does the trick. It does, however, need another PP attribute to work: collisionTime. You just have to love undocumented features. Especially at 3 a.m., when the shot is due at 9 a.m. dailies.

For convenience, I have created a simple collision scene that you can find on the companion disc: collisionAnnotation_start.ma. First of all, add collisionTime and collisionWorldPosition to the particleShape. One thing to note is that I have set the particle's max count to 2. This means that even though the emitter's rate is set to 100, there will only be two particles present in our scene. I did this to keep things simple and clear.

We will go through this expression piece by piece, starting with the most basic of information gathering and gradually build up to include all the bells and whistles.

First, store the collision position in a variable:

```
vector $collPos = particleShape1.collisionWorldPosition;
```

If you set Particle Render Type to Numeric and enter collisionTime as the attribute name, you will notice that collisionTime is always –1 *unless* at the frame of a collision. You will also notice that at the frame of collision, collisionTime spits out a value... in seconds. How very logical and consistent! Anyway, to get the collisionTime in frames, just multiply collisionTime with your frame rate. Store this in a variable as well.

```
float $collFrame = (particleShape1.collisionTime*24);
```

For starters, let's just print out the collision position and collision time in the Script Editor whenever there is a collision. To only get the information when there is a collision, we simply create a conditional that employs the fact that collisionTime is always –1 unless there is a collision.

Note: Due to the width of the pages in this book, some text wrapping has occurred. Please refer to the final scene file for the correct formatting.

```
if (particleShape1.collisionTime != -1)
{
    print ("particle ID " + particleShape1.particleId + " colliding at
        frame " + $collFrame + ".\n");
    print ("Creating locator at: " + ($collPos.x) +" , " + ($collPos.y)
        + " , " + ($collPos.z) + ".\n");
}
```

Open up the Script Editor and hit **Play**. It should spit out something similar to this:

```
particle ID 0 colliding at frame 92.83987513.
Creating locator at: -2.357551896 , -0.004957766074 , -2.279080616.
particle ID 0 colliding at frame 93.89070364.
Creating locator at: -2.384593182 , -0.004957766074 , -2.30522183.
particle ID 2 colliding at frame 93.22687399.
Creating locator at: -2.41718578 , -0.004957766074 , 2.942703742.
particle ID 0 colliding at frame 94.86516742.
Creating locator at: -2.409669351 , -0.004957766074 , -2.329463338.
```

We now have the information we need to create a locator at each collision and attach an annotation to it.

Creating Locators at the Collision Position

This is obviously a piece of cake and hence not very exciting. What we really need is cerebral puzzles and mind-twisting brain-teasers, riddled with undocumented features and massive bugs. Those, and only those, will get our juices flowing!

In any case, to create a locator at the point of collision, simply add the following code between the braces after the print statement:

```
//create locator
string $loc[] = `spaceLocator`;
// center pivot on locator
xform -cp $loc[0];

// move locator to collision position
setAttr ($loc[0]+".translateX") ($collPos.x);
setAttr ($loc[0]+".translateY") ($collPos.y);
setAttr ($loc[0]+".translateZ") ($collPos.z);
```

If you got lost somewhere, you can find the scene in the download files: collisionAnnotation_loc.ma.

Creating Annotations at the Collision Position

I want to have an annotation per collision that tells me the exact position in XYZ of the collision. This turned out to be a bit trickier than expected. The `annotate` command is not too smart, so the trick is not to try and do it all in one go in the `annotate` command. Rather than using the built-in `-text` and `-position` flags, I created a "naked" annotation at the center of the world and then adjusted that text and position using `setAttr`.

Here is the line-by-line explanation. Create an annotation with some dummy text at the origin. This command returns the shape of the annotation:

```
string $annotator = `annotate -tx "THIS SUCKS" -p 0 0 0`;
```

We need the transform so we can move it from the origin to the point of collision. Get the transform of the annotation (i.e., the parent of the shape node):

```
string $annTrans[] = `listRelatives -p $annotator`;
```

Using `setAttr`, we position the annotation at the point of collision. We move the annotation up five units in Y so it doesn't sit right on the collision object.

```
setAttr ($annTrans[0]+ ".translateX") ($collPos.x);
setAttr ($annTrans[0]+ ".translateY") ($collPos.y+5);
setAttr ($annTrans[0]+ ".translateZ") ($collPos.z);
```

collisionWorldPosition returns three rather long floats (–0.986083369, –0.004957766074, and –0.9532615149). Because we will use these values to annotate something, we will clean up the floats a bit by preserving only five decimals. To do this, we will multiply by 1e5, floor it, and then divide by 1e5. How does this work? 1e5 moves the decimal point five places to the right, `floor` throws away the fractional part, and /1e5 moves the decimal point five places to the left. Please note that generally it is a very bad idea to throw away data. However, in this case, we don't really use the floats; we only use the truncated data for display purposes.

```
float $annX = (floor ($collPos.x * 1e5))/1e5;
float $annY = (floor ($collPos.y * 1e5))/1e5;
float $annZ = (floor ($collPos.z * 1e5))/1e5;
```

Using `setAttr`, we set the text of the annotation:

```
setAttr -type "string" ($annotator + ".text") ($annX + " , " + $annY +
" , " + $annZ) ;
```

Finally, we parent the annotation under the collision locator:

```
parent $annTrans[0] $loc[0];
```

If you got lost somewhere, you can find the final scene on the companion disc: collisionAnnotation_final.ma.

8.4 **Adding Expressions with MEL**

8.4.1 **Overview**

Imagine you are working on a sequence of shots that all require debris that blasts out from explosions and object impacts. For the debris you are using geometry instanced on particles. This chapter illustrates how to avoid having to set up the instances (and especially the per-particle attributes and expressions) for each scene time and time again. We will write a small script that adds all the PPAs and expressions by simply executing one procedure. Of course, once the producer notices how efficient you are, he will triple your workload. Make sure you send me hate-mail. I thrive on expletives.

I will first explain the expression line by line, as if we were writing it for the first time. Then I will show you how to integrate it into a MEL script. Then I will open up a bottle of Pyrat XO and enjoy some of the world's smoothest rum.

8.4.2 **Workflow**

You can find a very simple instancer setup in the companion files download: instancer_start.ma. We will work from that scene.

Before we can write the expressions, we need to add some attributes that will be used by the expressions.

Add a float attribute called `rotMax` to the particle shape. For some unbeknownst reason, this is a bit tricky. To make sure the attribute gets added to the particle shape, select the shape in the Attribute Editor and hit the **Select** button at the bottom of the window. Then add the attribute. `rotMax` will control the speed of the rotation of the instances. Just like with the dust example, this attribute is kept outside the expression so the user doesn't have to touch the code.

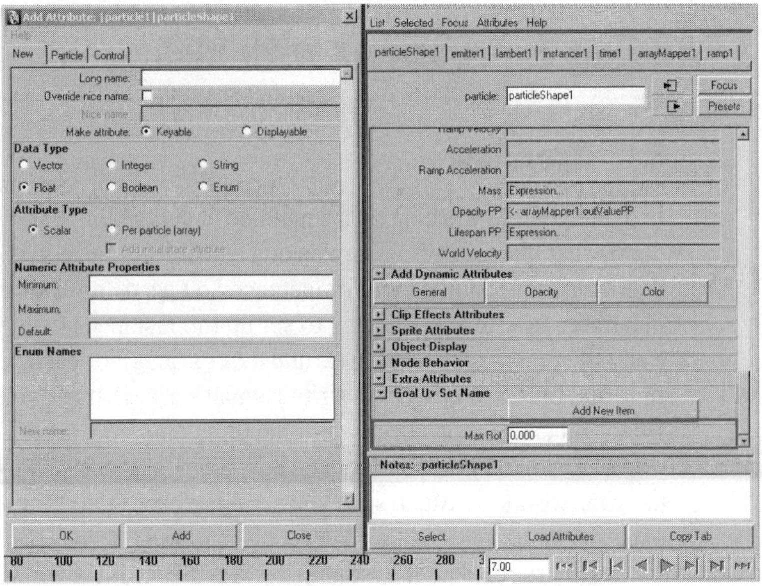

Figure 8-25

Also add these per-particle attributes:

- axisPP (per-particle float array): This attribute will hold a tag on which each particle's runtime rotation will be based.

- rotPP (per-particle vector array): This is a random rotation that each particle will get at birth.

- rotMaxRandPP (per-particle float array): This attribute holds a random value between –maxRot and +maxRot and will be the PP runtime rotation of each particle.

At birth each particle will get a random rotation. axisPP will return either 0, 1, or 2. Each particle will be "tagged" with one of these three possibilities. Based on this value, each particle will rotate in either X, Y, or Z in run time. The speed of this rotation (i.e., how fast the instance tumbles) is defined by the user-definable maxRot.

8.4.3 **The Creation Expression**

Use the `rand` command to get an integer (hence the `floor` command) value from 0 to 2. We tag each particle with this number. To verify this, you can set the render type to **Numeric** and enter **axisPP**. You will see that each particle has a value of 0, 1, or 2.

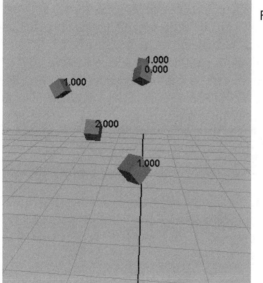

Figure 8-26

```
particleShape1.axisPP = floor(rand(3));
```

Something that is (unsurprisingly) not documented is that the value returned by the `rand` command is minValue <= value < maxValue. Hence, value will never be precisely maxValue, which obviously gains more importance when you are working with real floats (instead of flooring them like we do here).

Give the particles a random rotation at birth:

```
particleShape1.rotPP = <<rand(360),rand(360),rand(360)>>;
```

Get a random value between −rotMax and +rotMax. (rotMax is the speed of the rotation that the user can set in the extra attributes in the particle shape node Attribute Editor.)

> **Note:** The line wraps here due to the limited width of the printed page.

```
particleShape1.rotMaxRandPP = rand( 0 -
particleShape1.rotMax,particleShape1.rotMax);
```

8.4.4 **The Runtime Expression**

As mentioned before, `axisPP` will return 0, 1, or 2. Each particle will be "tagged" with one of these three possibilities. In the runtime expression, each particle will rotate in either X, Y, or Z based on this tag. The speed of this rotation is defined by `maxRot`.

Remember that x $+=$ y is shorthand for x $=$ x $+$ y. (Remember this, because this will also be used in the concatenation of the expression in the MEL script.)

```
// if a particle is tagged with 0, rotate it in the x-axis
if (particleShape1.axisPP == 0)
    particleShape1.rotPP += <<particleShape1.rotMaxRandPP,0,0>>;

// if a particle is tagged with 1, rotate it in the y-axis
else if (particleShape1.axisPP == 1)
    particleShape1.rotPP += << 0, particleShape1.rotMaxRandPP, 0 >>;

// if a particle is tagged with 2, rotate it in the z-axis
else
    particleShape1.rotPP += << 0, 0, particleShape1.rotMaxRandPP >>;
```

8.4.5 **Integrating Expressions in MEL**

Aside from some mind-draining concatenating and escaping a million characters, there is nothing to it.

getShapes Procedure

However, before we delve into that puddle of mud, let's write a small procedure that gets the shape node of a selected transform. I suggest you put it in your %MAYA_SCRIPTS_PATH, because it is an often-used procedure.

You will notice that we get the full path using the `listRelatives` command. This is because it is a good thing to be paranoid, Mr. Mulder. To avoid problems down the line, I like to know that I always have a full DAG path to any and all DAG nodes. That way there's no possibility of Maya getting confused.

```
proc string[] getShapes( string $xform )
{
    string $shapes[];
    $shapes[0] = $xform;

    if ( "transform" == `nodeType $xform` )
    {
        $shapes = `listRelatives -fullPath -shapes $xform`;
    }
    return $shapes;
}
```

randomInstanceRotation Procedure: Getting the Right Selection

```
//get selected particles
string $particleObject[] = `ls -sl`;

// (user will most likely select the transform)
// so get the shape of the particle
string $particleShape[] = `getShapes $particleObject[0]`;

//get instancer
string $instancer = $particleObject[1];
```

randomInstanceRotation Procedure: Adding the Attributes

Next we add all the aforementioned attributes with the addAttr command. You could type this out, or just add them manually and copy what the Script Editor spits out when you do so.

Interesting to note is the apparent inconsistency between the names of data types of variables (float) and attribute types (-attributeType) in the addAttr command (double). Float arrays are now called double arrays. In MEL, a float variable is really able to store a double. A node, however, (like the particle shape node to which we are here adding attributes through MEL) can have a doubleArray attribute, as well as float and double scalar attributes, but it can't have a floatArray. Hence the different names.

Mind you, in most languages (like C) there is a difference between a float and a double. If you are interested in computer numbering formats, you probably have no friends, but you can have a look at these web pages:

http://en.wikipedia.org/wiki/Single_precision
http://en.wikipedia.org/wiki/Double_precision

Anyway.

```
//add attributes needed for expression
//rotMax
addAttr -ln rotMax -at double $particleShape;
setAttr -e -keyable true ($particleShape[0]+ ".rotMax");


addAttr -ln axisPP -dt doubleArray $particleShape;
setAttr -e -keyable true ($particleShape[0]+ ".axisPP");


addAttr -ln rotPP -dt vectorArray $particleShape;
setAttr -e -keyable true ($particleShape[0]+ ".rotPP");


addAttr -ln rotMaxRandPP -dt doubleArray $particleShape;
setAttr -e -keyable true ($particleShape[0]+ ".rotMaxRandPP");
```

randomInstanceRotation Procedure: The Creation Expression

To add an expression to a particle shape node, we use the dynExpression command. The important thing is to use escaped new lines (\n) and tabs (\t) so the expression is nicely formatted when it gets passed to the Expression Editor. Also, quotes in an expression must be escaped (\") so that they are not confused by the system as the end of your string.

The general workflow is to create a concatenated variable that holds the expression and *not* slap your whole expression in the -string flag of the dynExpression command. It goes like this:

```
// CREATION expression
string $expressionC;
$expressionC = ($particleShape[0] + ".axisPP = floor(rand(3)); \n");
```

```
$expressionC += ($particleShape[0]+ ".rotPP =
<<rand(360),rand(360),rand(360)>>;\n");
$expressionC +=($particleShape[0]+ ".rotMaxRandPP = rand( 0 - " +
$particleShape[0]+ ".rotMax," + $particleShape[0]+ ".rotMax)/1000;\n");
```

> **Note:** Please check km_randomInstanceRotation.mel on the companion disc for the correct formatting.

Then we pass this variable to the `dynExpression` command:

```
//add string to expression
dynExpression -string $expressionC -creation $particleShape[0];
```

randomInstanceRotation Procedure: The Runtime Expression

As they say in Thailand: Same same, but different.

> **Note:** Please check km_randomInstanceRotation.mel on the companion disc for the correct formatting.

```
//==================================================
// RUNTIME expression
string $expressionR;
$expressionR = ("if (" + $particleShape[0]+ ".axisPP == 0)\n");
$expressionR += ($particleShape[0] + ".rotPP = " +$particleShape[0]+
".rotPP + <<" + $particleShape[0] + ".rotMaxRandPP,0,0>>;\n");
$expressionR += ("else if (" + $particleShape[0] + ".axisPP == 1)\n");
$expressionR += ($particleShape[0] + ".rotPP = " + $particleShape[0] +
".rotPP + << 0, " + $particleShape[0] + ".rotMaxRandPP, 0 >>;\n");
$expressionR += ("else\n");
$expressionR += ($particleShape[0] + ".rotPP = " + $particleShape[0]+
".rotPP + << 0, 0, " + $particleShape[0] + ".rotMaxRandPP >>;" );

//add string to expression
dynExpression -s $expressionR -rbd $particleShape[0];
```

Finally, we need to set the instance's rotation to `rotPP`:

```
particleInstancer -e -name $instancer -rotation rotPP $particleShape[0];
```

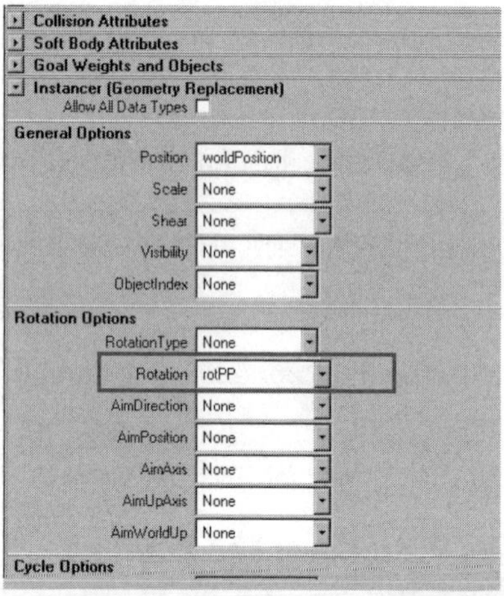

Figure 8-27

If that doesn't make you want to sing and dance in the streets, I
don't know what will!

Chapter 9

Annotating the Timeline: anno.mel

9.1 Introduction

9.1.1 Origin

The idea for this script comes from Graham Thompson at http://www.gt3d.net/, leeched by me and subsequently written by Craig Davies, who at the time of writing works at The Moving Picture Company. Craig is a programmer by trade (with a strong C/C++ background) and you will notice this immediately in the coding style and the overall logic of this script.

The procedures and workflows exhibited in anno.mel display a much greater depth and technical thoughtfulness than what you would normally see in MEL scripts thrown together by TDs. This of course stems from his profound knowledge of Maya's inner core. The reader will benefit greatly from this different approach to and application of MEL. It is a tremendous insight to realize how programming principles (like the usage of logical indices, complex attributes, and memory considerations) can be translated to MEL in such a way that the efficiency and stability of the script improves exponentially.

9.1.2 **What Does It Do?**

At its most basic, anno annotates the timeline with user-defined strings based on adjustable markers (in/out frames).

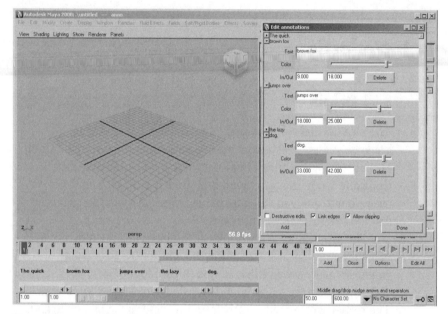

Figure 9-1

Figure 9-2

Graham originally saw the need for this tool (as an Australian, he baptized aniMate) in a caffeine-induced hallucination after 52 hours of consecutive lip-synch animation. As you might know, Maya and sound files don't play nice together. There is no such thing as real-time lip-synching. Most of the time, animators base the facial movements of a character on the wave sounds displayed in the timeline, which is not a pleasant task. In fact, it makes you want to fork out your own eyeballs and barbeque them.

Enter anno. This tool allows you to listen to the actual sound file (outside Maya if you prefer), precisely mark in and out frames of the words/sentences, and annotate the timeline accordingly. In doing so, you don't have to worry about screeching waveforms or 2 fps playback — you can just animate based on the annotations.

The usage and usefulness of anno doesn't stop there, of course. Being able to annotate the timeline is helpful for basically all the stuff you do in Maya.

- In modeling, for example, we normally make key poses on various frames. With anno, you could associate a label/annotation with each pose.

- In FX and animation, you can segment the scene into chunks, which is extremely useful for everyone working on the shot.

- In FX in particular, you can mark off pre-roll and other events that happen in the scene, annotate them descriptively, and as such speed up workflow and efficiency.

Graham was so kind as to make a video illustrating how he now uses anno in his day-to-day workflow. You can find the video on the companion disc and at this URL: http://mel4prod.mayawiki.com/.

It is *highly* advisable to watch this instructional video a couple of times before embarking on this chapter. That way you will know what each feature is designed to do, which will help enormously in understanding the code.

I *strongly* suggest you copy the anno scripts directory from the companion disc (mel\MEL4Prod_CH9_MELFiles\aniMate) in your $MAYA_SCRIPT_PATH and play around with it a bit before continuing to read. After sourcing anno.mel, you can run annoTest to generate some test annotations.

9.1.3 The Explanation

Given the advanced nature and considerable length of this script, it will not be possible to cover it line-by-line. Moreover, the mere fact that you have read this far assumes that you should be comfortable tackling any MEL problem thrown at you — even a cerebral triple whopper like anno. Due to the fact that the code is exhaustively commented, I will discuss this script in broader strokes, attempting to explain the logic and principles used within the procedures rather than focusing on syntax or commands.

Since I will only be explaining the key procedures of each script, I strongly urge you to have the script open in your editor while you are reading this chapter. In doing so, you can follow the actual (exhaustively commented) code, instead of relying entirely on the printed text in this book.

I repeat: I will only explain the key procedures of the script.

9.1.4 Syntax of Delimiters

If you are ever in the mood for a night of unadulterated fun, you should ask a couple of programmers which syntax of delimiters they prefer. Hours of fun guaranteed!

The compact, screen-space-saving flavor:

```
for ($idx in $all) {
    //$indexToSkip is for the edit-all dialog.
    if ($idx == $indexToSkip) {
    // don't touch this annotation
    continue;
    }
}
```

The clear, indented flavor:

```
for ($idx in $all)
{
//$indexToSkip is for the edit-all dialog.
    if ($idx == $indexToSkip)
    {
        // don't touch this annotation
        continue;
    }
}
```

Or the I-love-the-tab-key flavor:

```
for ($idx in $all)
    {
        //$indexToSkip is for the edit-all dialog.
```

```
if ($idx == $indexToSkip)
    {
        // don't touch this annotation
        continue;
    }
}
```

The bottom line is that it is a matter of personal preference. At least when it comes to delimiters, there is no right or wrong. Some people work on small monitors/laptops, so they want to keep their code readable yet compact.

Personally, I prefer the second flavor because it keeps code readable and visually synoptic even if there are a lot of nested conditionals. Craig, on the other hand, as you will see in the code of anno, prefers the C-like compact method.

As my mother says: *"De gustibus et coloribus non disputandum est."*

9.1.5 **The Structure**

The inquisitive mind might have already noticed that the anno script is composed of several files.

> **Note:** In order to follow the instructions in this chapter, I suggest you copy the aniMate folder into your own $MAYA_SCRIPT_PATH. By doing so, all anno scripts will be loaded when Maya starts.

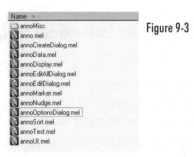

Figure 9-3

There are no fixed guidelines about when you should split a script in several files, but when you're scrolling up and down and you can't find things, then the file is probably too long. Personally, I'd say that anything longer than 1,000 lines needs to be split up. As Craig would say in technical terms only programmers are privy to: "It's just one of those undefined feeling type thingies."

The separate files are all stored in the same directory and sourced from the main procedure like so:

```
// store/edit annotations
source "annoData.mel";
// construct UI for one marker
source "annoMarker.mel";
// arrange markers under the time slider
source "annoDisplay.mel";
// sort annotations on time
source "annoSort.mel";
// create/edit/options dialogs
source "annoCreateDialog.mel";
source "annoEditDialog.mel";
source "annoEditAllDialog.mel";
source "annoOptionsDialog.mel";
// nudge a marker edge
source "annoNudge.mel";
// embed our UI under the time slider in the Maya window
source "annoUI.mel";
// test/debug procs
source "annoTest.mel";
```

There are a couple of other things going on in the anno procedure, but we'll discuss them as we look at each file individually.

9.1.6 The Functionality of the Individual Script Files

Let's start by taking a look at the functionality of each file in the anno structure. We will start at the lowest level (core functionality) and gradually work our way up (to the UI wiggly bits).

■ **anno:** This procedure sources all the other scripts and in doing so introduces the main UI. anno also declares some global variables that are used throughout the script, such as font types and tolerance values.

- **annoData:** This script takes care of the storage and manipulation of annotation data and how it'll save with the scene, not even worrying about displaying any UI yet.

- **annoSort:** This is a MEL implementation of a standard sorting algorithm, Quicksort, used throughout the script.

- **annoMarker:** These procedures create and edit the UI for a single annotation marker. A marker consists of a formLayout with some controls under it (text, canvases, separators, and buttons).

- **annoNudge:** This procedure nudges the edge of an annotation marker along the time slider, and optionally pulls the opposite edge of a neighbor with it.

- **annoDisplay:** These are the procedures that update our display of all annotations by arranging the markers in a formLayout under the time slider.

- **annoUI:** These procedures place all the previously created markers in the main Maya UI.

- **annoCreateDialog:** These procedures create a UI for making a new annotation.

- **annoEditAllDialog:** These procedures create a UI to edit all annotation markers.

- **annoEditDialog:** These procedures create a UI to edit a single, existing annotation.

- **annoOptionsDialog:** These procedures create a UI for settings affecting all annotations.

- **annoTest:** annoTest isn't really part of the functionality of the script, but it creates a test case/example of the entire script.

Did I mention I will only explain the key procedures of these scripts?

9.2 **Sourcing All the Scripts: anno.mel**

9.2.1 **Outline**

This script sources all the other scripts and in doing so introduces the main UI (which is integrated in the timeline). anno also declares some global variables that are used throughout the script, such as font types and tolerance values.

$gAnnoLockTolerance and $gAnnoMinSize are two tolerance values used throughout the scripts to avoid floating-point errors. As you remember from Chapter 7 (see "An Alternative to the Equality Conditional" in section 7.2.10), it is always a good idea to integrate catches for floating-point errors in your script. $gAnnoLock-Tolerance, for example, declares a tiny value that will be used to avoid floating-point inaccuracies such as when the user is dragging/sliding in/out points or clips annotations. The small tolerance helps us catch those inaccuracies by ignoring any differences smaller than that value.

The actual anno procedure:

- Adds an "annotations" menuItem to the time slider's right-click menu
- Creates or reads the node that has all the annotation data stored on it (annoDataGetStorage)
- Opens the annotation UI under the Maya time slider (annoUIOpen)

9.2.2 **Code and Comments**

```
// Distance between in and out points of neighboring blocks required
// for them to move together when nudging
global float $gAnnoLockTolerance = 1e-2;

// Don't allow our editing operations to make a marker smaller than this
global float $gAnnoMinSize = 1e-2;

// Number of formLayout divisions. Just any big number bigger than
```

```
// the likely screen resolution, so we don't lose the ability to
// achieve relative positioning to less than the size of a pixel
global int $gAnnoNumDivisions = 10000;

// The ones supported by the text control
global string $gAnnoTextFonts[] = {
    "boldLabelFont",
    "smallBoldLabelFont",
    "tinyBoldLabelFont",
    "plainLabelFont",
    "smallPlainLabelFont",
    "obliqueLabelFont",
    "smallObliqueLabelFont",
    "fixedWidthFont",
    "smallFixedWidthFont"};

// store/edit annotations
source "annoData.mel";
// construct UI for one marker
source "annoMarker.mel";
// arrange markers under the time slider
source "annoDisplay.mel";
// sort annotations on time
source "annoSort.mel";
// create/edit/options dialogs
source "annoCreateDialog.mel";
source "annoEditDialog.mel";
source "annoEditAllDialog.mel";
source "annoOptionsDialog.mel";
// nudge a marker edge
source "annoNudge.mel";
// embed our UI under the time slider in the Maya window
source "annoUI.mel";
// test/debug procs
source "annoTest.mel";


// Our main entry point
global proc anno() {
    // add a menu item onto the time slider to open the annotation UI
    if (!`menuItem -q -ex "AnnoTimeSliderMenuItem"`) {
```

Chapter 9

```
        menuItem -l "Show annotations" -p "TimeSliderMenu"
            -c "anno" "AnnoTimeSliderMenuItem";
    }
    string $node = annoDataGetStorage();
    annoUIOpen($node);
}
```

9.3 Storage and Manipulation of Annotation Data: annoData.mel

9.3.1 Outline

This script is a technical triple whammy that will require some background info. In essence, it takes care of the storage and manipulation of annotation data. The procedures in this script start at the lowest level with how the data about each annotation is stored and how it'll save with the scene, without worrying about displaying any UI. (That will be done in annoMarker.mel and annoDisplay.mel.)

9.3.2 Using a scriptNode to Store Annotation Data: annoDataAddAttrs and annoDataGetStorage

If you have followed my advice (and you should), you have executed the annoTest procedure and now have a test annotation scene. If you turn off Show DAG Objects Only in the outliner, you will see a node called "anno." This is our next topic of discussion.

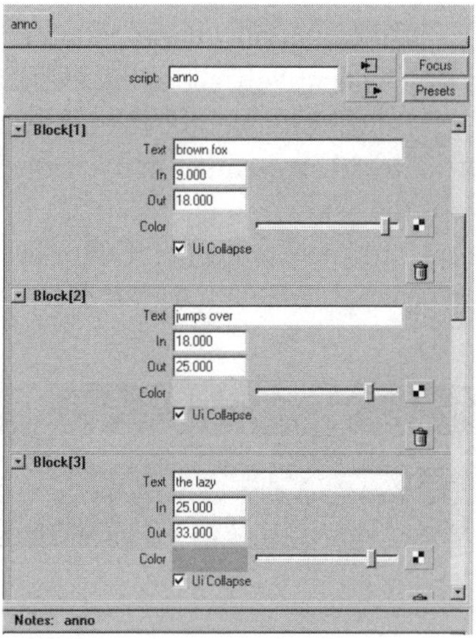

Figure 9-4

> **Important Note:** Do *not* use this node to edit the annotations. If you want to edit annotations, use the Edit All window instead.

We obviously want to give the user the ability to store his annotations with his scene. To achieve this we will create a so-called scriptNode (using the `createNode` command), which will store the user-created annotation data. A *script node* is a node that is saved with the scene and runs when a configurable event occurs. Just like any other node in Maya, this node (and with it all annotation data) will be saved with the scene.

Using `addAttr`, we will add a multi/array compound attribute to store the text, frame in/out points, and color of each annotation marker. Multi/array compound attribute, you say?

9.3.3 Complex Attributes: Introduction

By default, attributes have only one associated plug. These are called simple attributes. An attribute can also be defined as containing an arbitrarily long list of plugs. Attributes of this type are called *array attributes* or *multi attributes* and the plugs in the array are called *elements*. Each element plug can contain its own value and can have its own connection, and the array can be sparse. *Sparse* means that it is possible to have gaps between the indices. In other words, the indices do not have to be consecutively allocated; for example [1, 2, 5, 9, 143]. The data type of each element is the same and the type is specified by the attribute. Each element in the array is identified by its sparse index into the array.

Both Maya's Hypergraph and the Connection Editor display the index of an element plug in square brackets ([]) after the attribute name.

Figure 9-5

9.3.4 **What Is a Compound Attribute?**

A *compound attribute* is an attribute consisting of one or more other attributes. For example, a scale attribute could be a compound attribute that consists of three attributes: Scale X, Scale Y, and Scale Z.

The members of a compound attribute's collection are called *children*. Compound attributes are not defined as containing a particular data type — they are defined as the set of attributes that make up the collection.

In essence, compounds are a way to group other attributes into one unit, to treat them as one "family." This family analogy is also why we talk about the child attributes of a compound. The compound is the parent from the child's point of view. Another way to describe it would be *nestable attributes*.

As mentioned before, all translate/rotate/scales are compounds. You can get/set/connect their components individually, or treat them as a whole. (Note that for vectors/colors they're usually called components rather than children.)

Another example is the mentalrayControls compound on a camera, which groups lots of other mental ray-related attributes in one place. In this example, compound attributes are used more as an organizational tool.

Compound attributes are most often used as elements of multi attributes to ensure that "families" all have the same number and types of children.

Since Maya 2008, multi compound attributes are represented in the Attribute Editor. Before Maya 2008, there was no UI available for multi compounds. Just to give you an idea, the attribute representation of the anno node will look like this:

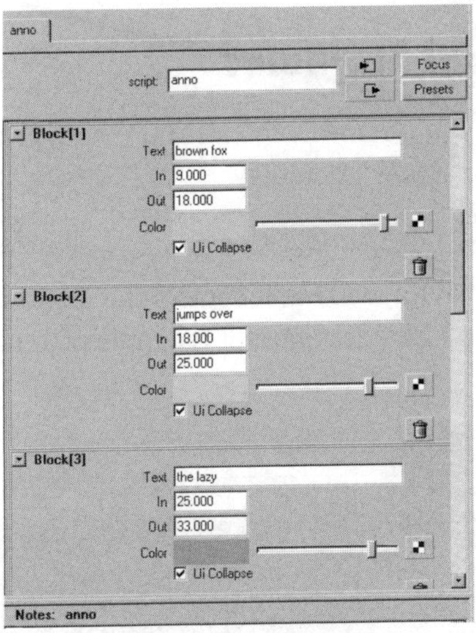

Figure 9-6

Important Note: Do *not* use this node to edit the annotations. If you want to edit annotations, use the Edit All window instead.

More about Child Attributes

A child attribute is treated like any other attribute. Child attributes have names and data types and can be defined as array attributes or compound attributes. A plug is associated with the compound attribute itself and is referred to as the parent plug to the members of the compound attribute.

Each child attribute also follows the same rules of connectability. A child is independently connectable, and if a child attribute is defined as an array attribute, its element plugs are also independently connectable. The plug of an entire compound attribute can be connected to another node's compound parent plug as long as the child attributes of each plug are defined identically. In this case, the data for all of the child plugs is sent along the connection. If a compound attribute is specified as an array attribute, then each element plug of the array will contain children plugs for each of the members of the compound attribute. The element plug will be the parent plug.

9.3.5 What Is a Multi Attribute?

A multi attribute means you can index the attribute with a value; for example, a worldMesh on a poly geometry.

```
pSphereShape1.worldMesh[2]
```

The elements of the displayLayerID that control the identification values of display layers in Maya are another example of a multi attribute.

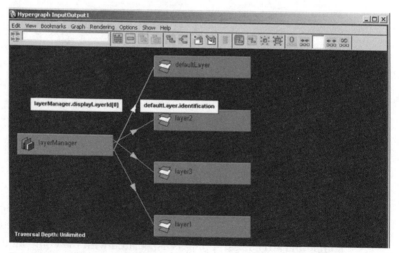

Figure 9-7

Another example is vertices on a poly. Each vertex of a poly object is identified through a multi attribute value. For example, to select the middle vertex of the poly shown in Figure 9-8, which is associated with the value of 12, use this:

```
select -r pPlane1.vtx[12] ;
```

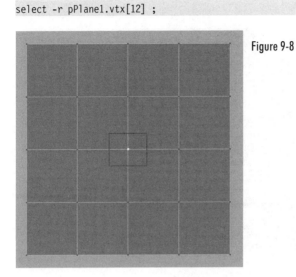

Figure 9-8

Multi attributes can be selected in pairs, such as the 11th and 12th vertices:

```
select -r pPlane1.vtx[11:12] ;
```

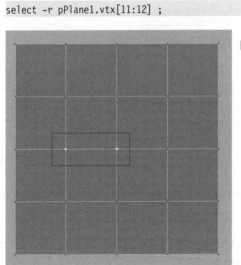

Figure 9-9

Attributes can also be in ranges; in this case, every vertex between and including the values of 11 and 13 is selected:

```
select -r pPlane1.vtx[11:13] ;
```

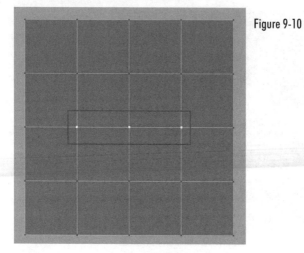

Figure 9-10

Complex Attributes: Summary

```
node.attr              // is a regular attribute
node.attr[5]           // is a multi attribute
node.attr.another      // is a compound attribute
node.attr[4].another   // is a multi compound attribute
```

We will use multi compound attributes when we create a node that will allow the user to save the settings from annotations with the scene. For example, each annotation will have several pieces of data associated with it stored as a compound: text, color, start/end frame. In other words, we will associate settings from our tool with that node and then that node will be saved with the scene, just like any other node.

In that case, a multi compound attribute will look like this:

```
anno.block[4].text
```

The number four in brackets ([4]) is called a *logical index*, which leads us to the realm of logical and physical indices. But first let's examine the procedures.

9.3.6 **Code and Comments of annoDataAddAttrs and annoDataGetStorage**

```
// Helper proc to add attributes to our storage node
// (Doesn't need to be global,
// it's not required outside that file, so it's kept localized.)

proc annoDataAddAttrs(string $node) {
    // We use attributeQuery here because it is faster than
    // attributeExists which is not actually a command,
    // but a MEL script.
    // See: attrLookUpSpeedComparisons.mel

    if (!`attributeQuery -ex -n $node "topform"`) {
        // the name of the top-level formLayout we build
        // the UI for this node under
        addAttr -ln "topform" -dt "string" $node;
    }
    if (!`attributeQuery -ex -n $node "nudgePixels"`) {
        // nudge distance in pixels
        addAttr -ln "nudgePixels" -at "long" $node;
        setAttr ($node+".nudgePixels") 5;
    }
    if (!`attributeQuery -ex -n $node "nudgeSnap"`) {
        // snap to frame when nudging?
        addAttr -ln "nudgeSnap" -at "bool" -dv 1 $node;
    }


    // Options controlling the behavior of the edit dialog.
    // In destructive editing mode, we allow the user's
    // time edits to destroy/split existing annotation
    // markers; otherwise we provide the option of whether
    // of not to clip existing markers, and pull the
    // edges of neighboring markers along with the one being
    // edited
    if (!`attributeQuery -ex -n $node "editOptionDestructive"`) {
        addAttr -ln "editOptionDestructive" -at "bool" -dv 0 $node;
    }
    if (!`attributeQuery -ex -n $node "editOptionDoLinkEdges"`) {
        addAttr -ln "editOptionDoLinkEdges" -at "bool" -dv 1 $node;
    }
```

```
    if (!`attributeQuery -ex -n $node "editOptionDoClip"`) {
        addAttr -ln "editOptionDoClip" -at "bool" -dv 1 $node;
    }
}


// Return a node that we can use to store the annotation data on,
// so it saves with the scene
global proc string annoDataGetStorage() {
    global string $gAnnoTextFonts[];

    string $attr = "isTimeAnnoNode";
    string $all[] = `ls -typ script`;
    string $node;
    for ($node in $all) {
        if (`attributeQuery -ex -n $node $attr`) {
            // got the node...

            // make sure nodes loading from old scenes have
            // all the attributes we need
            annoDataAddAttrs($node);

            return $node;
        }
    }

    // create a DG node we can store stuff on
    $node = `createNode -n "anno" script`;
    // dummy attr, so we can identify the node when the scene reloads
    addAttr -ln $attr -at "bool" $node;

    // multi/array compound to store the text, frame in/out points,
    // color of each annotation marker
    addAttr -ln "block" -nc 5 -at "compound" -m $node;
    addAttr -ln "text" -dt "string" -p "block" $node;
    addAttr -ln "in" -at "float" -p "block" $node;
    addAttr -ln "out" -at "float" -p "block" $node;
    addAttr -ln "color" -usedAsColor -at "float3" -p "block" $node;
    addAttr -ln "colorR" -at "float" -p "color" $node;
    addAttr -ln "colorG" -at "float" -p "color" $node;
    addAttr -ln "colorB" -at "float" -p "color" $node;
    // storage for the collapse state of the frameLayout in
```

```
// the edit-all dialog
addAttr -ln "uiCollapse" -at "bool" -dv 1 -p "block" $node;

// add some other attributes we need
annoDataAddAttrs($node);

return $node;
}
```

9.3.7 Why attributeQuery and Not attributeExists?

We use attributeQuery here because it is faster than attributeExists, which is not actually a command (compiled), but a MEL script (not compiled, but interpreted). For more information about compiled and interpreted languages check these articles: http://en.wikipedia.org/wiki/Compiled_language and http://en.wikipedia.org/wiki/Interpreted_language.

```
// The code below calculates the speed of attributeExists,
// attributeQuery, objExists
// This demonstrates that objExists is the fastest of the 3

{
    string $node = "perspShape";
    string $attr = "nearClipPlane";

    int $i;
    $t0 = `timerX`;
    for ($i=0; $i<10000; $i++) {
        attributeExists($attr, $node);
    }
    $t0 = `timerX -st $t0`;

    $t1 = `timerX`;
    for ($i=0; $i<10000; $i++) {
        attributeQuery -ex -n $node $attr;
    }
    $t1 = `timerX -st $t1`;

    $t2 = `timerX`;
```

```
    for ($i=0; $i<10000; $i++) {
        objExists ($node+"."+$attr);
    }
    $t2 = `timerX -st $t2`;
    print ($t0+" "+$t1+" "+$t2+"\n");
}
// 4.96 0.3 0.07
```

9.4 annoDataGetExistingElements

9.4.1 Outline

Have a look at the anno node in your Attribute Editor. You will notice that the data (text, in/out, color) of each individual annotation is stored in "blocks." Throughout anno, it will be vital to know which annotations actually exist in the scene, and what data they have attached to them. annoDataGetExistingElements gets an int array ($res[]) of the logical indices of existing array elements of a "block" on the anno node.

9.4.2 What Is a Logical Index?

As pointed out earlier, a multi attribute can hold many values. Each value is accessed by the user by logical index number. The thing is that the first element isn't *necessarily* at index 0. The values are, in fact, undefined.

For example:

```
getAttr node.myMulti[5];
```

The index number [5] in this example is a logical index. In order to minimize memory usage, though, Maya only allocates spots in the multi attribute when you set a value. This is possible because in Maya multi attributes are represented as sparse arrays. *Sparse* means that it is possible to have gaps between the indices like this: [0] [4] [5] [10] [14]. In other words, it is possible to have non-consecutive element indices.

This is the big difference between an array and a multi: arrays are *not* sparse and need to have their indices allocated consecutively. So, if you would do:

```
int $array[];
$array[1000000000] = 1;
```

Maya will allocate memory for 999999999 elements, although we only set the value of one.

With multis, however, if you've only set a value at logical index 5, Maya won't allocate memory for logical indices 0-4. The value at logical index 5 may be stored internally at a different physical index (in this case, physical index 0).

For example, if you have a multi attribute with the following values:

```
setAttr -type "string" node.myMulti[2] "a";
setAttr -type "string" node.myMulti[3] "b";
setAttr -type "string" node.myMulti[5] "c";
```

Internally, "a" would be stored at physical index 0, "b" at physical index 1, and "c" at physical index 2.

A good way to think about logical indices is to think of them as keys into a list rather than as indexes in an array. So for the following:

```
setAttr node.foo[5] 10;
setAttr node.foo[2] 20;
setAttr node.foo[7] 30;
```

The number 5 is actually the name of the key in the list and not the index in the list.

index (physical)	key (logical)	value
0	5	10
1	2	20
2	7	30

So in theory that means that 5 could actually be anything, including the string "five" or "fred."

index (physical)	key (logical)	value
0	fred	10
1	john	20
2	bob	30

The trick is to get your brain to realize that 5 doesn't mean the fifth element but 5 is just a name/handle to that element.

9.4.3 annoDataGetExistingElements as a Memory Efficient Procedure

annoDataGetExistingElements is a good example of how programmers approach MEL differently than TDs. Because TDs generally slave away in the trenches of production under the constant whiplashes of producers and supervisors, the most important feature of a script is that it *works*. Churning out pretty pictures often takes precedence over writing efficient code, so most TD-authored scripts are often hacked together over lunch with very little consideration for efficiency. (I can say this because I am a TD, and on numerous occasions am guilty as charged.)

In software development, however, programmers have to think much more about the resources (like memory) their tools will use. Memory efficiency is a major consideration and that trickles through when they write MEL.

If you'll remember, annoDataGetExistingElements receives an (initially empty) integer array. It then fills up that array in such a way that after the procedure returns, that integer array will hold the logical indices of the existing elements in the array. The $res array is modified through an argument (instead of being returned), because returning a local array variable would cause it to be duplicated. This would be slower and consume more memory.

Slightly rephrased: The procedure takes the name of the node on which all the annotation data is stored, and fills out the $res array such that it holds the indices of all the existing annotations. Since the annotations are stored within a multi compound (with one multi element per annotation), the integer index will be a logical index, i.e., sparse, non-consecutive. The proc is called anywhere in the script where we want to know which annotations currently exist.

It is important to understand that in MEL (in stark contrast to many other languages) only arrays are passed to procedures "by reference," so they can be modified from within the proc. All other data types (e.g., string, int, float) are passed "by value." This means that an array is not copied into a new local variable for the procedure, but that the procedure just references the existing array (wherever it is), and modifies it from within. You can compare this with how Maya works with references in which geometry or animation data is not copied to the actual scene, but read from a remote location on disk. Another example is pointers in C++, which allow you to pass the address of a (potentially large) object in memory around, instead of the object itself.

In other words, in MEL, arrays are passed "by reference" into procedures, which means they're not copied. You can clear the array and fill it up again from within the procedure. This is faster than returning the array from the proc, which would cause a copy of all the elements to be made.

Since arrays are passed by reference, if you pass an array as an argument to a procedure and modify that argument within the procedure, the array will have the modified values upon return from the procedure call. For example:

```
proc fred( string $myArray[] )
    {
        for ( $i=0; $i<size($myArray); ++$i )
        {
            $myArray[$i] = "fred";
        }

        $myArray[$i] = "flintstone";  // add to the end of the array.
    }

    string $a[] =`ls -geometry`;
    print("Before call to fred\n");
    print $a;
```

```
    fred($a);
    print("After call to fred\n");
    print $a;
```

The result of this is:

```
After call to fred
fred
fred
fred
fred
fred
fred
fred
fred
fred
fred
fred
fred
fred
fred
fred
fred
flintstone
```

You can read more about passing by value versus passing by reference at http://www.cs.princeton.edu/~lworthin/126/precepts/pass_val_ref.html.

To recap, the annoDataGetExistingElements procedure clears the $res[] array and fills it up again. The clear doesn't release the memory, it just wipes the elements. So there's a current size (the number of elements in the array), and also the capacity to which it has been allocated. If the code you write happens to repeatedly refill arrays, this workflow prevents it from releasing and reallocating memory over and over.

9.4.4 **Finer Points of annoDataGetExistingElements**

The listAttr bit gives all the names of attributes on the node, including multi elements.

For example:

```
block[1].text
block[1].color
// or
block[5].text
block[5].color
```

The match ignores everything that doesn't end in "text," so we end up with a list of attrs like the example below, where each element index appears only once:

```
block[1].text
block[5].text
```

The substring command prunes off the front six characters, so $at becomes

```
1].text
5].text
```

The last match pulls out the numeric digits from the front, and adds those onto the end of the array, so when we're done, $res looks like this:

```
1
5
```

We now have an array holding the logical indices of all existing elements of the block array. (Maya 2008 has a new flag for getAttr that gives you exactly that information, but it's not present in Maya 7/8.5, hence this procedure.)

use a swap operation: If the minimum value is greater than the maximum (which it shouldn't be), swap them around, so we know that the min is actually the minimum.

I bet you were expecting some procedure of cosmic complexity. Owned!

9.5.3 **Code and Comments**

```
global proc annoDataGetVisibleElements(
    string $node, int $res[],
    float $min, float $max
) {
    clear($res);
    // swap operation
    if ($min > $max) {
        float $tmp = $min;
        $min = $max;
        $max = $tmp;
    }
    // linear search
    int $all[];
    annoDataGetExistingElements($node, $all);
    int $i, $num = size($all);
    int $count = 0;
    for ($i=0; $i<$num; $i++) {
        int $idx = $all[$i];
        string $elemPlug = $node+".block["+$idx+"]";
        float $in = `getAttr ($elemPlug+".in")`;
        float $out = `getAttr ($elemPlug+".out")`;
        if ($in >= $max || $out <= $min) {
            continue;
        }
        $res[$count] = $idx;
        $count++;
    }
}
```

9.6 **annoDataCutExisting**

9.6.1 **Outline**

annoDataCutExisting clips or deletes existing annotations that lie within the min-max range (defined in the $min and $max arguments of the procedure). We use this procedure to make room for a new annotation when the user accesses the Create Annotation functionality under the Add button.

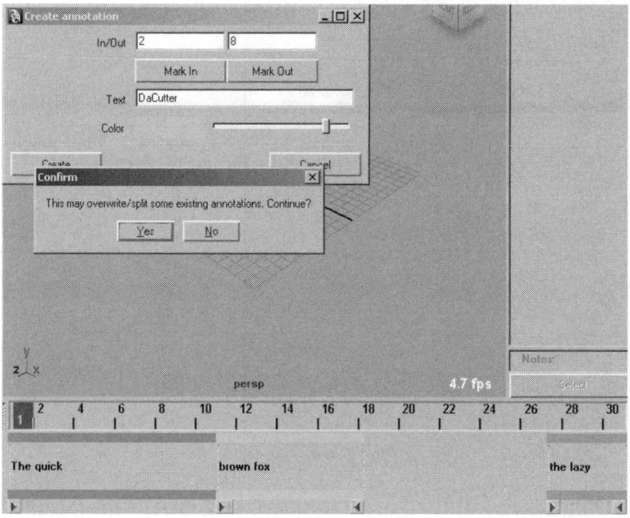

Figure 9-11

If $warnAboutOverwrite is non-zero, then we open a dialog to ask the user if he or she wishes to continue and destroy some existing annotations. The option box returns non-zero if the user decides not to destroy/clip/split existing annotations.

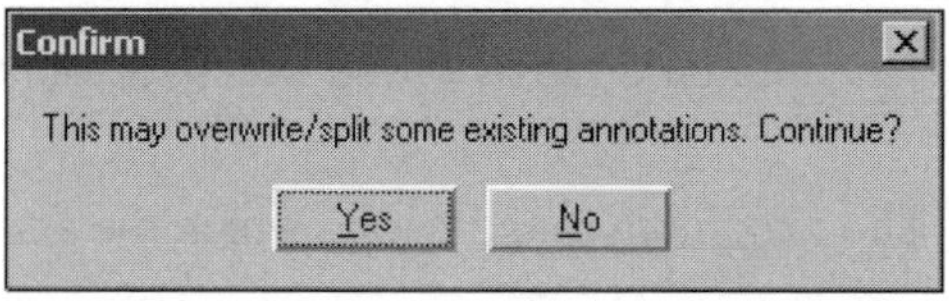

Figure 9-12

$indexToSkip is optionally the logical index of an annotation marker that we should not modify during this edit process. We make use of this when editing the in/out-point of an existing annotation. $indexToSkip is used in the Edit All window; when you change the value of the in/out-field of an annotation and destructive editing mode is on, then it cuts away other annotations. However, you don't want to cut away the particular annotation whose in/out-point you're changing.

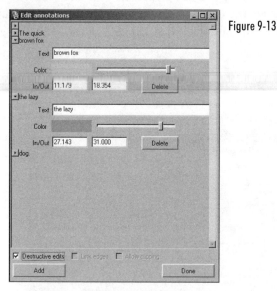

Figure 9-13

annoDataCutExisting is used in the annoEditAllTimeFieldChanged-Callback procedure, which takes care of the UI behavior when the user edits an in/out-point field.

9.6.2 The Arguments

- string $node: The node on which all annotations are stored. By default this is "anno".

- float $min: The minimum range within which the annotation will be clipped.

- float $max: The maximum range within which the annotation will be clipped.

- `int $warnAboutOverwrite`: If `$warnAboutOverwrite` is non-zero, then we open a dialog to ask the user whether or not to continue and destroy some existing annotations. Returns non-zero if the user decided not to destroy/clip/split existing annotations.

- `int $indexToSkip`: `$indexToSkip` is optionally the logical index of an annotation marker that we should not modify during this edit process.

9.6.3 **Finer Points of annoDataCutExisting**

Just to make sure you are with the program, I would like to reiterate that a piece of code like the one below refers to and gets data from the compounds on the anno node (shown in Figure 9-14).

```
// get the frame range of this annotation marker
string $elemPlug = $node+".block["+$idx+"]";
float $in = `getAttr ($elemPlug+".in")`;
float $out = `getAttr ($elemPlug+".out")`;
```

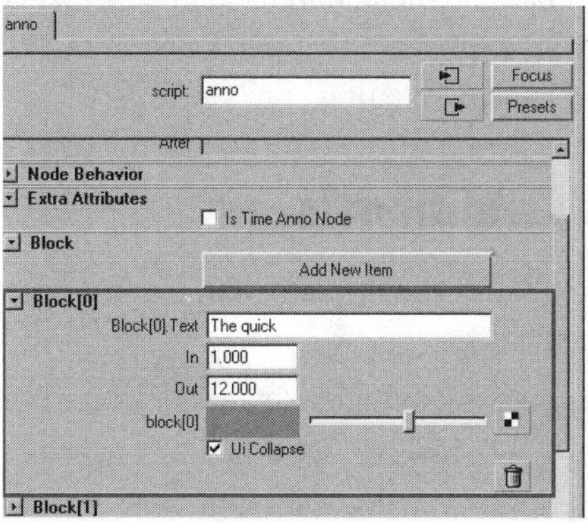

Figure 9-14

It is vital to note that you should *not* edit the annotations settings from the Attribute Editor. The anno node is a scriptNode that you shouldn't change the AE template for. You could, but not without messing with all the other scriptNodes (which is naughty). In retrospect, it would have been better to declare all the attributes hidden so they don't show in the Attribute Editor. Murphy's Law states that users will mess with sliders, especially the ones they shouldn't be messing with. Consider it a feature in the next version.

9.6.4 **The continue Command**

Take a look at this piece of code:

```
for ($idx in $all) {
    //$indexToSkip is for the edit-all dialog.
    if ($idx == $indexToSkip) {
    // don't touch this annotation
    continue;
    }
```

Is the `continue` command here really needed?

Yes. Or as Craig would say, "I do not write unnecessary code." `$indexToSkip` is the index of an annotation that should not be removed/split/clipped by the cutting procedure used by the Edit All window. When you edit the in/out-point field of an annotation, you could set the new value to a frame range that covers half a dozen annotations. Those annotations will be destroyed (if they lie entirely within the new in/out range) or partially clipped. Since annoDataCutExisting just cuts a hole into the annotation sequence, it would delete the annotation whose in/out-point was just edited. Hence the need for a way to prevent that particular annotation from being touched by annoDataCutExisting.

9.6.5 **Flow of the Conditionals**

Once we have the block[$idx], the in-point, and the out-point, the procedure makes some choices.

- If the annotation is entirely outside our range, skip it; see: `if ($out <= $min || $in >= $max)`.

- If the annotation is entirely inside, delete it; see: `if ($out < $max+$tolerance)`.

- If the annotation is partially intersecting, clip it. For the code where the in-point gets clipped, see: `if ($in > $min-$tolerance)`. For the code where the out-point gets clipped, see: `else if ($out < $max+$tolerance)`.

- If the annotation is larger than our range, split it into two pieces.

9.6.6 **The removeMultiInstance Command**

The `removeMultiInstance` command just deletes an element of a multi array attribute. The first time, it deletes an annotation that lies entirely within the min-max cutting range; the second time, it deletes one if it's become too small due to clipping.

If I may be allowed a little rant: `removeMultiInstance` is such an unintuitive name for a MEL command. Why not deleteArrayElement or removeMultiElement. Where does "instance" come from all of a sudden? It took me years to realize that command existed because I was always searching for something else.

9.7 **annoDataEditTime**

9.7.1 **Outline**

annoDataEditTime edits the in/out-point time of a marker without destroying any surrounding markers. This procedure is called by the drag/drop code, which allows the user to move the separator between two markers or move the nudge arrows.

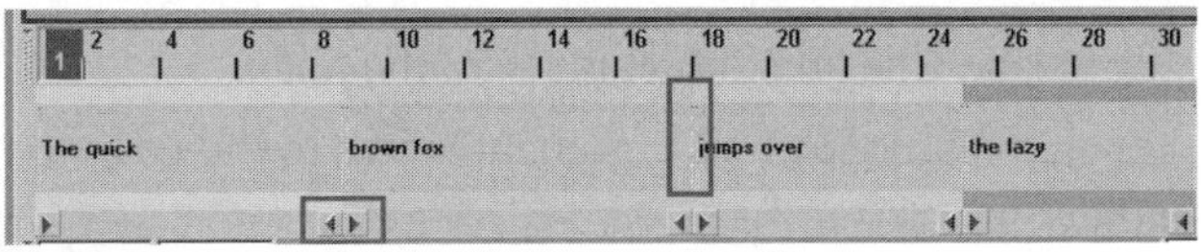

Figure 9-15

This procedure is also used by the Edit annotations dialog to adjust the in/out-point time of an existing marker.

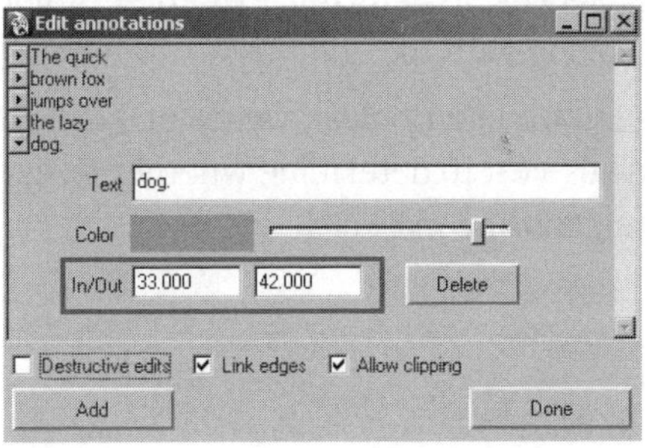

Figure 9-16

We prevent the user from shifting the in-point past the out-point (or vice versa), which would create an invalid marker: if ($lowerEdge > $upperEdge).

$doLinkEdges and $doClip are both either 0 or 1, and modify the behavior of this edit operation slightly, based on the settings in the Edit annotations dialog (see Figure 9-16). When $doLinkEdges is non-zero, we pull neighboring marker edges (that lie within $gAnnoLockTolerance of the edge we're moving) along with us; we use this when the user wants to slide the separator between two markers along the timeline (with the drag/drop operation). When $doClip is non-zero, we allow the immediate neighboring marker to be clipped by our edit operation, but not entirely destroyed or reduced to less than zero width. In the case that $doLinkEdges and $doClip are both zero, then we don't allow our edit operation to change the sizes of existing markers at all.

The annoDataEditTime procedure returns non-zero if the edit wasn't applied.

9.7.2 **The Arguments**

- string $node: The node on which all annotations are stored. By default this is "anno".

- int $idx: The annotation index of the node.

- string $handle: This argument refers to the edge to move either "in" or "out."

- float $newTime: The new time value for the marker edge after moving.

- int $doLinkEdges: We use Boolean values of 0 or 1, where 0 equals no and 1 equals yes, to determine whether or not to pull neighboring edges along with the edit.

- int $doClip: Again, we use Boolean values of 0 or 1, where 0 equals no and 1 equals yes, to determine whether or not to allow clipping of neighboring markers.

9.7.3 **Finer Points of annoDataEditTime**

The procedure consists of two similar blocks/chunks of code:

- First chunk after if ($handle == "in") moves the in-point of a marker.
- Second chunk after if ($handle == "out") moves the out-point of a marker.

Moving markers happens either by middle-mouse dragging on the dotted line between two annotations or by adjusting values in the Edit All window. (You can also move annotations by left-clicking the triangular nudge buttons, but that is done in another procedure.)

Again, it is important to realize that this procedure is a low-level procedure, as it does no actual UI-based moving. annoDataEditTime does the groundwork that will be used by the UI procedure (annoDisplay).

Each procedure goes through the following steps:

1. Say we get the in-point.
2. Get the marker to the left.
3. Get the out-point of that marker on the left.
4. If the edges are linked (based on annotations options), pull the left marker with the dragging.
5. If the edges are not linked (again, based on annotations options), clip (detach) the left marker and drag the in-point "alone."

9.7.4 **A Word about Global Variables**

We have discussed global variables before in this book, but this is a good opportunity to briefly discuss them again.

You can see that the first two lines of annoDataEditTime contain two global variables:

```
global float $gAnnoMinSize;
global float $gAnnoLockTolerance;
```

Chapter 9

These two global variables are originally declared in anno.mel:

```
// Distance between in and out points of neighboring blocks required
// for them to move together when nudging
global float $gAnnoLockTolerance = 1e-2;


// Don't allow our editing operations to make a marker smaller than this
global float $gAnnoMinSize = 1e-2;
```

As you probably know, although a global variable has already been declared, a procedure that wants to use that global variable has to say that it's accessing that global, or kind of declare it again inside the body of the procedure.

In other words, to reference a global variable, you must explicitly declare it in the scope in which it is used. This is necessary because MEL allows the implicit declaration of variables through assignment. The example below implicitly declares $flag to be an integer defined within the current scope. For more info about scope, you can refer to this page: http://en.wikipedia.org/wiki/Scope_(programming).

```
$flag = 42;
```

MEL can't discern whether you mean to reference a global variable $flag or to define your own locally. Requiring you to explicitly declare globals before referencing them relieves you from having to be aware of all the global data that can exist within Maya's system.

Also note the optional "g" prefix to the global variables, which is a commonly used convention that lets you immediately see that a variable is global without having to trace through the code.

9.8 **Creating a Single Annotation Marker: annoMarker.mel**

9.8.1 **Outline**

annoMarker.mel contains the procedures to create and edit the UI for a single annotation marker. In a later script (annoDisplay.mel) we will use this procedure to update the main Maya UI with all annotations.

A marker consists of a formLayout with some controls under it (text, canvases, iconTextStaticLabel, symbolButton).

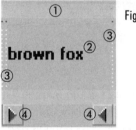

Figure 9-17

In Figure 9-17, the area labeled 1 is the canvas and 2 is the text. The areas labeled 3 are created with `iconTextStaticLabel -i "verticalCloseBar.xpm"`, and the arrow buttons (4) are created with `symbolButton -i "arrowRight.xpm"` and `symbolButton -i "arrowLeft.xpm"`.

However, in order to create the actual UI of a marker (with annoMarkerCreateUI), we need to gather and slightly manipulate the marker data (text, color, in/out-point, etc.) from the anno node. Once we are sure we have the data we need, we can pass it to annoMarkerCreateUI.

First let's have a look at some of the other procedures that precede the actual formLayout UI.

9.8.2 **Configuring the Text, Color, and Font of the Marker**

annoMarkerGetFont

This procedure gets the font type (specified by the user in the Annotation options dialog) that is stored on the anno node. If no font has been specified, smallBoldLabelFont will be used.

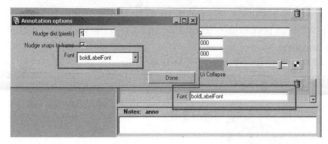

Figure 9-18

The font is obviously used in the text part of the marker. The first versions of the anno script didn't have this feature, but it soon became apparent that fonts that looked nice on one OS (e.g., Linux), looked crappy on another OS (e.g., Windows).

annoMarkerConfigureText

This procedure edits the text of an annotation marker, the actual text, and the in/out-point stored on the anno node. It also creates a tooltip or annotation that displays the in/out-point of each marker in the help line when the user holds his cursor over that specific marker.

One of the arguments of this procedure is called $elemPlug. The content and significance of this variable might need some explanation, as it is used throughout the script. In essence, it is some API terminology that is creeping into the script. In MEL, we mainly talk about "nodes" and "attributes." In the API, we talk about "nodes," "attributes," and "plugs." In MEL, you never get to do anything with an attribute that doesn't exist on a node; however, you do in API, so an attribute becomes this thing that doesn't exist on a node yet. The combination of a specific node and a specific attribute on that node (which you can then get/set/connect) is termed a "plug."

$elemPlug is the plug to one element of the block multi, which is a compound describing a single annotation. So, the "hierarchy" is as follows:

multi > element compound > member/child

Block is a multi compound; a single element of that multi is in itself a compound. Within that compound there are multiple members/children, such as text/color/in/out. $elemPlug references a single element of the multi, so it's a whole compound of attributes that collectively describe one annotation.

You might want to read that again.

annoMarkerConfigureColor

As you might not know, the -backgroundColor flag for controls such as buttons and text only works on Windows. Because we want our script to be cross platform, this means that we have to find another solution to color our markers. A little-used MEL command called canvas comes in handy. canvas creates a control capable of displaying a color swatch, as shown in Figure 9-19.

Figure 9-19

You may wonder why there is a loop iterating over all the children of the marker UI:

```
string $all[] = `layout -q -ca $marker`;
// find the canvas and set the color
string $kid;
for ($kid in $all) {
    string $kidPath = $marker+"|"+$kid;
    if ("canvas" == `objectTypeUI $kidPath`) {
        canvas -e -rgb $color[0] $color[1] $color[2] $kidPath;
    }
}
```

The reason for this is that at the time of coding we weren't sure if we were going to use two or four canvas controls. Instead of building internal names for all, we just inserted a linear search that looks for the name "canvas." Plus, it was a nice example of using objectTypeUI (a command so unhelpfully named it might have well been called didiFoofoo). The objectTypeUI command returns the type of UI element such as button or slider. Call me old-fashioned, but I think a name like UIType would have been more appropriate.

annoMarkerConfigureFont

This procedure gets the font from annoMarkerGetFont and edits the font on the text control under the marker accordingly.

9.8.3 **The Annotation Pop-up Callback**

If you right- or left-click on an annotation, you get a pop-up menu with two items: Edit and Delete. annoMarkerPostPopupMenu is the procedure that gets called when this pop-up menu is activated. *Callback* is a term that is not so much used in TD-written MEL scripts, but it simply means that a procedure "calls back to" another procedure. Wikipedia gives a broader definition: "In computer programming, a callback is executable code that is passed as an argument to other code. It allows a lower-level software layer to call a subroutine (or function) defined in a higher-level layer."

What is interesting in this procedure is the evalDeferred workaround. This workaround came about because of some rather annoying behavior of Maya on Linux — sometimes Maya completely freezes when pop-ups or the hotbox are called. A bit of investigation led to the realization that complex commands that take a long time to evaluate will stall Maya at times; simple quick ones won't. The root of the problem is unclear; it's either a bug in Maya or a quirk of a lower-level library that trips up Maya. In any case, evalDeferred schedules a command to run the next time Maya is idle. As far as the pop-up menu is concerned, evalDeferred arranges that the actual command gets evaluated *after* the menu closes; i.e., when Maya gets back to its event loop.

9.8.4 **Retrieving the Data, Storage Node, and Logical Index of a Marker UI**

annoMarkerGetData

annoMarkerGetData returns the custom data we attached to the marker UI, in the form of a string array of two elements: the node and the annotation logical index, which are set from annoMarkerConnect. For example:

```
// anno 3 //
```

If you want to get this procedure working on its own (i.e., not using it as a callback for other procedures), you have to pass the full path to a marker formLayout into it. This will be a very long string wandering down from the Maya window into the form layouts of the time slider to the marker.

Note that for the code below to work, you might have to explicitly redeclare annoDisplayGetTopForm and annoMarkerGetData, because they are local procedures.

(Some text wrapping has occurred due to the limited width of the page. Please refer to the code in the companion files for correct formatting.)

```
$node = "anno"
string $f = annoDisplayGetTopForm($node);
string $all[] = `layout -q -ca $f`;
string $kid;
for ($kid in $all) {
    string $marker = $f+"|"+$kid;
    string $data[] = annoMarkerGetData($marker);
    if (2 == size($data)) {
        print("\""+$data[0]+"\" \""+$data[1]+"\" marker
            \""+$marker+"\"\n");
    }
}
```

The result of the code above would be something like:

```
"anno" "0"    marker
"MayaWindow|mayaMainWindowForm|TimeSliderForm|formLayout16|formLayout17|
formLayout45|annoTopForm|formLayout100"

"anno" "1"    marker
"MayaWindow|mayaMainWindowForm|TimeSliderForm|formLayout16|formLayout17|
formLayout45|annoTopForm|formLayout101"

"anno" "2"    marker
"MayaWindow|mayaMainWindowForm|TimeSliderForm|formLayout16|formLayout17|
formLayout45|annoTopForm|formLayout102"

"anno" "3"    marker
"MayaWindow|mayaMainWindowForm|TimeSliderForm|formLayout16|formLayout17|
formLayout45|annoTopForm|formLayout103"
```

You can then pass such a marker into the annoMarkerGetData procedure:

```
annoMarkerGetData
("MayaWindow|mayaMainWindowForm|TimeSliderForm|formLayout16|
formLayout17|formLayout45|annoTopForm|formLayout103")
// anno 3 //
```

Next, a case of perversion and passion, of lust and murder: the -docTag flag.

```
string $data = `layout -q -docTag $marker`;
```

The line above shows how the -docTag flag was brutally hijacked because it is a convenient place to store some arbitrary data (the node and annotation logical index) with the marker UI, so we can refer to it later. It seems that -docTag is the only way to tightly associate an arbitrary string with a UI control. There's really no place (at least that I know of) to attach data to a MEL UI control/layout, so we place it in the -docTag flag.

In the annoMarkerGetData procedure there is a conditional that starts with if (size($tok) < 2). This conditional is there because it is always better to complain loudly with an error message than to fail silently and allow the problem to propagate further into the script, potentially screwing things up. This is yet another example of how careful programmers write code.

9.8.5 Connecting the Marker UI to a Particular Annotation

annoMarkerConnect connects our marker UI to a particular annotation. This procedure changes the text/color/font of a marker, and attaches a block[] index to it so we know which annotation it represents. It also creates a scriptJob to update the text/color of the marker when the attribute changes.

We create the scriptJobs so we know when annotation data (text, color) has changed. What is interesting is the -rp (-replacePrevious) flag. As you probably know, you normally parent a scriptJob to a UI so the scriptJob dies when the UI dies. We do this because scriptJobs tend to use a lot of memory. In the case of anno, the UI will always be visible, so we can't really use the -parent flag here to that effect. Our knight in shining armor is the -replacePrevious flag. It simply replaces the previous scriptJob. To quote the docs: "This flag can only be used with the -parent flag. Before the new scriptJob is created, any existing scriptJobs that have the same parent are first deleted."

A wise man once told me this: "Whenever you create something (anything), you usually have to worry about how and when it's going to be deleted."

9.8.6 Creating the UI Controls for a Marker

annoMarkerCreateUI creates UI controls for an annotation marker. This is achieved with a normal formLayout with some rather funky drag-and-drop behavior (which we will cover extensively below).

As mentioned before, we are using a formLayout and not a button because Maya doesn't handle overlapping controls very well, and that is putting it nicely. This forced us to use a formLayout with text, iconTextStaticLabel, symbolButton, and canvas rather than buttons with a background color. To add to the frustration, drag callbacks don't appear to work on separators or canvases, so we need to use iconTextStaticLabel instead. The two days it took me to figure that out were beyond exhilarating.

Some may wonder why `control -e` was used instead of the actual control names (`iconTextStaticLabel`, `symbolButton`). This was done purely out of aesthetic considerations, because it looked nicer on the page. The `control` command works on *all* controls and since there were four `-dragCallbacks` under each other, it was cleaner to use the command instead of the long and unattractive names. Yes, programmers have pride of appearance too.

9.9 Drag-and-drop Functionality

9.9.1 Grunts and Frustrations

As you might have guessed, a dragCallback allows you to attach a procedure to a middle-mouse button drag (and drop). In anno, we will access this functionality through the `-dragCallback` flag of the `control` command, which links to `iconTextStaticLabel` and `symbolButton`. The procedure that will be attached to the dragCallbacks (annoDisplayDragCallback) is defined in annoDisplay.mel.

To nobody's surprise, the docs are a bit obscure about dragCallbacks. This command is as straightforward as translating Wittgenstein's *Tractatus Logico-Philosophicus* into Russian. A Joe Pesci quote from *JFK* describes it best: *"It's a mystery wrapped in a riddle inside an enigma!"*

I am all about giving, so I will save you the countless nights of wide-eyed frustration by explaining dragCallbacks in human language below. I do so by relying on a tutorial from the mother of all MEL sites, Bryan Ewert's http://www.ewertb.com/, now sadly offline. It is my strong desire that this reference will revive, at least in some of us, the luster of a time when all things MEL had one common resource: Bryan Ewert.

(Some of his site is archived here: http://web.archive.org/web/20060721042910/www.ewertb.com/maya/mel/.)

9.9.2 **The Basics**

There are several key things you need to keep in mind regarding MEL's drag-and-drop functionality:

- MEL will register drop events *only* from other MEL controls that have been assigned a drag event. Simply assigning -dragCallback to a control does not mean that it will interact with every other control automatically.

- The drop callback will not trigger if the message array from the drag callback is empty. You *must* assign at least one item to the message array, even if it's an empty string.

For example, the following code block will not work because the callback returns nothing:

```
// A nonfunctional drag callback.
global proc string[] dragCallback( string $drag, int $x, int $y,
int $mods )
{
    string $msgs[];
    return $msgs;
}
```

However, the following code will work (as soon as we attach it to a UI control) because we explicitly stored an empty array in $msgs and returned that empty array:

```
// A drag callback that works.
global proc string[] dragCallback( string $drag, int $x, int $y,
int $mods )
{
    string $msgs[] = { "" };
    return $msgs;
}
```

How sneaky is that?

Before we look at a more practical and actual working example, let's take a look at the meaning of the arguments of both the drag and drop callbacks.

Drag callback:

- **$dragControl**: The control from which the "on drag" event was initiated; i.e., the control that gets dragged.

- **$x**: The X coordinate of the mouse where the drag event occurred.

- **$y**: The Y coordinate of the mouse where the drag event occurred.

- **$mods**: Any modifying keystrokes: 0 = None, 1 = Shift, 2 = Ctrl, 3 = Both. This means that you can attach different behavior to the drag if the user holds down Shift or Control during drag.

Drop callback:

- **$drag**: The control from which the "on drag" event was initiated.

- **$drop**: The control upon which the "on drop" event was invoked; i.e., the control on which the drop happens.

- **$msgs**: Array of messages sent from the "on drag" callback.

- **$x**: The X coordinate of the mouse where the drop event occurred.

- **$y**: The Y coordinate of the mouse where the drop event occurred.

- **$type**: For this argument, the docs state "$type can have values of 1 == Move, 2 == Copy, 3 == Link." Come again? Yet another fine example of descriptive and practical documentation. In any case, this seems to be Xt/Motif derived functionality. (Motif is a graphical user interface toolkit used in software development.) Maya sets the $type argument depending on what combination of modifier keys you held down during the drag-and-drop operation. It's just a feature of the UI toolkit that Maya happens to support. It's not Maya- or MEL-specific; it's just exposed so you can build a UI in which you can copy/move/link controls.

9.9.3 **Like Slowly Pulling Off a Band-Aid**

The code below shows a simple and very verbose example of drag-and-drop functionality. To test it, execute the UI proc and drag one button over the other. Check the Script Editor for information about the arguments.

```
// This proc MUST return something for drag/dropCallback to work
global proc string[] dragCallBackExample(
    string $dragControl,
    int $x,
    int $y,
    int $mods
    )
{
    print "=================== dragCallBackExample - START \n";
    print ("The drag control is: " + $dragControl + ".\n");
    print ("The X coordinate of the mouse is " + $x + ".\n");
    print ("The Y coordinate of the mouse is " + $y + ".\n");
    print ("The keystroke modifier is " + $mods + ".\n");
    print "=================== dragCallBackExample - END \n";

    string $msgs[] = { "We need to return something here"};
    return $msgs;

}
// The drop procedure
global proc dropCallBackExample(
    string $dragControl,
    string $dropControl,
    string $msg[],
    int $x,
    int $y,
    int $type
    )
{
    print "=================== dropCallBackExample - START \n";
    print ("The drag control is: " + $dragControl + ".\n");
    print ("The drop control is: " + $dropControl + ".\n");
    print ("The message sent from the drag control is: " + $msg[0] +
        ".\n");
```

```
        print ("The X coordinate of the mouse is " + $x + ".\n");
        print ("The Y coordinate of the mouse is " + $y + ".\n");
        print ("The type of the drop control is " + $type + ".\n");
        print "==================== dropCallBackExample - END \n";
}


// The UI proc
// To test drag and drop, drag button to other button.
global proc dropCallBackExampleWin()
{
    if (`window -exists dragWin`)
        deleteUI dragWin;
    window -title DragWindow dragWin;

        gridLayout -numberOfColumns 2 -cellWidthHeight 50 50 mainGrid;

            button
                -l "Drag me"
                -dragCallback dragCallBackExample
                -dropCallback dropCallBackExample
            button1;
            button
                -l "Drag me"
                -dragCallback dragCallBackExample
                -dropCallback dropCallBackExample
                button2;

    showWindow dragWin;
}
```

The example below takes it a bit further by rearranging the controls when you drop another control on it:

```
//Drag procedure
global proc string[] fooDrag(string $dragControl, int $x, int $y,
int $mods)
{
//find children array
string $children[] = `gridLayout -q -go mainGrid`;
return $children;
}
```

```
//Drop procedure
global proc fooDrop(string $dragControl, string $dropControl, string
$children[], int $x, int $y, int $type)
{
string $parts[];
tokenize $dropControl "|" $parts;
int $drop;
// loop through all children of the gridLayout
for ( $i = 0 ; $i < size($children) ; $i++)
    {
    // move the control dropped on up one position
    if ($parts[size($parts)-1] == $children[$i])
        $drop = $i+1;
    }
    gridLayout -e -pos $dragControl $drop mainGrid;
}

// UI procedure
global proc dropWin()
{
    if (`window -ex dropWinUI`)
        deleteUI dropWinUI;
    window -title "Re-organize!" dropWinUI;
    gridLayout -nc 1 -cw 120 mainGrid;
    button -l "Button1" -dgc "fooDrag" -dpc "fooDrop" foo_Button1;
    button -l "Button2" -dgc "fooDrag" -dpc "fooDrop" foo_Button2;
    button -l "Button3" -dgc "fooDrag" -dpc "fooDrop" foo_Button3;
    showWindow dropWinUI;
}
```

Chapter 9

9.9.4 Limitations of Drag-and-drop Functionality

Several controls do not support a user-customizable drag-and-drop:

■ Maya's native panels, such as the Outliner or its modelPanels,
cannot be assigned drag events that will propagate to your own
controls. For example, even though Maya provides a "drop cursor" when you attempt a drag from the Outliner to a MEL window, the dropCallback is never invoked. A MEL UI element will

only acknowledge a dropCallback from another MEL UI element that has initiated a dragCallback.

■ You cannot successfully capture a dropCallback directly upon a textField; the textField always offers a "Do not enter" cursor when you attempt a drop. A workaround is to use a textFieldGrp instead and drop on its label.

■ The "trash" control in Maya's shelfTabLayout is handled internally by the layout and not via a MEL callback. In other words, there's no way to assign a specific command to the trash can or intercept its operation.

■ The shelfLayout implements its own drag-and-drop functionality for managing shelfButtons; as a consequence, it is not possible to use the MEL `-dragCallback` or `-dropCallback` flags on shelf layouts or shelf buttons.

■ In general, controls such as shelfLayouts, shelfButtons, tabLayouts, textFields, and scrollFields cannot react to custom dragCallbacks assigned to controls as they have their own inherent drag-and-drop behaviors.

9.9.5 Illustration of Functionality and Limitations

Below is a slightly modified script from Bryan Ewert that illustrates some of the functionality and the limitations of the drag-and-drop in MEL. When using the UI, check the Maya help line for more information.

> **Note:** Some text wrapping has occurred. Please check the script dragCallBack_example_3.mel on the companion disc for correct formatting.

```
// Based on a script from
// Bryan Ewert's now offline www.ewertb.com


// Procedure that builds the UI
global proc dragDropHowTo()
{
    string $windowUI = "dragDropHowToUI";
```

```
if ( `window -exists $windowUI` )
deleteUI -window $windowUI;

window -title "Drag-and-drop How-To"
    -iconName "How-To #107"
    -wh 540 280 $windowUI;

string $form = `formLayout`;

    string $buttonLeftUI = `button leftButtonUI`;
    string $buttonRightUI = `button rightButtonUI`;

    string $shelfUI = `shelfLayout shelfUI`;

        string $sphereUI = `shelfButton
            -enableCommandRepeat 1
            -enable 1
            -width 34
            -height 34
            -manage 1
            -visible 1
            -label "Polygon Sphere"
            -image1 "polySphere.xpm"
            -style "iconOnly"
            -command ( "polySphere -r 1 -sx 16 -sy 8 -ax 0 1 0 " +
                        "-tx 1 -ch 1;\n" )
                sphereUI`;

        string $cubeUI = `shelfButton
            -enableCommandRepeat 1
            -enable 1
            -width 34
            -height 34
            -manage 1
            -visible 1
            -label "Polygon Cube"
            -image1 "polyCube.xpm"
            -style "iconOnly"
            -command ( "polyCube -w 1 -h 1 -d 1 -sx 1 -sy 1 -sz 1 "
                    + "-ax 0 1 0 -tx 1 -ch 1;\n" )
                cubeUI`;
```

Chapter 9

```
        setParent ..;

    string $tslUI = `textScrollList -height 64 tslUI`;

    string $scrollUI = `scrollField scrollUI`;

    setParent ..;

setParent ..;

formLayout -e

    -af $buttonLeftUI       "top"      2
    -af $buttonLeftUI       "left"     2
    -ap $buttonLeftUI       "right"    2    50

    -af $buttonRightUI      "top"      2
    -ap $buttonRightUI      "left"     2    50
    -af $buttonRightUI      "right"    2

    -ac $shelfUI            "top"      2    $buttonLeftUI
    -af $shelfUI            "left"     2
    -af $shelfUI            "right"    2

    -ac $tslUI             "top"      2    $shelfUI
    -af $tslUI             "left"     2
    -af $tslUI             "right"    2

    -ac $scrollUI          "top"      2    $tslUI
    -af $scrollUI          "left"     2
    -af $scrollUI          "right"    2
    -af $scrollUI          "bottom"   2

    $form;

showWindow;

button -e
    -dragCallback howToDragCB
    -dropCallback howToDropCB
```

```
            $buttonLeftUI;

button -e
    -dragCallback howToDragCB
    -dropCallback howToDropCB
        $buttonRightUI;

// The shelfLayout does not send or accept drag/drop callbacks.
//
shelfLayout -e
    -dragCallback howToDragCB
    -dropCallback howToDropCB
    -ann "The shelfLayout does not send or accept drag/drop
        callbacks."
        $shelfUI;

// The shelfButton does not send or accept drag/drop callbacks.
//
shelfButton -e
    -dragCallback howToDragCB
    -dropCallback howToDropCB
    -ann "The shelfButton does not send or accept drag/drop
        callbacks."
        $sphereUI;

// The shelfButton does not send or accept drag/drop callbacks.
//
shelfButton -e
    -dragCallback howToDragCB
    -dropCallback howToDropCB
    -ann "The shelfButton does not send or accept drag/drop
        callbacks."
        $cubeUI;

// The scrollField does not send or accept drag/drop callbacks.
//
scrollField -e
    -text ( "Drop shelf buttons on this scrollField to paste
        text;\n" + "This is not an effect of the '-dropCallback',
        but a native\n" + "behavior of the shelfButton and
        scrollField controls.\n" + "The button drag callbacks won't
```

```
                    trigger a drop here.\n" )
            -dragCallback howToDragCB
            -dropCallback howToDropCB
            -ann "The scrollField does not send or accept drag/drop
                callbacks."
                $scrollUI;

    // The textScrollList will send and accept drag/drop callbacks.
    //
    textScrollList -e
            -append ( "You may drag the button controls to this
                textScrollList, " + "but the shelfButtons will do
                nothing." )
            -dragCallback howToDragCB
            -dropCallback howToDropCB
            -ann "The textScrollList will send and accept drag/drop
                callbacks."
                $tslUI;
}


// -----------------------------------------------------------------------
// howToDragCB
// -----------------------------------------------------------------------
// $dragControl: The control from which the "on drag" event was
// initiated; i.e., the control that gets dragged.
// $x: The X coordinate of the mouse where the drag event occurred.
// $y: The Y coordinate of the mouse where the drag event occurred.
// $mods: Any modifying keystrokes:  0 = None, 1 = Shift, 2 = Ctrl,
// 3 = Both.

global proc string[] howToDragCB( string $dragControl,
                                    int $x, int $y, int $mods )
{
    print ( "Drag from " + $dragControl + "\n" );

    // The msg array returned from the drag callback must _not_ be
    // empty, else the drop callback will not trigger.
    //
    return { $dragControl };
}
```

```
// ------------------------------------------------------------------
// howToDropCB
// ------------------------------------------------------------------
// $drag: The control from which the "on drag" event was initiated.
// $drop: The control upon which the "on drop" event was invoked;
// i.e., the control on which the drop happens.
// $msgs: Array of messages sent from the "on drag" callback.
// $x: The X coordinate of the mouse where the drop event occurred.
// $y: The Y coordinate of the mouse where the drop event occurred.
// $type: For this argument, the docs state
// "$type can have values of 1 == Move, 2 == Copy, 3 == Link."


// ------------------------------------------------------------------
global proc howToDropCB( string $drag, string $drop, string $msgs[],
                         int $x, int $y, int $type )
{
    print ( "Drop on " + $drop + " from " + $msgs[0] + "\n" );

    // Special case for textScrollList.
    //
    if ( `textScrollList -q -exists $drop` )
    {
      textScrollList -e -append ( "Drop from " + $msgs[0] ) $drop;
    }
}
```

9.10 **Updating the Display of All Annotation Markers: annoDisplay.mel**

9.10.1 **Arranging the Annotation Markers under the Timeline**

annoFrameToPixel

This procedure makes sure that no matter what the size (in screenspace) the time slider is, the annotation markers will always line up with the frame ticks. This sounds easier than it is. Originally we tried achieving this with a pixel offset when attaching the marker to the formLayout. That works, but not when the window resizes. If you resize the window, Maya resizes the time slider but the markers stay put, which means that they no longer align with the correct points on the timeline. That's bad. The problem is that MEL does not allow you to register a callback with Maya that will be triggered when a window resize occurs.

The solution was to use relative positioning instead, in which the attach offset for the marker is specified as a fraction/percentage of the form's width. Think of it as a procedurally generated formLayout based on the width of the timeline.

First of all, we need a frame number (the in/out-point of the marker) in the range visible in the time slider (from playbackOptions). Then, in order to line up the edge of a marker with a specific time under the slider, we want to know at what fraction of the width along the slider (as it appears on screen) we need to place the marker. That fraction will be passed to formLayout -attachPosition. Note that that fraction is not strictly a percentage, as in 0 to 100 or 0 to 1, but from zero to whatever is in 0->$gAnnoNumDivisions because the formLayout requires that.

The arguments of annoFrameToPixel are:

■ $f is the frame, which is either the in- or out-point of a marker

■ $min is the minimum frame on the time slider (from playbackOptions)

- $max is the maximum frame on the time slider (again from playbackOptions)
- $width is the timeline width in pixels

annoPixelToFrame

From the dropCallback, however, we want to perform the mapping the other way. Given a pixel offset (the point on the form where the user dropped the separator edge when completing the drag-and-drop), we need the frame number. So it goes the other way — from pixels to frames — and then updates the appropriate edge of the marker with the new frame value.

In the annoPixelToFrame procedure, this line is intriguing:

```
return $min+(float)$x*($max-$min)/$width;
```

$x/$width is from 0 to 1, a fraction of the width of the time slider, so scale that up by the time duration visible on the slider in frames ($max-$min), then shift that along in time so it starts at $min (add $min). Given that $x is the X coordinate of the drop point in pixels on the form, and the form is the same width as the time slider, $x will be in the range 0 to $width-1.

Type Casting

(float)$x is a so-called type cast, in that it casts an integer to a float. Admittedly, this is a bit of overkill here, but it stems from an (irrational) lack of confidence that MEL would do what C does. MEL does it fine because (as we saw before) 1/3.0 or 1.0/3 gives a float division. However, in some languages (like C), when you combine two values of differing types with a binary arithmetic operator, the lesser (lesser as in ability to hold less information) of the two is promoted. In conclusion, type casting is not necessary here because the ($max-min) operand will be a float, so it'll do a float multiplication anyway. But it was a nice opportunity to illustrate that you can do type casting in MEL. On the subject, the links below are real page-turners:

http://en.wikipedia.org/wiki/Type_conversion
http://irc.essex.ac.uk/www.iota-six.co.uk/c/b3_float_double_and_sizeof.asp
http://www.cplusplus.com/doc/tutorial/typecasting.html

annoDisplayGetTopForm

annoDisplayGetTopForm is basically five different catches to make sure the topForm is still there. Remember the topForm is the formLayout that holds the markers and is stored in the anno node. annoDisplayGetTopForm gets used on annoDisplayUpdate to pass it the formLayout in which all the markers will be stored.

This procedure is another fine example of trying to think about all the things that could go wrong in a script and anticipating them.

We check:

- If the node is valid
- If the node still exists
- If the form is displayed in the UI
- If the form still exists
- If the UI is displaying the correct form

annoDisplayUpdate

This procedure updates the formLayout with the individual markers. It does so by gathering info about the number of visible markers, the marker in/out frame, the formLayout in which to place the markers, and the screen size of the timeline (so the markers line up with the correct frames; see also annoFrameToPixel and annoPixelToFrame). Note that annoDisplayUpdate only arranges the markers (formLayouts) horizontally in the main formLayout that will be placed under the time slider and does not display the markers yet in the main Maya UI; that is done in annoUI.mel.

The general flow of the procedure is as follows (see the code for more details):

1. Get the min and max frame of the timeline.
2. Get the time slider width so we can calculate the relative positioning with annoFrameToPixel.

3. Get the formLayouts of the markers, for example:

```
// formLayout60 formLayout61 formLayout62
// formLayout63 formLayout64
```

4. Get all the annotations that are potentially visible within the min/max frame range.

5. Get the frame range of the annotation.

6. Sync the marker with the annotation attribute data.

7. Do the relative positioning of the edges.

8. Move the marker to the correct position under the time port.

One thing to take into account is that layouts (like the formLayouts we are using here) can potentially be slow. This is because when you add controls to a layout, it resizes to accommodate the new controls. If you add lots of controls, it's faster to hide the layout, add all the controls, and show the layout again. The following line illustrates this workaround for potentially slow UIs:

```
// hide the form, rebuild the UI, then show it
layout -e -m 0 $f;
```

9.10.2 The Drag and Drop Callbacks: annoDisplayDragCallback and annoDisplayDropCallback

annoDisplayDragCallback

annoDisplayDragCallback is the procedure that will be attached to the middle-mouse-drag. This procedure will be called when the user starts to middle-mouse-drag a nudge handle under the edge of an annotation marker or one of the separators between two markers. If drag-and-drop functionality is still a bit hazy, please review the relevant section above.

The string "annoDragDrop" is set from the drag callback and tested in the drop callback. It's just a string that other scripts are highly unlikely to be using. That way, we can test from the drop callback that the incoming data is from our drag callback and not somebody else's. It is a further check on top of `if (size($msgs)`

!= 4). Such a further check is required because there is a small chance that other people could be passing four elements of user data between their drag/drop callbacks. This extreme caution is the result of years of bug fixing. Like a wise man once told me: "If it can f*** up, it will. It's only a matter of time."

annoDisplayDropCallback

annoDisplayDropCallback is called when the user ends the drag-and-drop.

The flow is as follows:

1. Get the required data from the marker/handle being dragged, which is supplied by the $msgs array and $marker:

   a. The path to the marker form.

   b. Which "handle" on the marker the user dragged (the in/out separator or nudge button).

   c. Which storage node the marker is on.

   d. The logical index of the annotation.

2. Map the drop coordinate onto a frame value.

3. Move the handles to the correct place.

4. Redraw the annoUI.

9.10.3 Getting a Marker's Neighbors: annoDisplayGetNeighbors

annoDisplayGetNeighbors gets the indices of neighboring annotations as they are laid out across the timeline. It returns an integer array of two elements containing the indices of the neighbors of the given annotation marker. Element 0 is the marker before logIdx in the timeline, and element 1 is the marker after it. Either or both elements are set to –1 if logIdx is invalid or if it's the first/last in the sequence (in which case there is no previous/next marker). annoDisplayGetNeighbors uses an exhaustive linear search, which is potentially slow for (very) large numbers of annotations. This procedure is very straightforward and gets used in annoNudge.mel.

9.10.4 **Nudging the Annotation Markers: annoNudge.mel**

annoNudge nudges the edge of an annotation marker along the time slider, and optionally pulls the opposite edge of a neighbor with it.

The procedure starts by getting the node (annoMarkerGetNode) and the corresponding index (annoMarkerGetIndex) of a marker. Then, based on the setting that the user specified in the options window, it gets the distance to nudge by (specified in pixels), then converts that to an equivalent value measured in frames ($deltaTime); i.e., the same units in which the in/out-point values are stored. (Don't forget that nudge distance is in pixels and as such needs to be converted to frames to get the positioning right.)

Based on the neighbors of the marker and on the Nudges Snap to Frame setting (from the options window), the procedure nudges either the in-point (if ($side == "in")) or the out-point (else if ($side == "out")), depending on the nudge button the user clicked.

The structure of both in- and out-point nudging is the same:

1. Get the in and out time of the marker, based on the node and the marker's index.

2. If Snap to Frame is on, adjust $deltaTime such that the marker edge is nudged to at least the next frame. In case the floor pushes the new time below the existing time, we make sure to move it to the right, at least up to the next frame.

3. Make sure that the user doesn't drag the in-point over the out-point (and vice versa).

4. Nudge the in/out-point of the adjacent marker with it.

9.11 **Displaying the annoUI in the Main Window: annoUI.mel**

This script slots a couple of new formLayouts into one of Maya's existing formLayouts: The first one holds the markers and the second one holds the Add, Options, Edit All, and Close buttons. Its procedures are pretty straightforward and are mostly the result of unraveling $MAYA_LOCATION/scripts/others/timeSlider.mel.

We had to work around two rather persistent crash scenarios in this script. The workarounds are explained in their appropriate procedures below.

9.11.1 **annoUIFindTimeControl**

As the name suggests, this procedure finds the name of the control that creates Maya's time slider. If you execute this procedure, you get something like this:

```
//MayaWindow|mayaMainWindowForm|TimeSliderForm|formLayout16|
formLayout17|formLayout45 MayaWindow|mayaMainWindowForm|TimeSliderForm|
formLayout16|formLayout17|formLayout45|frameLayout2//
```

The formLayout is the actual time slider and the frameLayout is the layout around the timeControl. As you might have guessed, we need to find these controls so we can slap the anno formLayout under it, which happens in annoUICreateUnderTimeSlider.

$gTimeSliderForm is a global variable set in $MAYA_LOCATION/scripts/others/timeSlider.mel. It holds the formLayout that attaches the time slider to its parent layout.

9.11.2 **annoUICreateUnderTimeSlider**

This procedure creates two formLayouts under Maya's time slider in the main window. The first formLayout will contain all the UI for our annotation blocks, which we regenerate whenever the playback range changes. The second formLayout will contain four buttons (Add, Close, Options, and Edit All).

The flow of the procedure is as follows:

1. Using annoUIFindTimeControl, get the layouts above the timeControl: $timeSlider and $timeFrame.

> **Note:** Only one timeControl can be created. The one Maya creates on startup can be accessed from the global string variable $gPlayBackSlider. Also, it is not a good idea to delete it. There is a similar command called timePort, which creates a stripped-down version of the timeSlider, of which you *can* have several instances. Unfortunately, the timePort control is unusable: There is no RMB functionality, no ability to set keys, no nothing. Why is this? To keep things fresh and interesting. You can find an example of the timePort in the hardware render buffer.

2. Un-manage the time slider. If you un-manage a layout, you basically turn it off so it doesn't take up any screen real estate. This line is a workaround for a crash on Linux and Mac, where Maya got angry when we messed with its default time slider. The general rule for adding controls to a layout that's already onscreen is to un-manage it, add the controls to the un-managed layout, then manage it again. This workflow is also used in annoUIDestroy.

3. Check if the anno formLayouts exist; if they do, destroy them. Obliterate them. Annihilate them.

4. Put the anno formLayouts (annoTopForm and annoButtons-Form) under the timeSlider. Here, we had to work around another crash. For some reason, Maya crashed when we added the anno formLayouts into the Maya time slider while having it constrained to the bottom of the frameLayout. The only explanation we could find was that we were venturing into voodoo Maya territory, a swamp not mentioned in the docs, inhabited by a vast population of platform-specific weirdness and over-constrained layouts. A few hours of psychotic trial and error and we came up with a workaround (and maybe a reason). Maya doesn't anchor the bottom edge of the timeFrame (see line 329 in $MAYA_LOCATION/scripts/others/timeSlider.mel) to anything (it's left as attachNone), so we need to anchor the top edge of our annoTopForm to a fixed distance from the top of our parent form. 34 pixels is enough to

Chapter 9

allow us to see the timeControl above. In `layout -e -h $height $mayaForm;` we make the parent Maya high enough so we can see our UI. The combination of these two settings is sufficient for Maya to be able to figure out the size of our form and not get itself into a mess.

9.11.3 annoUIDestroy and annoUIAuxiliaryControls

annoUIDestroy removes the annoUI from under the time slider and puts Maya's own forms back in place. In doing so, it uses the layout manage/un-manage trick to avoid slowdowns.

annoUIAuxiliaryControls creates the Add, Close, Options, and Edit All buttons under a parent formLayout, to go alongside the annotation markers. Both procedures are very straightforward.

9.11.4 annoUIOpen

This procedure, finally, opens the annotation UI under the Maya time slider.

The flow of the procedure is as follows:

1. Create the forms under Maya's time slider in the main window (annoUICreateUnderTimeSlider).

2. Edit the formLayout (under which the annotation blocks are constructed and lined up with the timeControl) and add a drag/drop callback so the user can move the nudge buttons at the edges of the blocks.

3. Attach the name of the node on which annotations are stored (by default anno) to the top form and the form name to the node.

4. Update our display when the playback range changes. We do this because when the user changes the min/max visible time in the time slider (by using the range slider), the annoUI needs to rearrange all the annotations so they continue to line up with the correct points on the timeline. Otherwise, the

markers would get out of sync with what the time slider was displaying, and you'd be looking at bogus information.

5. Close our UI when a new scene is created or one is opened. This is a fix/workaround for a crash scenario that would crash Maya (on Windows and Mac) when the user opened a scene with the annoUI already open. The solution was to destroy the UI when a (new) scene gets opened.

6. Finally, we create the auxiliary UI controls under the second form (annoUIAuxiliaryControls) and fill out the form with UI controls to display the annotations (annoUIUpdate).

9.11.5 **The Add/Close/Options/EditAll Dialog Scripts**

The annoCreateDialog.mel, annoEditAllDialog.mel, annoEditDialog.mel, and annoOptionsDialog.mel scripts take care of the display and functionality of the windows that allow the user to create and edit annotations.

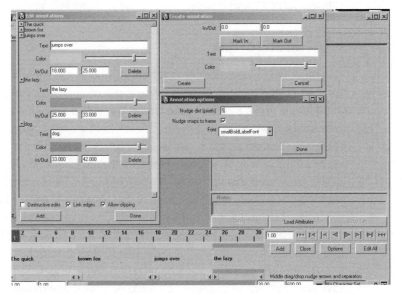

Figure 9-20

Chapter 9

These procedures are very straightforward and exhaustively commented, so I will leave it up to the discretion of the reader to dissect them.

9.12 MEL Implementation of the Quicksort Algorithm: annoSort.mel

In this section, we will venture yet again deep into the magical realm where the line between MEL and software engineering blurs. We will have a look at what a sorting algorithm is, what Quicksort is, how we can translate it in MEL, and how it can help us in managing, sorting, and searching huge amounts of data.

The procedure in question is annoSortElements. In this version of anno.mel, annoSortElements is only used in annoEditAll-Dialog.mel to sort annotations into ascending time order, but it could be used in many other instances where there is a need to search through large (huge) arrays.

9.12.1 Motivation

As you might have noticed throughout this book, we spend a lot of time searching for stuff in arrays: the name of a particle, the visible annotations given a certain time frame, the collision position of thousands of particles, and so on. The method we have been using to search through arrays so far is called *linear search*. Linear search is the simplest way of searching for something: Check all elements in the array until you find what you're looking for. This is perfectly usable for relatively small amounts of data, but can become slow if the arrays become larger and contain millions of elements. If Google used a linear search, for example, you would have to wait until the end of time before you could see the result of your search string.

As another example, say you were writing a renderer that raytraces millions of triangles. It would be impossible to use a linear search to test for a ray intersection, because you would have to test every single triangle one after the other in order to identify the nearest hit triangle. Instead, you could organize your geometry in a hierarchical/tree-like structure that would allow you to cull massive sections of the scene database and quickly home in on a small number of triangles of interest and gain speed by several orders of magnitude. One way this could be done is with what is called a binary search. In this particular example, the binary search lets you cull large chunks of elements that are not going to be visible on screen.

9.12.2 What Is a Binary Search?

In a *binary search*, assuming you have access to your data in sorted order, you compare the middle element to the value you're searching for, and then either discard the left or the right of the array, depending on whether the middle value is lower or higher than the target value. In essence, you repeatedly cull/prune half the data until you reach a single element. In other words, all the halving eventually gets you down to one element. A binary search is pretty quick in finding something in a large array and it scales well. But (and this is where sorting algorithms come in) you have to have sorted access to the data, which means you have to sort your array before searching it.

Repetitio mater studiorum est, so let's go over binary search once again, this time in the words of Wikipedia:

A binary search algorithm (or binary chop) is a technique for locating a particular value in a sorted list of values. To cast this in the frame of the guessing game, realize that we seek to guess the index, or numbered place, of the value in the list. The method makes progressively better guesses, and closes in on the location of the sought value by selecting the middle element in the span (which, because the list is in sorted order, is the median value), comparing its value to the target value, and determining if the selected value is greater than, less than, or equal to the target value. A guessed index whose value turns out to be too high becomes the new upper bound of the span, and if its value is too low that index becomes the new lower bound. Only the sign of the difference is inspected: There is no attempt at an interpolation search based on the size of the difference. Pursuing this strategy iteratively, the method reduces the search span by a factor of two each time, and soon finds the target value or else determines that it is not in the list at all. A binary search is an example of a *dichotomic divide and conquer search algorithm*.

I have a feeling you simply cannot get enough of dichotomic divide and conquer search algorithms, so please, by all means, type this URL in your browser: http://en.wikipedia.org/wiki/Binary_search.

9.12.3 **What Is Quicksort?**

First of all, what is a sorting algorithm? Quite simply, a *sorting algorithm* is an algorithm that puts elements of a list (e.g., an array) in a certain order. (An *algorithm* by the way is just a sequence of steps you follow to solve some problem. A programming language like MEL is a way of implementing algorithms.)

You can find a very nice animation of several kinds of sorting algorithms on this page: http://vision.bc.edu/~dmartin/teaching/sorting/anim-html/all.html.

Quicksort is a sorting algorithm that works very well with large arrays. Keep in mind that we are sorting arrays, so we can search them with a binary search (which requires a sorted array).

The basic idea of a Quicksort is as follows:

1. Pick one element in the array, which will be the *pivot*.

2. Make one pass through the array, called a *partition* step, rearranging the entries so that:

   ■ The pivot is in its proper place.

   ■ Entries smaller than the pivot are to the left of the pivot.

   ■ Entries larger than the pivot are to its right.

3. Recursively apply Quicksort to the part of the array that is to the left of the pivot and to the part to the right. (I bet those 60 pages about recursion you slogged through seem well worth it now.)

There is a rejuvenating animation illustrating Quicksort at the top-right corner of this page: http://en.wikipedia.org/wiki/Quicksort.

In pseudocode, Quicksort would look like this:

```
function partition(array, left, right, pivotIndex)
    pivotValue := array[pivotIndex]
    swap array[pivotIndex] and array[right] // Move pivot to end
    storeIndex := left
    for i  from  left to right - 1
        if array[i] ≤ pivotValue
            swap array[i] and array[storeIndex]
            storeIndex := storeIndex + 1
    swap array[storeIndex] and array[right] // Move pivot to its
                                            // final place

    return storeIndex


procedure quicksort(array, left, right)
    if right > left
        pivotNewIndex := partition(array, left, right, pivotIndex)
        quicksort(array, left, pivotNewIndex - 1)
        quicksort(array, pivotNewIndex + 1, right)
```

annoSortElements is nothing more then a MEL translation of this pseudocode.

9.12.4 Why Not Use the Built-in Sort Function MEL Already Has?

The inquisitive mind will rightly remark that MEL has a built-in sort function that is a lot faster than our MEL implementation of Quicksort. As we saw discussed earlier, built-in functions (and nodes) are faster because they are implemented in C++ (i.e., compiled) and bound to MEL, rather than being implemented in MEL itself (interpreted).

The problem, however, with the built-in sort function is that it just sorts a single array of data (be it strings, integers, or floats). With annoSortElements, we can sort two arrays (of the same size): one of indices into the block[] multi attribute, and the other of the corresponding in-point times of those blocks. annoSortElements was written because we wanted to sort the indices array not on the indices themselves, but on the time values. Think of it like a spreadsheet where you sort certain rows based on a particular column.

9.12.5 Code and Comments

Comments graciously contributed by Chris "The Gimp" Armsden.

```
// 'Quicksort' an array of logical indices based on the frame in-point

// as quicksort is a divide and conquer algorithm we
// rapidly divide and sort sublists rather
// than the list as a whole

// $log = array of indices for each time
// $time = array of times
// $min = min index of array we are dealing with
// $max = max index of array we are dealing with

// annoSortElements uses the in-place version of the algorithm -
// more efficient if a little more complex
// we only keep around one array rather than create new
// sub-arrays at each recurse.

global proc annoSortElements(int $log[], float $time[], int $low,
int $high)
{
    if ($high <= $low)
    {
        return;
    }

    // choose a pivot as the median of three elements. Picking the low
    // element as the pivot is okay for a random array, but if the
    // array is already sorted we generate worst-case behavior
    // for quicksort

    int $pivot;

    // initial pivot point
    int $mid = ($low+$high)/2;
```

```
// try to refine pivot to the most 'mid value'
// In theory this will create a more balanced tree,
// as we subdivide and sort the data,
// and thus a more efficient divide and conquer approach.

if ($time[$low] < $time[$mid])
{
    if ($time[$low] > $time[$high])
    {
        $pivot = $low;
    }
    else if ($time[$mid] > $time[$high])
    {
        $pivot = $high;
    }
    else
    {
        $pivot = $mid;
    }
}
else
{
    if ($time[$mid] > $time[$high])
    {
        $pivot = $mid;
    }
    else if ($time[$low] > $time[$high])
    {
        $pivot = $high;
    }
    else
    {
        $pivot = $low;
    }
}
// set our pivot value to be the value at this array index
float $pivotValue = $time[$pivot];


// swap pivot point value with the max index value of the
// (sub)array we are dealing with
```

```
    int $tmp = $log[$pivot];
    $log[$pivot] = $log[$high];
    $log[$high] = $tmp;

    float $tmp2 = $time[$pivot];
    $time[$pivot] = $time[$high];
    $time[$high] = $tmp2;

    int $i, $store = $low;

    // Iterate through all values in array
    // If value is less than or equal to our original pivot value,
    // move to beginning of (sub)array ($store)

    for ($i=$low; $i<$high; $i++)
    {
        // pivot value is still our original pivot
        if ($time[$i] <= $pivotValue)
        {
            // swap i/store
            $tmp = $log[$i];
            $log[$i] = $log[$store];
            $log[$store] = $tmp;

            $tmp2 = $time[$i];
            $time[$i] = $time[$store];
            $time[$store] = $tmp2;
            $store++;
        }
    }

    // swap values at new pivot and high indices
    $tmp = $log[$store];
    $log[$store] = $log[$high];
    $log[$high] = $tmp;

    $tmp2 = $time[$store];
    $time[$store] = $time[$high];
    $time[$high] = $tmp2;

    // recurse and sort elements that were less than the new pivot
```

```
    // (values that could not be sorted further)
    annoSortElements($log, $time, $low, $store-1);
    // recurse and sort elements that were greater than the new pivot
    annoSortElements($log, $time, $store+1, $high);
}
```

9.12.6 **Practical Example of annoSortElements**

Allow me to provide you with a verbose example of annoSort-
Elements to illustrate what it does. To do so, we will create two
arrays: The first one will hold a list of random floats that denote
time values; the second one will hold random integers that are individually linked to each time value. The idea is to sort the first array
according to time (smaller values first), but in such a way that the
elements of the second array stay "linked" to their initial time value.

We will create two procedures: one that handles the printing of
both rows of values with the correct spacing and one that generates
and sorts two arrays of numbers.

```
// print the time and id values under each other
// with appropriate spacing
global proc printAll(int $id[], float $time[]) {
    int $i, $n = size($id);
    print("\t");
    for ($i=0; $i<$n; $i++) {
        print($time[$i]+"\t");
    }
    print("\n\t");
    for ($i=0; $i<$n; $i++) {
        print($id[$i]+"    \t");
    }
    print("\n");
}

// Create two random arrays: one float, one int
// and sort
global proc testSort() {
    int $i, $n=6;
    int $id[];
    float $time[];
```

```
    seed 12345;
    for ($i=0; $i<$n; $i++) {
        $time[$i] = floor(rand(0,10)*100)/100;
        $id[$i] = floor(rand(0,25));
    }
    print("initial data:\n");
    printAll($id, $time);

    print("sorted on time:\n");
    annoSortElements($id, $time, 0, $n-1);
    printAll($id, $time);
}
```

If you execute testSort(), the printout will look something like this:

```
initial data:
    6.05     7.87     9.39     6.92     1.63     6.41
    12       11       5        22       14       10
sorted on time:
    1.63     6.05     6.41     6.92     7.87     9.39
    14       12       10       22       11       5
```

The initial data contains two arrays with random numbers, which then get sorted based on the time array. In the two rows below "sorted on time," you can see that the time array is now sorted, but the index array has gone with it such that the elements have maintained their original correspondence.

9.12.7 **Conclusion**

I expect anno.mel is probably one of the more advanced scripts you will encounter. Given its complex nature it might take a couple of sittings before you get a good grasp of the material. But even then, don't fret if there are still certain concepts that escape you. The fact that you worked through this book is only the beginning of a road that at times will prove to be slippery. It is now up to you to take the plunge and start writing your own code. Get ready for the fact that your first scripts will be crap — complete and utter crap. Don't worry about it; we have all been there. Remember that programming is not a spectator sport; you will only learn it when you are right in the middle. I suggest you close the blinds, cancel your gym membership, abandon all hope of a social life, stock up on coffee, and get comfortable in front of your favorite text editor. Once you have something, feel free to post it on our boards at http://mel4prod.mayawiki.com/.

We promise we will be nice.

Index

On the CD

The companion CD includes:

- All the scripts discussed in the book, meticulously formatted and commented
- Two educational videos illustrating the usage of the extended layer manager (explained in Chapter 6) and aniMate (explained in Chapter 9)
- All the Maya scene files needed for the discussion of MEL and expressions (Chapter 8)
- All of the images shown in the book

 Warning: By opening the CD package, you accept the terms and conditions of the CD/Source Code Usage License Agreement. Additionally, opening the CD package makes this book nonreturnable.

CD/Source Code Usage License Agreement

Please read the following CD/Source Code usage license agreement before opening the CD and using the contents therein:

1. By opening the accompanying software package, you are indicating that you have read and agree to be bound by all terms and conditions of this CD/Source Code usage license agreement.

2. The compilation of code and utilities contained on the CD and in the book are copyrighted and protected by both U.S. copyright law and international copyright treaties, and is owned by Wordware Publishing, Inc. Individual source code, example programs, help files, freeware, shareware, utilities, and evaluation packages, including their copyrights, are owned by the respective authors.

3. No part of the enclosed CD or this book, including all source code, help files, shareware, freeware, utilities, example programs, or evaluation programs, may be made available on a public forum (such as a World Wide Web page, FTP site, bulletin board, or Internet news group) without the express written permission of Wordware Publishing, Inc. or the author of the respective source code, help files, shareware, freeware, utilities, example programs, or evaluation programs.

4. You may not decompile, reverse engineer, disassemble, create a derivative work, or otherwise use the enclosed programs, help files, freeware, shareware, utilities, or evaluation programs except as stated in this agreement.

5. The software, contained on the CD and/or as source code in this book, is sold without warranty of any kind. Wordware Publishing, Inc. and the authors specifically disclaim all other warranties, express or implied, including but not limited to implied warranties of merchantability and fitness for a particular purpose with respect to defects in the disk, the program, source code, sample files, help files, freeware, shareware, utilities, and evaluation programs contained therein, and/or the techniques described in the book and implemented in the example programs. In no event shall Wordware Publishing, Inc., its dealers, its distributors, or the authors be liable or held responsible for any loss of profit or any other alleged or actual private or commercial damage, including but not limited to special, incidental, consequential, or other damages.

6. One (1) copy of the CD or any source code therein may be created for backup purposes. The CD and all accompanying source code, sample files, help files, freeware, shareware, utilities, and evaluation programs may be copied to your hard drive. With the exception of freeware and shareware programs, at no time can any part of the contents of this CD reside on more than one computer at one time. The contents of the CD can be copied to another computer, as long as the contents of the CD contained on the original computer are deleted.

7. You may not include any part of the CD contents, including all source code, example programs, shareware, freeware, help files, utilities, or evaluation programs in any compilation of source code, utilities, help files, example programs, freeware, shareware, or evaluation programs on any media, including but not limited to CD, disk, or Internet distribution, without the express written permission of Wordware Publishing, Inc. or the owner of the individual source code, utilities, help files, example programs, freeware, shareware, or evaluation programs.

8. You may use the source code, techniques, and example programs in your own commercial or private applications unless otherwise noted by additional usage agreements as found on the CD.

 Warning: By opening the CD package, you accept the terms and conditions of the CD/Source Code Usage License Agreement.
Additionally, opening the CD package makes this book nonreturnable.